THE SECRET
ADOPTION

THE SECRET ADOPTION

Thomas F. Liotti

iUniverse, Inc.
Bloomington

The Secret Adoption

iUniverse books may be ordered through booksellers or by contacting:

iUniverse
1663 Liberty Drive
Bloomington, IN 47403
www.iuniverse.com
1-800-Authors (1-800-288-4677)

ISBN: 978-1-4502-9556-7 (sc)
ISBN: 978-1-4502-9558-1 (hc)
ISBN: 978-1-4502-9557-4 (ebk)

Printed in the United States of America

iUniverse rev. date: 12/09/2011

Contents

Dedication

I dedicate this book to the only parents I ever knew, Louis J. (March 22, 1917 to April 2, 2008) and Eileen F. Liotti (August 8, 1920 to August 12, 2008). In life and death, love trumps all other emotions. The legacy which my parents gave to me is the unremitting love which they had for me and for each other. They were totally devoted to me and to each other, two extraordinary people who gave me everything they had. Their unselfish love is more powerful than the memory of anyone in history, any statesman, writer, warrior or rock star. It lives on in me and will exist for all of eternity. While none of us can truly know what awaits us after death, my father always had a spiritual connection to life after death as we know it. He would say: "Always have faith, it is the greatest thing." He meant that we should have faith in God, but he also meant that we should just have faith, in ourselves, in all others and in the fact that life is too great an experience to simply end when the physical body gives way. While I could never quite logically or fully accept the existence of a god, I did appreciate my father's awesome faith and it by itself has, throughout my life, given me pause to reconsider my beliefs. Even if he was wrong about the ultimate fact of the existence of God, there can be no doubt that his faith gave more meaning to his life and made it better. His belief in a broader context that all things are possible if you have faith is a concept that I accept. As Claude M. Bristol wrote in his book *The Magic of Believing* (Simon & Schuster, 1948), the power of positive thinking can never be underestimated. That energy, which my father had and which I have, does not die. So, my father was right. Faith, in that sense, really is the most important thing, and thanks to him, I believe. I have hope. I can still dream the dreams. This book is an attempt to pass along his profound message to others, faith on multiple levels. I am very proud and honored to have lived with and been raised and cared for by two people who dedicated their lives to me and loved me as much as they did.

We find solace in acknowledging the gifts of love given by those who loved us. If you believe, then that message may be received by them. Who can say that it will not be? In that sense, it is better to believe, and I do.

Even today as I visit their grave sites at Holy Rood Cemetery not far from my home in Westbury, I sit quietly pondering the mysteries of life and death, wondering whether I shall ever see them again and if so, in what context, in what form. Is this it? Is this all there is? I do not have faith but I do have hope. One day I may have both. I sit before them in search of these answers, remembering what my father said: "The most important thing is to always have faith." I respect his wisdom, his experience and his faith. They strongly suggest that I should have faith. His words pull at my conscience. It is not blind faith because of his great love for me and the secrets which are revealed in this book and which he kept for more than ninety years of his life.

My parents deserved this dedication and more. They died having faith that they will be reunited with each other and me. I do not have their faith yet, but I do not reject it either. In part, this book is the story of a search for facts relative to my own creation, but it is also about a search for the mysteries of life and death, a search for higher meaning and answers to questions which may be eternally metaphysical and existential. If there are answers, this is my attempt to find them. This is not a hopeless search and that is what I believe.

Mom and Dad at Dinner Dance

Preface

The writing of this book has not been easy. While the memories are fresh in my mind, I was conflicted emotionally as to whether this story should be told at all and what benefit, if any, might be derived from it. I conferred with my father about this book prior to his death and he urged me to write it. He thought it would be good for me because many parents would identify with it. In all likelihood this book would not have been written without his consent. My mother at the time that I discussed this with my father, had advanced Alzheimer's and was incapable of consent. She no longer recognized me; had little cognition and had lost her ability to walk and even chew. Alzheimer's has been described as a "Long Goodbye." That is true but in its advanced stages the "Long Goodbye" is not perceived by the recipient. Their quality of life is zero. They barely exist. They linger because their savings, insurance providers, Medicare and Medicaid allow for it. With each passing day I realized that Dr. Kevorkian has been right. The lives of many are needlessly prolonged by a health care, assisted living and nursing home industry that thrives on the deteriorating physical and mental health of many. In many cases, there is no hope of recovery or a better life so each day they are propped up, dressed, washed, fed and wheeled about by aides. Science and pharmacological advances can keep them alive for years in these miserable, zombie-like states, long past any productivity. This makes no sense.

On another level I did not want this book to be just factual. I wanted it to have a personal touch. That means honesty which can be both self-destructive and cruel. But it also requires a degree of faith in those who may read this book. While the book is dedicated to my parents there may be many others who will identify with what I have written. I have endeavored to be truthful but this is not an Act of Contrition. It is written for those who may read it. It is written for those from what Tom Brokaw has referred to as the Greatest Generation,[1] still alive and able to read or have it read to them; or those just after them in the next generations who were influenced by all that their parents accomplished during their lives, many long and some, regretfully short-lived. I hope that the book will instill a sense of pride in those reading it.

This book is also written for my children because they must one day look at my life and determine what meaning it has for them. In order for them to do that I must first crystallize in this book what meaning my life has for me, the lessons I have learned and whether they may be meaningful to others. I believe that most writers have that as a mission. It is not just about telling a story, it is about much more.

Writers must put themselves on the line each day if they have a love affair with their readers. In that sense, writing becomes an act of self-sacrifice where we give of ourselves, the events of our lives, our inner pain in order to help others through comparable situations. Life only has meaning if we derive and others derive meaning from it.

Most thinking people spend their lives searching for their true identity and the meaning of their lives. Some philosophers such as Rene Descartes have even questioned our very existence ("Cogito ergo sum, "I am thinking, therefore I exist"). This is a book searching for the inner self, myself. It is a book that examines the heart, the mind, the body and the gene pool which makes up each of us. There is the environment in which we were raised which gives us either stability or no foundation. Parents can give life but perhaps what is more significant is what they do with that life once it exists. This is a book that examines the influence that my parents had on me but then how that influence, later in life, transposed so that the foundation I was given would be given back to them. This is a book that focuses on the inner strengths of parents and children as they grow older when coping skills are tested and when the identity of self which you long ago believed that you had discovered, is shattered and you are forced to rediscover yourself for better or worse.

In a sense each of us goes through life experiences, challenges and crises which we can either learn from or choose to try and forget. I am choosing to find meaning from what is revealed in this book. It is more than a personal test while it is that as well. I write in the present tense because the mental and emotional challenge which I was forced to confront later in my life, is ongoing. It will continue after I am gone because the questions which I have been able to distill and the answers which I have been able to find are not enough. In a way, how I run the rest of my life is part of the answer but my perceptions of what occurred during my life and caused me to reach certain realizations about the present and even the future, is both reassuring and unsettling. But it does present a challenge for others who choose to accept it, to examine the present and the future for the connecting points that make us one. We are after all bits and pieces of a space which we currently call a universe. We have energy which some use to accelerate through life like meteors while others act like stars, fixed in their positions, some brighter than others, some distant and some close.

Each of us is confronted by the terrifying thought that death maybe final, that this is it, that we may never again see each other and that all we have are the dim memories of those we once knew. It is not a search for life that causes us to agonize over the unanswerable, the metaphysical. Rather, it is the question of how life begins, how it ends or if it does, and how these extremes are connected by what transpires in the middle, life itself.

The moment we are born we are moving toward what we call death. We spend our lives building the best lives that we can for ourselves and our offspring. That is all we know. Any other alternative is to give up. I am by no means giving up. Each generation moves a little closer to the answers to the questions which the last generation could not answer. In a cosmic sense, if we ever find those answers then these may be something called the end of the world as we know it since the meaning of life and death will be discovered. Until then we have the hope that those discoveries will either be made by us or forced upon us by nature or perhaps even supernatural events. That is the task of each generation, to search for those answers which may then unlock the door to those ultimate secrets. That is a duty that each of us has to all others, living and dead.

Coping with death, especially dealing with the death of both my parents within four months is hard, but I found solace in several things. First, while the separation, the alienation or the loss as many kept saying is difficult, I have come to accept that there is great hope that death is not final, that there may be life after death as we know it; that the spirit or energy force may move on, in an altered state and perhaps not to a heaven or hell. While I cannot fully accept the idea of reincarnation[2] any more than I can the belief in heaven or hell without hard evidence which, of course, is not available, nonetheless it and even cloning suggests that we may be immortal. That is an exhilarating prospect where faith combined with inquiry may one day bring us the ultimate answers to these vexing questions.

The search for your inner self does not provide answers to these monumental questions. It is just a baby step in that direction which I and others must follow.

In a profoundly written book review by Cristina Nehring appearing in New York Magazine, just as this book was going to press, I uncovered a deep meaning for the union between life and death, why we seek to continue our connection to the dearly departed and why we even seek to join them in whatever place they have gone. The empathy, sympathy and love which we feel can then, if we let it, give us more exuberance in our own lives. In reviewing Meghan O'Rourke's book: *The Long Goodbye* (Riverhead, $25.95) Nehring wrote:

> "For death is not merely a scourge and scoundrel; he's a teacher. For centuries he has taught poets and peasants alike to 'seize thee', as the phrase goes: to live more gratefully, generously, vocally, and urgently. Death teaches us to write love letters to absent parents, like O'Rourke or to absent daughters and husbands, like Joan Didion, whose surprising work, *The Year of Magical Thinking* (2005); inaugurated this current movement of end-of-life memoirs. If we're lucky, death even teaches us to write love poetry while those we cherish are still at our sides." See, *The End-Of-Life Memoir, Why Thinking About Death Isn't Morbid At All*. New York Magazine, May 9, 2011 at 104 and 109.

In a recent letter to me after reviewing a draft of this book the Most Reverend Timothy M. Dolan, Archbishop of New York wrote:

> Thank you most sincerely for your letter of April 29, 2011, together with the enclosed portion of your book, *The Secret Adoption*. Your thoughtfulness is deeply appreciated.
>
> While I enjoyed reading about your parents, it is not our practice [sic] to comment on or provide quotes for books that are not theological in nature, as I trust you will understand. I should add that some statements, particularly those concerning euthanasia/assisted suicide and heaven and hell, are not in accord with Church teachings. With prayerful best wishes for a blessed Easter season, I am,
>
> Faithfully in Christ,
>
> /S/

Suffice to say that a letter from the venerated Archbishop of New York gives me pause to reflect on my upbringing as a Roman Catholic; my respect for all who believe or cherish their faith; the constraints, guilt and fear that I have felt during my lifetime in questioning and in some cases rejecting the teachings of Roman Catholicism. I have admired the Church's opposition to the death penalty and its missionary work for the poor but resented its characterization of sin and sinners. My own sense of forgiveness tells me that it need not come from a confessional where penance is imposed. In our hearts and minds we have already imposed penalties against ourselves which last a lifetime in our consciences notwithstanding a soothsayer priest's absolution. This book is a breakout piece which rejects the rigidity of any faith or belief. It is not on rejection of any faith or those who believe. On the contrary, this book is written in praise of them. I can understand but will never accept how the church would accuse women who have undergone abortions of having committed mortal sins and murders. The lifelong emotional pain that a woman bears for making that decision then is exacerbated by the Church and its teachings.

Acknowledgments

Writing this book has been a much needed catharsis for me. It displaced my sorrow, transposing the loss I felt to a recognition of the meaning that I might derive from the lives of two people ostensibly, outwardly mainstream and average, yet inwardly extraordinary people. It has also allowed me to understand that while seemingly ordinary people who just go about their business each day while not celebrities, often have an inner strength that is remarkable, not flashy, but poignant for their acceptance of life as it is. Their steadfast adherence to moral, ethical and religious values allows them to stay the course in their own lives, but also to serve as a rock, an example, a firm foundation for others.

In my case just as I was feeling the loss of my parents, my tears were stopped by those friends and family who came forward to extend their condolences. What I saw in their words, their faces and actions is that they felt what I felt, they had been through it. We were identifying with each other, like brothers and sisters. They, collectively and individually, became surrogate parents, extended family, filling a void left by my parents' deaths.

Their deaths and the resurgence that I felt from those around me opened my eyes to seeing the worth in others, to how important we are to each other. It also allowed me to see the greater meaning in their lives and my own. What I felt at the end of their lives gave me an influx of new ideas, instilled in me stronger beliefs in the human potential, how each of us must strive to be role models for others and to take whatever our talents maybe to use and realize them so that others may do so. It also gave me a belief in positive thinking, keeping my dreams and those of others alive. I do that each day with my children, wife, co-workers and anyone with whom I come in contact. I go to more wakes and send notes of sympathy to others because I realize how much that meant to me and does to others.

Much of my effort today is spent telling and showing people how very special they are.

Discovering who we are and what we might become is the legacy we leave. A potential unrealized is also a legacy. The support which I received at the time of my parents' deaths has given me renewed strength to face down fear, to overcome it. We share common experiences, foibles and mistakes, but we must recognize them, learn from them, in a sense obtain an inner redemption for those errors and forgive others for their misdeeds.

My daughter Francesca gave me a book during 2008. It was a troubling time in my life, when I had to truly grapple with life's meaning. I glimpsed my own mortality. It was a book by Brian Weiss, M.D. about reincarnation therapy. While I am not necessarily a believer, I am not a disbeliever. Some would say that this makes me agnostic. I do not like that term. It sounds negative to me. I have been an Ethical Humanist so I believe in people, but I also respect and believe in them spiritually and in their inner strength. It has taken me a lifetime to fully appreciate others. I do not do so in desperation or in the depths of sorrow. I have spent a lifetime observing others, often bewildered by their faith and homage to gods and icons. Yet, it is too enduring and too powerful to ignore. The spirituality and energy of each of us should give us hope in what may follow this life. There is great pleasure in this recognition. This book is my acknowledgment of those who have helped me to realize, to believe in them, to believe in myself, to believe in us. Thank you.

Specifically I want to acknowledge all who expressed their sympathies to me and who, without knowing it, encouraged me to write this book. In particular, I want to thank my wife, Wendy and three children, Louis, Carole and Francesca; the Maria SS Dell'Assunta Society of Westbury, a religious and philanthropic organization; the Knights of Columbus of Westbury; the United States Army; Debora Pitman; Father Ralph from St. Brigid's Church of Westbury; my entire office staff; Joan and Paul Echausse; Mary Giordano, Esq.; Joan and Larry Boes; Maryann and Mayor Ernest Strada; my aunt, Carol Melzig and my cousin, Geralyn Volpe. I must also thank Maria Albano, my former secretary, for typing this manuscript and Rosemary Ellerby, my co-worker who painstakingly put the finishing touches on this book from formatting to spell checking and everything else that goes with completing a project of this enormity.

A special thank you to Rosemary because without her diligence, this work would not have happened.

It also goes almost without saying it, but I do believe that they deserve credit for their actions. I write of adoptive parents everywhere, both celebrities and those less known, for their valiant efforts to make the world a better place by adopting children, many who might otherwise be destined to lead miserable lives. For rescue parents who may not have realized such grandiose accomplishments and simply acted out of love or for other reasons, I thank you on behalf of all adopted children and to those of us who are adopted, we share a special bond that makes us, in a sense, brothers and sisters. I share with you and we share with each other our loneliness, our separation, our identities, our independence, our courage and our connectedness to each other through love and understanding. We more than others, must realize that we are each other's keepers. My thoughts are with all of you.

Lullaby In Blue

Lyrics by Bette Midler

I know that I'm no saint.
My head is in the clouds.
They called you a mistake,
but I still, I still say your name out loud.

They called me a stupid girl,
just like my mom.
Too many men passed through my arms.
At seventeen I looked into your eyes,
knew I could never comfort your cries.
Every April still reminds me of you.
The child I never knew.
My lullaby in blue.

It all goes by so fast.
How lovely you must be.
Why you've reached the age at last
that I was when your daddy lived with me.

How I wish we could meet somewhere,
talk it through.
There is so much I would say to you.
There are others, I'm not alone.
A younger brother you've never known,
and a baby girl who so reminds me of you.
The child I never knew.
My lullaby in blue.

As the years go by,
try not to think of us sadly.
Believe it if you can,
I wanna see you so badly.
On your birthday, Mama's thinking of you.
The child I never knew.
My lullaby in blue.
My lullaby in blue.
My lullaby . . .

Chapter I

<u>Finding a Home</u>

In 2002, my dad, Louis Joseph Liotti, was 85 and my mother, Eileen Frances Liotti, was 82. Eight years before that my dad had triple bypass surgery, and one year before that, in 2001, mom was diagnosed with Alzheimer's. They had lived in the same split-level house in Westbury, Long Island for forty-two years. Mom was having increasing difficulty cleaning it and dad was having a hard time just navigating the stairs.

Dad had been a contract negotiator for Western Electric Company, and prior to that President of the Communication Workers of America (CWA), the Office Workers Local in Manhattan. For twenty years, mom was a keypunch operator for Nassau County and later, a recorder of deeds. In her youth she was a model. They retired together in 1982 and went on one major trip. It was a two week trip to Italy with Perillo Tours. I felt guilty about that because when I went to Italy with my wife in 1983, we stayed at the finest hotels and resorts including Villa d' Este, the former Cardinal's home on Lake Como just outside of Milan. Indeed, I played on the same tennis court used by the Pope just a week before, next to the border of Switzerland. I went to La Scalla to see a German opera and ate Osso Bucco, Caruso's favorite meal, at his favorite restaurant and sat at his table. I saw *The Last Supper* painting which was being restored, hanging at the back of an old church. No security, just hanging there. I had lunch at the Hotel Cipriani in Venice and we finished our stay at San Pietro in Positano, the world-famous resort built on the side of the Amalfi coast, on which I drove my own car, a Lancha. The beach consisted of a massive piece of rock perhaps one hundred yards long with the upper portion blown out to create a massive granite-looking-type slab of flat rock and the feeling that you are in a cave with the sun shining on you, with the

1

Island of Capri off the coast. It was in San Pietro that I read in the hotel log book: "Living well is the best revenge."

My wife Wendy and I had a small house about a mile west from my parents, also in the Village of Westbury. We have three children and all were living with us at the time. In 2002, our twins, Louis and Carole, were seventeen and Francesca, our youngest daughter, was thirteen.

After some careful planning we agreed with my parents that they would sell their home and use the money from the proceeds of the sale of their home to renovate our home to accommodate their moving in with us. Selling a home that they had lived in for over forty-two years was heartbreaking for them and for me. I had lived in that house with them for sixteen years, not leaving until 1977 when I was thirty and had just gotten married.

My parents married in 1941 and dated for five years before that. My dad went off to war in Europe. He was an infantryman, a corporal in the U.S. Army and participated in the invasion of France. He never talked about his many friends who died during the war, except to say that he made God a promise while he was there. He promised that if his life were spared he would pray everyday. He did say his prayers everyday. He said the rosary at least once a day, he became a daily communicant and an usher in his church, St. Brigid's of Westbury. He was a member of the Knights of Columbus and the Holy Name Society.

I can remember when my dad and I went to see the movie, *Saving Private Ryan*. At one point in the movie I looked at my father and noticed that he was crying. I told him to "Take it easy, it's okay," but he did not stop for awhile. As people get older they often become more emotional, nostalgic and cry a lot. My father also spoke of having to return home on an emergency leave to tend to my mother who had miscarried. Thereafter this happened a few more times to my mom, at least three times and possibly as much as seven. Years later when I was nine or ten, my father told me about the miscarriages and I cried over the brothers and sisters I would never know.

One can only imagine how devastating this must have been for both my parents in that era. Reproduction was a cultural and religious mandate. When my dad learned of my mother's miscarriage he made special arrangements to return home on military leave. At the time, if a woman could not have a child, her friends, family and neighbors questioned her entire worth or value to society. Feelings of remorse and depression might ensue. I do not know if that ever happened to my mother, she was an optimist by nature. My father was totally supportive of her even when faced with the fact that he might not ever have a child of his own. They never thought of divorce. They believed in their marital vows of "love, honor and obey, in sickness and in health." The obey part was also never an issue. I never saw my father or mother order one another and I can recall no serious arguments between them. They certainly had some financial issues, but their love for each other was an enduring commitment. If you are blessed by being able to love another in your lifetime and, if you have that love returned, then all else is secondary. Next to faith, to love and to be loved is the most compelling life experience. In that respect, they were so lucky.

From the man's standpoint, his virility might be questioned by himself. The loss of self esteem for each could be overpowering, deflating all other emotions. Only the very strong can survive and remain together. Louis and Eileen stayed together until their deaths in 2008. Love overcame all other emotions. They lived up to their marital vows and then some. The natural fears of not having a place in history or a legacy, were annihilated by their faith and love.

After the war my parents moved to a one room apartment in Brooklyn on Martense Street. I was born on May 29, 1947. My dad went to work for AT&T and my mom stayed at home. My dad became involved in the union movement during its bare knuckle days. He became friendly with Alex Rose of the Ladies' Garment Workers Union and United States Senator Robert Wagner, Sr. after successfully negotiating contracts for his fellow employees, he went to work for Western Electric Company as a contract negotiator predominantly with the Department of Defense. He had top security clearance.

During and following the war my mother, of Scotch-Irish decent, became a model. She did that until my parents moved to a Levitt home in 1951, settling into a home in the Salisbury section of Westbury. They bought the home for $7,999.00 on the G.I. Bill, which provided for low interest mortgages. It had four rooms, no basement, an unfinished attic and a carport. It was a wood frame house, no bricks, with radiant floor heating. A main selling point was that each home came with a television. (black and white, of course). That cost an extra one hundred dollars. *Milton Berle, I Love Lucy, Ozzie & Harriet* and *Abbott and Costello* were some of the early television shows available, together with *Amos and Andy* as well as reruns of *Laurel & Hardy*. The Million Dollar movie on Channel 9 also made its debut. We watched them like a religious rite together with Channel 11, the Brooklyn Dodgers, the New York Yankees and on occasion, the New York Giants (if Willie Mays was playing centerfield, we might catch a glimpse of one of his spectacular catches). I can still hear the announcer, Mel Allen's voice. It was mainstream America, the suburbs, a new term that became a part of our national lexicon.

Much of Long Island, or at least the central part of it, had been potato fields which, developer Bill Levitt purchased just after the war in the late 1940's. Nassau is one of sixty two counties in New York State. The name has a German derivation. It is the first County east of Queens County and the City of New York. It is a mere sixteen miles long and the same distance wide. After the war and for the rest of the twentieth century it was predominantly Republican with a population of nearly one and one-half million at the century's end. Fifty years after his acquisition, Levitt died a broken and poor man, but back then his vision brought people from the City to affordable housing on Long Island. Instead of a one room apartment, my parents now had a home, an investment. Of course the returning G.I.'s were not sure if these homes would hold up against hurricanes and the like, but they have. They are still there, built up and out, many now resembling small mansions still on plots of about sixty by one hundred feet.

While millions were moving out of the City, Robert Moses[3], the master planner, was complimenting Levitt's ideas with those of his own. He had already developed Jones Beach with appurtenant access roads. Many of his tunnels and bridges were also completed by then. The middle class joined the super wealthy who had already built their massive estates on the Gold Coast, the north shore of Long Island. Northern State Parkway became a main access road for trips to and from Long Island. The Long Island Expressway (L.I.E.) also known as "the largest parking lot in the world," came into existence in the early 1950's.

Life was good. Many of the ex-G.I.'s secured jobs in Long Island's defense industry including Grumman Corporation, Sperry, and others. Still others kept their jobs in the City and commuted on the Long Island Railroad each day. My dad had a gray Plymouth which he would drive to the Westbury railroad station, take the train to Jamaica and then to Penn Station at 34th Street and Seventh Avenue. From there he would take the subway downtown. He did that everyday, five days a week until he retired, more than thirty years later. Occasionally when the train fare became too expensive, he would drive to Queens and take a subway from there. The whole train trip would take one and a half hours each way. The trains were dangerous and overcrowded, running on diesel fuel and billowing huge clouds of smoke into the air. Even then, the pollution seemed unfathomable to me.

For the white G.I.'s, a Levitt home was a good bet. We had no Hispanics or Asians or African Americans in the neighborhood. By the century's end the demographics showed twenty eight percent to be Italian American; nineteen percent Irish Catholic; eleven percent Jewish and nine percent African American and other minority groups. The Hispanic population grew but much of it was still undocumented. Levitt built schools, miniature shopping malls which usually consisted of a grocery store, a five and dime with a luncheonette and a hardware store. He also built outdoor swimming pools, schools and baseball fields.

My father got to work almost immediately. He turned our carport into a garage using a broken hand saw, used lumber and a borrowed hammer. He did the same thing in the backyard when he put up a fence, mixing and pouring his own cement for the posts. He laid a brick patio and built a porch over it. He never had any engineering, architectural, or carpentry training.

The backyard soon became a home for our first pet, a boxer puppy we named Duke. He was the first of many boxers which we owned and later showed in local dog shows around New York, not including Westminster. Duke was friendly and loving toward me. We would play in the backyard. He would run at me and knock me down. Then he would bite the cuffs of my pants and drag me around the backyard. I loved it. We were pals and I would fall asleep in front of the television with my head on Duke's back or with him at the foot of my bed. He was a very strong animal, living for thirteen years, a long time for a boxer at that time. Using the times seven formulae for determining the duration of a dog's life, that was ninety-one years. Duke was fairly docile unless he thought that you were going to harm me or my mother. My father used to play a game with him where he would raise his hand pretending to strike me. Duke would come over and bite down on his forearm. Not hard, but just enough to stop my father by his grip.

The mailman and milkman also had their problems with Duke. Boxers have very strong hind legs and jump straight up nine or ten feet.

The mail would be pushed through the mail slot and it was always a race to get there before Duke, lest your mail would be eaten or shredded by him. Duke went through thirteen windows in his pursuit of mailmen. He never caught one or hurt one. He almost bled to death once on cut glass and we finally had to reconstruct the windows in front of the house so he could not run through them. Like the entire community, Duke was spirited. None of our neighbors had dogs and Duke became the unofficial mascot for this rugged community.

In 1952, I attended kindergarten at the Bowling Green Public School, which catered to children in the kindergarten through fifth grades. Not much was memorable except a block fight and my first kiss by Beverly Lamont, a beautiful blond with whom I have been infatuated and in love ever since. Many years later I tried to reconnect with my long lost love. She had moved to California. I wrote to her. She wrote back, stating that she had never been the same since the death of her son. I did not write back. I hope that she is okay and that she has had a good life. Beautiful people should have beautiful lives.

First, Second, and Third grades are a blur. The old class photos show neatly dressed boys and girls. Some of us wore ties and jackets. There was pride in how children were sent dressed to school. By then I became interested in sports. My dad provided a guiding hand. At first I was not very good at anything, but I liked sports and played everything all the time. We also used to play a game called "Get Your Guns." It was just a pretend game where we would get air rifles which did not fire anything, they just made a loud pop. I had toy guns everywhere and we would run around the neighborhood pretending to shoot each other, hiding behind bushes and trees. We pretended to be cowboys and gunslingers like Jesse James and Billy the Kid. It was so much fun. But it also cured me of having any interest in guns. I got all of that out of my system when I was a little kid. We played make believe games. Today even toy guns are unpopular. Students referring to guns of any type today are suspended from school. School officials appear to think that they can prevent reenactment of the Columbine High School shooting spree by banning all references to guns.[4]

First, I played for the Levittown Red Devils transition football team. I was eight. Today they are a legend. I did not really take to football. Someone gave me the nickname "swivel hips," but I was not very good at it. In a picture of me in a team photo I look like a long, lost, sad sack. I did not really understand the game and disliked the hitting.

My dad next gave me a basketball and that was one of my games. Today I am six three and a quarter so I would not have been tall enough but I could play, at least for a white kid at the time. My dad touted Bob Cousy, the short star of the Boston Celtics. When my dad played basketball, it was with two handed set shots, something that was outmoded by the time I took up the game.

I took that ball up to the asphalt, outdoor steel rim basketball courts at Bowling Green. I would stay there for hours, outdoors, all during the winter and summer, nothing bothered me. Sometimes I would go up there and a lot of the older boys were there. We would do a "shoot around" or foul shots and I would always get picked even though I was the youngest at the time. I would drive past all those guys. I did not care—big or small, I went through them. I practiced a lot. I would stay on the court for hours and just kept shooting, often by myself, in the winter, until my hands were nearly frost bitten and cracked from the cold.

I do not remember much studying then although I do remember my mom teaching me to read. I have some recollection of bringing books home, but almost none of doing anything with them once they were there. Whatever learning took place was by absorption and osmosis, a trickle-down affect just by being around. Art, finger painting, and drawing were a pleasant side of school. Trying to learn to play the trumpet with an unusable, rusty musical instrument was not. I never received a lesson although I really did like music. In the 1950s, I collected 45 RPM records and acted out the singing and movements of Elvis Presley, Fabian, Frankie Avalon, the Big Bopper, Richie Valens and others. No one could replicate the provocative movements of Elvis with his shoulders back, legs apart and bent, on the balls of his feet, holding a mic, jacket open, hair black and flipped up in a loose pompadour, hips moving side to side. Photos of him which were brought to school by a friend showed his incomparable acrobatic prowess. Most of us were too inhibited to venture a try at his movements but the lyrics to his songs were imitated and his movies such as *Jailhouse Rock* were favorites. We did karaoke before there was karaoke. In his own rock/country/blues way, Elvis represented a rebellious lifestyle which we envied. On Friday and Saturday nights from 11:30 p.m. to 1:00 a.m. we would tune into Zacherly and watch old Sci-Fi movies—*Frankenstein* with Boris Karloff; the *Wolfman* with Lon Chaney; the *Invisible Man* with Claude Rains and *Dracula* with Bela Lugosi. Usually I had a friend sleep over and my mom would make us steaks, French fries and milk shakes.

We would play knock hockey; poker and Monopoly while we waited for the shows to start. I also had my own eight by four foot pool table which we used. It was heaven.

My dad was active in his church, St. Brigid's, the largest parish on Long Island, back then fifty-two square miles. My mother, like her Scotch father, was Episcopalian so she rarely went to church with us. I took catechism classes there and every Friday night I was dragged to confession, which I detested due to the long lines and having to confess to sins which I felt I had not committed. The confessional was a fearful place, located in a dark part of the church with a foreboding priest on the other side of a perforated wall who would, as a rule, politely listen to your Act of Contrition and then impose Hail Mary's and Our Father's as your penance. The Hail Mary was the shorter prayer of the two so it was better to get those. I do not think I ever got more than ten. It seemed that penance was always imposed irrespective of the gravamen of the sins confessed. This may explain my later aversion to uncreative sentencing proceedings as an attorney. After confession, I would join my father in the pews where I would say my penance, kneeling at the altar before entering and leaving, repeatedly making the sign of the cross and dabbing my forehead with holy water as I entered the church and left it. This mindless recital of prayers seemed to me to be a tedious waste of time even then. You say these prayers to yourself, always keeping track of the number while my mind would wander.

After my penance and my father finished his prayers, we would usually light candles, saying another prayer on our knees on the hard marble or granite floors. The church is magnificent as most Catholic churches are. It was built in about 1880 by Italian immigrants who first settled in Breezy Hill, the Italian neighborhood just across the way from it. Many Italians came from southern Italy, the poorest part of the country but the home of many artisans, masons and more recently, landscapers. They worked on the estates in Old Westbury. My father's parents came from Calabria, in the southern part of Italy and my dad spoke fluent Italian. I do not, but I was told by many who heard him that his Italian was perfect, beautiful, and sounded aristocratic.

My father was not aristocratic, but his parents had some appreciation for better things. My father's father was a barber and had his shop on Ninth Avenue in Manhattan beginning in the teens after World War I. My grandfather served in the Italian army. My grandparent's names are on

Lee Iacocca's wall at Ellis Island. My father was baptized at Our Lady of Pompeii Church in Soho (south of Houston St.), one of New York's oldest churches and one that catered to New York's new immigrant community which settled in lower Manhattan or on the west side of New York in an area known as Hell's Kitchen. These were mostly white enclaves inhabited by Jews, Irish and Italians, the "Melting Pot."

My father's father, Thomas, was a little guy, a very nice man. The family's first apartment was in Tribeca, just north of Ground Zero. He was a District Leader in Tammany Hall and favored Mayor Fiorello LaGuardia. My father often spoke about how politics worked in those days, how he would go with his father to deliver groceries to the poor or how jobs would be dolled out by the political machine.

One of my grandfather's stories was about members of the Black Hand, the forerunner to the Mafia, coming into his shop and trying to shake him down for protection money. My grandfather, who was very mild mannered and never bothered anyone, took a straight edge razor and held it to the throat of one of the men, explaining that he would kill him if he ever returned. They never did. There were no fire bombings or explosions or reinforcements or machine guns or anything else. This was fifty years before New York's Knapp Commission found rampant corruption in the Police Department of bribes, kickbacks and payoffs to police on a massive scale. But my grandfather, like most immigrants of that era believed in hard work for his family, never bothering anyone or expecting to be bothered.

My mother was raised in Bellerose, Queens, before the Great Depression. Her parents also had a summer home in the Rockaways. Her father was born in Glasgow, Scotland in 1880. He owned a successful bar and restaurant on Braddock Avenue in Queens. His name was Francis Lambe. My mother was proudly named after him, Eileen Frances. My mother's mother was second generation from Dublin, Ireland. Her maiden name was Anna Burke. These strong Scotch-Irish genes meant that my mother was fated to be stubborn, highly intelligent, literate, pretty with a touch of what the Irish call "the disease," a thirst for alcohol. It has been said, mostly by the Irish, that but for "the drink," they would rule the world. She abstained from alcohol for her entire adult life.

My grandfather lost his business in the Depression and his family was forced to move to a walk-up, cold water flat in Brooklyn. It was a five room, railroad style apartment with a pot belly stove in the kitchen. My mom dropped out of Jamaica High School at sixteen so that her sister Carol could finish. It was common practice in those days for the older siblings to drop out of school to work in order to contribute to household expenses. The youngest could then finish their schooling. My grandfather developed Parkinson's Disease. In 1955, he fell, broke his hip and died of pneumonia at age 75. Later, my mother earned her G.E.D.

My grandmother went to work in a dress pattern factory. The patterns were sold to women who could then make their dresses at home. In later years when my grandmother would come for visits to our home she would always bring with her a dress pattern that she and my mother would then work on. My mother became an accomplished seamstress, making her own dresses. My grandmother also taught her to knit and she made many beautiful afghans. I became so fascinated by it that I too took it up for a very brief period. I never really produced anything but I did master some of the complicated stitching in the more elaborate knitting patterns.

During the war and just after it, my mother worked as a model in New York. I still have photos from her portfolio. She was always beautiful; more pretty than many of the famous actresses from that era. She and my father married in 1941. They were together for five years before that. They were married 67 years when my father died in 2008 at the age of 91. They were always in love, deeply in love. To me they always seemed like newlyweds, perpetually on a honeymoon or like a young couple on their first date. They were always together and never separated. But they had a rare relationship that allowed them to work toward a common goal, the rearing of me. I was born on May 29, 1947, the same day as President John F. Kennedy, who was born the same year as my father, 1917.

My parents had a one room apartment on Martense Street in Brooklyn, New York, an area which in later years became apart of "the hood." But from the time of my birth in 1947 until we moved to Long Island in 1951, it was a pristine neighborhood, filled with young couples and G.I.s who had returned home after the war.

I was a bit of a devil back then. One Christmas my parents had given me a toy rifle that shot ping pong balls and I managed to shoot all the ornaments off of the tree. I was an only child.

In the 1940's and after the war my father became a union organizer where he rose to the Office of President of the Communication Workers of America, the Local for office workers in Manhattan. It was still a tough time for the union movement and management employed thugs, private security firms to curtail unionization. My father got the idea and had his own tough guys standing beside him at negotiating sessions.

As a young man, my father had fought in the Golden Gloves. He would kid with me by putting his dukes up. He had quick, good moves. He knew how to feint. We would play slap fight. He would laugh if I landed a punch. That rarely happened. He was in command, just fooling around but teaching me how to fight, to box and defend myself in case I ever needed it. Although he was short at five feet, eight inches and weighed just one hundred sixty pounds, he could defend himself and feared no earthly being. He was awarded medals from the AFL-CIO for his efforts. I have pictures of him attending the huge union conventions of that era. He was a rising star.

He later left the union and went to work for American Telephone and Telegraph Company at their main headquarters at 195 Broadway in lower Manhattan. This was considered to be a coveted position at the time because it was a "white collar" job. He deeply regretted leaving the union. He felt that he had sold out, but at the same time, he did it for the good of his family. After that he worked for their subsidiary Western Electric Company, spending most of his career negotiating defense contracts with the military. He was without a doubt, the toughest and most brilliant negotiator I have ever seen. That was also his reputation among members of his union, his corporate co-workers and his adversaries. The lesson he taught me from this was not to be afraid to pursue your dreams and natural talents. Much of life is about taking calculated risks. Rather than just playing it safe all the time, you must be prepared to take those risks in order to improve yourself and those around you. If you are not born wealthy or with power, then through hard work and a willingness to gamble it all, you may reach a higher station in life where you can help your family and others. My father gave me hardcore lessons in life and politics. In his view, nothing would come easy and there are few you can trust. He taught me to know the enemy and to be ready for them.

I remember my father taking me into the City for annual Christmas parties for the kids of the employees at Western Electric. I would get all dressed up with a jacket and tie. We would ride the Long Island Railroad into the City and take the subway downtown. After that party we had a routine. We would go to St. Francis of Assisi Church on 34th Street where they have two beautiful chapels and Christmas decorations. We would say a few prayers and move on. Usually our next stop was the Empire

State Building at 34th Street, riding to the observation deck atop that 102 story edifice. Then we would go up to Fifth Avenue to Rockefeller Plaza to watch the skaters, see the big tree and walk around inside St. Patrick's Cathedral across the street. In back of the main altar there would usually be an impressive manger. Television cameras were set up for midnight Mass on Christmas Eve and a wax, life size figure of Pope Pius was near the entranceway. Behind the altar was the tomb for all the Cardinals serving as Archbishops of New York, and if you looked to the top of the Cathedral, their red hats with black tassels hung from the ceiling. This was familiar territory for my father and he would give me a guided tour.

Then we would go back downtown to 42nd Street where we would have hot dogs at a corner store catering to all comers, including the local riff raff. This was probably my first encounter with the poor, beggars, and hobos, as we called them then. They were homeless people living on the streets, surviving on hot dogs, black coffee, cigarettes and alcohol. My father wanted me to see them and another side of life. We had just come from Fifth Avenue, one of the wealthiest parts of New York City and then to 42nd Street, which gave me a glimpse of the poor. The contrast opened my eyes. It was appalling.

It was cash and carry. We would eat our hotdogs standing up usually on the street or at one of those round stand up tables. When you were with my father being in the City was fun but also serious business. If you looked up at the skyscrapers while you were walking along the street he would say: "Hey, watch where you are walking. Look straight ahead. You look like a hick." Watching those poor souls made me feel grateful. I had parents and a home. I was loved. They had only themselves. They were disheveled, laden with black dirt covering their skins, under their nails and their clothes. They smelled of human excrement, alcohol, tobacco and sweat. The dirt was so encrusted that large blackheads covered their severely lined, fissured faces. Many were bent over with early osteoporosis or simply defeated spirits. Their shoes were work boots, worn, and covered with dark dirt and grease.

Even at my young age I thought of how lucky I was; how any of us could wind up in similar circumstances—alone, with no one to care for us or to love us. Learning to give love takes maturity. On Christmas Eve these poor would not be huddled by the fireplace waiting for Santa. There were no presents under the tree for them. They were like so many characters out of a Dickens novel. Their lives were a banishment from society, a destitution and I wondered if my father was trying to show me contrasts in how people live, that I should not be ungrateful for the benefits of life which I was fortunate to receive. Oddly, most of those I saw were Caucasian. Even the poor seemed to be segregated. I was left to imagine what was the far worse plight of those living in places like Harlem, at the time a national scandal, symbolic for poverty, drugs and the shortened life expectancies of African Americans living in those deplorable conditions.

But was there also another message that my father was attempting to convey? That we should help the poor but the problems of poverty are much larger than what we in cloistered suburbia imagined. Before President John F. Kennedy sought to instill these values in us all, I think Louis J. Liotti was doing so with me, whether he realized it or not. I think he probably did realize it but he also knew the difference between our humble, middle class existence and the plight of the poor. He believed: "That there but for the grace of God, go [all]."

He told me that I should not want to be a laborer or to work with my hands. He would tell me to study and use my brain. I believe that there was an inculcation that he was giving me to make something of myself, to be a leader, to help the poor and one day my own family. He and my mother set examples of what caring parents should be.

After the hotdogs we would usually take in a movie on 42nd Street. While the sex trade was then making its inroads into the area, you could easily find a respectable Walt Disney movie there, which is what we did. We would also sometimes stop by a big store on Broadway called Playland which was owned by my father's childhood friend, Freddy Carnara. Playland was filled with coin games of the type seen in video parlors today. Mr. Carnara was a large, impressive gentleman, who easily could have been a character in any *Godfather* movie. He had an all-cash business of video games. He had great respect for my father as someone who had made his way as an Italian American from the old neighborhood into corporate America. Mr. Carnara made his way on the streets of New York. My father respected him as a lifelong, loyal friend. As young men growing up together, they would have died for each other. You could feel that coming from them.

Traveling to and from the City was meant to add to my sophistication, to give me a more worldly, cosmopolitan demeanor. It made me want to grow up in the City and live there. It was so much more exciting than the dull suburbs that did not even have a playhouse where musicals or shows might be seen and heard. We had movie theaters, but that was about it.

Much of what I saw in New York City seemed to be for the super-rich, not us—but we never counted ourselves out. That's the nice thing about living in the City (or close to it), you feel like you are always trying out for the Big Leagues, where the action is, the center of the universe, where everything that can happen, does. People of different colors, races, religions, languages and cultures abound. That is the true richness of New York and that is why it remains the greatest city in the world.

I can remember my mom taking me to the movies on Post Avenue in Westbury, an ornate former Vaudeville Playhouse, to see "Old Yella, Shane, Black Beauty and other Walt Disney films such as Twenty Thousand Leagues Under The Sea, Snow White, Fantasia and Alice In Wonderland. Sometimes these movies would cause me to cry and at other times they would fill me with a sense of joy over the possibilities that were ahead. I did not see myself as a creator but merely as the beneficiary of these wonderful works of art. They took me to the moon and stars, under the oceans and even to outer space, beyond our universe. Such creativity filled you with a sense of optimism about life. We won the Second World War. We were a nation of high achievers, capable of accomplishing anything, reaching any heights. Failure was not on anyone's agenda.

At the same time there are con men, hustlers and even some deranged people walking the streets. I was always taught to "mind my own business" when traveling in or around the City. I was also taught to be careful, to keep my eyes and ears open, not speak to strangers and avoid confrontation. Yet, New Yorkers are known for their toughness and no one walks over us.

There is something called subway etiquette. I was instructed not to stare at people or make fun of them or make physical contact with them. I was told to act like I knew where I was going and what I was doing. I was told how to fold the New York Times the long way so that it could be read without interfering with fellow passengers. Once my dad and I were riding on the subway seated next to each other. The car was pretty empty but a deranged man was sitting across the way from us. He started to get loud and was cursing. My father was avoiding eye contact with him. The man appeared drunk, angry, and probably rode the subways all day to stay warm and panhandle. My dad had an umbrella. He lifted it and pounded the metal end of it on the ground two times, hard. It made a loud noise. The man got the message and left us alone. As we exited the subway, my father said: "Did you see that?" "Yes," I said. I asked: "What were you going to do if he came across the car?" "I would have hit him with the point of my umbrella right in the chest. Remember that, do not be afraid, think ahead about what to do. Hit him where it is unexpected." That's when he told me about a fight he had where he hit his opponent in the solar plexus. "He wasn't ready for it. I took his breath away. He couldn't do anything. The fight was over." He showed me where the solar plexus is. Years later that came in handy when I got into a few physical fights of my own.

After the movie we would head home by train. Everything was so festive; people seemed to be bustling about everywhere, most were happy. It was an exciting time; Christmas and the scent of pine was in the air. A decorated tree waited for us at home; a fireplace; gifts under the tree and a black and white television which allowed us to celebrate with all others. It was America in the 1950s.

From the top of the world's tallest building

EMPIRE STATE

I was photographed in LIFE Color 1472 feet above the street and looking out over the most fabulous skyline of the world.

Every Christmas my Dad would take me to the city
and invariably the Empire State Building was one of our favorite stops.

Chapter II

<u>Making Of Middle America</u>

In the 1950s Bowling Green Public School was drab and boring. I was a student there from kindergarten through fifth grade. I remember how students would be forced to sit down in the hallways, hands clasped behind their heads which they then placed between their legs, (some said "to kiss their asses goodbye") in the event of an atomic bomb attack. They also had air raid sirens which they would sound and we would ignore. Bomb shelters were built. It was the era of Senator Joseph McCarthy, so fear of a communist threat transcended to the suburbs and existed even in my elementary school. I had no concept of it or that there had been a World War just ten years earlier. The Cold War followed the World War because Russia was suddenly no longer our ally and Lenin's and Stalin's socialism were deemed a threat to democracy, free markets, and capitalism. As a youth, I had difficulty deciphering these conflicts but nationalism and patriotism were indoctrinated into the young. We were the land of the free and the home of the brave. Left out of our history books were references to Columbus or early settlers slaughtering the Indians or that segregation existed, not just in the South but in our neighborhoods and places of work. There was no enlightenment in that sense. I was not taught these things at the dinner table either. It would be many years before I had the courage to question our form of Government or the righteousness of the United States. With time I developed those questions with vehemence and resentment that I had not learned them sooner. I later felt that I had been brainwashed, not by my parents but by society as a whole and our tolerance of error-ridden foreign and domestic policies, all under the banner of patriotism.

In fifth grade I had a terrific teacher, Mr. Claus. He wore a suit and bow tie everyday to class, but he was also a jock. During lunch he would pitch to us in baseball. After school the guy would play full court basketball with us in the gymnasium. It was real men-type stuff.

I was good—very good—his best player. He would challenge me every chance he had. One day it was a duel between us, chest passing at ten yards These are two hand passes from the chest, taking one step forward to throw and one step back to catch. The ball is thrown to your upper chest area, hard. If your hands are too far apart, the ball will go through the receiver's hands, hitting him in the throat or in the face. We would rifle the ball like a bullet back and forth. If you dropped the ball, missed the catch or backed away from the fire, you did not meet the challenge. I not only accepted the challenge and met it, but Mr. Claus called it a draw when he gave up. I believe I rocked him back with the force of my passes, jolting him on each volley.

Growing up my parents gave me things that no other kids had: my own room and television, Duke, and a motorized go-cart. It was terrific and I would load it into my dad's car and he would drive me up to the empty Bowling Green School parking lot where I would drive it around for a half hour or so. I was probably traveling only twenty or thirty miles per hour but it was fun.

I was starting to play little league baseball and my dad was getting active in the league. He did not like the fact that none of the kids had real uniforms. They were all wearing little league shirts and hats, but no uniforms.

The little league started as the Central Nassau Little League which my father renamed the Central Nassau Athletic Association. He became the President of it. He built it up to a Pony League, Babe Ruth League and Connie Mack League, everyone got uniforms and he even started a winter basketball league. He did all of that for me. It was a massive organization. All the local stores and businesses sponsored teams. The annual parade was a major community event attended by many politicians and elected officials. These were community events where literally everyone was involved

My dad also organized annual awards dinners where every kid got a trophy. No one was excluded. At one pep rally at Levittown Hall, Governor Nelson Rockefeller came over to my dad saying: "Lou, how are you doing? Is this the little guy, Tom?" He patted me on the head, touched my shoulder, shook my father's hand and then mine. "Nice job, keep up the good work, good luck." He nodded to my father and me, then made his way through the crowd and back to his limousine. My father turned to me and said: "You see that, it is important to remember people's names, always remember their names." Since then I have made a conscious effort to always remember people's names.

We were all about baseball. My dad had tried out for the New York Giants and the Brooklyn Dodgers. He played in the minor leagues, sandlot ball as they then called it, the Queens Alliance. He got to know all the greats from that era. One day he took me to Ebbetts Field and into to the locker room. There I met Emmet Kelly, the Dodgers' famous clown. I met Gil Hodges, Pee Wee Reese, Duke Snider and Roy Campanella. They all knew my dad and played up to him, autographing a baseball for him which I cherished for years until one day I decided to play catch with it. Those signatures were gone forever.

After my grandfather, "Pop Pop" Lambe passed away in 1955 at age 75, my mother gave me three silver dollars which he owned as remembrances of him. I kept them for many years and then used them. It was stupid of me but at the time I had little concept of their material or nostalgic value.

When I first started playing baseball, my dad wanted me to be a pitcher. He said it was the best position. The pitchers control everything. There was one problem though—I could not pitch. So, every night in the spring and summer when my dad came home and while it was still light out, we would go into the backyard and I would pitch. He would catch. He really knew his stuff because he had been a pitcher and a great all-around athlete with no training. He would show me how to place my fingers on the ball; working the seams to my advantage; how to throw a breaking pitch, especially a curve ball. Then he showed me a "change-up," side arm, submarine and three quarter arm pitching. He showed me how to pick off a runner and how to follow through. At our backyard sessions he taught me control. If I threw a wild pitch the session was over and he would walk into the house. One time this got me particularly upset and I started crying. It was one of the few times I ever broke down in front of my father or gave in to him. I pounded him on his chest with an open fist as a young boy might and sobbed. He hugged me and apologized. It is the only time in my life that I remember him apologizing to me about anything or us showing nearly uncontrolled affection for each other. I do not recall my parents ever saying the word love. It was implicit in everything they said and did. My mom, after having cooked dinner, was watching us from the back door. She expressed her dismay to my father, but it made no difference, he was determined to teach me control and concentration. He did. It worked and I learned how to pitch. Baseball became my game and I played it all the time, pick up games all day long, every chance I got. Some of the kids I played with went on to play professional baseball. I did not.

Kids then and now have few recreational programs available to them. Sports and other goal oriented programs keep kids away from drugs, alcohol, and gangs. In those days kids still had time to play in wholesome activities. We did not have stoops in front of our homes so we could not play the favorite past time of some City kids, stoop ball. Instead, fathers and their sons played stickball in the street. We used wiffle ball bats or broom handles and had a Spalding. There was no pitching. As the batter, you bounce the ball and swing. A home run is over the lamp post, about seventy-five yards away. I got pretty good at stick ball. I could usually hit a home run almost every time at bat.

One day some of the older boys were angry that I had beaten them in a game. They were about thirteen and I was ten. They had their bats and were ready to beat me up. My father came out of the house and spoke to them. "So you want to fight him?" he asked. "Yeah," came back from the four boys, each holding a bat. I had only my mitt. My father then said, to my shock and surprise: "Okay, he'll fight you. One at a time. Put down your bats. Who's first?" My father taught me a lesson about bullies. He called their bluff and they went away like the cowards that they were.

Stick ball could be played in the street or sometimes we would play with pitching against a wall. In chalk we would draw a box on the wall behind the batter equal to the strike zone and the pitcher would pitch and call the strikes. That is another thing that I learned from my father in that era. You never made an excuse for losing and you never questioned an umpire's call. If the umpire called it a strike, it was. We were on the honor system and lived by it. This was called sportsmanship and we prided ourselves on it.

Saturday mornings were a great time. In the Bowling Green gym they had a recreation program where we played dodge ball and just dodge ball for three hours. We would divide up into two teams with a line in the middle of the gym separating the teams. If you caught the ball on a fly, the thrower was out. If you just got hit, you were out. Near the end of the session we would have a free for all dodge ball game. It was the best. The coach would throw the ball into the air and everyone would run freely about the gym. Someone would field the ball and keep throwing until they lost possession of the ball. As kids got hit with the ball, they were out. We played in socks so you could slide on the gymnasium floors, running with abandon, ducking and dodging. I was usually the winner. There was a sense of community, simple pleasures and competition.

Another past time was Chinese handball. In back of the Grand Union supermarket there were cement boxes marked in the sidewalk. Each was about six feet wide by ten feet long going from wall to curb. Chinese handball, as we called it, was played on a bounce to the wall and off of it. It is different than regular handball which requires hitting the front wall on a fly. The other difference was that you had to stay in your box. There might be six or eight players in boxes down a horizontal line. The server was in the first box and he could serve to anyone. You hit the ball with your hand to any of the boxes, keeping the ball as low to the ground as possible or hitting a "killer shot" which meant that the Spalding had to hit the wall and sidewalk in the crack where they both met. You would get points based upon your successful shots. If you scored you stayed in or moved up to the service box. If you lost a point you moved to the end of the line of players.

Chinese handball was started by the high school kids who had cars and were starting to hang out around the stores. The boys wore tee shirts, jeans, slicked back hair, and packs of cigarettes rolled up in their sleeves. They were not considered to be academics or jocks. Sometimes they wore black leather jackets and engineer boots. We called them "hoods."

My father smoked up to four packs of cigarettes a day and had four heaping teaspoons of sugar with each cup of coffee. His breakfast was never more than a buttered roll which he would dip into his coffee. He said that he got the habit of smoking in the Army where the cigarette companies gave the soldiers free cigarettes. I guess those companies knew what they were doing, getting G.I.'s addicted to cigarettes. I never developed a taste for tobacco. Even though we did not then appreciate the cancer-causing effects of it, I had no interest in it and it conflicted with my sports. One day there was a cigar in the house and I started fooling around with it in front of my parents, saying I wanted to smoke. My father said fine and lit the cigar. I was acting like a big shot, puffing away, chatting up a storm. My father and mother just waited for the inevitable, me turning green, getting very sick, and throwing up. That cured me of any interest in tobacco.

My mom had been diagnosed with epilepsy. She had some seizures which I vaguely remember. My dad was distraught by them. He brought her to a top neurologist who prescribed medication that brought it under control and kept it there.

In 1955 we had purchased a new Ford. My parents liked Fords. This one was tan on the sides and white on top. It had some chrome on the sides and a big, powerful engine which not only sustained it for many years but gave my dad the opportunity on a few occasions to "let it out." This was before the days of Ralph Nader's *Unsafe At Any Speed: The Designed-In Dangers of the American Automobile*, Grossman Publishers (1965). Cars were made to last a long time. In fact, most of the antique cars that you see at car shows are from that era. Men seemed to identify more with cars than women and were overly proud and protective of them.

My dad taught my mom to drive. She received her license and became an excellent driver. In all the years that she drove, she did not have an accident. Women tend to be better drivers than men, just ask any insurance company.

Learning to drive was an event. I would sit in the back of the car. My parents were up front and my mom was behind the wheel while my dad coached her from the front passenger seat. She practiced in parking lots. There were no driving schools then and she was one of the first women in our neighborhood to have a driver's license. She passed her test on the first try, never disclosing that she was an epileptic, which would have prevented her from securing one. In more than thirty years of driving after that, she never had an accident and never received a ticket of any kind, not even a parking ticket.

She was very proud of that. I can remember my dad telling her to do this or that as she drove. Naturally, I would chime in from the back seat with some needless, childlike comment such as: "Yeah mom, keep both hands on the wheel." Instead of being perturbed, my mother would politely reply: "Yes, Tom."

Levitt built his planned communities with shopping centers, schools, ball fields and swimming pools. One block from my home was the Carman Avenue Swimming Pool, equipped with two one-meter and one three-meter diving boards. It was twenty five yards across and about fifty yards long. The only pools to rival them were the Jones Beach salt water bath house pool built by Robert Moses and the City Parks Department pools which were older and massive. For example, the Astoria Pool was one hundred meters long and fifty meters wide with a separate diving well which included a tower for ten meter diving. It had seating all around for thousands and the 1964 Olympic Team Trials were held there. The Carman Avenue Pool like all the others Levitt built had a separate kiddy pool and you needed a pool tag evidencing your residence in order to get in for free. In the summer, Memorial Day to Labor Day, I did not miss a day at the pool. I slept in my Ocean Pool nylon swim suit. My dad could not swim. My mom had a passable freestyle for that era allowing her to navigate up to fifty yards, non-stop, with an open turn. Playing underwater tag was terrific because you got to use the people in the pool as an obstacle course, swimming underwater around them. My mom would let me swim between her legs and sometimes back again if I really held my breath.

When I first started going to the pool, I was four and five. I was always with my mom and in the kiddy pool. I wore boxer trunks and it had little spray water spouts at each end. It was about a foot deep. The mothers would gather around the concrete perimeter. The kids would wade by walking on their hands, heads out of the water and legs behind. We did not realize it then but it was excellent training for the dog paddle which is usually a natural first step in learning how to swim.

The lifeguards started to give us swimming lessons, first in the kiddy pool. I do not remember what they were, because they were really nothing. Gradually, though, the younger kids made their way to the bigger pool adjacent to the kiddy pool. It was at the shallow end, in three feet of water. The kids would gather there and hold onto the sides. They were told to flutter kick and breathe to the side. We would count to ten while our faces were in the water, blow bubbles out and turn our heads to the side to inhale. I do not remember how I learned to do arm strokes. More than likely though it was just by replicating what I saw my mom do. She learned to swim from her father who taught her in the ocean at the Rockaways, off the Atlantic Ocean coastline of Queens, New York.

Carman Avenue Pool (1952). Learning to swim.

Swimming or being under water presents another reality. There are different sounds, no human voices. You become more in tune with your body because you hear it breathing; your eyes must adjust to blurred vision; you must control your breathing by not breathing in; you do not hear human voices and you do not speak. Once you get past the panic of being in the water, you start to enjoy it and it is a time for introspection. Being under water also forces you to realize that you are in a foreign element. The animals who make their home in the sea are obviously equipped to be there and we are unwanted aliens with limited visiting privileges. The subterranean forces of the deep are among the most powerful known to man and in light of that, swimming on top of the water is a humbling experience. We are so inadequate, in comparison to the creatures beneath us.

Being around the water as much as I was, you had to learn to swim. At the end of everyday of playing ball, I would wind up at the pool to cool off. When I was eight, I was at the pool with my mom and dad. It was overcast and I have a recollection of the pool being empty of people. An older woman had apparently convinced my parents that I had some swimming prowess and that I should swim in the deep end of the pool. I had never swam in deep water before but I was told to dive in and swim across the twenty five yard distance. I was terrified. I dove in, looking underwater at the deep end, far below, where no humans abide. It was blue, with some black dirt in the crevices making the outline of a rectangle at the very bottom. The vacuuming of pools occurred infrequently back then. I swam as fast as I could in order to get over it. As I approached the incline below on the other side of the pool, a sense of relief came over me as I hit the wall and climbed out. The lifeguard coach said that I swam the distance in a relatively straight line despite the fact that there were no painted lines on the bottom of the pool. Apparently my body instinctively realized that the shortest distance between two points is still a straight line. I just know I was scared and wanted to get it over with as soon as possible. It was an overcast and dreary day. I remember not taking a breath and keeping my head down the entire time. I miraculously completed the distance, without drowning, in fifteen seconds flat. Unbeknownst to me the woman had held a stop watch on me. She explained to my parents that this was an excellent time. It was 1955.[5]

My parents gradually wound up becoming the swim coaches for the Carman Avenue swim team, but leading up to that I was supposed to go to practices each morning. I hated it. I would take baby steps in walking to the pool, arriving late or I would make excuses for not going at all. I disliked the competition, always being timed and swimming in the deep water during workouts. I had not gotten over my fears. I did not want to race or have anyone expect anything of me. After years of just frolicking in the pool, the fun was gone. Now I was being told each day that I must go into the cold water, early in the morning. It was not how I wanted to spend my day.

My parents won the team championship for the Levittown Swimming Association, a big deal held each and every year at the end of the summer. They were both thrown in the pool, the deep end. My mom could swim so that was not a problem. My father could not swim. He was jubilant, kept smiling, but barely made it back to the side of the pool.

Chapter III

<u>Looking For More</u>

This newfound interest in competitive swimming encouraged my parents to consider my continuing swimming during the winter months. There were few indoor pools on Long Island and none where they held workouts. My mom had her license then and from the time I was eight until ten years of age, each Monday and Wednesday after school she would pick me up and drive me to Brooklyn Technical High School for swim workouts with the Knickerbocker Swim Club and their famous coach, Bob Alexander. Bob later became the Maccabiah Games Coach, the Jewish Olympics as we called it. He was also a coach of other international teams, producing several world champions and Olympic medalists. I published an article about him which contributed to him being inducted into the International Swimming Hall of Fame in Fort Lauderdale.

Each Monday and Wednesday afternoon my mom would meet me after school. She usually had a hamburger, French fries and a container of chocolate milk or a Coke waiting for me. She would take Northern State Parkway to the Grand Central Parkway to the Interboro which is now known as the Jackie Robinson Parkway to Atlantic Avenue toward Brooklyn Technical High School located near the downtown part of Brooklyn. My dad would take a subway over from his job in lower Manhattan. I did not understand it then but the subway runs under the East River and New York Harbor between lower Manhattan and Brooklyn. During the Revolutionary War, George Washington made this trip at night and on the water in order to escape from Brooklyn Heights which the British had won. He made an outpost across the river in lower Manhattan now known as the Battery. There he at first unsuccessfully defended against an attack by four hundred British war ships.[6] Later, of course, he became victorious.

Brooklyn Tech was and remains one of three special admission public schools in the City of New York. In other words, the best students went there. The other schools are Stuyvesant High School in Manhattan and the Bronx High School of Science.

Brooklyn Tech had a pool in its basement. It had about four lanes and a diving board. It was all white tiles. Our coach, Robert Alexander from North Jersey, would drive in for the practices. The Knickerbocker Swim Club was one of the first established in New York. Its predecessor was the Orbach's Swim Club named after the Department store and founded in the early 1950s. New York, being in the cold northeast, was not known for producing great swimmers back then mostly because we did not have many competition pools. The Mecca for competitive swimming that was beginning to emerge was California. There were no teams in New York with any national prominence except for the New York Athletic Club (N.Y.A.C.) on 59th Street in Manhattan. The N.Y.A.C. uptown (the downtown club by the Battery gave the Heisman Trophy every year to the nation's most outstanding college football player) had great swimmers who were given free memberships there after they graduated from college. They would come to New York to work and join the N.Y.A.C. The N.Y.A.C. also had championship water polo teams for the same reason. Ironically though in the 1950s, African Americans, Jews and women were not allowed to become members of the N.Y.A.C. Jackie Robinson had made it into the big leagues but would not be eligible to become a member of the N.Y.A.C.

The Knickerbocker Swim Club was different, mostly because of Jack Abramson, a tremendous businessman and go-getter from Jamaica Estates who had three wonderful sons, David, Alan and Richie. Two became medical doctors and one became a stockbroker. Jack Abramson and his wife Ruth were dynamos who really brought competitive swimming to New York and even more importantly, broke down the barriers of racism and anti-Semitism. All three of their sons attended Brooklyn Tech. Jack was the President of the Club. For a few moments during each practice he could be counted on to say a few words, usually about upcoming meets. He was instrumental in bringing the U.S. Olympic Team Trials to New York in 1964 and later fielded a U.S. Team for the Maccabiah Games in Israel.

During the workouts, the younger kids would finally get a chance to swim a few laps, not many. I remember, one lap and then later in the practice, two laps or fifty yards. That is where I had trouble. I would work myself up into a panic half way back on the second lap. I just did not take to the racing and had the same problem in meets. I was beginning to feel like a coward or a quitter. I would have to go to the side before completing the second lap. My parents were never critical but I sensed their disappointment.

To this day I am not sure why it happened, but it bothered me for years. There is an expression in sports having to do with becoming a champion. It is a phrase taken from the runners at the Boston Marathon who encounter "Heart Break Hill" around the twenty third mile and who are in excruciating pain, ready to give up, to back down or hold themselves back. It is said that real champions have the capacity to overcome the pain and "go through the wall." The wall being a wall of pain.

The water at Brooklyn Tech was dark green. You could not see the bottom of the pool. I may have been worried about monsters down there or I might have run out of breath on the second lap, perhaps not breathing properly. I think that was probably the latter, together with not acclimating to the water, and possibly getting just a little sea sick from the turbulence (yes, that can happen to you even if you are just bobbing on the surface).

My parents took me to all those practices and indoor and outdoor swim meets all over New York, but I really did not seem to be taking to it. So as I entered the sixth grade, the competitive swimming stopped for awhile. I would get back to it a few years later in a big way. But in the meantime, my parents wanted me to get a better education. With that I was also taking a break from sports, at least during the school year.

The summers on Long Island are beautiful. Riding my bike along the bike path of Wantagh Parkway almost to Jones Beach, was a treat. Even better was a real swimming hole that we found in Merrick. The water was clean, the foliage around it was lush. It had a sandy beach, no lifeguards, a tire to swing on and a parkway bridge to dive off—it was idyllic.

My mom would take me to Jones Beach three or four times during the summer. The first time I saw the ocean I ran for it. Sometimes we would go with my dad and pack a picnic lunch. We would park by the big parking lots in back of Fields 3 or 4 and walk through the tunnel to the boardwalk. There you could play miniature golf or shuffle board or stay late and watch Guy Lombardo, the great band leader, come up to the theater in his magnificent mahogany speedboat out of his summer home in Freeport.

New York was safe, clean, on the move and the center of the universe. Each summer right before school my mom would take me to Coney Island in Brooklyn. It was the best recreation and amusement park in America, better than Disney which was just starting in California and better than Disney World in Florida which did not yet exist. There was no Great Adventure. Coney Island had the Steeple Chase, painted horses that would take you on a ride; it had the sky high parachute jump; giant wooden slides that my mom also rode down; mirrors that made you look funny and the Cyclone Roller Coaster which was too big and scary for me. It had Ferris wheels and a fun house, Nathan's hot dogs, cotton candy, popcorn and lots of ice cream. It also had a scary fun house with make believe monsters inside.

Today, probably no sane parent would allow their children on these rides for fear of liability. They had no seat belts or extra cushions to prevent knocks or whiplash. But they did have the watchful eye of my mother and others like her.

Chapter IV

<u>The Nuns</u>

Sixth grade brought about a change in gears. My parents wanted me to focus more on academics. They were determined to give me the best education possible. They believed that that was possible at Sacred Heart Seminary in Hempstead, situated next to Sacred Heart Academy, the premier Roman Catholic girls high school in Nassau County. The grade school which I attended conducted classes for students from kindergarten through eighth grade. Some of Nassau's wealthier Catholics sent their children there. It was run by the nuns from the Order of St. Joseph, an elite Order of highly disciplined, rigid, academic nuns, many still attending graduate school at St. John's University in Jamaica or at Fordham in the Bronx. The nuns of St. Joseph had the reputation for being like the Jesuits—very serious and purposeful, motivating students to make something of themselves and to receive a classical education, including Latin and Greek. My parents enrolled me in Sacred Heart Seminary in the sixth grade. It would prove to be a difficult transition.

My father told me how he had been taught by Brothers who disciplined students by striking them on the knuckles with rulers. He said it was painful and I am sure it was. By the time I arrived at Sacred Heart I was afraid of brothers, priests and nuns, all dressed in black, always serious and wearing their crosses. They were on the side of God and I was not—or so I thought at the time. How could a lowly, insignificant sinner and child like me ever feel comfortable in such a place?

At the start of sixth grade I was off to Sacred Heart Seminary. All of the students wore uniforms. The girls had a green and blue plaid uniform with the SHS logo, side shoulder straps and white blouses. The skirt of it was below the knee and the girls were required to wear stockings and horrible flat shoes that almost looked like male wing tips, but abbreviated to comport with the slight stature and figures of the young girls. The shoes were so ugly. No matter how pretty the girls were, their beauty—their eventual womanhood—was repressed from blossoming. Perhaps this is why Billy Joel's lyrics read, "Catholic girls start much too late." This repression revolted me even then and I was merely eleven. The girls were being treated differently and I thought unfairly. Why not let their natural beauty evolve? Nothing flashy, but it just seemed that the repression at a natural time of pre-pubescent development would ultimately produce more rebellion, resentment, and anger later in life. At some point, if they were to realize their true inner selves, they would have to overcompensate to make up for this lag in development. The dress policy seemed counter intuitive, against natural law and it, together with the entire Catholic school experience, was a cultural shock to my system.

I had developed such a severe anxiety over the Catholic school experience that when I first started attending the school and for at least two months thereafter, I threw up every single day. I no doubt disliked the separation caused by leaving my home community, attending school with kids from all over Nassau. The differences and alienation was first felt when I had to ride the bus to school. When I attended Bowling Green I would walk to school. If I had gone on to Tresper Clark Junior High School, a brand new edifice in the East Meadow School District, I would have walked there as well. But now I had to take the bus from Stewart Avenue, boarding two blocks from my home. My mother would drive me to the bus stop. It would then wind its way through the East Meadow community, north and south of Hempstead Turnpike and finally through Hempstead to the school. Hempstead at that time was a pristine community, vibrant and more of a developed county seat than the neighboring community of Mineola, the actual county seat and the home of the County Executive Offices and the courts. But Hempstead was special. It had an Abraham & Strauss store, a hugely popular department store before the Roosevelt Field Mall existed. The Mall and nearby Mitchell Field is the spot from which Charles Lindbergh made his famous flight in 1927 across the Atlantic in the Spirit of St. Louis. The Mall was developed into the largest of its kind in the world. It subsumed all the neighborhood shopping areas of surrounding Villages and Towns, taking away customers and becoming a magnet for business. Once that happened, Hempstead went downhill. But until then, it was the Mecca for shopping.

Arnold Constable was also in Hempstead together with the Men's Clothier, Browning King Fifth Avenue and of course, Cookies, a restaurant on the corner of Hempstead Turnpike and Hilton Avenue, a favorite for everyone at Sacred Heart and for most of Nassau's residents.

Sacred Heart Seminary was a large home converted into a school with classrooms throughout. It sat on the northwest side of Hilton Avenue and Hempstead Turnpike, next to Sacred Heart Academy, a modern, large brick building to its north. Next to that sat the convent and next to that, recreation fields and another home converted to classrooms. Sacred Heart Seminary had no after-school programs. You simply got on the bus and were returned home.

For those first several months I could not stop throwing up. Finally, instead of riding the bus, my mother would drive me to the school. Sometimes I would arrive later or my mother would have to coax me out of the car. Sometimes I had to be taken home. The only friendly face that I could find in the place was a white-haired, little, old Italian custodian who seemed to empathize with my condition, telling me to take it easy and not worry so much. I have forgotten his name. I knew him only as Tony. I wish I could remember it—what a nice man!

The nuns did little to quell my fears. The nuns of St. Joseph wore black habits from the tops of their heads to their toes. They looked so uncomfortable. I could not understand how they could wear those habits year-round, but they did. Covering their hair and all but the oval of their faces were heavily starched white headpieces which culminated at the top in a triangle and descended across the chest in a half circle with the center of the semi-circle coming up to the throat, covering the chin and shoulders. All of that was then covered by a black veil which was draped out to the sides and back of the head extending down toward the elbows in front and the hip, pelvis area at the rear. The only flesh that could be seen were the white oval faces and hands. I say white because there were no nuns who were not Caucasian at that time, at least at Sacred Heart.

In addition, they had large crosses showing at the neck, chest area and large rosary beads around their waist with decades and another cross hanging from the hip area off to one side. They would sometimes say their rosaries while standing. They wore black stockings and heavy, black shoes with short, block heels. The nuns never seemed to smile except when speaking to parents. They were all about serious business, educating and disciplining children, whipping them into shape, making them into productive members of society. The nuns were also very devoted, rigidly following their vows, early to bed and early to rise, saying their prayers multiple times each day. The nuns of St. Joseph were not social reformers, but they were highly disciplined, smart and very hard working. I later came to have great respect for them.

I should point out the obvious, namely that nuns, at least in that era, did not wear makeup or perfume. I never saw the hair of a nun. They were also very clean. Their habits were neatly starched and pressed each day. Nothing was ever out of place. This by itself made students more self-disciplined and more caring about their own appearances. The nuns of St. Joseph appeared to be elite, a cut above other nuns—they lived in better quarters and taught in better schools. It made you feel that you were elite also or at least special for being able to attend such a fine school.

If nuns clapped their hands just once, that meant that you were to stop everything and come to attention. If you did not, then you would have a problem because the nuns of St. Joseph did use corporal punishment. Parents in that era though did not sue the school—they trusted in the judgment of the nuns. I do not ever remember a parent or student complaining about a student being hit or anything else at the school. The nuns were always right. Certainly they were better educated than most of the parents. These were the days when teachers were well respected as professionals—as much or more than doctors and lawyers. The thinking then was that nothing is more important than raising and nurturing the young. What a wonderful time in America it was. I had no concept of the Korean War; politics or Senator Joseph McCarthy. Those things were not discussed in school. Had I known about them I might have felt very differently about the complacency of so many in the heartland of middle America where I was being raised. I had not yet learned of Adolf Hitler; the threat of communism; the atomic bomb; discrimination or anti-Semitism. These things were also not discussed at our dinner table or in our home. I missed that. I do not ever recall my father reading a book. He read the newspaper each day and watched the news on television. The 1954 case of *Brown v. The Board of Education of Topeka*, 347 U.S. 483 (1954) dethroning the 1896 case of *Plessy v. Ferguson*, 163 U.S. 537 (1896) and the "separate but equal" legal doctrine, did not impact on us because we were students in an exclusive, private school; we were in the North and since there was discrimination in housing which still prevented blacks from moving into white neighborhoods, the *Brown* case had no ripple effect at that time in suburbia and where we lived. In the 1950s children and even adults were often protected from the harsh realities of the real world. I vaguely remember driving through Harlem in that era and seeing African Americans for the first time. It was after the decline of Harlem yet before its resurgence and there were neighborhoods where people were living in deplorable, squalid conditions. As we drove by, I remember my parents simply saying that these people were the poor. There was no discussion of slavery or the racial divide or the epidemic of heroin and drugs that engulfed that community.

My sixth grade class had a lot of students in it, but no minorities. My recollection is that we had over thirty students in our second floor classroom. Our desks sat on oak floors, with the teacher's desk in front, off to one side. Blackboards were on the two walls. Windows were on the other two walls at our backs and to the left. We had no air conditioning, but we were never cold.

Sister Bridgitine was our teacher. She stood not more than five feet and had a very stern look. As she faced the class, the boys were on her left and the girls on her right, all in rows. All of our desks had ink wells and all of us used fountain pens. There was great emphasis on the Palmer method of penmanship, practiced each day like Tibetan monks engaged in a religious rite of calligraphy.

Everyone had on uniforms except for me. Since I was new to the school, my uniform had to be fitted for me, prepared, altered, etc., once I arrived. It took a few months for that to happen. Until then I had some sport jackets which I wore, one was brown camel hair so I stood out. The boys all had blue blazers with white shirts and blue ties with the SHS logo on them, black shoes and pants that were a lighter blue with a black cord strip on the side. I liked the militaristic style of it, even though it was boring having to wear it everyday. It made you feel a little like a soldier, a warrior. My mother always pressed all of my clothes and they were neatly laid out for me each day. A blue overcoat was part of the uniform during the winter months. It too had the SHS logo and extended past the buttocks. But, when I first came to the school, I did not have any of these things.

My father and mother taught me how to dress. My father had to wear a suit to work everyday. When he came home at night, like the adoring son that I was, I would usually accompany him to his bedroom where he would change into his casual clothes. He always wore dress hats and tied perfect Windsor knots. The only person who I have seen tie comparable knots is our former President, the late Ronald Reagan.

Our sixth grade class had boys seated on one side of the room and girls on the other. Naturally the girls were all well behaved. I do not recall a girl ever being disciplined. The boys on the other hand were, to say the least, mischievous. Spit balls were fired from lunch room straws and some used more high powered canons such as pea shooters. The boys would chew up paper into little balls which then became their fodder. Notebooks were used to block the oncoming fire or one had to duck without attracting any attention from Sister Bridgitine. Spit balls are quiet but really quite disgusting when they hit because they flatten or splatter.

Once a week we would have art instruction and Sister Bridgitine would leave us alone with the art teacher. No one worried too much about not passing art, but we had school supplies including rubber type erasers that were used to correct our drawings. In lieu of spit balls, pieces of the erasers were broken off and hurled as projectiles. At the end of the one hour session, the floor of the classroom felt like a rubberized astro turf. The art teacher "ratted us out" to Sister Bridgitine and the Sister, the next day, pulled out five boys as the primary trouble makers. I was not one of them.

She had them turn around and face the wall. Then one at a time they were called to the front of the class and directed to throw the large black board erasers at the other boys as hard as they could. The erasers were then thrown in a wind up pitch at the boys. They ricocheted off the backs of their heads leaving white chalk marks. It was like being in a firing squad but the squad was being fired at by a single shooter. Those of us who remained in our seats would wince and gasp as each eraser hit its intended target. The boys would flinch as they were hit, their manhood being tested by their willingness to stand there and take it. It occurred to me then and now that the purpose of this punishment was to force conformity on the children, to beat down rebellion, creativity and independence in its burgeoning stages. The nuns who engaged in corporal punishment had a repressed anger which was unleashed with beatings of students. I do not recall a single student ever being seriously hurt by these episodes of violence on the part of the nuns, but it was so unprofessional and primitive. Rather than giving Catholic education a good name, I resented this treatment and this infliction of violence by the nuns. It scarred all of the students in a variety of ways. At the time it was done and condoned with the best of intentions. There was not one courageous voice questioning the wisdom of authority that would allow this kind of physical punishment to be inflicted upon children who were eleven years of age at the time. What I was watching is one of the things that has made Catholic education so financially successful. They do not advertise it, but they market discipline and corporal punishment. After military schools, this is the next-most-popular institution for promoting discipline by means that would not be tolerated in public schools then or now.

There were three rows of boys facing the front. There were about six of us in a row and probably six rows in the classroom, the others were occupied by the girls. I sat at the back of the classroom next to a row of girls. The boys in the class put me up to saying to the girl next to me, Gail: "You wear falsies, boom, boom, boom." I still remember her last name. She at first turned in my direction and then looked straight ahead. I had no idea what I had just said or what falsies were. I still did not have my uniform. This was still during the period when I was throwing up each day.

The boys were laughing. I had forgotten the incident until the next day when Sister Bridgitine called me out of the classroom by myself into the hallway. We stood face to face. I towered above her. Then she said: "what did you say to Gail yesterday?" Oh boy, this was really traumatic. I thought that I might be thrown out of school. Gail had given me up. I replied: "Nothing, Sister." Poor Gail. I did not mean to offend her. She was a pretty girl, neatly dressed in her uniform, whose breasts had matured. Sister Bridgitine was not believing and with my answer she hit me with a hard slap across the face. I had to stand at attention with eyes open and just take it like a man. This was really learning how to take a punch, what fighters call "rolling with a punch." You can not show that you are in pain or embarrassed. That would be admitting to a "glass jaw." I just turned my head slightly to avoid the direct hit, moving away from her hand. She still made some contact but it softened the blow. My father taught me how to" roll with a punch." I was not sure yet what the repercussions would be, but she told me to go back to my desk. Class resumed and I never heard anything more about it. I was not directed to apologize to Gail. I was not asked to implicate the boys who put me up to it. My father always drummed into me that I should "be a leader, never a follower." This incident drove home a point for me. I would never again be a follower. I would always lead or try to do so. If my parents were told anything about it, they never told me. I was never again hit by a nun.

My dad bought us both a set of golf clubs. I was the only kid to have them. We would go to the driving range and I was soon able to hit the ball more than two hundred yards almost every time. I would hop the fence at Salisbury Park (later it became known as Eisenhower Park) and play a quick nine holes after supper on one of the three courses there. Back then there were not many golfers. Few people could afford that leisure time or the expenses involved. Although I was far from royalty or being an aristocrat, I felt that I had more privileges and better rearing than the kids I knew. That made me feel instinctively proud. I was taught to play chess at a young age by relatives. It is a nobleman's game and one that none of my contemporaries knew how to play.

By seventh grade our class was too large and had to be broken up into two sections. Our teacher was an older nun, Sister Osmond. She looked very mean but had a heart of gold. Everyday she would give us extra play time, but when she came to the window of the class, you lined up to come back inside. We would play "Kill the Man with the Ball" in our uniforms. The game is like a rugby free for all. The man with the ball just keeps running until subdued.

During the luncheon recess the girls would stand and chat. They were not permitted to be unlady like and we did not have physical education classes at Sacred Heart. After lunch we would say the rosary. To me it was astounding how much time was devoted to lunch, recreation in the schoolyard and prayers. There did not seem to be much time left for anything else except diagramming of sentences, at which Sister Osmond was an expert.

Sister Osmond never had any discipline problems. Her stern look scared you. She never smiled and seemed so unhappy. But if you did not bother her she would not bother you. My mom started getting active in the school and was unofficially acting as the class mother. My mom ran fashion shows for the school. In particular my mom brought in handmade hat makers for luncheon lectures and to sell their wares. All the women bought them. They were beautiful. Mom, who was not employed also became very active in the Mercy League. This was a Catholic women's group on Long Island that raised money for Mercy Hospital, a Catholic hospital in Rockville Centre. My mom would often go there to volunteer her time at the hospital. My mother's father was Episcopalian and her mother was Catholic, but never went to church for as long as I knew her.

The nuns appreciated what my mom was doing for the school. I remember her bringing Italian pastries for all the nuns at Christmas and other holidays. The nuns who were always fasting or abstaining from something, really appreciated these treats. So, because of my mom I was no longer an outsider, I was an insider. Now I was respected by the nuns and the other kids. Of course, it did not hurt that I was the second tallest kid in our class.

Once a week at Sacred Heart we had ballroom dancing lessons with Professor Reilly. Professor Reilly was always impeccably dressed in a suit and each class would begin with the Grand March. The boys would be on one side of the room and the girls on the other. The John Philip Sousa 75 rpm music would play from Professor Reilly's phonograph. The students would briskly walk to the center of the room. The boys would bow to the girls, all of whom were required to wear white gloves for dance class. The boys would extend their right elbows and couples formed a line facing Professor Reilly. We would then march around in circles, from couples to four across to eight across. After the Grand March we would return to our side of the room. For each class the boys would come across the room, bow again and ask another young lady to dance. No one ever refused these entreaties. Girls like to dance. So now we would learn to waltz, cha-cha, rumba. We were not permitted to get too close to the girls. So our hands went under their elbows and hands and forearms wrapped around ours and landed on our elbows. We were always at least a foot apart. While I started to have my favorite dance partners, I still was not thinking of the girls sexually and I doubt they had any such thoughts of us. I did not become eleven until the end of sixth grade.

I was starting to learn to become a gentleman, with all the chivalry and good manners that entails. My parents were pleased with my development. I had my own charge card at Browning King Fifth Avenue, a well known men's clothier at the time located in Hempstead next to Abraham and Strauss and with a main store in New York City. This was before the woman's movement so there were few clothing shops for women. Few women went to work or needed clothes for that purpose. Men controlled the purse strings.

I never used it to buy clothes on my own, but when I walked through that store with or without my parents, the salesmen would stop whatever they were doing to say: "Good day, Master Liotti." Later it became Mister Liotti. My parents were not wealthy but the salesmen did not know that. At the time, being regular customers at Browning King was a big deal, none of my classmates or neighbors did likewise.

Chapter V

<u>Hardball And Learning To Steal Home</u>

My parents always had simple, good taste. My father taught me how a suit should be tailored or fit. Ultimately it was my mother who would smile, nod and wink, signaling her approval of the fit and purchase. My mom would stand by and wait for the tailor and my father to finish. My father and I would then look to my mom. She rarely had anything to add to my father's fastidious, meticulous instructions to the tailor. My shoes were always purchased at Browning King and since I did not have much of an arch in my feet, they were specially fit for me so that the bones in my feet would reconfigure with the help of a "cookie," always inserted in my shoes to create an arch.

We did not have summer schools back then and I never went to camp. Summers were a time of baseball, stick ball, swimming, playing, hanging out and outdoor barbeques on the grills that started to appear. Back then it was nothing fancy, mostly hotdogs and hamburgers. We did not really barbeque anything else at the time and barbeque sauces were not yet being marketed. We always had delicious Long Island corn and sometimes baked potatoes, also from Long Island and not Idaho. We had farm stands nearby where you could buy fresh fruit and vegetables, including watermelon, which we had for dessert. A second dessert would come later in the evening when the Good Humor or other ice cream trucks like Mr. Softee would come by ringing their bells. The kids would come running out of their homes with ten or fifteen cents in their hands calling out to the truck, which would then stop. The kids would line up at the side and the driver, dressed in a neat white uniform would open the back freezer door and fill the orders. One of my favorites was vanilla ice cream with toasted almonds.

That summer I was still playing in the majors of the little league. I was twelve. My dad was president of the league and also the manager of the team. We only had about three pitchers in our rotation and we were playing two games a week, usually one during the week at night and one on the weekends, on Saturday mornings. We played seven innings, not nine, but I was pitching at least every third game. When I was not pitching I played the outfield or I also was a catcher which I liked because there's lots of action. Even though I practiced my batting all the time at a range in East Meadow, I still could not hit.

My dad was still playing in a softball league then. I would go to his games. He always played with gusto, doing the unexpected. He would tell me about the great Jackie Robinson and how he would steal home. My father did likewise. He loved the game, the competition, to win. He usually played second base or short stop. He had his opponents believing that when he slid into base, it was with spikes up high. They were metal spikes. You did that if you wanted to hurt or cut somebody. My father never did that but he was so scrappy in other respects, players who were looking to tag him out would back away from the bag and miss the tag because they were afraid that he would spike them. If someone dared to attempt to spike him, he would start fighting with them. Some of his spirited bravado rubbed off on me.

My father told me that he could always get a hit by placing the ball or sometimes just doing a drag bunt down the first or third base lines and then outrunning the pitcher and third baseman. So while bunting was an option for me (because I could not hit), I did not use it if I had a third baseman, pitcher and catcher who were fast on their feet. Also, a bunt is viewed as kind of a cheap hit or cheater's hit that requires some degree of luck. It does not have the respect of a regular hit. So I did not want to break up the no hitter with a bunt. Instead, I decided to switch hit. I usually batted righty and this time I got up to the plate lefty. I was in no way ambidextrous. I did not tell my father beforehand that I was going to do it, but I could see him smirking from the bench. First, he saw me catching that season which he had not expected and he admired that because I was overcoming my fear of the ball by being behind the plate. Fear of the ball is felt by infielders if they get a "bad hop" and get hit in the face or miss the play. This happens a lot on poorly maintained Little League infields. Infielders have a really quick reaction time which I did not have. So, I could never be an infielder. Catchers are really in the war zone of baseball even though they are wearing equipment. As the pitch comes in you are looking at the ball and following it with your glove. If the batter does not swing or swings and misses, it is an easy catch. But if the batter hits a foul tip, the ball comes back at the catcher even faster than the pitch because now the ball is spun off the bat and it is in a different position than the path of the pitched ball. Great catchers like Jorge Posada or Yogi Berra have an ability and quickness to catch foul tips, foul balls, field bunts, stand firm in blocking the plate when a runner is sliding in and "pegging" the ball to second base on a steal.

Pegging is a term usually applied to the throws of outfielders after they catch a fly ball with a man on base. The man on base has to wait for the catch and tag up or not leave the bag he is on until the catch is made. The outfielder, if deep in the outfield, may not be able to reach the base that the runner is going to, so the infield, usually the shortstop or second baseman, will come into the outfield to take the throw on one hop or a single bounce. If the runners are heading home the better outfielders may try to throw all the way home to the catcher, on a line, meaning as close to the ground as possible and to the left field side of home plate. "Pegging" describes this relay throwing system but also usually the throw by the catcher over the mound, like a bullet, low for the tag out at second. If the runner is coming from first base, the ball must be thrown as close to the right field side of the second base bag as possible. When the catcher receives the pitch and the runner is going for a steal, the catcher has to stand, throw off his mask and fire the ball to second usually on a fly but sometimes on a peg where the ball is thrown low to the ground and skids on a low fast hop to the second baseman or shortstop, for the tag out. The catcher has more physical contact than any other player on the field. Being a catcher at twelve was one of my first conquests over my own fear.

In one game, Billy Janek had a no hitter going and it was the bottom of the seventh inning and the other team was winning. There were two outs and I was at bat. Janek was smiling. He figured I was an easy out. I figured that we were not going to win the game but there would be a victory, albeit a personal one, if I was able to get the hit. Janek was a righty. So, like most righties, his breaking pitch if he had one would break against a right handed batter. A left handed batter has to follow the breaking pitch to see if it's inside or outside the strike zone. Since the ball generally comes across the plate on a diagonal from the release on his right side to his left, as a batter you have to bring your left elbow down a little and bring the angle of the bat back a little more so you have firm contact with the ball. I had a slow reaction time and that's why I usually struck out. I was afraid of the ball, closed my eyes and did not follow it from the pitcher's hand release. I decided to bat lefty, figuring that if I could break his no hitter batting lefty that would add to my pyrrhic victory and be more humiliating for him. I was a bad hitter to begin with, but having the audacity to bat lefty would defy his ego and unsettle his stance.

Well, this time it was different. I followed the ball. It was heading toward the outside of the plate. I swung late, but I punched the ball just over the third baseman's head for a hit and broke up Janek's no hitter.

We all have opportunities to overcome fear. When, how, and if we do that is a personal matter. Champions meet it everyday. There is a fear that each of us has about harm, injury or death. Some have more survival instincts than others. But facing down fear of whatever our fears may be is a measure of our character and productivity. If we do not face off against our fears we never realize our true inner selves or our greatest potential. So I learned to identify my fears and started to face off against them. In life this is one of our great tests. We can ignore our fears, be timid and unchallenged or we can face off against them and try to conquer them. I chose the latter. In some ways, I am still doing so.

Not all of us are gifted. And in fact many of the people around us are imperfect. If we are not born with pure, natural talent then we must learn from others, their perfections and their mistakes. My father would remind me of that if I was sitting on the bench day dreaming and not watching the game. He would tap me on my head and say: "Watch that guy. See what he does. He knows how to hit. Watch him step into the ball. You see how he takes a cut?" That taught me to pay attention, to watch the good and the bad, the natural talents and those who were struggling. I then tried to replicate the best. Being able to watch sports on television was helpful because you could watch the stars and learn from them. This technique for learning has stayed with me. I have used it time and again in sports, in life and in my career. Later in life when I was asked how I learned my craft as a trial lawyer I said that I never had a mentor in my profession, but I did have the best teacher—myself. I learned by watching others and replicating the actions of the best people.

I taught myself a pick off motion. A good pick off motion makes the pitcher into a liar and fake. This is so because he has to make the runner think that he is throwing home when in fact he is throwing for a pick off. The right handed pitcher has no problem in picking off at third base because all he has to do is step forward with his left foot and throw to the third baseman who is right in front of him. A second base pick off means that the pitcher must turn one hundred eighty degrees and throw. That takes longer and runners easily return to the bag. So naturally with some gamesmanship, I would have the second baseman cover the bag and the short stop would come behind the runner and go to the top of the infield and behind second. I would turn and pretend to overthrow the second baseman. It's an old trick. The runner would see the ball go over the head of the second baseman and think that it was a wild throw. He would run toward third. I was throwing to the short stop and he would throw to third base and cut the runner off. He would then be caught in the "squeeze" and tagged out.

First base was more of a chore. The runner would take a lead. As a right hand pitcher I would look over my shoulder. I would lift my leg in the same fashion as throwing home. Then instead of coming forward and down with the left leg, you turn your leg out and to the left.

Marty Rivard was a great athlete. He was an opponent on the mound. His team was playing ours. We were not expected to win but we did. The crucial part of the game was my pick off of Marty Rivard. He had it all. Speed, agility, coordination—he could hit, pitch and field. He was a natural all around athlete but over-confident and cocky. That made him my target—someone who needed a lesson in humility. But if I could beat him then my status among my teammates would grow. He was really quick but I managed to pick him off at first after he had gotten a single. I bested him pitcher to pitcher but also when he was on the field. It gave me another notch in my gun belt. He fought with the umpire. That made it worse for him because he made it appear that it was an important event for him. If he had just taken his lumps and walked off the field it would not have been as noticed. That taught me something. Take the hit like a man and you can come back. Be a cry baby about losing and you will lose again because you have shown a flaw in your personality—you cannot take the loss. You build the other guy's ego by showing you're sore and distracted, still thinking about your defeat. It is far better to get over it by planning for how you will get even with or cause an even greater loss for your adversary.

In eighth grade I was back at Sacred Heart in Sister Theresa's class. She was a heavy set woman. She was very nice, if you behaved yourself.

But if you did not then she would attack you with a flurry of punches and slaps. She never hit me but I saw her go after many students. Now the question was whether we could learn from her or were we just going to be intimidated by her all year. Our two seventh grade classes had merged and we were again one.

Leadership can be established in a variety of ways. My first taste of it came in eighth grade. Vincent was a nice boy but as he developed he was becoming a bit of a hoodlum. He was perceived as a troublemaker, the toughest kid in the class, so everyone was afraid of him. The other students would follow him for that reason. He had a clique of young men that always seemed to be up to no good. I was neither here nor there, content to just let life run its course until one day I had a show down with Vincent.

We were in the basement coatroom at the start of school. There were other students milling about when Vincent announced his prank of the day. He intended to take one of the large fire extinguishers off the wall and set it off producing foam all over, disruption and a mess that might damage the students' winter clothes, among other things. Sister Theresa had not anointed me as Class President or as her agent but something told me that this was a moment when I could either be a follower or a leader.

Vincent looked tough in addition to being that way. He would go into the pawn shops in Hempstead and buy switch blade knives, bring them to school and show them to his fellow students. We were in awe, but also believed that he was capable of using those knives. So with Vincent you were not sure if you would be in a fair fist fight or whether it would become a knife fight. Vincent ruled by fear of expected consequences. So you either went with him or you might have to deal with the consequences of not doing so. While I certainly did not want to be in a knife fight, I had some idea of how to defend against one. You use your feet to fight in order to keep the knife away from your body. You wrap a coat around your left wrist and use it to block. And you use anything bigger than the knife to attack. A light chair is usually your best bet. You must also be prepared to kill or to be killed or cut.

This was a moment that changed my life but Vincent's also. Leadership is something that is hard to define but I believe that there are influences that shape it. It may be part genetic but it is also taught. I was taught that you should not work on an assembly line if you can own the plant or be President of the United States or a famous lawyer. But there are opportunities and tests along the way in life. Those who seize them may become leaders. Those who do not may be condemning themselves to mediocrity, an unchallenged existence, just cruising through life. That was not for me but I did not know it yet. My leadership skills were evolving.

I told Vincent that he was not going to take the extinguisher off the wall, but he was going to defy me. We stood facing each other. Some other students were around so word of this would carry. Each of us had an opportunity to back down or blink. Neither of us would.

In my head I could hear my father say "Take the first punch." Vincent stood there, arms at his side, each of us "called out." The tone would be set by which of us did something first. If you put your "dukes up," it would be a fist fight. If he pulled a knife, it would be a knife fight. I did not have a knife.

Then it happened. I hit him with a left hook. He did nothing except step back. He had tears in his eyes. He was not hurt, just stunned that I had the courage to do that. With that single act he lost his leadership role and I acquired it. That all happened because I stood up to him. At some point each of us have a moral and ethical fiber or component that says to us, "that's enough, I will not do that." That's when we stake a claim to leadership. We begin to realize who we are and start to act on our own volition. I was not going to join with Vincent. I made my stand against him and liked it. The bullies had lost.

Sister Theresa began to take a liking to me. I appreciated that. I did not get into trouble and kept the other boys out of it. We were still boys but no longer ruled by Vincent and his friends. We set our own agenda which did not involve creating trouble but did involve an interest in the opposite sex and meeting girls at the Calderone Theater in Hempstead on Saturdays and seeing movies like *Butterfield 8* with Elizabeth Taylor and Lawrence Harvey while "making out." Taylor was in her prime. She played the provocative role of a prostitute and was probably suggestive to the girls we were with or so we no doubt had fantasies of at the time.

My first girlfriend was Janice Casey. She lived around the corner from the school and later moved to Hicksville. She came from a big family. We were THE couple. We never did much of anything except kiss now and then, but we had strong feelings for each other which never quite evolved. Our knowledge of sex as a class was extremely limited. In those days Catholic schools did not teach health or sex education. We were naive and childish about sex. But then again, we were children. The nuns seemed oblivious to sex. The word was never spoken. A "dirty thought" was a venial sin.

One of the male students managed to take a black and white photo out of his father's military albums. It was a photo of his father's male organ dressed up to look like a face. It had glasses and the big nose was the penis with whiskers or a mustache underneath and then a large chin which was the scrotum. We were saying the rosary aloud after lunch and the photo was making the rounds among the boys on our side of the classroom. We were giggling quietly. Then one of the boys passed it to the girls' rows and it was being circulated among the girls. They were not smiling or laughing. It went to the front of the class where it was intercepted by Sister Theresa who looked at it, said nothing and thumb tacked it to the bulletin board so that the owner might claim it later. There was the male organ hanging there, staring out at us as we said the rosary aloud. An hour later the photo was redeemed by the student who brought it to school. It was not seen again.

I was not the teacher's pet but Sister Theresa liked me. She would give me extra help and reported to my parents, much to my surprise, that: "he is very smart and can do anything he sets his mind to." According to Sister Theresa, it was all about focus, which I did not yet possess.

I probably had Attention Deficit Disorder then which I have resolved on my own, over time. What I have learned is that once you overcame the disorder your concentration can become more powerful than those who never had the disorder or never challenged themselves to overcome it. What I have learned is that due to the disorder, I have probably lost some skills that I could have developed earlier in life if I had the attention span at that time. So now, for example, I read slower but I do not take my comprehension for granted. I do not go on to another sentence or even a word until I understand what I have read.

Part of the problem was that I never considered academic subjects to be very important or difficult. I took them for granted and figured, much to my own and my parents' consternation, that I could always catch up or learn it later on if I needed to do so. I was simply far more interested in sports.

It was prophetic that I did not go to a Catholic high school. My parents had looked at military schools for me including LaSalle Military Academy in Oakdale, Long Island, at that time a prestigious Catholic high school and Eastern Military Academy in Woodbury, the former Otto

Kahn Estate, the second largest home in North America, now known as Oheka Castle. Both were boarding schools although within easy driving distance from our home in East Meadow. My parents also looked at prep schools including Williston Prep in Massachusetts and Lawrenceville Prep in New Jersey. I did not attend any of them. I do not think it was a money issue as much as my parents not liking the schools, not wanting to deal with the separation that would come from sending me away and feeling that they could do a better job of nurturing me. But a few things happened in the summer after eighth grade. First I made it to the Pony League All-Star team as a third string pitcher. I doubt that I would have made it to the team had it not been for my father pulling a few strings for me. So rather than have people think that, I wanted to show them that I belonged there. I did not want my father embarrassed. I never told him that but I knew it was up to me to measure up.

As fate would have it, we had a great team but in the first round we drew as our opponents the Levittown Pony League, a truly star studded team with amazing players and a fast ball pitcher who was occasionally a bit out of control. He was what we then called a "bean baller." He was fearsome. It was a nine inning game. Our first pitcher got clobbered and our second string pitcher was no better. After six innings we knew we were going to lose. I took the mound. The best I could do is show everyone that I should have been the starter. I wanted everyone to think that their judgment about me was wrong; that I was the best Pony League pitcher and if they had started with me they might have won. I wanted to singlehandedly win the game if I could. I wanted to create the impression that it was just me against the other team.

All those years of practice with my dad had taught me to concentrate and focus. Now I was the center of attention. No one was expecting much from me. The other team had bigger guys on it and a couple of sluggers, one hitting a home run at a prior at bat.

They did not know me. As the third string pitcher they figured I must be worse than the first two guys they had already smeared. A couple of them snickered as they came to the plate. It was show down time. They were underestimating me which is exactly what I wanted. They would not be as intense whereas I was all fired up, not showing it of course because I did not want to give it away that they were in my cross-hairs—mano-a-mano.

Part of what an athlete does is establish his or her unique personality during a contest. I had to stake my claim to the plate. Confident batters will sometimes crowd the plate. That is done to intimidate the pitcher but also to distort his view of the strike zone and to get him to throw outside.

My father had taught me how to back up the batters by "dusting them off." My dad was a tough player, he would fight with anyone. He told me that he would throw at the batters to back them up, scare them. He even hit a few. He did not care. He was playing for keeps in every game. He taught me how to throw a breaking pitch, an unbelievable curve ball which I would throw directly at the right handed batters. They would step back from the plate and the ball would break over it for a strike. If they swung at it after stepping back, they were off balance, without power on their right, back leg. They would either pop up for an easy out or strike out. My breaking pitch went from the batters left shoulder down to his knees on the outside of the plate, about a three foot break, high to low, which is unbelievable. I was not that fast, but each pitch was a deception. I used a change up, a side arm and even a submarine. These were techniques that were rare even in the big leagues, but these guys had never before seen anything like it. They were unsettled. They did not know what to expect. I faced nine batters in three innings and struck them all out, but our team was not hitting and I was not a hitter. Nonetheless, to add to the drama of what I could do if they had only picked me first, I stepped up to the plate. I was determined to not "go down looking," meaning striking out without swinging.

The pitcher was still that "bean baller" but I decided I would swing on his first pitch. Since I always swung late, I decided I would start earlier. I batted righty. It was a fast ball heading near the plate, I closed my eyes and swung. The ball lofted near the fence at right centerfield. It was nearly a home run. It was caught and it was game over except everyone said that they should have started with me. Mission accomplished!

From that game on I felt that I could have gone a lot further in baseball. I liked the game and I had become very good at it. But other events intervened that sent me on a different path.

Chapter VI

<u>Finding My Niche In Sports</u>

That summer without any training I competed in the Levittown Swimming Association Championships. I was thirteen and my events were the one hundred yard freestyle and the one hundred yard backstroke. I won both events and no longer had any fear of the water. Maybe it was the three-year hiatus. I do not know.

After that meet my father went to work. East Meadow Public Schools did not have a winter swim team or pool, but just over the line of Old Country Road, in the neighboring community of Westbury, they did have an indoor pool and team. So my dad made arrangements for me to use the address of friends in Westbury so that I could attend school there. Their son was using someone's address in East Meadow so that he could play baseball there.

I was also learning that there were other cultures, races and religions. My father taught me more than racial tolerance or acceptance. He viewed that as an insult to African Americans who had been enslaved, and discriminated against for two hundred years. My father felt that they had every right to live, to be in peace among us, to grow their families and to prosper just as his parents were able to do so even though they too were discriminated against. He told me that Italians, Jews, and all minorities have everything in common in that they have all been the victims of discrimination.

My dad became friendly with a wonderful African American family—the Forsters. They had a home at the corner of Grand Blvd. and Brushhollow Road, directly across the street from one of the oldest African churches in America, AME Zion. It has former slaves buried in its graveyard just across the street from the Forster's home. The Forsters lived in New Cassel which was then becoming integrated. The Forsters were a large family and all hard-working. Mr. Forster was, among other things, a painter who did work on our home. Back then this was a shock to our all white neighborhood because white and black people did not mix. Blacks did not come into white neighborhoods even to do work. *De facto* and *de jure* discrimination existed in the north. We had our own form of Jim Crow. My parents would give the Forsters food and clothing around the holidays. Although we never got around to socializing, we became lifelong friends.

I attended Westbury Junior High School on Rockland Street in Westbury and my mother would drive me there everyday. Since the swimming season did not start until November, I decided that I would tryout for the football team. The coach was a great guy, an Algebra teacher. His name was Annunziata and he took a liking to me although I was not very good. I played end on offense and linebacker on defense. I made the team. I did not like getting hit especially in the knees where bones might break. But I felt proud. I was in very good shape for the first time. My parents were proud and came to all the games.

October, 1955 Levittown Hall after awards ceremony.
My father congratulating me on my first trophy. It was for the Little League
baseball farm team. I was eight.

Westbury Junior High School was an integrated school. In ninth grade our music teacher was Rufus Norris. He had a reputation at the time for being crazy and a racist. We started every class by singing the Star Spangled Banner and God Bless America. Naturally we all stood and faced the flag in doing so except one courageous African American girl in the rear of the classroom, Diane. She would not stand or sing. One day Mr. Norris saw this and stopped everything. He stood up and came around to her, speaking in a loud voice chastising her for not standing or singing. He began by telling her that she was unpatriotic and did not respect the soldiers who had given their lives in defense of our country. Diane bravely kept her composure and simply said that she was a Jehovah's Witness and that it was against her religion to worship the flag. This was a confusing moment for me and my white classmates. I was in a public school and with African Americans for the first time. Rufus struck me as a dangerous lunatic whereas Diane seemed mature and smart, but I was not a part of her world. We were about the business of public education and at the time I failed to see what Rufus' tirades had to do with that. In retrospect I later learned how heroic Diane was. I wish I could remember her last name or speak with her.

As the football season unceremoniously came to an end I made my way into the swim season. As a freshman I made the Varsity swim team, earning a high school letter. Our coach was Bob Otto. I went to his so-called practices each day which were almost non-existent. I became good friends with a star sprinter and senior on the team, Jim Beck, who was also our Captain. Because Jim was a sprinter, I gravitated toward the two-hundred-yard and four-hundred-yard freestyles. Without much training that first year, I finished seventh in the County championships. As I watched the Section Eight finals from the stands at the Long Beach Municipal Pool on Magnolia Boulevard, I remember turning to a swimmer from Plainview High School, Al Bishop, and saying that next year I am going to beat that guy and win this meet. The guy I was referring to was Gary Weinstein, a standout, extremely talented swimmer from Plainview-Old Bethpage High School who was far ahead of the field. In fact, I remember him swimming part of the four-hundred-yard freestyle championship competition on his back and still winning. It was the ultimate humiliation of the competition.

I won my varsity letter, a big green "W" which my mom sewed onto a beautiful, white button down sweater. I proudly wore it all the time.

By the end of ninth grade I was beginning to believe that competitive swimming was going to be my sport. Even then sports enthusiasts were starting to realize that the days of "three letter men" were gone. In order to excel in sports you had to concentrate on one sport. It was 1961. I was fourteen. A year before, a young girl from Flushing YMCA, Lynn Burke, won two gold medals in backstroke at the Rome Olympics. Lynn retired from swimming but she had a younger brother, Bobby Burke, who was a competitive swimmer and competed with me.

Lynn had gone out to California to train in Santa Clara in 1958. As a result, she made the 1960 Olympic Team. She showed that New Yorkers, without a warm climate or appropriate pool facilities could become world class swimmers with the right training.

The Olympic Swim Team just prior to departing for the Rome Olympics had to have a place to train. Bob Burke, Lynn's father, made arrangements for the team to train at the Renaissance Country Club in Roslyn, New York. The Club had an eight lane, fifty meter, unheated, outdoor pool and the owners of it, the Martucci family, were agreeable to a competitive swimming training program in the summer of 1961. Our coach was Dick Krempecki, the Head Coach at St. John's University during the academic year. The program attracted some of the best swimmers in the metropolitan area because before that there was nothing like it. We would be training for two workouts a day, long course, meaning fifty meters. At that time the Amateur Athletic Union ran national championships in the summers and winters. The summer championships were also held in a long course fifty meter pool, whereas the winter championships were held in a short course pool of twenty five yards. In short course there are more turns. In long course there are fewer turns but the races were also longer since a meter is thirty nine inches. It was then commonly felt that in order to successfully compete on a national level, you had to train in a long course which, up until the Renaissance program, New York had not had.

So I trained that summer doing two-hour workouts in the morning and another two hours at night, five days per week and a two-hour workout on Saturday morning. This was state-of-the-art training, at the time replicating the California model.

We were also starting to train with big yardage and doing something that was totally new called interval training. You would pick a distance (say one hundred meters) and repeat it ten times with an interval of rest of about thirty seconds in between each one hundred meters. The coach would call out your time on each swim and send you off again after the rest. The objective was to swim faster on each interval and to shorten your recovery time so that ultimately you were simulating the actual race distance at a faster pace broken by short rest periods.

There has been quite a bit written about the synergistic effects of music on athletic performance. I did not know anything about that but I did like playing the song "Locomotion" by Little Eva in my head. It got me moving faster and distracted me from the hard work that I was doing. Instead of idle thoughts, the music causes you to pay attention to the power of your body moving through the water. Your timing and rhythm pick up with the music.

We also adopted something called circle swimming whereby you could put ten or more swimmers in each lane and they would stay to their right of the black lane markers on the bottom of the pool going down a lap on one side and coming back on the other side of the lane. So there were few collisions. The swimmers would be sent off five seconds apart with the slower ones going last. I started in the last place position but quickly started passing those in front of me. As I came up on the swimmer in front of me I would give them one tap on the foot and they would move more to the right while I would pass them in the center of the lane, avoiding contact with the swimmer coming back on the next lap on my left. I also started in the slowest lane with the worst swimmers but by the summer's end, I was in the fastest lane where it was harder to pass the better swimmers. Those out in front wanted to stay there or expand their leads. Those behind were eager to pass. If the swimmers up front slowed, we would be up on their heels and they would lose their slot or position. If that happened often enough then they would lose their position not just on that item but for that workout and maybe into the future. It is a bit like being taken out of the lineup in a ball game. For the swimmers who are coming up, you must never lose your slot and you have to keep moving up. Stars can be born in workouts or at least you know that they are coming. All they need to do is transform their workout performance into meet performance. Once they get past the "jitters" and get used to winning, this is accomplished. Anyone can stay with the best for twenty five yards, but pulling away from the field is exhilarating while falling behind is defeating. As you go along you are measuring your opponent. You are looking for weaknesses. You make a move. Are they with you, or are they backing down? If there is no change, you may just ride your position and wait to make your move. They may try to pull away but if you stay with them, they will know that you are just pacing and will move on them at the last part of the race. Even though you are behind, you have a psychological edge because your opponent thinks that he has expended too much energy by staying out in front without taking a commanding lead. The swimmer just behind has taken control of the race. He or she might be moving up slightly each lap seeing how much time and space they need to catch up and pass. Sometimes it's just a half a stroke or a stroke back.

One of the tricks used by middle distance and distance swimmers is to ride the eddy currents of your opponent. When you are swimming in a circle, the first swimmers are going over and through placid water. It is not churning up or down. There are no bubbles. The swimmers behind are traveling in the wake of the first swimmer who has broken the water. The swimmers behind are riding over those bubbles and the water is moving up and back. Swimming is easier. In a race, it is different because you are swimming side by side. There are waves created by the hands entering the water and the head moving through it. If you are swimming side by side then you are not going to experience too much turbulence that will hurt your performance. Yet, if you are further back, then you want to be further away laterally in order to give the waves more time to flatten out. The best thing about swimming in clear water is that you can see your opponent's weaknesses under the surface. That is why I always preferred swimming in pools as opposed to lakes or oceans. You have to always watch your opponents under the water, never on top. You cannot see anything on top.

Some of these things may involve just fractions of a second but swimmers want to go faster and faster, getting an edge anyway that they can. Learning about physics, hydrodynamics, physiology, kinesiology, and anatomy are all very much a part of what you must learn to be a champion. Newton's Third Law became an important part of my lexicon—"For every action, there is an opposite and equal reaction." You cannot be jerky in the water. You must go through it as smoothly as possible, streamlined. Understanding Newton's Laws helps you to do that.

It was also during that summer at Renaissance that I got my first Speedo swimsuit. It has less material. It was one layer of nylon all around except in the front where it had two layers. It flattened your body parts and was the closest thing to swimming naked, only better because it held in those body parts which add to your drag in the water.

At the end of the year, at Renaissance, I also learned about "shaving down." The pubescent girls on our team were training hard. They had little time for cosmetics. Their foremost concern was swimming faster. Although they had little hair on their bodies, they waited until the end of the summer to shave their legs, arms and arm pits. Although the girls were more accustomed to shaving, they claimed that they were getting something out of it. Shaving cut down on drag and friction. It made you feel lighter in the water and gave you a better feel for it. So that summer and every year thereafter for the balance of my career, I would shave down at the end of the season for championship meets. It felt great. It, together with "peaking," just gave me what I wanted when I hit it right. Peaking is the most important thing. Peaking had to do with gradually reducing the workload as we got closer to big meets. We would concentrate more on speed while also maintaining endurance and weight. With less yardage you can put on weight so that has to be carefully monitored. I would weigh myself each day. "Shaving down" is just icing on the cake, the final edge that you need. Back then not everyone was doing it so it was more of an advantage. "Crew cuts" or very short hair, even shaved heads became popular among male swimmers for the same reasons. My parents seemed to adjust to all these quirky aspects of sports, never questioning it, but supporting everything that I did.

Now I was working out and training for the first time. My mom would drive me to the workouts in the morning and my dad would pick me up at night. In the mornings it was 8 a.m. to 10 a.m. and at night it was 5 p.m. to 7 p.m. My dad would always arrive a little early before the end of the evening workout to see my progress.

As a rule, I would stay at Renaissance all day. I had convinced a friend from Westbury to join the program so he went with me everyday. We would often do a short extra workout for fun during the day. The rest of the time we would hang out watching the women play mahjong or we would go exploring on the Country Club property which bordered on Roslyn Estates and later a County park known as Christopher Morley. It was beautiful, cool and terrific for hiking.

One of our better swimmers that summer was a young man by the name of Billy Shrout, a talent from Flushing YMCA and Brooklyn Technical High School who a few years later went on to Harvard. In a book written by Don Schollander, the famous four gold medal winner in the 1964 Tokyo Olympics, he referred to a dual meet against Harvard when he was then swimming for Yale. He described Billy Shrout as one of the toughest competitors he ever had. One year after Renaissance in 1962, Billy Shrout placed fifth in the Men's Senior National Outdoor Championships in the two hundred meter freestyle. The nationals were always televised on ABC's Wide World of Sports with Jim Mackay and we were able to see Billy in that race. How inspiring it was. Even in 1962, Billy, who was a year older than me, appeared destined to one day make the Olympic Team. One of the great tragedies in New York competitive swimming history is that he never made it. He should have, but I always felt that he had not gotten enough of the right training. This was a problem that all New York competitive swimmers faced at that time. We had the coaches and the athletes, but we did not have enlightened elected officials who would give us enough pool time so that we could pursue our goals of excellence in sports. There always was a clash between recreational swimmers, the inner tube crowd as I then called them, and competitive swimmers. Competitive swimmers did not vote so the mahjong ladies who wanted to wade in "just to clean off" or "get their feet wet" took up valuable time and space that should have been devoted to serious athletes in pursuit of excellence. It was not until years later when older people started to workout and train for the Master's competition that municipal and other pool operators started to loosen up, allowing for more competitive swimming and workout time. But I am sure that it is still a problem and that a large number of outstanding athletes have not been able to excel in their chosen sport because of it. It is a sad commentary about us as a nation to know that for years and years, we supported casual recreational swimming instead of excellence in sports. We have gotten lazy as a nation. We do not pursue excellence as a nation as we once did.

Chapter VII

<u>First Breakthrough Into The Big Time</u>

During that summer of 1962, my parents took me around from swim meet to swim meet in the metropolitan area but I did not have my big breakthrough until the end of the summer. It was at a meet at Traver's Island, the New York Athletic Club summer home in Westchester, also known as Winged Foot, a description of their logo and often used to describe their famous golf course.

The Traver's Island outdoor salt water pool was six, narrow lanes. Salt water enables you to float a little better. It was dark, cold and you could not see the bottom or the walls for turns. I was in the end lane, meaning that I was the worst in the field of six. The top swimmers in that race were David Abramson and Bill Shrout, going head to head for 400 meters, that's eight long laps of the pool; pain and agony lasting about five minutes. Also in the race were Henry Frey, another brilliant swimmer and student, albeit eccentric, who also went to Harvard, and Bob Burke, who was my age but starting to emerge as a new star. He was a student at Brooklyn Prep and later went on to Michigan State as a scholarship athlete.

The gun went off and I was in my own world not even thinking about the others because I just figured that they were so much better than me that I was lucky to be in the race at all. It was a saltwater pool which made everyone more buoyant but at night you could not see. It turned out to be my breakthrough meet. At the time the statisticians of swimming had concluded that there was roughly a thirty-six second differential between four hundred yards freestyle and four hundred meters freestyle. In that race I dropped more than thirty seconds off of my winter time at four hundred yards. In doing the math I had a better time than Gary Weinstein or anybody else in my county in the previous winter. Dick Krempecki was really pleased. Although I finished behind the others, I had come into the upper echelons of the sport, at least in New York. Now I was a "comer" and someone to watch.

The importance of this success was not unnoticed by my parents. They decided that it would be better for me socially, academically and in swimming if they moved to the Westbury School District. So, in 1961 we moved from 26 Lace Lane in the East Meadow School District to 193 Staab Lane in the Westbury School District, a corner house in a development called the Viceroy Homes. The wealthy community of Old Westbury was just across Jericho Turnpike, a block away from our home. They were split level homes and my parents painted it barn red. I could walk to school. I had graduated from the Westbury Junior High School and would now attend the Westbury Senior High School for my sophomore year. The new high school had been built in 1959 on Post Road in Old Westbury on the southern cusp of the heart of Long Island's Gold Coast, one of the most affluent communities in the world. It was nine tenths of a mile from my home and I would walk there everyday from Staab Lane to McKenna to Queens Street to Cambridge and into the rear yard of the school by the administration building.

The school was pristine, absolutely beautiful. It was modern in its design and by comparison with other like structures, was among the very best in Nassau and Suffolk Counties. Most importantly, we thought at the time, it had a six lane, twenty five yard pool. Unfortunately, as I later learned, its coach was far from being state of the art and swimming at the school took a back seat to traditional sports, especially basketball. Westbury's basketball team produced a number of professionals. At that time, the star was Rudy Waterman who called me "Motor Boat." Rudy was really cool. We shared respect for each other, but he was a senior. He wore all black and looked ominous, a Darth Vader or Batman. Just being around him made you feel like a star. He was from the City and a proud African American whose talents on the basketball court were unrivaled. Then he was like Michael Jordan, only better. The coach was Ed Krinsky, a nationally known high school basketball star coach. I longed to have a coach like him. "What a leader," I thought.

Chapter VIII

The Road To Excellence

The swim team that everyone envied was Plainview-Old Bethpage High School and its innovative, demanding coach, Charles Schlegel. But Plainview was the subject of controversy due to alleged illegal recruiting practices. Oddly, one of Charlie's first recruits was Peter McGrain from East Meadow. Peter was two years older than me and was the County Champion at one hundred yards butterfly. He later went on to North Carolina State where he continued to swim on scholarship and later went on to earn a Ph.D.

Charlie would pick Peter up everyday, driving each morning from his home in Plainview to East Meadow in his two seater, white MG. He also drove Peter home at night. After attending Ohio State University and graduating from Long Island University, Charlie first came to Long Island as an Assistant Coach at Uniondale High School. In 1959 he moved to Plainview-Old Bethpage High School and became Head Coach there. He had a new indoor pool with five lanes, remarkable because it had no gutters and a flush deck.

Because of Peter, Bob Newman, Gary Weinstein and others at Plainview, Charlie had the best team by far and he was emerging as a star coach, not just locally, but nationally as well. The only rival he had was George Haines from Santa Clara High School and Swim Club in California who was producing Olympic Athletes by the dozens including Don Schollander and Mark Spitz.

My dad had learned of and became friendly with Vinny Santos, a Junior High School history teacher at Westbury who was the Assistant Swimming Coach at Adelphi University and who had been an NCAA All-American in swimming from Adelphi just the year before in 1960 and 1961. The Head Swimming Coach at Adelphi was Reavis Frye of North Carolina who also doubled as a baseball coach. Reavis was a nice man whose knowledge of swimming was non-existent but he was smart enough to turnover the coaching responsibilities to Vinny. Although it was probably legally improper for him to do it at the time, as a sophomore in high school, I began to train each day with Vinny Santos. I was back to one workout a day but Vinny was a terrific coach. He knew what he was doing. I was giving his swimmers a good workout. I do not recall swimming at Adelphi on weekends much and there were no morning workouts. On weekends I would try to work myself out every Saturday evening and Sunday morning at the Magnolia Boulevard Pool in Long Beach. My dad would hold the watch. But each weekday I was at Adelphi to swim in an ozone pool that had four lanes and was built in 1927. The ozone was heavier than oxygen and lay in your lungs like cement but unlike chlorine, did not bother your eyes at all. My mom would drive me to and from the University each day.

In tenth grade I was now single-minded in my devotion to one sport: swimming. When Westbury swam in dual meets they were usually resoundingly beaten but yet we did have our bright spots—me. I won every race in dual meet competition that year. When we swam against Plainview away, I knew that they would be gunning for me. I was certainly nervous but could not back down. I swam the four hundred yard freestyle but they did not put their big guns up against me, Tom Azzara or Gary Weinstein. Coach Schlegel may have felt that he wanted to just check me out or not have any of his swimmers suffer a defeat prior to the championship at the end of the season. Nonetheless, my time in Plainview set a new pool record of 4:29.9. That's a ridiculously slow time by today's standards but back then it was quite sensational, especially in New York. The four-hundred-yard freestyle, although a middle distance event was considered a long race in high school competition so many swimmers shied away from it. It also required more training than sprints. All swimmers and coaches were in awe of anyone who braved the event much as most people respect milers in track and field. I think that that is what first attracted me to it.

My parents attended every meet. My dad would come home early from work in order to be present for the 4 p.m. start times. I often wondered how he could do that without losing his job.

The high school swim season in New York at that time went from November through March. County Championships were held at the end of March followed by the New York State Championship. In 1963 the Championships were held at Uniondale High School. I was fifteen. My big race in that meet was the four hundred yard freestyle. Earlier I swam the two-hundred-yard freestyle finishing just behind Gary Weinstein, whose star was beginning to fade.

In the four hundred, Azzara and I took off together and went stroke for stroke. It was a grueling contest. On the last two of the sixteen laps I tried to pull away but Azzara hung with me. As we approached the last turn I did a flip turn while Azzara did an open one. I pulled slightly ahead but with that surprise move I demoralized him. Now I poured it on touching him out and winning at 4:24.0 to his 4:24.4. Now I was the County Champ and heading to the New York State Championships in two events.

Near the end of my sophomore year the head of the Physical Education Department at Westbury High School, Harvey Kulchin, was adamant about my having to take gym. I had won the County Championship and took two fifth place finishes in the New York State Championships. I was a credit to the school. What Kulchin did not understand or did not care about was that being a great swimmer does not mean that you are adaptable to dry land sports. It is odd but the use of different muscle groups in swimming does not mean that you are well coordinated or in shape for dry land sports such as basketball. I explained to Kulchin that I was still competing in post season A.A.U. competition; that I was competing in the YMCA Nationals for the Flushing YMCA, and that having me participate in gym ran the risk of my getting injured. Kulchin did not listen, so I had to take gym. The unit was basketball.

On day one I was guarding a fellow student from behind and he gave me an elbow in the solar plexus. It was intentional, it hurt, and it took my breath away. He may have been able to score because of it. I recovered, caught my breath, and went back to play. Now I had the ball and he was guarding me from behind. I waited. He was just off to my right and leaning over me. I took my right arm up in a cocked, ninety degree angle and brought it all the way back as hard as I could and hit him in the solar plexus. I hit him so hard, his feet left the ground. He was really hurting but tried to come at me right away. That was a mistake. I had backed away and I was waiting for him, primed in a furtive boxing position with my left foot out in front and my dukes up. He came at me charging with his left and getting ready to hit with his right. I have a long reach. My arms are thirty five inches from my shoulders to my wrists. Before he could make contact I got him with a left hook. He winced, was thrown back. He tried to shake it off but was having difficulty regrouping because he still had not caught his breath. Now he seemed more determined. When men box, they never look at their hands or their feet. They do not blink because in that instant you might get hit. It is staring at each other, eyeball to eyeball. With a few quick steps, he was at me again, charging. If you hold your breath after getting hit in the solar plexus, you can defend yourself, but you are still not recovered. A blow to that area of the body is paralyzing but angry, spontaneous, unthinking fighters are always eager to lash out. I was poised, backing up and again waiting for him. Once again he was looking at me dead on and did not see the left hook coming at him. This time I hit him even harder. He was stunned. He had to shake it off. He was bending over trying to catch his breath. He knew I could have moved in close on him and really finished him off but I did not. I waited a few more seconds. He was a beaten man. That was it. He never bothered me or spoke to me again. If I had let that go down without a fight, then I might have been bullied. The white kids and black kids in the school separated a lot. When they interacted neither one wanted to give the upper hand. But you could not show your fear either because then you might be easy prey.

I was not quite done with gym and one day during a gym class basketball game I was doing a lay up. I came down on my left ankle, twisted it and broke it. I had to be taken from the school by ambulette. My mom came up to get me. The ankle blew up like a balloon. Kulchin was all apologetic, but it was too late. I kept thinking that he was an asshole. I was not able to swim in the YMCA Nationals. I was in a cast and watched from the sidelines. The team won. I should have sued Kulchin and the school but did not. While I did not realize it at the time, Kulchin was instrumental in causing me to leave Westbury High School because I deeply resented his lack of respect for what I was attempting to achieve as an athlete.

The Westbury coaching situation was so deplorable that I really had to fend for myself. I did not know how long I would be exiled in Westbury so I determined that I had to be my own coach, learning more about it than the coaches. I started subscribing to *Swimming World* and *Swimming Technique* magazines. I read everything I could find on competitive swimming. I attended swim clinics where famous coaches would talk about the latest training techniques and stroke mechanics. America was then the international leader in competitive swimming adopting most of our techniques from the Australians who had considerable success in the 1950s and early 1960s with mostly big yardage programs and a coach there, Forbes Carlisle. Australia produced Murray Rose, the middle distance and distance swimmer who won Olympic medals in four Olympic Games from 1956 through 1968. His father (Ian F. Rose) wrote a book entitled: *Faith, Love and Seaweed*, Prentice Hall, Inc., 1963. I bought it. It was about how they raised Murray to become an Olympic champion with their faith, love and a vegetarian diet.

> Eileen Rose, Murray's mother later authored, *The Torch Within*, Double Day & Co., Inc.,1965, where she wrote of her son:

> "This fascinating story makes the Olympic torch the symbol of the inspiration which burns within everyone. Its flame, once alight, can be used to direct and strengthen the everyday lives of us all."

> "We have all had a picture of things we want to do-the persons we want to be. What has become of that picture? Was it put away as too good to be true? Then it is time to take it out again and hold it clearly in front of you. Reach out for it! Plan and work for it! Bring it nearer to you everyday! You build your own life-*only you*! The materials are all there. Remember, there's never been a truly great person who wasn't once an untried, immature little child. Each of us is capable of so much more. Great things, if we so wish. There are unlimited, untapped powers in reach-yet how few of us take those first steps to something better than our usual, mediocre selves!

> "Though this is the story of Murray, our son, it could just as well be your story, or that of your son, your daughter, or anyone else in whom you believe. It is essentially a story showing that these castles we all build in the air can-and should-be formed into a wonderful reality.

"This book is concerned largely with sport, especially with swimming, because that was the first medium through which Murray chose to express himself. It was through this that he was able to rise above many early difficulties and prove the power of faith and love and courage.

"But as you read and apply the principles to yourself, don't think only of swimming . . . or even of sport. Choose any medium that comes naturally to you or your child. We confidently send out thoughts to all who would enrich their lives, and the lives of their children-especially to those with a problem: a frail body, a nervous temperament, or any imperfection which they wish to overcome. If the desire is great enough, you will find the energy, ability, and inspiration to make those wishes come true. The greatest strength can grow from weakness." From the jacket cover of *The Torch Within.*

I also followed the career of Dawn Fraser, a world class sprinter from Down Under" who won four gold medals from 1956-1968 in the one hundred meter freestyle. Al Oerter, a discus thrower from Long Island accomplished the same amazing feat. After her 1968 triumph with Harry Gordon, Dawn wrote a book entitled: *Below The Surface* (William Morrow & Company, 1968) which, of course, I bought and later she autographed it for me. She may have been nine thousand miles away but I felt a bond with her as I did with all the great athletes. Some were more naturally gifted than others, but the struggle to become a world class athlete was something with which all of us could identify. Their quest was for Olympic Gold and world records. So was mine. It was my total, single minded purpose, nothing was more important than that goal. But to get there I had to track the careers of everyone, all of my actual and potential competitors—their times, their training, virtually everything about them. Many were fortuitously lucky to be born, raised or transplanted to places like Santa Clara, California where competitive swimmers were treated with respect and afforded the best training facilities and coaches. I did not have that so I had to improvise. I had to learn more about the sport than anyone. I should have moved out to California then. It is the one major regret that I will always have about my athletic career. The moral of that is that each of us should strive to be the best. To get there we need to be near the best, a part of their lives, do what they do, and improve on it. But training in a vacuum with no one to chase day after day, while admirable, does not bring you as close to the Gold as you need to be. No matter how motivated you are, it is always far better to be around greatness, because you watch the ups and downs of the competition. You can compare their mood swings to yours, their bio-feedback, their body mechanics, where they excel, where they are weak, and how you can ultimately beat them. When you are training by yourself and against yourself, it requires a concentrated focus on the competition. You have to imagine that they are there and what they are doing in each workout. In order to do that, you have to know them inside and out. It is more than just showing up for practices each day, it is striving to be the best every single moment—to out-work, out-think and ultimately out-perform the competition. While I did not have the opportunities of many of the greats, I could and would make up the difference by hard work. That, too, is a lesson which I have adopted throughout life. We cannot always be associated with those whom we most admire for their success. So we must be leaders, setting our own high standards, above the bar and in pursuit of excellence.

My mother and father were there every step of the way. My father played traditional sports without cardiovascular conditioning so he would give me bits and pieces of information that would improve my performance. When I first started, he gave me oranges for energy then it was glucose/dextrose tabs. Although I was not yet fast enough to compete in them, I would attend the national meets for both the NCAA and the AAU. I would sneak past security in places like the Payne Whitney Gym at Yale University, get into a suit and warm up with the greats. I would introduce myself to the famous coaches, broadcasters, and referees. At one of the clinics at Yale held in conjunction with the NCAAs, I met Adolph Kiefer, a 1936 Gold Medalist from Michigan who was an entrepreneur and an inventor. He developed the Kiefer gym which contained sand weights and a bench press rack for dryland weight training. It was the beginning of concentrating on strength by dryland weight exercises and training. My dad also purchased a set of Dan Laurie barbell and dumbbell weights for me. My dad bought me a Kiefer gym which I kept in my basement and used for years. Kiefer was even more famous and made his fortune a few years later by developing Keifer lane lines which they still use today to separate the lanes but also to break the waves of competitive swimmers.

They are perforated, circular plastic disks modeled somewhat like those on a human spinal cord.

My mother put together ledger sheets for me which contained the weekly times of swimmers throughout the nation. I studied those times closely every week and soon memorized them. I could tell you what they were for any swimmer in the country to the tenth of a second. I would have been able to do it to hundredths of a second but we did not have timing devices at that point that went to hundredths. We were still using stop watches read by the naked eye.

I started to take vitamins everyday—wheat germ capsules and large doses of vitamin C to ward off colds. We did not know much about diet, so steak for dinner and eggs for breakfast was the mistaken staple upon which I existed. In order to supply me with these accoutrements my parents made many sacrifices but never complained about them or threw them up to me in any way. They would eat leftovers while I had sirloin. What I needed to further my athletics and academics was always obtained by them for me without fanfare. I used whatever I received.

Billy Shrout told me of one of his trade secrets. Instead of pulley weights, which not everyone could afford, he obtained surgical tubing from a medical supply store. It works like a bungee chord. At a mid point in the tubing he wrapped it around a doorknob, stepping back with the two ends. He then would wrap his hands around them, bend over and replicate a downward swimming motion with both hands. It was a terrific simulation. I started to use surgical tubing everyday as well as bent-leg sit-ups and push-ups. I would also often jog a mile or two at night wearing heavy combat boots. As the years went by and we learned more about sports, we learned that each sport uses some well defined muscle groups for its activity and training must be very specific. But back then we did not know any better.

I was sixteen and still in Westbury. Charlie Schlegel had seen what I did and invited me to train with his swimmers at Woodbury Country Club that summer in 1963. Charlie was a terrific coach. He was on the move. He had developed amazing teams and had lots of talent at Plainview/Old Bethpage High School. I was in awe of him. It was an honor, I felt, to be invited to train with him. He was dynamic, highly energized, motivational, dedicated, knowledgeable and a clear, provocative public speaker. Charlie was on his way to becoming one of the truly best high school coaches in the history of high school sports in any era. In short, he was "the man." I liked everything about him but especially what he demanded in the way of a tough regimen of training. It seemed very militaristic in the way he administered it. He had an aura about him which showed that he was a winner. His greatness had a way of rubbing off on anyone he touched. He was charismatic, a showman beyond compare.

Being a County champ gave me a little taste of notoriety, celebrity, and fame. I liked it. I liked the fact that other swimmers feared me, that things got very quiet when I stepped up to the blocks. But I also knew that just as I had passed others I would have to work to maintain my position or improve upon it. My answer was Spartan-like training, self-discipline, working harder than anyone else. I did not have a girlfriend, I did not socialize. I did not drink alcohol or smoke pot. I worked out and competed. That was my life together with just enough school work to get by.

After the County Championships I kept working out. The high school swim season started in November and went through most of March. When it was over and until it started again, most high school swimmers stopped training. Few in the east had coaches like Charlie Schlegel, who worked his athletes year round. Even when the New York State Public High School Athletic Association (NYSPHSAA) rules limited the times of training, Charlie found ways around it. He was state of the art. He was a California coach in New York, the equal of any coach in the nation or better. His fellow coaches were jealous of him. But Charlie had a work ethic which no one could match and he imparted that to his athletes. He was all about winning but he showed us how to win as a team. He was a sport celebrity in competitive swimming and he made all of us feel that we were as well. He carried himself with pride and confidence. He was "larger than life."

The public schools did not finish until almost the end of June, so we were not getting started until then. The deal was that the swimmers got a free country club membership if we acted as lifeguards during the day.

One of Charlie's secrets was that his swimmers (or at least many of them), would train year round. I felt that I needed to work harder than Charlie's guys to be better than them. I knew also that they would be measuring their own performance against mine. When I was at Westbury they did not work out with me, so they did not know what to expect. But, working out with me every day, they would know my strengths and weaknesses. I would have to work harder and beat them in everything, which meant that I had to touch the wall first on every item, in every workout. That summer was one of the hardest that I ever had. I really pushed myself far beyond what I did at Renaissance and with more work than anyone was doing anywhere. It was 1963, the summer before the Olympic trials, but I was not thinking in those terms yet.

Chapter IX

Working Harder Than Anyone To Reach The Goal

The schedule that I set for myself was incredible. I would set my alarm to wake me at 5 a.m. each morning. If I did not get up, my dad would wake me. My breakfast was two raw eggs mixed with honey, orange juice and wheat germ. Then my dad would drive me to the country club, which was about ten miles east on Jericho Turnpike. The club was closed at that hour so I would break in, let my father in and get things going. There was a pond adjacent to the pool so I first had to chase the ducks and geese out of the pool. Sometimes there was bird dung in the water. I would take out the lane lines that divided up the recreational areas so I could swim long course.

The Woodbury pool was "T" shaped. The top of the "T" was fifty five yards across with no lane markers on the bottom of the pool. It was only about three feet deep at the ends. The middle of the "T" was twenty five meters and had six lanes marked on the bottom with black tile.

I was in the water each morning by 5:30 a.m. I was alone except for my dad who would stay with me while I did my workout. The water temperature was cold, in the low 70's or colder. My dad held a stop watch. I did what I could to make my workout harder. I invented a device to create resistance. I used a gallon can which I dragged behind me and I wore special rubber hand paddles which created a larger surface area and more resistance. I swam for the next hour and a half putting in 3,000 to 4,500 yards, roughly two to three miles. Coach Schlegel would arrive at 7 a.m. Other swimmers would come at that time. Charlie's workouts would end at 9 a.m. where I would do another three to four miles. By

9 a.m. I had completed anywhere from four to seven miles or anywhere from 6,000 to 11,000 yards. My dad would usually stay until about 7:30 a.m. and then head off to work. From 9 a.m. to 11:30 a.m. I would have a little more breakfast, clean up the pool and do some lifeguarding, all to earn my keep as a member. Charlie set us up with these jobs so that we could train.

We would clean up the pool and lifeguard from 9:00 a.m. to 11:30 a.m. At 11:30 a.m. my mom took turns with another mother. One would pick us up at Woodbury and take us to Plainview/Old Bethpage High School where we could workout with Charlie from 12 noon to 1:30 and log in another two to three miles of swimming. Then the other mom picked us up and drove us back to Woodbury County Club where we would lifeguard from about 2:30 to 5:30 p.m. At 5:30 p.m. Charlie ran his evening practice short course, two to three miles of sprints at Woodbury. For that I would usually wear a five to ten pound weight on my back or a scuba diver's belt. I used goggles during most of the day workouts but not at night. My dad would come directly from work and watch the second part of every practice. This was our routine five days per week and on Saturday mornings. Most days I was swimming 15-20,000 yards or ten miles. This would be like a track athlete running forty miles per day. But that was not all. After the evening workout, I would go home to my steak dinner, lift weights and then run one to two miles. If I jogged around the neighborhood I would do it by myself. If I ran on the desolate roads of Old Westbury, my dad would ride behind me in his car with the headlights on. After that I would read a bit about swimming and hit the hay, only to get up seven hours later with the same routine. The amount of traveling or driving that my parents did was remarkable. During that summer, just for workouts, my dad would drive one and a half hours to and from the country club and then take the train and subway each way to work for another three hours. All the travel time is tiring but my father was undeterred. I never saw him nod out or sleep on the train or anywhere else. He never complained.

Many of Charlie's swimmers did not compete in A.A.U. meets in the off-season. I did. I entered every single race that I could. During the summer Charlie invited me to attend Plainview/Old Bethpage High School. He said he would get me a scholarship to college. But there were a few problems, I did not live in Plainview and if I changed schools, I would attract much attention since I was a County Champ. Rumors were already circulating about Charlie achieving success by illegal recruiting so a change by me was bound to add to those troubles. But Charlie was a man of courage, an innovator in pursuit of excellence. He had disdain for mediocrity. He could have been just like all the other coaches, waiting for retirement and cruising. But Charlie was far from mediocre. His athletes saw his dedication. Few of us could match it although each of us would try. He was a model of what sports should be all about but too often athletes and even coaches are relegated to the pursuit of high salaries and profits instead of excellence.

Swimming is an amateur sport. There is no reward as a professional. Swimming is pure and those who engage in it understand that. It is still the toughest sport I know because it is just you, you alone, fighting against the elements, against yourself and your urge to give up and to stop trying. It is just you against equally relentless peers all striving to beat the clock.

I never saw the white light of death during a workout or a race but I thought about it as I pushed my body to the outer limits of its potential. The white light comes sooner or later. Competition at its highest levels can be a near death experience. Your brain says stop or die. Your heart is beating faster than you can count. As you hit the wall for a final touch, you have arrived safely, beating your opponents and the light of death, once again, ever again.

A summer with that much work gave me background for the school year. I decided to take up Charlie's invitation. I would change schools from Westbury to Plainview.

Charlie introduced us to the Stack family. They lived at 10 Wilben Lane in Plainview. Their oldest son Mike had just graduated. He was a terrific backstroker. He went on to Long Island University. Their daughter was not a swimmer. Their younger son Christopher was just starting his competitive swimming career. They were wonderful people and gave me an address. I had a room there which was outfitted with a few books and some of my clothes. I never spent a day or a night in it.

As I entered Plainview, the New York State Public High School Athletic Association (NYSPHSAA) began an investigation regarding my transfer. They held hearings at which Charlie and others testified. Without Bob Burke, Dick Krempecki, Vinny Santos and Charlie Schlegel, what would have become of me? They rescued me from a life of mediocrity. I thank all of them and others each day of my life for giving me the opportunities which I had. If given more I might have done better but each of us must play the best hand we are dealt. I had to keep upping the ante.

I was being followed to and from school by NYSPHSAA officials. Charlie was dragged through the mud but what could he do if talented swimmers kept coming to him because he was a winner? Stories of the investigation appeared in the *Long Island Press* everyday. Thurlow Childs, a writer for the *Long Island Press,* covered the hearings and investigation.

Charlie was friendly with the School Board attorney. His kids swam for Charlie. His name was Campanella and Charlie never made a move without speaking to him. I was allowed to stay in Plainview and I was never asked to pay tuition there. Everyday my mom would drive me to Plainview, getting on the LIE at Exit 40, traveling to Exit 44 and Route 135, getting off at Wallace Drive, making a left over the bridge and a right into the Plainview parking lot. It was a twenty minute drive. Westbury had been the home of the Dragons. Now I was a student at the Plainview Gulls, (as in "seagulls"). Even the name brought me closer to the water. The pool was in the first part of the building at the end of the parking lot.

It was 1963. I was sixteen. Morning workouts began at 6 a.m. and we would swim until 8 a.m. every weekday and on Saturdays. No matter what the weather or how sick I might be with a cold or fever, I never missed a workout. My mom got me there everyday, no matter how she felt. She too never complained.

During the day I had a 45-minute study hall and swam during it. The lunch period was 25 minutes and I swam during it. I would swim 50 yards butterfly stroke, climb out, and do it again. I was becoming like a finely tuned machine. After school I would squeeze in a workout with Charlie's A.A.U. (Amateur Athlete Union) team. This was Charlie's club for children up to high school and a number of female stars. It was less work than I did during the summer, but still a lot. At night my dad would often drive me down to the Magnolia Boulevard Pool in Long Beach where I would do some more work. My dad would hold the watch. I would workout with Charlie on Saturday mornings and on Sunday morning with the Smith family from East Meadow at the Long Beach pool. I was trying to get the edge on Charlie's swimmers, so I put in extra workouts without telling anyone, not even Charlie.

In the Fall I was invited to the Sadie Hawkins dance by Linda Kirsch. She became my girlfriend for the next four-and-one-half years. Linda lived in Bethpage. After Sadie Hawkins, my Friday and Saturday nights were with Linda. She was fifteen. She was a wonderful, very pretty girl and we shared our dreams. Next to swimming, she was the most important part of my life. But as an athlete, I felt that I had to also resist that temptation. Usually on Friday nights we would go to the movies and on Saturdays I would go to her home. We would watch television. Generally I would also play ping pong with her father, Lewis Kirsch. He was a fine guy, with four daughters. He played tennis, bowled, occasionally smoked a cigar, and would play ping pong with me. In and around those ping pong games, Linda and I were getting pretty serious. She came to all my meets and my parents started taking her to my away meets as well.

In 1963, The Beatles came to America and performed on the Ed Sullivan Show. Not since Elvis had there been a cultural revolution, an antidote for the Red Scare, the inhibiting Joe McCarthy era of the 1950s. Elvis' love songs like "Love Me Tender" were not revolutionary, but a young man from the South shaking his hips to the screams of millions of young girls went far beyond the "bobby sockers" at the Paramount for Frank Sinatra. Sinatra was about sex appeal; Elvis was more about exhibitionism and raw sexual movement on stage. Both had wonderful voices, but it was sex that sold both of them. The Beatles were different, although most of their songs were love songs. It was their hair, their accents, their youthful exuberance, and their new style of rock 'n roll that created an interest in them. They were different and a real alternative to the boring, hum-drum fifties. With the Beatles you just never knew quite what to expect. With them, anything could happen and did. They were the talk of every town and high school in America, including Plainview.

Later, of course, with their *Magical Mystery Tour* album and others they, together with The Rolling Stones with their *Paint It Black* album, gave us psychedelic music, a counter-cultural enhancement to the anti-establishment political rhetoric of the 60's and an addenda to the "Turn On, Turn In, Drop Out" philosophy of Dr. Timothy Leary and his disciples from that era.

A metamorphosis was taking place in our minds and bodies but athletes were left out of that equation until Tommie Smith and Juan Carlos, the famous American track athletes raised their black gloved fists into the air on the awards platform at the Mexico City Olympics in 1968. In 1963-1965, most of us, particularly high school students such as myself, were far behind that level of political awareness. Unlike Smith and Carlos, who had the courage to do what they did, and were sent home by our own Olympic Committee and the International Olympic Committees, we were concerned about our futures and the punishment that might follow from too much rebellion. We laid back, enjoyed the Beatles, but did not join the cultural revolution just then.

It was a selfish attitude, there were political activists in the front lines who were taking the heat (and the bullets) and being jailed for their civil disobedience and rhetoric. The adolescents of my generation and I were kept under protective wraps by our parents. They feared for our safety and where our liberated minds and bodies would take us (and them).

My parents' generation was oblivious to the cultural and political revolution then taking place. They were the "silent majority," with money and power. Either we had to convince them that we were right or beat them by acquiring political and financial power. We were still in the early throes of the revolution. I for one was not a full-fledged member yet but there were changes taking place in my own awareness. New ideas were beginning to filter through and my instincts were simply telling me that the *status quo* was wrong.

I remember a high school biology class where we were instructed to dissect frogs. Each student received his own creature, alive and well, but given a death sentence by the teacher. The teacher explained how to anesthetize the frog by inserting a sharp pin into the back of its head and then move it about inside of the frog's cranium. It was like a lobotomy used on humans but was applied at the back of the head instead of the front. We were next told to place the frog on its back onto a hard rubber dissection tray. Then pins were inserted into their appendages to keep them from jumping off the trays. Then we were told that we had to make a capital "I" incision, pull back the flaps of skin and observe their internal organs. The heart was still beating. Other signs of life were apparent but we were told that they could not feel a thing. Then we were given vials of epinephrine which we applied to the helpless creatures with eye droppers. Then we were able to see their muscles twitch, in response to the stimuli.

I cringed with each aspect of the laboratory exercise. I felt the frog's pain, wondering why a simple photo would not suffice. I did not intend to become a medical doctor. Why did I need to see this, to know it, to participate in it with such excruciating detail? As much as the frog was allegedly anesthetized, I felt that I was being desensitized by participating in the killing of a living thing. It seemed so unnecessary, just as human lives are unnecessarily wasted in war. What gave us the right to kill in the name of science, in the name of education? As far as I was concerned, we were high school students being taught to kill, to accept death. I cannot say that I was cognizant of this at the time, but not too many years later I realized that I had trivialized this event and that it had made a lasting impression on me at a point when public education was perhaps unknowingly dehumanizing students' spirits. School officials and some teachers had a callous, unknowing disregard for life that I was foolish to accept. I still had no ability to question what authority figures were telling me to do. But something was brewing deep within me—my anger, my resentment, were repressed by schools, teachers, parents, coaches, society and most horribly, myself.

Plainview had many stars. One was Mike Golub, a fantastic sprinter with natural talents. He was a perfect mesomorph in his body build. I nick named him "Rivet Arms" because he had an ability to churn his arms. There was no dislocation or change in the position of his arms as they cycled through the water. He swam the fifty and one-hundred-yard freestyles. He did not swim during the summer and hardly worked out. Yet, he had what one might today call a type "A" personality. He was not aggressively in your face, but you could tell that he had supreme confidence in his own abilities. We did not swim directly against each other, but Charlie would use us from time to time in head to head matches in dual meets or practices since almost no one could challenge us in our events. Charlie would create a little rivalry between us for a day or a week or for one meet, and build the speculation about who would win. He created the excitement.

In one of those meets where we had nothing to lose he put us both in the hundred. In practice with a little jump or roll start, that means starting yourself, I was pushing fifty seconds in repeat one hundred-yard swims. Golub had a flat start time from a gun for a one hundred yard freestyle of fifty seconds. That was about four seconds off of the American record at that point which was held by Steve Clarke of Yale University, later a world record holder and Olympic Champion. Clarke was also from Santa Clara.

What I learned over the years is that kids who participate in sports generally do better in school. Some of their enthusiasm and self-discipline that sports teaches often transcends to school work. Because of the competing disciplines of mind and body, they must make good use of their time. Every minute counts.

Golub and I went head-to-head. He had the center lane and got the jump on the start. He hit the water first and started swimming first. His first turn was a good one, mine was too deep. After that I started to gain but it was too late. He had too much of a lead in that first fifty yards and I could not catch him. He got me. I wanted a re-match but Coach Schlegel would not give it to me. Golub's ego was intact. He had to know that he was still the best in his event and he was. I admired his natural talent.

My usual event was the four-hundred-yard freestyle. I was improving in each meet, cutting my time from the County Championships the previous year. I was also developing my backstroke and individual medley. I became the first male swimmer in New York State to break a minute for one hundred yards backstroke. These times are totally irrelevant by today's standards.

Our chief rival was West Islip High School. Plainview usually beat them but in the 1963-64 season they had some stand-outs too. Charlie would have to be creative in the line-up. Islip's star was Norman Zahn, a year older, but also threatening the State record at four-hundred-yards freestyle and Mike Golub in the shorter distances. Zahn was a tough competitor who looked hard. Some people can scare you just by their looks and demeanor. Zahn was one of those guys but he also had some weaknesses which I learned about—namely he smoked and did not train very hard.

The key to us winning against Islip was Charlie changing the lineup. In order for us to win, I would swim the one-hundred-yard backstroke against Islip's star and then back to back, in the next event face off against Zahn in an even more grueling event, the four-hundred-yard freestyle. This meant that I would go against Zahn with almost no rest between events. If I could pull it off, Plainview would win and I would be a hero. If not, then I might still be admired for Coach Schlegel having enough confidence in me to give me that assignment and for giving it my all to carry it off. Feeling special in the eyes of Charlie Schlegel meant a lot to me because he was special. His recognition was important. Athletes crave recognition from their coaches who often have a more profound and deeper relationship than parents have with their children. The most important thing to a child is the coach who has the knowledge of the sport. The athlete who makes that connection to the coach and the coach who makes that connection to the athlete, have a special bond, beyond friendship and respect. The coach usually spends more time with the athlete than the parents. The coach has them at their best times of the day. The parents get them when they are going to and from practice, as school work awaits, after dinner, when they are tired with eyes laden with chlorine and when they are ready for bed. Parents may know the medical and early history of their children, but coaches later become more intimate with them, learning what makes them tick.

The Islip stands were packed to capacity. We were running neck and neck as we got to the diving competition when there was a break in the program. After that there were two more events before we got to the one hundred yard backstroke. My opponent was Hargraves. You could see that the Islip team was surprised by this change in strategy and lineup. Now they were scrambling. They had already used Zahn in the one-hundred-yard freestyle and were saving him for either the four hundred or the relay at the end.

Hargraves was considered the premier backstroker at that time, but I was versatile and had established myself as a contender in anything except breaststroke and butterfly. Now people were beginning to appreciate Charlie's strategy. I lost by a touch, but stayed near the starting blocks waiting for them to announce the next event, not knowing if Zahn would be my competition. A low hush filled the air as the tension built on whether Zahn and I would face off against each other. As the announcement was made, he was not in the race and I cruised to victory.

Islip won the meet by a few points. Even though I lost, as I walked out to the waiting area to my parents and Linda, I was given applause for the valiant attempt I had made. I felt like a hero because Charlie trusted me with the responsibility for carrying the whole meet. Although I was not the Captain, I felt like one. Coach Schlegel had just treated me that way and I had nothing to be ashamed of. I gave it my best. One thing about Charlie, he never criticized any race that I swam. He knew I was trying my best and that is all that should be required of any athlete. Charlie honored me with that assignment and I have never forgotten that.

My junior year culminated by my taking second place in the four-hundred-yard freestyle behind Bill Shrout in the Eastern Interscholastic Championships held annually at Lawrenceville Prep School in New Jersey. It was for the best high school swimmers in the East and our most important contest.

At that time we were starting to learn about peaking. Charlie would taper us as we got near big meets. We would have shorter practices with less yardage and we would swim shorter distances, take more rest in between workout items and work on speed or whatever fine points we needed to sharpen our performances. The key to measuring the effectiveness of the peaking was to take your warm-up. At the end of the warm-up we would stand behind the block in the end lane. Charlie would be down at the far end. One at a time we would clip off twenty five yard sprints. The closer you got to ten seconds, the more ready you were.

In the County Championships, a few weeks after the Easterns, I swam the medley relay and the four-hundred-yard freestyle winning both, but also setting a State record of four minutes, eight seconds and dropping my time by sixteen seconds from the previous year. It was a milestone. I went on to the State Championships which I won as well and also where we won the medley relay. Plainview was the best in New York State and one of the best teams in the East. Billy Shrout was graduating and I was the top gun. That year I became a member of the N.Y.A.C. All City, Metropolitan All Star team and received a coveted plaque for it.

Chapter X

<u>Eye On The Olympics</u>

Now there were A.A.U. meets and the finish of my junior year. It was also an Olympic year, 1964. The Olympic trials were to be held in Astoria in August and the games were scheduled for Tokyo in October.

Athletes must always look for better training programs. They must also be around the best in order to be the best. I started out my summer like the previous summer and went to a meet at Traver's Island. My dad reminisced with Jack Abramson and others from the old days. Jack invited us to come to the North Jersey Swimming Association in Wayne, New Jersey where my old coach, Bob Alexander, also fondly known as "Mr. A" from Knickerbocker Swim Club was holding workouts. Some of the best swimmers in the nation were there, all trying to make the Olympic Team. I was seventeen and had not seen Mr. A for seven years. He was still the same, a large man in his late 60's who you never saw in a swim suit.

I was not terribly excited going into my training during the summer of 1964 because it was an Olympic summer and my teammates from Plainview did not express much interest in training. Serious athletes consider their sports to be full time jobs. I could not just take the summer off when all the best swimmers were seriously training in California and elsewhere to make the Olympic Team. My dad spoke with Jack Abramson and he told my father to get me to Bob Alexander in North Jersey. He was running a training camp in a lake in Wayne, New Jersey. The camp was about one-and-a-half hours from my home in Long Island. Mr. A had poured concrete on the edge of a lake creating a fifty meter course. The lake was on Mr. A's property. I did not like the idea of going to New Jersey or swimming in a lake with snakes and turtles.

When my dad and mom first drove me to North Jersey it was a weekend. They did not say it was a tryout but that was what it was. My dad tried to smooth things over by helping the men build a large porch and picnic area adjacent to the small cement building which we used as a locker room. My dad was carrying these large pieces of plywood and sweating profusely. He later told me that he almost had a heart attack doing it. All of us joined in to hoist the I-beams up to give it support. Mr. A had an office between the men's and women's bathrooms.

Mr. A was a big man, about six feet but well over three hundred pounds with a large protuberance. The talent assembled in North Jersey was the equal of almost any team in the nation. One of the stars was Dick McDonough of Villanova. He later attended the University of Michigan School of Law. He had won the Pan American games the previous year, set a world record and had beaten Don Schollander. Dick had a bout in his senior year with mononucleosis and was still recovering from that. He was shooting for spots on the Olympic team at the one-hundred and two-hundred-meter freestyle races and one-hundred-meter butterfly. His fellow teammates from Villanova were also there, including Rick Girdler, a playboy but who one year later would establish a world record at 100 meters short course (a 25 meter pool). Jack Geoghegan from Villanova and New York had been a finalist in the NCAA's and AAU nationals. Bill Stuek, not a long course swimmer but a powerful sprinter and All American from Colgate with the second or third best time in the nation for fifty yards freestyle and Billy Shrout, were there. Also two tremendous All-American prep school starts from the Hill School in Pennsylvania, Mike Fitzmaurice, a sprinter on his way to Villanova and Tommy Johnson, a versatile medley swimmer. Jed Graef of Princeton and Thompson Mann from the University of North Carolina were also there. Both were among the best backstrokers in the nation. Lastly, there was Patience Sherman, a beautiful girl and top freestyle swimmer who later became Don Schollander's girlfriend.

There was no circle swimming in North Jersey. It was all straight away sprinting. Everything was fast and usually not more than one hundred fifty meters. We would line up usually two to a lane, straight across, head to head. The stars were in the first heat or wave. I was in the second and there was one more behind us. In the second wave I usually swam next to Thompson Mann. He would swim backstroke and I would swim freestyle. I was seventeen. He was twenty two and on his way to medical school. I acted like his rabbit. His best friend was Jed Graef. They lived together at Jed's parents' home in Jersey. Jed was very tall at six feet, six inches. He excelled at two hundred meters and Thompson's forte had been one hundred yards, short course. He was unproven in long course and had been ranked about number five in the country in short course events.

Thompson had a goal that summer. Although he did not advertise it, it was to beat Jed in every single item, in every workout, and in every meet. This would give Thompson the option of competing at both one hundred and two hundred meters. At five feet, ten inches, Thompson's arms were about thirty-three inches. Jed's were about thirty-seven inches. Jed had more pulling power because of that but could not turn over as fast as Thompson. Jed would take fewer strokes per length than Thompson, neither one expending more energy than the other, but Thompson building more lactic acid and viscosity faster because of his rapid churning motion. Ultimately that factor inhibits speed and flexibility; so part of Thompson's mission that summer was to condition himself to ward off the onset of those problems for the whole two hundred meter distance while maintaining his speed at one hundred meters. The world record at that time for one hundred meters backstroke was one minute and nine tenths of a second.

Mr. A was old school. His workouts were too short for me. I was not made to be a sprinter. For the first few weeks of the camp, my mom drove me each day to Richie Abramson's home in Jamaica Estates. Richie, Jack's youngest son, was a student at the Air Force Academy. He drove me to and from Jersey each day. My mom would pick me up at night from his home. That lasted a few weeks until my dad took out an ad in a Jersey church bulletin asking parishioners if there was someone who would board me. The Demarest family came forward. They had two sons and two daughters. They had no connection to swimming. I do not know what my dad paid them. Every Saturday my parents would pick me up and drive me back home. Usually Linda was with them. They would bring food for the following week which consisted of steaks almost every night. I am sure they were expensive. They meant nothing to me. Mrs. Demarest always cooked them for me and after a while I was embarrassed to eat them because the Demarests were not having steak.

The Demarests lived just down the road from Mr. A and his training camp. I would walk there and back early in the morning and back at night. Sometimes I would walk back after dinner for a few more laps of swimming by myself. No one else was around. It was a lonely existence. That is what athletic training is. The loneliness of it can drive you mad. You are isolated, away from the real world. For athletes playing professional sports there is a goal or something to look forward to after college, a professional contract. But for competitive swimmers at the time, there was none of that. It was just the glory of the moment and the possibility of a college scholarship. The glory was never as much as what was generated in the media for athletes playing professional sports such as football, basketball and baseball. That was really a source of great irritation to me in that I knew how hard competitive swimmers had to work in return for few rewards. I always felt that this was unfair and sprang from the public's and the media's ignorance of the sport.

After dinner I would watch a little television with the Demarests and then head for bed in a non-air-conditioned, upstairs bedroom. I would come back to Long Island on Saturday afternoons and my mother would drive me back on Monday morning. I did not have a car or a license.

The workouts were not hard but the drudgery of being away from home and from Linda was depressing. Nonetheless, my dad had to be credited on several levels for getting me into the camp and supporting me. Even though he was not a swimmer, he had a sense of what athletes must do to excel. He was taking me to higher levels by giving me one opportunity after another.

I sensed that I was not improving. I did not like lake water and not being able to see my opponents or the bottom of the pool. I could not tell if I was swimming in a straight line. Backstrokers did not have these problems since, except for their turns, they hardly go under water. They can watch a marker above the surface.

Thompson was on schedule with his plan. He was beating Jed in every item. Mr. A had something called "time studies" which happened once during every workout. This was the most important item in the workout where everyone would go all out at top speed. You had to know your time at the end. Freestylers were trying to get under one minute thirty seconds for one hundred fifty meters, while backstrokers were trying to get between one minute thirty five and one minute forty seconds. Based upon national times it could then be projected that anyone achieving those times in practice had an excellent chance of making the Olympic Team. Thompson was beating Jed in those as well and because they were one-hundred-fifty-meters, they showed Thompson's promise at two hundred meters. He was showing his endurance. If he could beat Jed at one hundred fifty meters in practice, then all he had to do was hang on for another fifty meters or pace himself and he would be a top contender at two hundred meters as well.

Because I swam next to Thompson I knew how he was doing. He was keeping pace with me, his backstroke to my freestyle. One day during a break I asked Thompson why he was not telling people about his success in practice. He was literally breaking the world record in practice. Wouldn't that psyche them out? "No," he said. "Where I come from we believe in 'poor mouthin'. We don't brag. We talk ourselves down so that nothing is expected of us. Then at the end we have a surprise for our opponents. That's the 'southern gentleman's way."

So no one except those in our camp knew what Thompson was achieving. Then we started swimming in meets and Thompson was winning everything. His times showed that he was at the cusp of greatness. He won the Eastern U.S.A. Outdoor Swimming Championships at the John B. Kelly Pool in Philadelphia just weeks before the trials at both one hundred and two hundred meters. Jed took disappointing second places.

The greatest story in Olympic swimming history of which I am aware occurred in August at Astoria's outdoor New York City pool which had been completely remodeled for the Olympic Trials, thanks to Jack Abramson, an incomparable leader and businessman who did more for competitive swimming in the East than anyone. We had a friend at the *Long Island Press*, Mike Lee, a famous sports writer who supported every aspiring athlete in every sport. My dad got to know him during his days in baseball and would always brag about me to Mike. Mike then wrote a number of stories about me that appeared in his column. He wrote how I was training for the Olympics. Those stories were terrific and Mike followed my career for its duration, always writing about it, taking me to the next level at least in my mind even if I was not ready physically. Mike has passed on. But he inspired many athletes. Years later my dad and I attended a testimonial dinner to thank him. At the Shea Stadium podium Governor Mario Cuomo said a few words on Mike's behalf. The room was filled with professional and Olympic athletes. Mike was retiring and the *Long Island Press* was closing down. Firmly stationed at the microphone was the organizer of the event who did not give an inch of his physical position away to the Governor—that man was Jack Abramson.

In any event, I did not qualify for the trials but attended every bit of them. So did my dad, who was a timer. They had three timers per lane. All were dressed in white. My dad was assigned a lane with Mrs. Schollander, Don's mother.

In the backstroke events the two hundred meter event was first. Both Jed and Thompson qualified for the final, the top eight. The first two finishers would make the Olympic Team and the third would be an alternate. This would be Jed's only chance. If he failed here, he would not make the team.

Thompson was out first ahead of the field by ten meters. I clocked his first one hundred meters at one minute and two seconds. While he had one hundred meters to go, he appeared strong and in command. His split time was one second and one tenth off the world record at one hundred meters. At the one hundred and fifty meter mark, Thompson had picked up another two meters as he came off the third turn. For another twenty five meters he was way out front. Jed was grouped in a pack with others. Eyes were on Thompson, the leader, but he was looking back at this best friend, Jed. Although he might have easily finished first, he allowed Jed to come up and place second. Jed was on the team. Thompson was not. He would have another chance in two days at one hundred meters but anything could happen in those two days, an accident, sickness, whatever. Thompson gave up his spot on the team for his best friend, Jed.

Mr. A was infuriated. He pulled Thompson aside. I could overhear the conversation. He accused him of throwing the race. Thompson denied it. It was an unparalleled sacrifice for friendship which I have never seen before or since in any sport. It was simply incredible. Two days later Thompson made the Olympic Team at one hundred meters and set a world record. In Tokyo that October Thompson and Jed both won Gold Medals and set world records at their respective distances.

Patience Sherman made the Team as an alternate for one hundred meters. She swam on a Gold Medal relay team in Tokyo. The rest of those superb athletes from Jersey did not make the Team. If nothing else, being around those stars built my confidence for my senior year at Plainview. In the Fall of 1964, I was back.

I resumed my big workouts with Charlie. Linda was my steady girlfriend. I was spending more and more time with her. My dad questioned the amount of time I was spending with her, indicating that it was taking away from my athletics. I argued, but he was right. The downfall of male athletes in that era was too much alcohol or women. Drugs were not prevalent. My dad's statements produced a heated argument between us. Swimming was still the most important thing in my life, but Linda had become a close second. Linda lived in Bethpage and I was still in Westbury. I was with her every Friday and Saturday night. I was still not driving, so my parents had to drive us wherever we might go. That was usually just to the movies. There was no night life to speak of, no "clubbing."

In the fall we had our usual early morning workouts and at night, after dinner, my dad would drive me down to Magnolia Boulevard Pool in Long Beach. I would do a workout on my own with my dad holding the watch. I was probably overcompensating at the time, overworking and too tired. I broke my own state record in the first dual meet of the season, but I wanted to go under four minutes and exceed Bill Shrout's times from the previous winter. Swimming was everything. I was coasting in school, just getting by. My parents hired tutors for me but I was doing almost no school work. I would take off on any day when there was a meet. I slept late and stayed at home to rest. Neglecting my school work and being so myopically focused on competitive swimming was not good. It was certainly not good for my long term development, but something where I was being recognized for the first time. It goes to your head. It is a good thing, but I was too young to put it into perspective. Competitive swimming should have been one part of my life, not all of it.

I was in the newspapers every week and over a two or three year period, I had become a bit of a celebrity in competitive swimming circles, at least in New York and on the East Coast. With celebrity status you are expected to perform each and every time you get on the blocks. I tried to do that by setting records in the backstroke and even in the individual medley. Charlie was working me hard. In one workout he put me in a narrow lane between Tom Azzara and Billy Rome, another great freestyler. We were going head to head in repeat two hundreds. The water was hot and Charlie had lowered the water level to make it more turbulent. We were hitting each other on every stroke. It was one of the toughest workouts I ever did.

There is no future in competitive swimming after college so it is all about the Olympics and college scholarships. I did not know what to do about colleges, but with my mom's help I started writing to college coaches whose names I knew. I wrote to every "name" coach expressing an interest in attending their school. The responses came back. Nearly everyone I wrote to was interested and some I did not write to were writing to me. Coaches talk among themselves and sometimes they share with their fellow coaches their prospects and new recruits. If a kid cannot get into Harvard, their coach may tell another coach (not necessarily a rival), what they have learned about this promising young athlete and how he or she might be a candidate for another school. I was popular among college coaches. They liked me, my interest in the sport and my enthusiasm for possibly attending their school.

In 1964 and 1965 we started the season with the fastest two hundred yard freestyle relay team in the nation at one minute twenty nine seconds and two tenths. That was 22.3 seconds per man. There were five of us on that team, one of us acting as an alternate. I chose to come off of it so we could spread out our strength in individual events. I remember one workout after a dual meet which we resoundingly won as we always did. Charlie was not happy with our times. So he kept the five of us after the meet and each of us, one at a time, from a rolling block start, (meaning you start yourself), had to put five fifty-yard swims under 22.5 seconds. It took us almost two hours but we did it. The other four members of that relay were Mike Golub, Mike Sinkinson, Tom Azzara and Fred Schneider. They all became High School All-Americans that year, which meant they finished in the top twenty times in the nation. They finished the season in twelfth place nationally. Golub also made All-American in the fifty yard freestyle.

We made our way to the Easterns. I had the best times for two and four hundred yard freestyles going into the meet. Something terrible happened to me in the trial heats. I barely qualified. I left the pool exhausted. I had only a few hours to rest. My times were way off. My legs were hurting but I did not know why. I saw a whole year of work going down the tubes. I was in deep trouble. No college scholarships, no career, game over. I was lucky to get into the finals. I went to the Howard Johnson's Hotel room to lay down. I could not sleep. My dad put some hot compresses on my legs and covered my eyes with cold compresses. I lay there exhausted trying to figure out what went wrong. I do not remember if I had anything to eat.

That night I came back to the Lawrenceville Prep School Pool and the place was packed. There was excitement in the air but I was wondering whether I would again succumb to the same mysterious fatigue. It had never happened to me before in any sport that I played. My first event would be the two-hundred-yard freestyle. My main opponent was

Terry Robinson from Rye, New York who later went on to become an NCAA All-American at Dartmouth College and for a time was moving into position for a possible spot on the 1968 Olympic Team. I do not know how I did it, but I went by him in the last fifty yards to win the two-hundred-yard freestyle. As I hit the wall I looked to Charlie who had a big smile and his fist was in the air. The crowd gave a standing ovation. My father and mother were beaming but the night was far from over. The four-hundred-yard freestyle was awaiting and my opponent would be Eugene McElroy who had also trained at North Jersey with Mr. A. McElroy was tough. He was a fighter and cunning, saving himself for a surge by me at the end of the race. This time I got him, hitting the wall first for a double victory in the Easterns. Charlie was thrilled. Mike Golub won the fifty and our relay team won. Other members of our team had placed in the finals and won some medals. Plainview was the best in the East.

Now it was on to the County Championships. We would pretty much dominate every event especially the freestyle events, but we were weak in the individual medley. I had worked on it during the year because I was bored with just swimming freestyle. Plus, I wanted to take myself away from the guys on my team who were swimming freestyle everyday. I felt that I could keep my edge against them by diversifying and conditioning myself in other strokes. It was a little bit like being a switch hitter in baseball. I was more versatile and could help the team in other events although I had the second fastest fifty yard freestyle time just behind Mike Golub. Charlie would have kept me on that relay team if I had pressed it but to me it was more of a challenge to try something different.

The 200 yard medley had two laps of butterfly, two of backstroke, two of breaststroke and two in freestyle. My butterfly was passable, my backstroke and freestyle were strong but my breaststroke was just about illegal because I had a scissor kick which if detected could disqualify me. I won the medley and the four-hundred-yard freestyle. We were limited to entering two individual events although I could have won four events plus been on a victorious medley relay, swimming the backstroke leg or on the record setting 200 yard freestyle relay. I was voted by the coaches as the Outstanding Swimmer in the County. I shared the award with Ron Hoffman, a diver from East Meadow.

I probably was not too popular among the coaches due to the recruiting scandal, but my dad had gotten friendly with many of them.

He was working his diplomatic relationships with many which helped to diffuse any residual anger.

I went on to win two events in the New York State Championships—the medley and four hundred yard freestyle, setting a State record in the later. Now it was time to look to college. Competitive swimmers cannot turn professional. For us, it was "get a college scholarship and try to make the Olympic Team." There would not be any multi-million dollar contracts for me, an amateur athlete.

Male athletes reach their physical peak between the ages of 25-27. Few compete after college because they lack the ability to earn income through swimming as a professional sport. Many great athletes have had their careers cut short because of this. As more people take on swimming as a lifetime activity, interest in the sport will grow and eventually it may become a professional sport. All we need is the financial justification for it.

The new Yankee Stadium was built for $1.3 billion and the new Mets Stadium for $600 million. Yet, with seating for 60,000 people and television rights to sell, they will soon pay for themselves. Baseball is big business. By contrast the construction of the Eisenhower Park Pool in Nassau County is 50 meters and cost $43 million to build. It loses money every year. It has an indoor seating capacity for about 3,000 people.

But there is hope, in that I have observed that people who are interested in swimming, particularly as they get older, are fascinated by stroke mechanics and techniques much as golfers are intrigued by those things. A friend, Terry Laughlin, has made a small fortune writing books, giving lectures and selling videos on that subject.[7] Swimmers like golfers can enjoy the sport for a lifetime either competitively through Master's competition or just for recreation.

I had a few months left of school and I had not yet chosen a college or university. I was wait listed at Yale, but Insley Clarke the Admissions Director at Yale did away with athletic scholarships that year. I went to West Point on a visit. My dad was with me as always. The West Point Team was working out, getting ready for a championship meet. I decided to show off and try to impress the coach, Jack Ryan. My dad was on the deck with a stop watch. I swam in the end lane. I swam five one hundred yard swims on two minutes so I was getting about one minute rest between them. I did them from a push off, no dive. Each one was around fifty seconds and at least two were under that. It was very impressive since the American record from a dive was 45.6 seconds at that time. That afternoon

Coach Ryan offered me an appointment to West Point, an all expenses paid education. He explained that each Congressman and Senator had two appointments to each of the federal academies—Air Force; Annapolis (the Naval Academy); West Point (Army) and the United States Merchant Marine Academy at Kings Point. The Coast Guard Academy had a different system for admission. Not all of the members of Congress and Senators used all of their appointments, so if my representatives had used theirs', then he could easily get me in from any of the elected representatives in the United States who had not used their appointments. There would be no problem in getting it. It made no difference that I did not live in their Congressional District.

That night we had dinner in the Mess Hall. My dad and I sat with the cadets. The officer in charge (I think they called him the Commandant), was on the stage in the center of the room. It was impressive. He announced us as invited guests. All of the cadets then rose to salute me. I stood and saluted back. They patted me on the back and applauded. Grace was said with references to soldiers who died; the Pledge of Allegiance was said and "God Bless America" was sung by the Cadet Corps. Near the end of the meal the Lord's Prayer was said. The meal was plentiful—steak and potatoes. They cut the dessert, chocolate cake, with great precision. Most of the cadets at my table were studying Engineering.

My dad was not very keen on the military. The Viet Nam War was raging and I did not like the idea of a four year hitch in the military following graduation. As impressive as it was, I viewed it as an attractive nuisance because the discipline, *esprit de corps*, heroism and being among the greats of military history such as General Douglas MacArthur appealed to me, I was not ready to hang up my swimming career for a bullet in Southeast Asia. My dad did not want me to go into the Army and take on unnecessary risks created by poor political leadership at home. It was not unpatriotic, just smart. He was thinking ahead of the curve. Most Americans were still bewildered by what was happening in Viet Nam at the time. It was just beginning to heat up, but my father's instincts as a World War II veteran told him that this was a misguided War without a clear objective or opportunity for success. Although we appreciated the hospitality and spirit of West Point, the disadvantages, namely possibly catching a bullet in Southeast Asia, outweighed the advantages of going to West Point. Also, and more importantly, West Point had never produced an N.C.A.A. Champion or Olympian. The academics and military regimen competed unfavorably against what one had to do to succeed in competitive swimming. Their program was seasonal from November through March and I needed year round training. So, reluctantly I said "No" to West Point.

Long before it became fashionable for high school students to tour the schools they might attend, my dad had me on a circuit. In the Fall of 1964 I went to the University of Maryland in College Park and received a fully paid weekend at the University of South Carolina in Columbia. I was recruited by Frank McGuire, a legendary professional basketball star from New York who had gone on to the Gamecocks and was trying to build a sports program in all sports. South Carolina at first offered me a half scholarship which they later changed to a full scholarship. I was brought to their Homecoming football game where my name was announced and appeared on the scoreboard before sixty thousand people. A barbecue was held in my honor at the coach's home. Once again my dad and I were impressed by the southern hospitality. But something about a Scotch-Irish/Italian boy from New York going to school in the south made me feel uneasy. I was not terribly conscious of racism or the Klan, but I felt some bridled tension in the air. The Civil War did not seem to be over and South Carolina did not have a proven track record in competitive swimming.

Chapter XI

Three And One Half Yards And
A Cloud Of Dust

Charlie Schlegel had attended Ohio State University and was partial to the school. I applied and I was accepted. We arranged a weekend visit. Ohio State in Columbus had an unparalleled history in sports. It was the heart of the Big Ten. Mike Pepe, its former coach who retired just after the 1963 season when Ohio State won the NCAA's, was an amazing recruiter. He was succeeded by Bob Bartels, a Ph.D., a first class gentleman and scholar, but without Pepe's charisma and ability to motivate. The Assistant Coach was Ron O'Brien who was earning his Ph.D. at that time and later went on to become an Olympic Diving Coach. He was a motivator. One of the Graduate Assistants helping out with the team was Ernest Maglisco who later went on to become a well regarded coach at, of all places, Chico State in California.

Ohio State had won more NCAA Championships than any other school in the country. As of 1963 it had won eleven championships to Michigan's ten. Michigan's coach had been Matt Mann who coined the phrase: "When the going gets tough, the tough get going."

Innumerable greats attended Ohio State—golfer Jack Nicklaus (who attended but did not graduate) and basketball great Jerry Lukas. It was also the home of football coach Woody Hayes, a god of the gridiron whose famous teams were known as: "Three and One Half Yards and a Cloud of Dust."

In coming to Ohio State, you are first impressed by the size of the campus, a veritable city with the fifteen-story William Oxley Thompson Library standing at its center. Not far from that is the Ohio State football stadium which set national attendance records back then, drawing an average of 87,000 plus people per home game, more attendance per game than any other university in the country. The natatorium had two pools side by side, with a seating capacity of about four thousand. It was majestic—framed photos of the great teams and stars from the past graced every wall in and around the facility. Ohio State honored their athletes and there was a sense of history everywhere.

At that time Ohio State had 50,000 students, so it was both enticing and intimidating at the same time. Bob Bartels scheduled a lunch for us in the Faculty Dining Room. I was seated between Woody Hayes and the Athletic Director. Bob Bartels and my father were also at the table. I was taking in the ambiance and noticed an oil painting hanging on the wall. There was some idle chit chat going on. The painting was one of track athletes coming out of the blocks, the first figure being an African American dressed in United States Olympic colors. As I was looking at the painting, an elegantly dressed African American gentleman in a sport coat and tie suddenly appeared under it. He walked over to our table and over to me. Everyone became silent. He extended his hand to me and I stood up to shake it. "Tom Liotti, welcome to Ohio State. We're glad to have you. You'll love it here. My name is Jesse Owens. Where's your dad? I've heard about him." He shook my father's hand. I bowed and thanked him. Woody reached around my back, not standing and said: "Hey Jesse, how ya' doin'?" "Just fine, Mr. Hayes, just fine, thank you sir." I thanked Mr. Owens and again I was in awe. I bowed slightly. The four time 1936 Olympic track Gold Medalist and an Ohio State alum left our table and rejoined his party. No school in the country could compete against that kind of a greeting. Jesse Owens won in Munich and many believe that he single-handedly defeated Adolf Hitler's vision of Aryans as a "Master Race." Yet, I felt embarrassed because, aside from my father and I, no one else stood. Mr. Owens had the dignity and class to address Woody Hayes with a Mister and a sir, but Hayes did not stand to greet one of the best athletes in history. In my mind he and Jim Thorpe were among the very best in the first part of the twentieth century.

Jesse Owens was an athlete and Woody Hayes was just a coach. In the world of sports no matter how great the coach, he can never measure up to the athletes because his physical abilities have not been tested. Athletes share a special bond which coaches, unless they have also been great athletes, can never share. I felt a bond with Owens. Maybe others at the table realized that. While I respected the power of Woody Hayes, I disliked the fact that he had not treated Jesse Owens with respect and that Mr. Owens felt the need to act like a waiter before him. I sensed that racism was alive at Ohio State. Years later, after an almost unsurpassed record, Woody Hayes was forced to step down as Ohio State's coach due to his belligerent conduct toward his players. He would beat them and they were compelled, as scholarship athletes, to take his abuse. They did for years. I did not like him from day one. But I did respect him.

I was hot on Ohio State University. Ohio State divided their sports program into amateur and professional sports. There were five professional sports at Ohio State and they received all the scholarships. The professional sports were football, basketball, baseball, wrestling and swimming. Football got thirty two full athletic scholarships per year. It produced more revenue than all the other sports combined. The swimming team got eight full scholarships per year. In the Big Ten, if you were not on scholarship, it made no sense to try out for a team. Everyone on our team was on scholarship.

I told my dad I wanted to go to Ohio State University. They offered me a full scholarship and it was too good to turn down. Bob Hopper, an NCAA Champion in the 200 yard individual medley in 1965, escorted me around the campus. I went home to think about it but I was pretty sure that I wanted to attend.

I was accepted at the University of Southern California without a scholarship and at Indiana University also without a scholarship. Indiana had the hot team in the country. Their coach, James E. Councilman, Ph.D., also known as Doc Councilman, was a graduate of Ohio State. He recruited many greats in that era and one of the incentives was that there was a Manager on the team who was a genius at allegedly taking Graduate Record Exams; LSAT and MCATs for swimmers. If you went to Indiana there was a promise that you would be admitted to the professional school at Indiana of your choice. I am sure that there were many, if not all swimmers at Indiana who made it to professional schools on their own without this kind of illicit help. Nonetheless it was an enticing statement made by Councilman perhaps said just to draw athletes into the school but never used by them. For example, Mark Spitz who won seven gold medals in the1972 Olympics, graduated from Indiana and went to their Dental School. Mark may not have ever practiced Dentistry, I doubt that he had to. His fame led to many endorsements at the time. He was a world class swimmer from California and wound up in Indiana. Aside from Doc Councilman, being the most knowledgeable coach in the country, there may have been other reasons for all those stars going to Indiana. Indeed whenever you see a college team coming out of nowhere to reach the pinnacle of a sport, you have to wonder what recruiting methods they used to attract the most talented athletes from the furthest reaches of the country. Councilman's record was so impressive at the time that if he placed his stock in you, it gave you great hope of achieving success. He studied the science of swimming and wrote a book by the same title. He was Indiana's main attraction, a genius in body mechanics, physiology and kinesiology. Many athletes wanted to emulate the inspiring accomplishments of Doc Councilman, if not in sports, then in the professions or academia.

The obscure Indiana program became a Mecca under Doc Councilman, but did not offer me a scholarship. Oddly, I was also interested in Foothill Junior College in California which was emerging as a powerhouse. They had attracted Mike Burton, later a world record holder at 1500 meters at Foothill Junior College and then UCLA. In retrospect, I wish I had attended Foothill.

More acceptances and scholarships came in but I was partial to Ohio State and signed my tender, a contract, for a "full ride" in May, 1965. That June I graduated from Plainview with more college acceptances and scholarships than any other student in the graduating class. Azzara would be joining me at Ohio State, but not on an athletic scholarship; Golub went to Maryland and Mike Sinkinson was off to Bucknell. My girlfriend Linda had another year of high school.

During the summer of 1965, I was back training at North Jersey and living with the Roland family. The Rolands lived in North Jersey on Franklin Lakes. They had a magnificent home on the lake. Ralph Roland was the head of International Sales or American Cyanamid, an international pharmaceutical conglomerate. This time, though, my dad had bought me a car. Some of the monotony was broken up, but it was largely an uneventful summer where I accomplished little.

The five hundred seventy mile journey to Columbus took my parents and I twelve hours. I felt like I was going to another planet. I had a foot locker filled with everything I might need, including some new clothes. The amazing thing about a school like Ohio State is that you had better be very mature, self-assured and well adjusted because you lose your identity, no matter how great an athlete or student you may be. Its history is venerated and the talent in all sports is phenomenal. Not only that, but there is nothing that you can accomplish that has not already been achieved by someone else. There are stars everywhere. From the moment I arrived I felt alone and isolated, left out of the mainstream. As an only child in an individual sport I was accustomed to loneliness. But, once my parents left, it was a traumatic, tearful departure for me. I missed them, New York, and Linda. In high school I always felt like a star. At Ohio State, I was just a number.

I got to Ohio State early, at least one week before anyone else. I was there just after Labor Day, eager to start my practices and to engage in a campus routine. My first year, I was assigned a room in Stradley Hall, a regular dorm. My roommates were George Horton, a swimmer from California who hated Ohio State from the moment he arrived, and Ed Becker, a non-athlete, agriculture student, who came from a farm in Ohio. George was distant; Ed was friendlier, a good guy.

As I settled into Ohio State I started to compile a swimming log. It was like a diary that grew to three thousand pages and ten volumes five years later when I stopped swimming. It was a compilation of each day of my experiences, feelings and training. I started it so that I would be able to more closely follow my progress, the ups and downs. When I went home, I would occasionally allow Linda and even my parents to read it. But generally my reflections were private and personal. The log also became cathartic, expressing my loneliness and frustration at being away from home.

The next Olympic Trials was three years away. I was in Ohio, at a great school, but one that did not have a personal touch.

I did not like the looks of the Ohio State sweats with gray bottoms and red tops. They were not tapered and did not look cool. Athletes must always dress cool, even in their sweats—it is part of the intimidation factor. So I told my parents that I wanted custom-made sweats. I had them made for me at a local sporting goods store in Columbus. They were solid red fleece with silk lining and zippered pants. No one at Ohio State or in the Big Ten had a pair of sweats that looked that good except my good friend Tom Fritz from Michigan, a year older than me at Ohio State and a nationally ranked butterflier. He too took his sports attire very seriously. We were, after all, the best that our school and sport had to offer and we wanted to play that to the "nines."

Linda and I were now together for two years. I was calling her and my parents every night. My parents' phone bill was well over two hundred dollars a month, a big number back then. My dad mentioned it once, but everyone knew I was homesick. My parents wanted to hear from me as much as I wanted to hear from them. I wrote letters almost everyday to my parents and Linda. My parents were not letter-writers so I rarely got letters from them, but I had a bank account and they always kept it supplied with money, as needed. I am sure that it was a great sacrifice for them even though I was on scholarship. I am sure that I did not express my appreciation enough, but my parents were as devoted to me as any parents could be. Like most young people, my full realization of their love and sacrifice would not come until much later in life.

At that time, freshmen could train with the varsity but not compete with them. I had everything at Ohio State: free room and board, tuition, books, supplies, tutoring, and Sunday meal money when the cafeteria was closed. I ate at a training table with as much food as I wanted. I had carte blanche at the University Book Store. I could pick up free jerseys and tee shirts at the stadium. Once a week Bob Hopper and I would go to the trainer and get Vitamin B12 shots. A masseuse was assigned to our team and nearly everyday I would get a massage after practice. The masseuse would crack your neck. I learned how to do that from him. I got all the home football and basketball tickets I wanted, usually at the fifty yard line and center court.

The locker next to mine was occupied by Mike Finneran, whose sister Sharon, a swimmer, had been on the 1964 Olympic Team out of Santa Clara. Mike later made the Olympic Team in 1968 and became the only diver in Olympic history to score perfect tens in the three-meter event. Chuck Knorr, an Olympic Tower Diving Champion was with us and Randy Larsen, an NCAA diving champion. Ohio State's team had fallen off somewhat. We were ranked third in the Big Ten behind Indiana and Michigan. Michigan State was also gaining ground.

The competition was fierce. Gus Steiger, the coach at Michigan at the time, walked into a practice in early November and told his team that anyone who was not in the top six in the Big Ten time-wise, had to leave the team. The Big Ten and Swimming World Magazine published times every week and we compared our times against everyone nationally and in the Big Ten. This was about as close as you could get to being a professional as an amateur athlete without being one.

I was recruited by Beta Theta Pi, a national fraternity and probably the most popular at Ohio State. Fraternity and Sorority Row at Ohio State was spectacular. The Homecoming floats built in front of the houses were major construction projects. The barn fires and pep rallies the night before homecoming games attracted thousands. Columbus was a genuine college town. The merchants supported the athletes with free haircuts and, in some cases, the use of cars, new and old, by local car dealers. I did not ask for or receive one of those.

Fall is a pretty time in Columbus. The seasons are the same as they are in New York. The leaves turn a golden brown and there is a nip in the cool air. My parents and Linda came to Homecoming. Linda looked just beautiful. She was seen by some of my teammates on Friday and all they could do was talk about her. It was very nice to hear. Young men, especially athletes, were into collecting girls as trophies. While I did not consider Linda to be a trophy, I was proud that she was my girlfriend. When other young men recognized that, it built my self-esteem and image. I was, after all, just a freshman from New York. Midwesterners and people from other parts of the country had a disdain for New Yorkers. Their acknowledgment of me on any level was worth noting.

Many of the Ohio State athletes and football players, in particular, came from the coal country of Pennsylvania or Massilon, Ohio. In Massilon, every baby boy gets a present at birth, an Ohio State football. Their high school football stadium seated over fifteen thousand.

I was enrolled as a Liberal Arts student. I had no political awareness. A flame of interest in academics had not yet ignited. I had taken advanced composition in high school. I figured that I had some ability to write so that freshman English would not be too much of a problem. I was wrong. Ohio State was on a quarter system. Basically, it was ten weeks of classes, then exams and a break. There were seven themes in the first quarter of English. The class was taught by a Graduate Assistant. It was horrible. I never got above a C. They were taking from me one of the subjects I always liked. Most students received C's in English. It was a school policy where allegedly we would learn to write by receiving low grades. I found it to be demoralizing and absurd. All it did was defeat our egos and remind us that undergraduates were academically non-entities.

There were approximately nine thousand students enrolled in my freshman math class which consisted of forty-minute classes where a senior professor would lecture to the masses over closed circuit television for half the class. Then a Graduate Assistant would come into the class and answer any questions. Usually we had time for only one question and answer. Psychology was more of the same. Instead of Freudian analysis we studied B.F. Skinner and conditioned responses, learning all about how you can program the behavior of mice with food pellets as a reward or electric shock as a punishment. Frankly, this did not seem very enlightening and I became distracted by those poor mice spending their lives inside of boxes, pressing levers for food or being shocked. The comparison to my own existence was unavoidable. I identified with those mice, their hopeless, dull routine. Like the mice, my box was the pool. Up and down that pool each day in a seemingly mindless regimen with the only reward being possible praise for a good workout and the possible expectation that I was getting closer to my dream of Olympic gold, a world record and NCAA All American.

Instead of a relatively simple history class on the Civil War or the 20th Century, I found myself in the midst of the French Revolution, which, at that time, once again had no relevance for me. What I noticed is that football players often had their courses and teachers hand picked for them by the Athletic Department which then rewarded certain faculty for the high or at least passing grades bestowed with good seats at athletic events, tutoring assignments and other rewards. Football players were allowed to defer on their major and take easier courses in their freshman and sophomore years. Many never graduated. There was a disparity between the treatment that football players received and the rest of us. There was an unending supply of resources devoted to football. For example, there were two large football practice fields adjacent to the stadium. It had rained and Woody Hayes did not want his players practicing on wet grass where they might sustain injuries, so he had two helicopters stationed above the fields for an hour or so to dry the grass. Woody Hayes was easily more powerful than the President of the University or anyone else in Ohio. He was like a god. He instilled fear in everyone but aside from the hoopla, I detested the football mentality that went with it. I did not fully understand why at that time but I was not getting a true university education where I might learn to question authority or engage in critical thinking. Instead I was being trained and conditioned to be a part of what Vice President Spiro Agnew later referred to as the "Silent Majority." Jocks were not allowed to question or to think. You certainly were not encouraged to do that as a pledge to a fraternity.

On November 22, 1963, President John F. Kennedy was assassinated, one hundred years after the Great Emancipator, Abraham Lincoln, met a similar fate at the hands of John Wilkes Booth. I was in high school then and like most of the nation, saddened by Kennedy's death but had little awareness of what that might mean politically. By my freshman year I still had not matured. The war in Southeast Asia was accelerating. More troops were being sent and every college student, even with deferments, had to worry about being one of them. Meanwhile, the poor kids from the ghetto who were not on scholarship or could not afford to go to college were being drafted and sent off to war. Lyndon Johnson would start each speech with his tired phrase: "My fellow Americans . . .". Robert McNamara, the Secretary of Defense and a holdover from the Kennedy Administration, was joined at the hip with Johnson, sending more and more troops there. By the war's end seven years later, 58,000 Americans had been killed and more than 500,000 Vietnamese. The number of dead in Cambodia, the so-called "Killing Fields" and Laos was estimated to be at least another 500,000.

Political awareness was developing first at Berkeley with the rhetoric of student Mario Savio and what would come to be known as the "Free Speech Movement." By 1965, Norman Mailer had published *Armies Of The Night*, a book about the first marches on the Pentagon which expressed dissent over the War. This political awareness had not yet reached the Columbus campus, or if it had, I was in no way aware of it. Instead, like all of the male freshman, I was compelled to join the R.O.T.C. The promise was that I would graduate from Ohio State as an Officer in the United States Army. The theory was that you were deferring military service until after college and if you had to serve, it would be as an Officer. Obviously overlooked in all of this was the fact that we were killing hundreds of thousands of Vietnamese, Cambodians and Laotians without a clear mission except to thwart an ill-defined Communist threat. We had not learned our lessons in Korea and Viet Nam was a replay on the same theme. In addition, the United States was engaged in a form of chemical warfare, the spraying of the defoliant, Agent Orange. Twenty years later in a lawsuit against Dow Chemical, the manufacturer/producer of napalm and Agent Orange, in the United States District Court for the Eastern District of New York, 320,000 Viet Nam veterans claimed that Agent Orange had caused them to suffer irreparable maladies, such as cancer. Their case against Dow Chemical was settled in the early 1990's for one hundred eighty million dollars plus interest of at least another fifty million.

It was assumed by university administrators, particularly in the south and mid-west, that all athletes were patriots and as such would favor war, any war. We were fighters in sports so it was assumed that we would naturally, enthusiastically fight in wars. The R.O.T.C. favored athletes for this reason. Most of the athletes were too involved in their sports to pay much attention to the political unrest that was starting to foment on college campuses.

My father and mother were not concerned since I was safe for the time-being. My father was calculating and could not see risking my life for such an unworthy cause. He served in WWII under General Patton in Europe. He saw many of his friends die. He survived but had no respect for white elected officials who did not serve in the military and would not allow their children to serve. My father was not going to allow my life to be wasted. He never discouraged me from anything but I knew he did not want me to be in the military, especially in any place where my life would be in jeopardy. Maybe I was a coward but I could not reconcile the human devastation against the limited foreign policy objectives that we were attempting to achieve. Still it was not a concern because I was in college and R.O.T.C. was just a two credit course which the jocks all took for the grades. Once again, the officers who taught R.O.T.C. were rewarded by the Athletic Department with free football tickets and invitations to sports banquets. If an audit were ever done on attendance at football games and disparities between attendance and actual ticket sales, the results would be surprising (and not just at Ohio State but at every major football school in the country).

The R.O.T.C. students were a weird lot. We had our uniforms, but I noticed that some of the students were very serious about the R.O.T.C. to the point where they would polish all the brass buttons on their uniforms and spit shine their Army issued shoes so that they looked like patent leather. Some of these guys would take hours and hours to spit shine their shoes. I could not quite believe that this was a priority in their lives.

I would often study late into the night and I met a Jamaican janitor, an older man, in one of the study rooms downstairs at my dormitory. We struck up a conversation and I learned that he had a Ph.D. in physics but could not get a job because of the color of his skin. He needed this job for the money and his family. He often used the word "Man" so he acquired the nickname "Man." I was astounded by the sacrifices he was making and the indignity which he faced everyday of his life. He was obviously well-educated. He could sense my sorrow over his plight. He turned to me with a big smile as he swept the floor. "Always remember, Man, the job does not make the man." Those words proved to be prophetic. At the same time Martin Luther King, Jr. gave one of his usual spellbinding speeches where he said that each of us should be the best at what we are. So if you are a janitor, as Man was, be the best you can be at that job. I did not think less of Man because he was a janitor, I thought more of him because he endured the racism that brought him to that position, yet he maintained his self-respect. I was in awe of him. I considered him a giant of a human being. I was honored that he took the time to speak with me.[8]

I was restless and packed with energy. I could swim three or four miles per day, but still I could not sit still and just read or study. At night I would lay on the bottom bunk talking to Horton above or Becker until they fell asleep. During the day, and at night instead of studying in my dorm, I would go to the stacks of the William Oxley Thompson Library where I found quiet and isolation.

College students are pranksters, but we carried it to absurd, immature extremes. On our floor there was a Graduate Assistant who was in charge of our floor which was a bit like being Nurse Rachet in *One Flew Over The Cuckoos Nest*. Undergraduates would "penny" him into his room. They did that by taking four pennies and wedging them between the doorframe and the front of the door. Once that is done he was locked into his room from the outside. I am sure he may have missed a few eight o'clock classes because of it. Finally extricating himself as he opened the door to his room he was met with more surprises such as a thirty gallon waste basket filled with water from the shower being placed against his door on an angle. As he opened the door, water would come crashing in, all thirty gallons.

One time while he was "pennied in," they went downstairs to a construction site in the middle of the night and brought up wheel barrows filled with new sod. When you awoke in the morning and looked down the hallway, it looked like a massive putting green or a well kept fairway. Some guys were literally out in the hallway teeing off and calling "fore!" The hallway was only about five feet across, so this was really quite something. They had mapped out a course with holes and everything. Before John Belushi and the movie *Animal House*, there were the students at Ohio

State and, I am sure, college students everywhere. Nonetheless, most of these pranks were a cultural shock for me.

The jocks on our floor were relentless, taking rolls of toilet paper and making a giant wet ball with it and pushing it out of a dorm window to land on a Graduate Resident's Porsche convertible down below. One of the non-jocks on the floor had his only pair of shoes filled each night with water and placed in the ice box. At 7:30 each morning he was seen pounding ice out of his shoes. Another time they tied this same guy up in a chair after stripping him of all of his clothing. They put shaving cream and eggs on him and sent him downstairs in the elevator during an Open House on Parents' weekend. Believe it or not parents and girlfriends of other students just got on the elevator and pretended like he was not even there. His name was Johnny, and he rode up and down in that elevator for a few hours that day. Once they stripped the poor guy naked and tied him up in a large laundry bin and covered him in sheets. He was taken across campus by truck to the laundry center where he was found hours later by the African American female workers there who reportedly had quite a time teasing him.

If the Peter Principle is that everyone reaches their highest level of incompetency, then I was beginning to feel that I was well on my way. While I admired the athletic abilities of the athletes around me and the size of the Ohio State campus, the backward, punitive side of some of those around me was beginning to make me feel like I was regressing from the careful upbringing that my parents provided. There was no doubt that success as an athlete at Ohio State would mean something to me, but I was beginning to feel unfulfilled and thirsting for something more, something academic, something that would inspire me and take me beyond competitive swimming and sports.

But still I had to earn my keep as an athlete. I had to produce because tenders (scholarship contracts) back then went from year to year. If the coach did not like you or if you did not produce or if you became academically ineligible, you could lose your scholarship. Coaches bet on your ability to succeed in college. They bet on your potential and sometimes they are wrong. The best coaches it turns out are the best gamblers. By that I mean that they have made winning bets on the athletes they have recruited. This is even more true of pro-sports. After picking the right recruits, the coach must bring out the potential. The school must act *in loco parentis*, or in place of the parents, to aid in the athlete's development and insure that he or she matures as a total person with academic and athletic prowess, but also with a maturity that allows students to establish their independence and then embark upon a productive life after sports and the university, allowing each to be a contributing member of society. Perhaps I was not seizing all opportunities that were given to me or perhaps I was not being given what the German philosophers have described as the "Weltanschauung," or world view. I did not see it. I felt that I was being worn down in sports and in life, just not growing and not developing. Concrete goals were missing. I would go through the motions each day but I did not feel that I was really a part of anything. I was proud to be there, proud of Ohio State, but not a full-fledged member. I am sure that this was partly my fault being brought up as an only child in a somewhat cloistered and protected environment. My parents no doubt wanted to see me establish my independence, to grow and flourish. Since neither had been university students or athletes, they were trusting in me and Ohio State. I just was not ready to launch, to go it alone, to be set apart from my roots, my foundation, my home. This is a confession of my own frailties. I wanted to be on my own but I still desperately needed love, affection, and human interaction that my life in New York provided and which the venerated Columbus, Ohio could not match, at least for me. I am sorry that I was not stronger or a better person. In the end I regret much but could do little at the time to address my personal failings. I am sure I owe an apology to Ohio State; to my former Coach there, Bob Bartels, who bet on me and placed his career and faith in me; to Coach Charlie Schlegel and my teammates at Plainview who looked up to me; to my parents; Linda and a great many others. I belatedly apologize to you whether you read this or not and even if you are not alive to accept it, I convey it to your spirit, to you in retrospect, with all my heart. I apologize for being inadequate, for not being up to the task. While I can never make it right or make it up to you, I have endeavored to become and will continue to be what you expected of me. I remember the faith and trust which you placed in me and I will forever continue to strive to live up to it. In the meantime, know that I have not forgotten you and what you did for me.

I squeezed through my freshman year, switching my major from Liberal Arts to Commerce. I earned my Letter which was a beautiful grey and red sweater inscribed in script at the waist with my name and with one red armband and Ohio State on the front. I was a part of the venerated tradition of Ohio State University. I completed my freshman year with an end for the season time trial rather than a meet or competition which they did not have back then for freshman. The equivalent college event for middle distance freestylers was the 500-yard freestyle instead of the 400-yard freestyle as in high school. It was an extra minute of swimming. My time improved marginally over what it had been in high school.

Bob Bartels invited me to stay in Ohio that summer but his training program seemed inadequate. I also wanted to get home. I should have gone to California but I did not. Instead I returned to North Jersey. This time I stayed at the home of Ralph and Marion Roland in Franklin Lakes, New Jersey, a pristine setting, adjacent to the prestigious Indian Trails Country Club. Their home was perched on a hillside overlooking the beautiful Franklin Lakes. Ralph was a graduate of the Wharton School and Chairman of American Cyanamide where he was also in charge of their International Sales Division. He was a brilliant businessman and Marion was a homemaker. They had three children and Mr. A had made arrangements for me to stay with them. I had my own air conditioned room overlooking the lake and drove their three children to practice each day in the family's Mustang convertible. It was idyllic. Marion cooked all the meals and each night I would chat with Ralph and Marion. Ralph and I would engage in somewhat of a debate format. Of course, I was no match for him, but I must say that he was always respectful, appeared to enjoy our discussions and encouraged more of them like a ritual every evening after dinner, just the three of us. We never had an argument and always parted with friendly differences of opinion. Ralph was incredibly well informed in matters of business, reading the *Wall Street Journal, Barrons,* and a variety of business journals everyday. Except for the Rolands, the summer of 1966 was a replay of what had occurred in the summer of 1965 with no startling improvements. It was my third summer in New Jersey.

Linda was still my girlfriend in the fall of 1966. She had been to Ohio State and was impressed. She came to visit on a Homecoming weekend. She came on Friday with my parents driving the usual twelve hours from New York. She had to be exhausted but we were lusting after each other. My pledging a fraternity did not work out. I could not bring myself to memorize the fraternity lore, which seemed so ridiculous. So was the hazing. I met some terrific guys there, but also some nuts who were totally whetted to or obsessed with the traditions of the fraternity.

That fall I returned to Ohio State with renewed ambition to try and make it in the Big Ten. This time I had a different room and I was in a double (two beds) instead of the triple that I had in my freshman year. George Horton transferred back to a Junior College in California and later went on to U.C.L.A. Ed Becker wound up rooming with a high school buddy. Linda was a freshman at Hofstra University in Long Island, New York. I received a so-called "Dear John" letter from Linda's mother Helen. She wrote that she did not want her daughter tied down and wanted her "to play the field." I was devastated. It did not come from Linda. I understood a mother's concerns for her daughter. Linda and I had not dated others during our courtship. It was called "going steady." That letter further exacerbated my sense of separation, anxiety, and alienation. I had lost another anchor. My foundation was slipping away. It was forced independence for which I was not ready.

That semester was a nightmare. I had transferred from Liberal Arts to Commerce and now I was in the School of Education taking some Physical Education classes but taking a core curriculum in math, science, English, history and the like. I hated my existence. The only records I had set at Ohio State were in the physical tests they administered to all freshmen. I was able to do 123 bent leg sit-ups in two minutes with my hands behind my head. I also climbed a thirty foot rope in nine seconds. This was not what I was looking for but perhaps the event that really drove me away in mind and body was a physiology class I took that semester in the medical school. It was a large class taught by a senior professor who also taught in the medical school. I did not like the course to begin with, but this was the icing on the cake. I walked into class which was held in an amphitheater. As I walked past the front of the room, the professor was standing in front and there was a dog laying on its back next to him. The dog was dissected with his paws spread. His heart was hooked up to a speaker and we could hear it and other bodily functions of the poor animal as the professor lectured. I could not stand it. The cruelty to me was overpowering. I wanted to throw up. At the end of the hour class, the professor invited us up to the front to get a closer look at the animal. I declined and left the room as quickly as I could.

I was back in the routine at Ohio State and bored to tears. I still hated being away from home. I would sit in front of my books for hours but could not concentrate. At the end of the fall quarter I took a bus ride from Columbus to Fort Lauderdale's Swimming Hall of Fame for the College

Swim Forum. I stayed there for a week or so training. I watched Buster Crabbe, Johnny Weismuller, Eleanor Holm, and Esther Williams be inducted into the Hall of Fame. I competed against Mark Spitz, who was emerging as a child protégée but still a high school student. While Mark later won seven gold medals in the 1972 Olympics, he might have won more in 1968 had he not gotten psyched out by Don Schollander, who had won four gold medals in the Tokyo Olympics and was still considered the star.

Chapter XII

Goodbye Columbus

I flew back to New York. My father, mother and Linda were waiting for me. There was silence in the car coming home until my dad broke the news that my grades had dropped to the point where I was ineligible. There was no such thing as academic probation, so I was out of Ohio State. If I wanted to return there, I would lose a year of eligibility. Linda clutched my hand. I think she thought I would be openly distraught or break down. I would not do that in front of her or my parents. I may have been in shock, a fugue-like state where your mind wanders into an abyss, while others sit in silence waiting for a reaction, a cogent phrase acknowledging that the message has been received. My father looked in his rearview mirror for me. He drove on. Linda and my mother said nothing.

I had just returned from the front lines, a week or two of training at the International Swimming Hall of Fame in Florida. I went there via Greyhound Bus through Pittsburgh. It took me thirty two hours to get there. My uncle Mario lived in Hollywood, Florida and he found a cheap hotel for my stay. He also gave me a broken down car to drive to and from Ft. Lauderdale each day. It barely ran. The hotel and the car were even more disgusting than the bus ride. Being on a bus with the same people for thirty two hours, without a shower, change of clothes and only one bathroom, created a pungent odor which made me feel as if I was traveling with prisoners to a concentration camp.

My room must have been part of a welfare motel with long term guests since I noticed a number of animal stains in the carpet, akin to the remnants of dog poop. If these were the sacrifices that I had to make in order to become the best, I was prepared to make them. The room was just a place to crash. I would spend all day, everyday at the Hall of Fame, training or sitting on the beach. I was alone which is the athlete's way. Being Spartan, pure and devoted, I was focused on athletic achievement. The top swimmers and divers in that era were like that. Sports was our lives. Nothing else except for family and in my case, a girlfriend, mattered. I might have stayed in Ohio to train or just returned home to swim with Coach Schlegel. That is probably what I should have done and that way I could have spent more time with Linda. My parents thought I needed the sunshine and training that Florida would provide. I wanted to go because I figured I could train harder there than anywhere else. I was right about that. I still was not swimming as fast as I wanted to, but I was training with Olympians and future Olympians in what was known as the College Swim Forum.

I was getting ready to take on the stars of the Big Ten, but that was suddenly gone, my dreams ended, my fate decided for me and the harsh realization that all things are not always possible at least not for me. Until then I had been on a steady climb, overcoming all obstacles and meeting with much success along the way. This was my first failure. Now I would return to all those that I had left behind when I thought I was onto more fame and fortune at Ohio State. All that training was for naught. I was like a soldier ready for battle only to be told that the war was over.

It is in times such as these when well-to-do and connected families can make a difference in your ability to overcome your personal catastrophe. But, that was not my plight. My father might find a solution, but unlike the rich and powerful who can often raise their magic wands and make everything better, that was not anything that I had. No one could make me whole, there was no such thing. The most important thing in my life had just been taken from me. Now what? Instead of deciding my own destiny, I was on automatic pilot controlled by others. Whether I would be off to war, school, work or some combination of them were not even in my thoughts. The prospect of separation from Linda and my parents was on my mind, so was the thought of possibly being killed in Vietnam. I was learning to accept my fate, not liking it, but accepting it. I should not have but at the time I was not sophisticated and my view of the world was confined to two ends of a swimming pool. I spent days at home alone, going nowhere, contemplating the future. What would become of me? My parents were off to work. Linda was now a freshman at Hofstra and I was nowhere.

I must have been expecting it because I did not react. One thing I thought for sure—my goals to reach the Olympics were over. Everything I had worked for was gone. My entire life was in flux. I did not know what I was going to do. I thought that I might wind up being drafted. I was emotionally distraught and devastated, but not showing it. My parents and Linda could feel my pain, my disappointment.

For anyone who has ever had a dream of achieving something of note and failed, the after shock forces you to come to grips with yourself as a person and how strong or weak you really are. Can you face the uncertainty that follows failure and rejection? Can you go on? How? Where? What?

Linda and I had talked about marriage but neither of us was ready for that. Certainly my new status as a non-athlete and not being in college caused our relationship to fall on the rocks. As much as I had lost my competitive swimming career and goal of Olympic Gold, I was going to lose the love of my life (at that time). I was crushed, down and out, imagining that I would soon be drafted. I lost my celebrity status in sports. My senses were dulled. I could have been cast in any direction and doubt that I would have cared. I accepted my fate. I had lost everything that was important to me. Plus, as a New York swimming celebrity I would have to endure the embarrassment of returning home—not only without success, but worse, having failed. The rumors would abound. Many would speculate that I had blown a golden opportunity. I was resigned to believing that what they would say about me was secondary to what I was sensing—that my life as I knew it was over.

Once back in New York, I accounted to myself. I continued writing in my swimming log but I was not working out. I did not send for my belongings at Ohio State so I do not know what became of them. I never got the chance to say goodbye or to thank anyone. I thought that I would soon be in Southeast Asia. I could not find a ray of hope. It would be months before I smiled.

As always, my father went to church to seek the advice of a priest. I, on the other hand, just sat around the house wondering whether I would decide my own fate or whether it would be decided for me. I felt more isolated than ever. I had no coach, no pool to train in, no job and now I would be a burden to my parents, financially and emotionally. I was powerless to control my own destiny or my future. I had nothing that made me special or that set me apart from all others. In fact, since I was in a perilous state of limbo, I could not even point to college as a special aspect of my life that would set me apart from those not fortunate enough to be at a university. I was identifying more with them.

I was not perfect. I was not unstoppable. I could be beaten and I was. Good parenting teaches us that our potential is limitless. We later learn throughout our lives that is not the case. A little at a time we incrementally accept failure together with success. The real egomaniacs among us continue to believe throughout their lives that they are infallible. They can be quite happy in their deluded, narcissistic world. But I was being confronted at the age of nineteen with the fact that my goals and aspirations were not going to be realized. The immaturity that I had as a college freshman was now pushing me at lightning speed into an uncertain future, without a compass to guide me or a dream to which I might look forward. It was a dark, dismal time for me, exacerbated by the deaths of so many in Southeast Asia, a foreboding place. Going there might take me to another lifetime—to death, or perhaps I would be severely disabled or wounded in battle like so many bloodied soldiers I had seen in the media. It would be a totally different me—perhaps to a fate I deserved. I was resigned to accept whatever might come. I was not consumed by fear, only uncertainty.

When you are winning, you are conditioned to win. You feel like a winner and you think like one. When you are losing though, it takes a strong person to still think like a winner, to keep the flame of hope alive. What is life after all if not the ability to achieve and experience? Both were taken from me. Now I needed to rebound but I was not ready.

This was one of the hardest things that I have ever had to do. Facing your own shortcomings, your own failures, teaches you honesty. It is also a matter of overcoming fear about your future, wondering what it will be. The fear is gradually overcome by a curiosity about your destiny. If I had been raised as a Kennedy then my life might be planned out for me—each move, each school, and later, each elected office. I was not so lucky. My parents wanted me to have a better life, to have all the advantages of the Kennedys. But my parents were not the Kennedys. They were in the middle economic class and so was I. Their power, money, influence, knowledge and experiences, unlike the Kennedys, were limited. The planning of futures that comes with wealth was not there. The comfort of security that comes from wealth was not my lot. While my parents endeavored to guide me, now self-determination would either take over or my fate would be entirely decided by others. This would be a turning point for me which I did not realize then but would later. I was crossing the Rubicon of life-engaging in a war within myself to reach a higher level of maturity. I was demoted, but in this sea of uncertainty I would have to find a positive outcome. Everyone has skeletons in their closets, i.e. what they might consider dark secrets about their past, something that shows their fallibility as human beings. Mine were right out in the open, but now what? For the wealthy, projections about their futures are born out of a sense of entitlement. For the rest of us, it is considered grandiose.

I did not have a job. I never had to look for one before this. As in the case of other athletes, especially world-class athletes in sports such as competitive swimming, there was not time or energy left for anything aside from sports. You train five to six hours a day, almost everyday and the rest of the time is spent sleeping (you need nine hours of sleep a night, plus an afternoon nap of an hour). There are 168 hours in the week. At least 36 of those are devoted to hard-core training.

My father and mother had concern for me, worrying that I might be drafted or that I was emotionally or psychologically troubled. They were smart to secure medical opinions. I was told that I must not ever discuss this with anyone, but I was being brought to two different psychiatrists. One was in Manhattan. I was told that he was a world-renowned psychiatrist. His Park Avenue office and his affiliations with New York's finest hospitals exemplified the trappings of a highly regarded and acclaimed Medical Doctor. He was giving me a serious check-up from the neck up. I had just one visit with him. I was in awe of his office, his sophisticated, urbane bearing, a distinguished appearance in a finely tailored navy blue suit. He was Asian American, very calm, thoughtful and incisive. You could just tell that he was a master in his field. He gave me a clean bill of health. I did not feel like I deserved it, but my parents were satisfied. I still felt lost.

Later in life I have come to read a great many psychological reports and to frequently work with clinicians. I use the Diagnostic and Statistical Manual for Mental Disorders (DSM IV) in my work. It is published by the American Psychiatric Association and used as the bible in the field of psychiatry. I have learned that according to competent clinicians who base nearly every diagnosis in part on references to DSM, that every person has disorders to a greater or lesser degree. That is a given. The issue of greater importance is whether the disorder leaves them functional or dysfunctional and what effect their disorder has on them and those around them.

I may have been depressed, but I was not suffering from suicidal ideation and I was not delusional. I was not psychotic. I had, in no way, departed from a firm sense of reality. I was not paranoiac and I was not blaming anyone else for my own personal failings or ability to cope and succeed. I simply had to face the fact, as we all must, that I was not invincible. This harsh reality is one that we must all accept sooner or later. It was my reality to accept sooner.

The acceptance of failure in not being able to reach all of our dreams is something with which we must cope. Rationalization sets in later. As we grow older, our mortality gives us still more questions to ponder. The extent to which we submit to failure or how we rebound from it, is what often contributes to our future course.

My father then brought me to a second psychiatrist. This was not serious. This was for use in order to possibly avoid military service. If needed, it might be used for a 4F deferment. That would simply mean that, for medical reasons, I would not be qualified for military service. I went to him a few times. This is where I became acquainted with the so-called indirect psychotherapeutic method of analysis and treatment where the psychiatrist is not didactic but instead turns the patient's statements into questions. The patient in essence answers his own questions. Once you realize that is the sum total of what the analyst is doing, and not giving you feedback, it becomes unnecessary because you are going through an introspective, existential phase of your life in either case. You are constantly asking yourself questions, inquiring about the meaningfulness of your existence. Unless the psychiatrist can help you directly by offering answers, even possible answers, the sessions become irrelevant and a waste of money. But I was not there for answers, I was there for a deferment if it became necessary. The doctor was being used, and that may have been unfair to him, but he was being paid for it and the old expression of "All's fair in love and war" seemed to apply. I do not even remember his name. My father thought the guy was a menace. Not at first, but he came to believe that.

My father did not stop there. Most people consider Italian men of his generation to be conservative and bigoted. He was not that way at all. He recommended that I attend Conscientious Objector meetings at the Ethical Humanist Society of Long Island. I started to do that once a week. At the Society, I learned that for one hundred dollars there was a certified psychologist who would write a 4F deferment letter for anyone.

While I was still at Ohio State, the Selective Service had a lottery. I drew a fairly high number but at that time the Department of Defense was offering an exam for college students. If you scored high enough on it you were exempt from the Draft (in those days they changed Selective Service policies to meet the needs of an escalating war). Many of my friends chose not to take the exam which we were told might expose them to the Draft if student deferments were eliminated. They were afraid that they would not score high enough. They viewed it as the government's trap. I took the test and scored high enough to keep my deferment but also had an exemption.

Once I was home and had to listen to President Lyndon Johnson's speeches every night regarding the war, my parents and I became convinced that we were losing the war and that the United States was simply going to keep sending troops in greater and greater numbers. The war was pointless. In fact, it was not even a declared war. It was a military action, much like Korea, unilaterally initiated by the United States President. For many, its justification had as its genesis a continuation of the war in the Pacific during World War II and our fight with Japan. After Pearl Harbor and our retaliation of dropping atomic bombs in Nagasaki and Hiroshima, our further involvement in Indochina could be justified by politicians used to the indiscriminate killing, even extermination of "yellow people." The deaths of 1,300 Americans in Pearl Harbor then became a war cry for justifying the killing of more than 200,000 Japanese with two bombs and more than 500,000 Vietnamese and another 200,000 Cambodians and Laotians.

The expansion of communism did not seem to be the menace that Johnson, Nixon, and others were making it out to be. To my way of thinking, communism was an idea which could be defeated by better ideas, not war. It could also be defeated by responsible capitalism.

My father then suggested another backup plan. My mother had epilepsy and he knew that unless a neurologist could see a seizure as it was occurring or could hook a patient up to an electroencephalogram (EEG) while it is happening, there is no way for the medical doctor to concretely know if one has epilepsy. All he or she can do is base their diagnosis on the symptoms provided by the patient. My father told me what to say, that I bit my tongue and tasted blood in my mouth, that I passed out, that I was sore afterwards from hitting the ground, and had jerky movements, and that people gathered around me and told me afterwards what they saw. I was taken to a top neurologist who informally diagnosed me with epilepsy and prescribed Dilantin, one of the drugs used to control seizures. Epilepsy was a 4F deferment. I never used this diagnosis for anything. It was a backup plan to avoid the Draft, if needed. I have never had a seizure and I have never taken Dilantin. My father said "You will fill the prescription and either mom will use them or you can flush them down the toilet".

As a final backup plan, as a last resort, I would be off to Canada or Europe. Was I being unpatriotic? On the contrary—while my efforts at the time were personal, there were thousands of young people doing what I was doing and more. Some were burning draft cards, going to jail, and even renouncing their citizenship. They were starting to protest against the war and politicians who supported it. What was patriotism? Was it more patriotic to go to Southeast Asia and lose a life or limb or was it more patriotic to stay at home, to resist the draft, and fight for the end of the war? I opted for the latter but I also knew that there were many poor young men from Appalachia and elsewhere who would enlist or who would submit to the draft because they had no better alternative and because their parents or teachers had not enlightened them to choose another course. In time, my personal, self-serving resistance would evolve into one where I would fight to end the war, to stop others from participating in it, and to bring our men and women home.

The military establishment's marketing program used the heroism of soldiers to recruit and exploit our young. The thought of becoming a hero by killing others did not appeal to me. The idea of becoming a hero by saving the lives of our own soldiers, who should not have been in Southeast Asia in the first place, seemed pointless. What became more meaningful to me over time was taking down elected and appointed officials who sought to further our involvement in that misguided war and others. The search for world peace, however unpopular that cause may have seemed to some at the time, represented a different kind of patriotism, one upon which our nation was founded. Just as our Founders had questioned the rule of the King of England, so too I and many other young people at the time questioned our national political leadership. Toppling Presidents in the name of peace is what we set out to do. It was no easy task.

Taking on the President, the Pentagon, and all of the special interests associated with them is a formidable task. Their first attack is usually to say that those who question the government's policies are un-American, unpatriotic or threatening national security interests. My parents knew that as my political awareness was changing, such accusations would be made against me. Nonetheless, though they sometimes questioned my actions, they stood by the decisions I made. They would question my reasoning, as good parents should, to make sure that I had thought things through and considered all the consequences. My mother told me of a book she had read entitled: *The Ugly American*, an account of failing U.S. diplomatic efforts and why America was hated in many parts of the world.

Politicians and others pander to the public, labeling those who question a war as outsiders, enemies of the state. So-called radicals of the era such as Jerry Rubin and Abby Hoffman had to draw attention to themselves in order to acquire a public voice. They were not necessarily the best examples of dissension, but they had an important place in the public fora.

Dissidents ran up against those who served in the military and lost relatives or friends. Persuading those people that we were as patriotic as those who died fighting against Hitler was no easy task. But Viet Nam was different—very different. Getting everyday folks to understand that, was the mission. At the same time we were totally supportive of all Viet Nam veterans, though not the mission that they had been erroneously forced to pursue.

People who have not been an only child themselves think that those without brothers and sisters must be spoiled because they never had to share the love of their parents or because their parents would spend all of their money on their only offspring. Naively, perhaps, I never considered myself to be spoiled. Yes, I probably got more because I was an only child, but my parents were not wealthy. I never expected anything. My parents never spoke of money, especially not at the dinner table. I had a sense of what was possible and what was not. I always knew that my parents would do what they could for me, but I never demanded anything. I was never very concerned with money. Having just enough to get by was fine with me.

What people with siblings do not realize is that there is strength in numbers. Siblings can agree and parents have less time to question. Only children stand alone often against parents who agree. It is two against, or for, one. The only child learns that she or he must persuade both parents. This can be a daunting task. Parents with only children maybe more protective of them because they have no more to spare. Establishing your independence as a young adult then becomes more difficult.

Chapter XIII

<u>Coming Back</u>

My father remembered Adelphi University, how I swam there in high school. He used some of those old contacts. I think he was also hoping that I might start pitching again. In January, 1967 I was at the school to take a look around.

Adelphi was founded in 1896 in Brooklyn as a women's college, primarily producing teachers and nurses. After the Second World War, soldiers returning home from military service took advantage of the G.I. Bill. By then, Adelphi had opened its main campus in Garden City. At first it was a commuter school with four large brick buildings and some athletic fields. It was, and has remained throughout its history, a commuter school, with some dormitories.

Once there I met some of the men on the swim team at Woodruff Hall, the home of the natatorium. I was also introduced to Bill Irwin, the Chairman of Swimming at the New York Athletic Club and who had become Adelphi's Head Swim Coach the year before that. I next met Jim Bedell, an active Adelphi alum, star athlete and Athletic Director. Bedell was a mountain of energy, a doer, he made things happen and before I knew it, I had an interview with Dan Bratton, the Dean of Admissions. I remember waiting in the reception area at Levermore Hall and being brought into his large office with subdued lighting. He was wearing a suit and looked very distinguished sitting behind a large desk. Adelphi was then trying to field a club football team, so he was known to have a passion for that. I was not being interviewed as a prospective athlete but rather, as a student being given his last chance. Dan gave me my chance. I would be an evening student. In order to avoid the draft, I had to matriculate, meaning pursue a degree. I took twelve credits at night and started working out with the swim team in the afternoon. As a transfer student, I could not compete. I was ineligible. I did continue to compete in Amateur Athletic Union competition.

In my first semester at Adelphi I was back to taking a Liberal Arts curriculum. I took Sociology, Linguistics, Speech, and Literature. It was my last stop before Southeast Asia, but that by itself did not create an interest in academics. The distraction of swimming was removed. I felt that the pressure had been taken off of me. The size of the school, the personal connection which professors had with us, being back in New York, and other factors ignited an interest in Adelphi and academics. I did well because I had to—more importantly, because I wanted to do well. I remember reading on my own, and not as an assignment, William Buckley's first book, *Man And God At Yale*. I wrote a short review of it which was published in the school paper, The *Delphian*. I then began to write a weekly sports column for the student paper called "Circle of Sports" where I featured athletes from all of the programs at Adelphi. I was then nominated and accepted for membership in Pi Delta Epsilon, the National Journalism Honor Society. I was being acknowledged and accepted for something other than sports. My confidence was gradually coming back. I had published an article on competitive swimming in *Swimming Technique* magazine, an international journal. I was seventeen then. I published two more articles in *Swimming World* and *Swimming Technique* magazines while in college. I wrote one with a physics student from Adelphi. I had determined that the distance in an Olympic size pool from the starter's position to the starting block for the swimmer in lane eight was at least twenty-one meters and since swimmers reacted to the sound of the gun, the signal by the speed of sound was reaching the swimmer in lane eight one-tenth of a second later than the swimmer in lane one. One-tenth of a second could make the difference in making the Olympic Team or not. More than a decade later, due to my article, the starting systems were changed so that all swimmers would get the signal at the same time and an electronic clock starts at that time so that you do not have another variable with hand held stop watches. Now touch plates at the finish give you the reading to hundredths of a second of each swimmer. In 2008, Michael Phelps won the 100 meter butterfly at the Beijing Olympics by one-hundredth of a second.

In the summer of 1967, I commuted to and from North Jersey, occasionally staying at the Rolands'. But I was also taking two courses at night at Adelphi, Psychology and Philosophy. I became interested in both and again did well. Nothing very eventful was happening in swimming. I was not working hard enough there.

I still dressed like a college kid from the 1950's and early sixties. I was not a hippie. I was neatly groomed, wearing cuffed pants, pressed shirts, sweaters and shoes that were shined. Any other style would have been frowned upon by my fellow students and the faculty who were not in anyway plugged into the student protests and quiet student revolution which were building at universities elsewhere. Mark Rudd and students at Columbia University had taken over the Lowe Library at Columbia to protest plans to build a gymnasium in Morningside Heights. But it was much more than that—it was the era of sit-ins when suddenly passive resistance became active. Students were going to the front lines of protests and taking on personal risks, in some cases going to jail. The song lyrics and political rhetoric which had been brewing a revolution for half a decade or more, perhaps beginning with Lenny Bruce, the famous comedian from the 1950's and 60's, had created the first steps of a revolution.

Chapter XIV

Political Awareness

An organization called the Students for a Democratic Society (SDS) was formed at Harvard and took credit for the events at Columbia which were decried by middle America. Being closer to middle America at a suburban campus, our parents spoke to us. They who were reserved, and worked, did not have time to pay attention to the political unrest occurring on college campuses. Protests at suburban schools like Adelphi were occurring gradually. We were not the models for the revolution, though later became the copycats of it.

At Columbia and elsewhere students objected to their University's involvement with research for the Defense Department. Most schools wanted the ROTC off their campuses. In 1965, New York City Mayor John Lindsay started open admissions to the City University of New York. That meant that poor kids from the ghetto could go to college if they graduated from high school. At that time, the City University had the second highest paid faculty in the country and it was a truly venerated institution of higher learning. Lindsay, a Yale graduate, was a pioneer who understood that barriers of racism existed even in exalted institutions of higher learning. Students at the elitist, Ivy League Columbia recognized these issues perhaps because they were intellectually gifted, but many were also well-to-do with parents able to pay for their schooling. Academic success for them was a given. City College, the main part of the City University, was a short distance from Columbia. The disparities between open enrollment at the City College and elitist admissions at a private university such as Columbia, were glaring. Columbia was the largest landowner in Manhattan. It had faculty members and students critical of its posture.[9]

My parents were paying for my education at considerable sacrifice. In deference to them, even if I was aware of the torrents of political change that were sweeping the country and I was not, I was also not ready to assume risk or to jeopardize what my parents and others were trying to do for me. My inner self was being pulled in two directions: one was the safe culture of sports and middle America, the other, academia and the politics of dissent. This duality of thought produced a conflict within me which I have spent a lifetime trying to reconcile. It was a dichotomy between a mainstream lifestyle or launching into the unknown. I was being pulled into the direction of the unknown, charting my own course without maps or mentors. *I have since come to realize that I spent the first part of my life hedging my bets and the second part of my life trying to figure out why I did.*

Once I came over to Adelphi, my parents also became involved in the school. They revived the Parents' Association. My dad became so involved that we wound up giving him the nickname "The Dean." In reality, he could have been one, because just like his little league days, he was totally for the students. He was a born leader and organizer.

I had taken a liking to radio and every Saturday night I had a campus radio show which few people listened to but which enabled me to learn a bit about broadcasting, voice, and the use of a microphone. Adelphi had about five to six thousand undergraduates and approximately one thousand dormitory students in the five dorms they had built. The school had about fifteen thousand students all together when you counted graduate programs on all campuses. In any event, my show was potentially available for anyone on campus who might listen in on a Saturday night. I had three engineers who helped me with the programming and quite a few well known national radio personalities emerged from that station known as WALI. Mel Granick (formerly with CBS) and Dick Kneer (formerly with WNEW-FM) were among them.

My dad became the President of the Parents' Association and with a Dean at the school, managed to acquire for Adelphi an FM radio license. The station then became known as WBAU.

Dan Bratton urged me to participate in campus life and I took his advice. By the end of 1967, I ran in a contested election, my first one, for President of the Men's Athletic Association. That meant that I would fight for my fellow athletes to make sure that they had what they needed to excel in sports. I also ran the Annual Awards Dinner.

I was having a long dry spell without much competition in sports, but I was studying hard and attending campus events, such as lectures, plays, and concerts. I was becoming a fixture at the school, even attending art show openings. I was taking classes in Education, Astronomy, Physical Education, Interior Design, and English. I had fallen in love with learning. I had to take a class in physiology, which all my fellow students dreaded because it was very difficult. My fear factor was high. I did not want to relapse into failure so I studied hard. This time, without a dog on the table in front of me, but with the same course work, I received the highest grade in the class, a 98. Now I started to feel more confident in school.

It was time to pick a major and I felt pushed into Education simply because of my circumstances. But I was not your typical jock. My father always wanted to be a lawyer, but never had the opportunity. He would have been an amazing lawyer, probably the top labor lawyer in New York. Of this, I have no doubt. I knew that he wanted that for me but I had to get out of school with a major and a career. Teaching seemed like the easiest and best bet. But, I was being pulled into another direction where I might make a difference in the lives of others. I had some natural leadership skills which I was rekindling.

Senator Eugene McCarthy was making headlines as a Presidential candidate who wanted to end the war in Vietnam. He was taking on President Johnson and it looked like Richard Nixon was going to be the Republican nominee. I am ashamed to say it now, but I voted for Richard Nixon in 1968 because he said he had an undisclosed plan to end the Vietnam War. Little did I realize that his plan included bombing the North Vietnamese "back to the Stone Age."[10]

I was a Democrat and so was my father. My mother was a registered Republican. As a County employee, she had to be. I registered at age eighteen just after the Twenty Fifth Amendment was passed. I voted in every election. My father spoke of politics everyday. He encouraged me to read the papers and watch the news. Teaching was a nice mainstream idea but my father hoped for more. He did not expect it or demand it but on the other hand, John F. Kennedy and Bobby Kennedy had inspired young people, like no others before, to believe that we can and must change the world for the better, collectively and individually. The Peace Corps had been established and I was developing a commitment to humanity that was much bigger than coaching swimming or teaching in a classroom each day. I was still watching from the sidelines as McCarthy won the New Hampshire Democratic primary in February, 1968.

I remembered years before when I was in seventh grade, my father had a great many law books in the house. He acquired them from the Blackstone School of Law, a correspondence law school in Chicago. My dad never got around to doing much with those books, so they just collected dust until I started to read them. My dad would come home from work, I would tell him about the cases, and we would debate them. With my dad, all talk was of politics, law and sports, and the strengths and weaknesses of anyone in those fields of endeavor.

At the same time, my father's attorney was Jules Buckbinder, Esq. Mr. Buckbinder was a very successful practitioner with a mansion in Kings Point and a large office in the Woolworth Building in downtown New York City, just across from City Hall. Each Saturday morning my father would drop me off at Mr. Buckbinder's home and his chauffeur would drive us into the City. Mr. Buckbinder did not have children. Mr. Buckbinder would regale me with stories about politics and law—what you had to do to get things done in New York, how to make money. His African American chauffeur was dressed meticulously in a gray uniform with gold buttons, high black knee boots which had a high shine, and a black and grey cap. He wore white gloves. When we got to his office, his chauffeur would double park. Mr. Buckbinder and I would stay seated until he came around to curbside to open the door for us. "Jim, the usual time," Mr. Buckbinder would say. That usually meant 12:30 p.m. when we would be driven to DelMonico's Steak House for lunch or uptown to the 21 Club. Mr. Buckbinder had a table at each. He also had a phone at his tables.

At his office I would sit next to him as he sat behind his large desk in his spacious office which overlooked lower Manhattan and the Statue of Liberty. I sat upright in my suit, paying attention as the clients were shown in by the secretary who called me "Master Tom." Associates, always dressed neatly in suits with their jackets on, would hover next to Mr. Buckbinder waiting for his direction, his orders. Their response was always "yes, sir" and they would leave his office with the clients to carry out his direction. Mr. Buckbinder would whisper to me who the talented lawyers were and why. He said they would stay with him for a few years, learn all they could from him and then move on to their own practices.

Mr. Buckbinder would dress more flamboyantly on Saturdays than he did during the week. He always wore a homburg hat, a well-tailored tweed or cashmere coat with felt collar, and a walking stick which was purely ornamental and added to his already exuberant, regal presence. He also wore a pocket watch, fob and gold chain in his vest. He always wore beautiful cuff links and had fresh pocket hankies in his suit pocket to dab his face.

I also remember my mother being a voracious reader and fan of *Perry Mason*. We would watch the television show together and marvel at Raymond Burr's eloquence, his style, his unflappable delivery.

While I was still involved in sports and headed toward a teaching degree, my interest in politics and law was growing. I was resigned to complete my teaching degree requirements but I was not content with that, I wanted more, I was starting to see a bigger picture.

In March, 1968 I was finally re-entering collegiate competition. Adelphi had decided to compete in the National Association of Intercollegiate Athletics (N.A.I.A.) Championships in St. Cloud, Minnesota. I was entered in three events, the two hundred, five hundred and sixteen hundred and fifty yard freestyle events and a relay. I felt rusty. It had been three years since the High School Easterns. I had won the Regional Championships during the summer at two hundred and four hundred meters. My parents wanted me to keep striving. Staying involved in swimming kept my sanity which I might have otherwise lost to failure. The message was not to give up, ever. Go to your goal—take the hits and set backs, but keep going.

In St. Cloud I won the two-hundred-yard freestyle and won a birth to the 1968 Olympic Team Trials. I took second place in my other events and false started in the relay which regrettably deprived two of my teammates from ever making All-American.

I was now an N.A.I.A. All-American, but the coaches from the other universities wanted to challenge my eligibility based upon what happened to me at Ohio State. My Athletic Director, Jim Bedell, woke up the Dean of Students in the middle of the night, got my transcripts and flew out to Minnesota. Jim and Bill Irwin fought for me. They established my eligibility and I kept my championship.

Adelphi was thrilled with my success. It was not the Olympic Games, but it was a National Championship.

In the summer of 1968 I left New Jersey and decided to swim for Bill Irwin. He had become my coach and a very good friend. We were with each other everyday. He had arranged for us to train at the Manorhaven Pool in Long Island, an unheated fifty-meter pool. One of his swimmers, Mary Beth Tomaselli, a breaststroker, had qualified for the trials. Also Lenny Galuzzi, who had graduated from Adelphi that year had qualified in the two hundred meter breaststroke event. He did not work out with us that summer. The only other New Yorker to go to the trials that year was Paul Katz of Seward Park High School. He was from lower Manhattan. Paul had scored a perfect 1600 on the SATs and was headed to Yale as a Physics major. His mother and father both taught Physics at branches of the City University.

Morning workouts were from 6 a.m. to 8 a.m. at Manorhaven. Irwin was there every morning and was not even being paid. He made so many sacrifices for me and other swimmers that we must all be eternally grateful. Irwin was also the Pool Director at North Hempstead Country Club so I would generally workout there, short course, from 8:30 a.m. to 10 a.m. I would then grab breakfast on the run and head into the City where I would work out with Paul Katz at the Hamilton-Fisch Pool on Pitt Street in lower Manhattan, a bad neighborhood on the lower East Side. On hot summer nights people from the neighborhood would hop the fences and be in the pool all night.

I would swim with Paul from 11:30 a.m. to 1 p.m. everyday and then drive back to Long Island. I would sleep in the afternoon for a few hours and either return to North Hempstead at night for a workout from 5-7 p.m. or more often I would train by myself at night at the Cantiague Pool in Hicksville. It is a 50-meter pool. My father would hold the stop watch for me, calling out my times on the repeats as the kids from the neighboring area would swim across my lane. I had to set up my own lane line. The young recreation swimmers would always cross it and interfere with my workout.

I tried at the start of that summer to propose the use of County pools for training. My proposal was rejected. So, I was on my own. They gave me one lane at Cantiague between 5-7 p.m. at night while recreation swimming in the rest of the pool was still taking place. These were not ideal conditions at all. Once again, I should have gone to California.

I was not working, just training each day. My father underwrote the cost of everything. I was competing in the Olympic Trials. It was a great honor. I had to do what I could to make the team. I still was not getting enough training in the right conditions with the best athletes at my side.

You can not train in isolation, all by yourself. You need partners, people to chase and others who are chasing you. California had the system. We were trying to replicate it without much support from elected officials who controlled the pools. They catered to the recreation swimmers, the voters.

In early 1968, I presented the County with a program that would use its facilities to start an Olympic Development Program to train competitive swimmers in their long course pools. I had it all mapped out in a paper that explained everything. I was twenty-one and told that I should present it to a Park Director. I did and it got nowhere. Instead they gave me one end lane in Cantiague Pool at night. I had to string my own lane line. It was a waste of precious time. My dad helped me.

In 1968, "Doc" Councilman published the book *The Science of Swimming*. It was state of the art and explained technique and training. I read it from cover to cover many times. By 1968 I was getting pretty good at coaching myself and designing my own workouts. In fact, during the previous winter, 1967 to 1968, I coached, as a volunteer, the St. Mary's High School team at the Pierce Country Day School in Roslyn. Really, I just worked them out and never attended one of their meets. I liked coaching but it is very difficult to train yourself no matter how much you know. I pressed myself pretty hard but did not have anyone pushing me. That means that you give into the pain, the boredom, and the monotony. You have a sense that life is passing you by when really your whole existence should be about training.

I had been making daily log entries for three years and I was starting to see trends in my performance. I was learning to be a student of bio-feedback. I was essentially on a three day cycle where one day I was down, the next day mediocre, and then finally a day when I was really up, swimming faster and far better than the other days. This is when you really have to test your limits. In plotting your bio-feedback, what you are trying to do is plan your training so that you can reach a peak at the end of the season. In my case that would be in August at the Olympic Trials which were held at the Belmont Plaza Pool in Long Beach, California.

Summer, 1968, Olympic trials, Long Beach, California waiting for my heat.

I had not seen Linda in over one year. She had transferred to the University of Miami and understandably lost interest in me. It took me a long time to get over that. I cried a lot. I was not leading a normal life. I still had not tasted alcohol or even a beer. I had not tried marijuana or any other drugs. But Paul Katz convinced me that I should come into the City on weekends for a little relaxation. I did. We went to the Electric Circus on St. Mark's Place in the East Village. It was the psychedelic era and in that night club I saw strobe lighting for the first time. I loved it and danced as often as I could with a partner or without one, it did not really matter. The Filmore East was just around the corner. A large airplane was parked in front of it signifying that the Jefferson Airplane was playing there. Grace Slick, the Airplane's lead singer, was so sexy to me, but as a non-musician I could not really be a part of that life.

Still as an athlete I was reserved, guarded, and could not have too much fun. I could not abuse my body where my physical performance might be hurt, plus I did not really have extra money to waste on those endeavors. Nonetheless, the East Village showed me that there was another culture, a counter culture that I longed to be apart of and which I envied. I did not play music or sing and probably had no talent for either, but I loved the freedom that rock 'n roll represented. I loved wild and crazy dancing, feeling the fast pace of the music in every stroke I took. At the same time LSD was everywhere. A part of the culture seemed to be testing the outer limits of human potential, but at times that caused some very severe self-destructive results.

It was a few weeks before the Olympic Trials and Paul convinced me to meet him at Maxwell's Plum in New York City. Maxwell's Plum was a famous bar in uptown New York on the east side. It was a pick up place where people like Truman Capote would hang out. I was there and tried some tequila with worms in the bottom of my glass. I did not like it. We left and were heading downtown to Paul's sister's apartment. She was away. Along the way I spied a beautiful African American hooker coming across the street. I told Paul to stop the car. She came over to the window, there were police everywhere. I asked: "How much for everything for both of us?" We agreed on the price. I told her to get in, and we headed to the apartment. She had a double scotch. It was before the days of AIDS. We were young and liberated. Two hours later we dropped her off.

My newfound political awareness had not overcome my physical desire for fun, sexual exploration or a release from the tension of physical training. My actions were no doubt chauvinistic, but at the same time, consensual. I have had some regrets about them, but as I look back on it, it was another break away from the protective, inhibiting culture that surrounded me. As for the woman, it was her work and she benefitted financially from our brief encounter. When I think of her today, I remember her as kind, friendly and tender. I hope that she had a decent life. If I had more political awareness then I doubt that I would have done anything different. I was thinking or not thinking with the wrong head.

I do not write that to be flip, but it was a different time. Experiences such as these have given me greater empathy for those committing moral and ethical transgressions. I have matured and perhaps I owe all women an apology for some of my actions. If so, then here it is, my candid admissions of mistakes that I have made. There is hypocrisy in denial and deceit. I choose not to conceal my own hypocrisy because that in itself teaches us only to lie. Today I would like to think that I am and have always been an advocate for the rights of all women and minorities. These experiences have shown me another side of this life. I do not know what became of the woman we met on the streets of New York, but a part of me speaks for her whenever I raise my voice for equality. I will not forget her. Even now, she is with me, in my thoughts.

Workouts continued and one day returning from Pitt Street I had the choke out on my car, heading east on the Brooklyn Queens Expressway near the Kosciuszko Bridge. I had forgotten that I left the choke out and my car stalled. It was raining. I had my flashers on but in my rear view mirror, I saw a car skidding and it slammed into my car sending me up onto the center meridian and nearly into the oncoming lane of traffic. I had to be towed away. I was still in one piece, but stiff. I continued my workouts.

A day or so later, I was at Cantiague and started peaking for the trials. The peaking phase of my training generally lasted about two weeks. I was hot and swimming very fast. From a push off, I swam under my best time for four hundred meters. It was at Cantiague Pool during recreation with kids cutting in front of me. The pool was poorly constructed for competitive swimming. It had narrow lanes, dark water and lots of turbulence. My dad held the stop watch and was not always exacting in starting and stopping it. My time was somewhere between 4:16 and 4:20. With a dive, a better pool, and more peaking, I was hoping to shave another four seconds off of that time. To make the final at the trials I figured that I would have to be around 4:12 and to make the Olympic Team probably around 4:08. I knew that in the final of the Olympic Trials, just like in the final of the Olympic Games, anything can happen, and upsets occur and that might be me, but I first had to get into the final.

Two weeks later we were in California without a coach. Our parents also stayed home. Paul and I roomed together in the student dorms at Long Beach State College. We rode by shuttle bus to the pool each day. When I arrived for the first day prior to the trials, I went to the Belmont Plaza Pool. It was breathtaking. Excitement was in the air. I looked up at the large score board above the starting blocks. On the marquise they displayed the motto for the trials, which I have since adopted for my life: *In Great Attempts, It Is Glorious Even To Fail.* Some very kind and compassionate people had put that up there so that the losers might feel better. There were an estimated five hundred thousand swimmers in the United States and the chances of making the Olympic Team were about one-thousandth of one percent, but the point was that it was an honor just to be there. I felt that honor, but wanted more.

For those who make the Team or who win a medal, it may well be the highest achievement in their lives. That is also true of those who try out but do not make it. But, no matter what, I did not intend to stop at trying to achieve in life. The lessons which I learned in sports would carry over into life. I did not get to the Olympic Trials on the basis of natural talent. I got there through perseverance.

I do not know why our parents did not come to the trials. It was probably a money issue, but I do not recall any of the four New Yorkers having their parents there except for Mary Beth, who was accompanied by her mom.

The atmosphere was intense. All of the Olympic water sports trials were being held in Southern California. In the Belmont Plaza Pool they held the trials for swimming, diving, water polo, and synchronized swimming.

At that time, the United States dominated world swimming. If you could make the U.S. Team you were almost guaranteed a medal in the Games, but the competition in the U.S. was fierce. Our athletes held world records in every event. I could have made the team of any other nation.

We were warming up and practicing for a few days. Paul and I were coming back on the bus from the pool one day and I told Paul I was thinking about shaving my head for the meet. We stopped the bus. The driver and the other athletes cheered me on. They waited for me while I went into a barber shop and had my head shaved. That night I would shave the rest of my body.

This was such a big meet that I thought we would be seeing a lot of shaved heads at it. I was wrong. There were only about four of us.

My first event was two hundred meters. I was in the first heat of the first event. Swimming next to me was Mike Burton, the world record holder at fifteen hundred meters.

I did not make the final in that event or any other. My best finish was fourteenth in the four hundred meter race. None of the New Yorkers made a final in any event. Once at Yale, Paul later became a member of their National Championship relay team.

Looking back I remember the assassinations of Martin Luther King, Jr. and a month later that of Bobby Kennedy. You could not ignore the campus upheaval and unrest, but as I later learned, that usually happens in the Spring on college campuses, once graduation occurs, things quiet down for the summer. This was a different year though. It was a Presidential election year.

Allard Lowenstein, a political activist from Long Beach, Long Island had organized the "Dump Johnson" movement. He supported Bobby Kennedy, a United States Senator from New York at the time. Lowenstein had been the President of NSA, the National Student Association, said by some to be a front for the C.I.A.[11] Al graduated from the University of North Carolina at Chapel Hill and later, the Yale Law School. Al was running for Congress that year. He won and served one term in the House of Representatives. He was a non-stop organizer and activist. He had a huge following of young people, over one thousand came to his Congressional District to work in his campaign. He and Bobby Kennedy exemplified what I wanted to be. I found time to work for him in the summer and fall of 1968. Al's campaign was a part of The Movement, as we then called the political activism of the 60's.

It was not that I was oblivious to these things. On the contrary, I was deeply touched by them, especially when I looked around at my fellow swimmers and could not see a black face among them. What was it that kept blacks away from the Olympic Trials? The answer is a simple one. They did not have suitable facilities and coaches in their neighborhoods. Their parents could not afford to let them swim.

I was trying to keep my focus. That summer the Democratic National Convention was unfolding. With Johnson out of the race and Bobby Kennedy assassinated, interest in Senator Eugene McCarthy had waned and that left Vice President Hubert Humphrey, an uninspiring figure who was unable to distance himself from Johnson's failed policies in Southeast Asia. Johnson had presided over the successful sheperding of the Civil Rights Act of 1964 and his Great Society programs commendably followed those of Kennedy's New Frontier. Yet all of that was being criticized because of the debacle of Viet Nam. Johnson himself was being severely criticized for his slow, pedantic delivery. He was inflicting a national depression upon the American people. The nation was in a state of despair because we were in a war that we could not win and we were morally wrong for continuing to wage it. The marches on Washington had started in 1965, but by 1968 they were getting bigger and bigger. Busloads of people were going to Washington to protest.

I was following news accounts closely. I wanted to be more a part of what was happening nationally. The Convention was being held in

Mayor Daly's Chicago. The Yuppies were there to nominate a pig for the Presidency. Jerry Rubin and Abbie Hoffman were focal points, but young people generally were in the front lines and I identified more with those masses, as I was not a public figure. When they were beaten by police, you could hear the chant in the background on national television: "The Whole World Is Watching." It was a culminating event for me, finally pushing me to become more involved in the so-called Peace Movement and student rights. I still did not consider myself to be a prime mover. There was, I felt, a conflict between athletics and politics, in that most athletes in that era were not activists or even politically aware. Figures like Mohammed Ali were few and far between. My father admired Mohammed Ali and the political protesters. He was in his early 50's. He always respected free speech and resented the police using force against young people in order to quell debate. My father liked Mohammed Ali's courage but said Rocky Marciano was a better fighter. My father, without fear, said that he would like to go fifteen rounds with Mohammed himself. He was always ready to take on anyone.

I was watching David Susskind, a somewhat liberal alternative to William Buckley's Firing Line, which I also watched. I came to follow and admire the Chicago Seven, alleged conspirators, and their counsel Bill Kunstler and Gerry Lefcourt, and to decry the judge who presided over their case, Hon. Julius Hoffman. The Chicago Seven and particularly their counsel, demonstrated to me what was right with America and Julius Hoffman represented what was wrong with it.[12] The defendants and their counsel were about free speech and exposing the extent to which the Government would go to stop criticism of it. To me, they were championing the Bill of Rights, much as our Founders had. Listening to or reading the works of Tom Hayden, a former student at the University of Michigan, and later a State Legislator in California and husband to actress Jane Fonda, was illuminating. Hayden was one of the defendants. He was also a poet. The eighth defendant was Bobby Seale, an African American who was gagged and shackled by Judge Hoffman and later removed from the courtroom to be tried *in absentia*. I saw in these defendants a rejection of the *status quo*, a beacon to the future. They had achieved what I was trying to learn—independence, courage, eloquence, leadership and critical thinking. A metamorphosis was taking place in me and college students around the nation. It was also beginning to foment a climate of change in the electorate, but in my Republican dominated county, the torrents of change had not reached the community as a whole. Rather the patronage laden local and state government seemed to control mind, body and spirit. The politics which I was beginning to appreciate was anathema to the politics of old. Most people were comfortable in their Government jobs and saw new ideas and rebellious young people as a threat to them, indeed, to a post World War II culture which they had come to accept and appreciate. They ignored racism and anti-Semitism which were predominant features of American life. For them it was all about hard work and reward. There were no political questions, the way of life could not be questioned—well manicured lawns took a priority over challenging government policies. People in the suburbs just were not "sitting in" and viewed anyone who did as a communist or worse.

The anger among those content with their existences was palpable. You could see the hate in their faces. The young were not given slack, they were treated as the enemy. Those with some money and power would do whatever was necessary to preserve the American way of life and to crush those who challenged it or wanted no part of it. I wanted a part of it, but I wanted fairness and equality, innocuous and seemingly unthreatening terms, yet supported over time with a vast array of evidence and a life-long commitment to human and civil rights and the Bill of Rights. I was not brought up to be the servant of any master. I would not do what the Speaker of the House of Representatives had once recommended to aspiring politicians, namely: "To go along, get along." That was not me. I was not raised to be a follower. If there was a cookie-cutter mold, I was intent on breaking it.

In the fall of 1968, I was working out and now attending student council meetings. I was participating in all my classes and came to know Dr. Jeffrey Kirk, an Ed.D., Professor of Education at Adelphi who competed in the 1948 Olympics in the hurdles. I also became friendly with Dr. Menaheim Less, a Ph.D. physiologist from Penn State who was state of the art in sports. He recruited Israelis and took Adelphi to the NCAA University Division Championships in soccer. The guy was a masterful, positive thinker and motivator. I saw his brilliant creativity in sports which he later used to become a success in business. Then I got to know Ron Bazil, the track coach who produced a world record indoor mile relay team and brought the Olympic broad jump champion and world record holder, Bob Beamon, to Adelphi.

Then there was Paul Dougherty, an Adelphi Alum who worked in admissions and who coached the Lacrosse Team to an NCAA University Division Championship. Paul took me on a trip to Detroit for a University Admissions conference. He later remarked that my bed stayed made for three days and that after arrival he never saw me again until we were ready to depart.

The Athletic Department under Jim Bedell, was very strong and the coaching staff was tolerant of my budding political awareness because I was supportive of the sports programs, the athletes and coaches. It was a cooperative effort which I was not seeking to undermine, but rather to build upon it.

Adelphi had an outstanding speaker and concert series. At that time it was probably the best in the nation. Famous writers, politicians, lawyers and even Supreme Court Justices were among those attending. They included Justice William O. Douglas, the reigning liberal on the Court who had written *Points of Rebellion*[13], a comparison between the Revolutionary War and the revolution then occurring on college campuses. Douglas was a boring speaker but the substance of his opinions, life story[14] and rhetoric were inspiring. In any event, irrespective of what was said, the fact that it was being said and said at Adelphi was to me an awakening. So I plodded along going about my day to day business but paying close attention to what was happening nationally, locally and at Adelphi.

That academic year I was inducted into Flambeau, the Senior Men's Honor Society. My grade point average was now well above a 3.0 and climbing. I was not in an Ivy League school or even Ohio State, but I had taken Dan Bratton's advice and gotten involved with the University. It made a great difference in my life, and my outlook. Now I was beginning to see a life after sports, oddly in politics and in law.

In dual meet competition I was undefeated. My parents came to every meet and many of my practices. My dad would often come to my practices on Saturday mornings. He was always a welcome sight.

In March, 1969 I attended the NCAA College Division Championships at Springfield College in Massachusetts. I finished second in two events, the 500 yard and 1650 yard freestyles behind Mike Martin, a gifted athlete from the University of California at Irvine. I placed tenth in the 200 yard freestyle and became an All-American in three events.

That spring I decided to run for Vice President of the Students' Association. Most of the jocks were not involved in student politics and wanted nothing to do with anything outside of their fraternities, sports and degrees. To my surprise, I won. That summer I trained with Bill Irwin at the Garden City Pool and at Adelphi. I also became one of two Presidential Interns that summer working with incoming students, counseling them on the courses they should take and orienting them on life at Adelphi. The President of the University who had chosen me was Charles Vevier (dec.), a former Dean and Historian from Cornell, a brilliant academic, but an abrasive, non-leader.

Canadian Nationals. Summer, 1969, 400 meter freestyle. Fourth Place.

That summer, I won the Regionals for the fourth time and competed in the Canadian Nationals, finishing fourth. Coming back from the Nationals through upstate New York, I wanted to divert through Woodstock, but my friend John Quinn, a fellow swimmer from Adelphi and later a lawyer himself, was driving. His dad was a Sergeant in the Nassau County Police Department. Much to my dismay and regret we went around the Woodstock Music Festival. We were so close, but did not attend. I could barely believe it. I was in shock, but to me it showed that I was still not a full-fledged member of the 1960's revolution. If I had been I would have gotten out of the car and walked or hitched a ride. Instead I acquiesced to the comfort and security of Quinn's vehicle.

That summer I met an incoming student from Alexandria, Virginia. She had beautiful, long, natural blond hair and high cheek bones. She was stunning and I promised myself that I would look her up in the fall. I remember looking at her intake form and seeing that her father was a lawyer, a graduate of the University of Michigan and was Assistant Under Secretary for United Nations Affairs in Washington. Deborah Allen caught my attention because she was beautiful and because her father was a lawyer with contacts in Washington.

Fall is a time on every college campus when the air is filled with excitement. The protests from the previous spring had subsided, you could feel tension. Students were optimistically looking forward to a year of good grades; new achievements and relationships. In my case I was looking forward to graduating, but I was still uncertain about my future. More and more I was becoming involved in politics both on and off campus. I was still trying to workout twice a day but my political involvement was now occupying much of my time. Al Fischer, the Student Association President, was called up by the National Guard for military service. He had to leave school and the Presidency. The By-Laws of the Association provided that I would ascend to the Presidency which I did. I became Co-President with Cynthia Favata, now a United States District Court Judge in the Eastern District of Pennsylvania. I was an activist on campus. I began to monitor the policies of the new President seeing many of them as far too grandiose for a small university. For example, he decided to hold an elaborate inauguration for himself, which I referred to as a coronation. In 1969 dollars that represented more than $90,000 in order to invite representatives from all United States colleges and universities. Following economists' Rule of Seven, by today that money could be worth nearly three million dollars.

President Charles Vevier then became a focus of my attention since he seemed to be the embodiment of Nixonian policies. His inauguration convinced me that he was more interested in himself than he was in the welfare of society.

At every meeting of the Student Council I pushed legislation that was oriented entirely toward student rights. I convinced the Council to hire an attorney to protect the rights of the students. I became the first Student Trustee on the University's Board of Trustees. I used the student newspaper to excoriate Vevier. Dan Bratton begged me to let up. While I felt a loyalty to Dan, I could not betray the students whom I was elected to represent. Besides, I reasoned that I was following Dan's advice when I first came to Adelphi two and one-half years earlier. Dan had tied himself to Vevier. If Vevier succeeded, so would Dan. If he failed, so would Dan. I graduated from Adelphi in 1970, but two years later when Vevier resigned in a speech before the Faculty-Student Senate, where I was not present, he referred to me and only me by name as being the cause of his resignation (which really was more in the nature of an ouster). Unfortunately, Dan left with him. Vevier has since passed away. I am not sure about Dan.

In the fall of 1969, I was determined to find Deborah Allen, which I finally did. We began dating and seeing each other throughout my senior year. We had a great time. We did everything with each other. In the last six months of my senior year she was really living at my home. My parents had no objection. They liked any girl I liked, and my mother started telling a few close friends and relatives that she thought Deborah would be the one for me and that I would marry her. My mother was not wrong about my intentions, although I never told her that.

By March of 1970 I was back for the NCAA College Division Championships where I again placed second in the five hundred and third in the sixteen hundred and fifty yard freestyle events. I made All-American again. I had the previous year and this year won the Metropolitan Collegiate Championships and I was undefeated in dual meet competition. I qualified for the NCAA University Division Championships and attended those at Indiana University. That effectively marked the end of my active swimming career. After fifteen years I called it quits at age twenty-three. I should have graduated a year earlier in 1969 but lost credits in transferring to Adelphi.

The spring of 1970 was turbulent. There were more marches on Washington and peace demonstrations. I was speaking at every campus rally. I formed the Metropolitan Association of Student Governments, consisting of all the representative student governments at the universities in the New York area. Instead of protests and violence, it was our plan to use all these students in the Metropolitan area to lobby for change and student rights. We held many meetings and drafted bylaws, but could not agree on all terms and ultimately stopped meeting.

In the Spring of 1970 students at Kent and Jackson State Universities were killed. One of the four students shot and killed by the National Guard at Kent State in Ohio was Jeffrey Miller. I did not know Jeff, but he came from Plainview-Kennedy High School, a neighboring school to my high school, Plainview-Old Bethpage High School. That event really pushed me over the edge politically. Now, I had a life-long commitment, in Jeffrey's memory, to civil and human rights. I would not stop unless they took me down with a bullet, as they did Jeff. In 2005 when I was interviewed by the Governor's Federal Judiciary Committee I listed the song Ohio by Crosby, Stills, Nash and Young as my favorite while favorite is the wrong word when applied to death.

I was elected by my fellow students to be Commencement Speaker. President Vevier tried for weeks beforehand to find out what my topic would be. I refused to tell him. On Commencement Day I sat next to Margaret Chase Smith, the Republican United States Senator from Maine who was to give the keynote address. There were F.B.I. Agents and Nassau County Detectives everywhere, many assigned to me.

I had pre-arranged to have a nine minute long montage of rock music and speeches from the 1960s played. It came out over Stiles Field. You could hear music, the words of President Kennedy, Martin Luther King, Jr. and Sebastian Cabot reading the lyrics from Bob Dylan's "Like A Rolling Stone." You could hear graduates and faculty members in the front rows saying: "Far out." My actual speech was another eight minutes. I could hear Vevier saying from behind me that he was going to shut it down, but he did not. I had Deborah, Irwin and my father all watching the sound track to make sure no one interfered with it. At the end I received a standing ovation from the ten thousand people present. Smith and Vevier were booed.

The next day daily papers carried my speech as the lead story with a quote from it across the top of the page in bold letters: "For those too busy surviving, will they hear us?" Some heard, more did not. There were white arm bands and peace logos everywhere but the war still raged.

Just prior to graduation I was named as the Outstanding Senior Athlete at Adelphi. The Spring prior to graduation was noteworthy because campuses across the nation shut down except for political rallies and teach-ins, primarily on topics relating to the War but also political discussions involving the Kent and Jackson State shootings and the assassinations of the sixties.[15] There was almost no discussion about the death of Malcolm X, although there should have been.

I was student-teaching in Great Neck South High School under Dutch Hess, a legend in Long Island High School sports. I was getting to Adelphi in the afternoon. At South, a smart student by the name of Bobby Sacks was fomenting political discussions at the school. He was getting students to walk out of classes, to sit in and finally he brought his focus to the flagpole in front of the school. His claim was that the flag should be taken down or at least flown at half-mast in honor of the Jackson and Kent State students. I agreed with him. He was courageous and forward thinking. The Superintendent of Schools, the Principal, teachers and about one hundred students gathered around that flagpole, many holding on to the rope that would bring it down or keep it up. Because I was a little closer in age and a student leader myself, I was able to intercede. I may have been trying to "suck up" to the administration so that I might get a job. However, they wanted the flag to stay up and I wanted it at half mast. In any event, we got the flag down to half-mast and the students left at the end of the day. For the rest of the school year the flag disappeared and the students more or less continued attending classes. I do not know where Sacks wound up, but he reminded me of a youthful Jerry Rubin or Abbie Hoffman. I was hoping for big things from him. Among the students at South, he was clearly ahead of his time and a future leader. That guy would stand out anywhere because he was not afraid to put himself at risk for the sake of a political cause.[16]

There was another very important event that occurred in 1970. It was the publication of a book by a little known law professor at the Yale Law School, Charles Alan Reich. The book was entitled *The Greening of America*. Professor Reich had clearly distilled the essence of the 1960's into his book.

> "We have all known the loneliness, the emptiness, the plastic isolation of contemporary America. Our forebears came thousands of miles for the promise of a better life. Now there is a new promise. Shall we not seize it? Shall we not be pioneers once more, since luck and fortune have given us a vision of hope?

The extraordinary thing about this new consciousness is that it has emerged out of the wasteland of the Corporate State, like flowers pushing up through the concrete pavement. Whatever it touches it beautifies and renews: a freeway entrance is festooned with happy hitchhikers, the sidewalk is decorated with street people, the humorless steps of an official building are given warmth by a group of musicians. And every barrier falls before it. We have been dulled and blinded to the injustice and ugliness of slums, but it sees them as just that—injustice and ugliness—as if they had been there to see all along. We have all been persuaded that giant organizations are necessary, but it sees that they are absurd, as if the absurdity had always been obvious and apparent. We have all been induced to give up our dreams of adventure and romance in favor of the escalator of success, but it says that the escalator is a sham and the dream is real. And these things, buried, hidden, and disowned in so many of us, are shouted out loud, believed in, affirmed by a growing multitude of young people who seem too healthy, intelligent, and alive to be wholly insane, who appear, in their collective strength, capable of making it happen. For one almost convinced that it was necessary to accept ugliness and evil, that it was necessary to be a miser of dreams, it is an invitation to cry or laugh. For one who thought the world was irretrievably encased in metal and plastic and sterile stone, it seems a veritable greening of America."[17]

There was yet another person who influenced me in my senior year, Professor Gerald Edwards. He was the Chair of the Health and Physical Education Department but also a pioneer in the field of "Sensitivity Training." It sounded like nonsense at the time but it was an eye-opening experience. My parents' generation had been brought up to believe that all drugs were bad and addictive. This was most likely an attitude that was pervasive among white people during Prohibition. While white people were flooding speakeasies and drinking themselves to death, some African Americans particularly in the jazz clubs of New York and Chicago were beginning to use marijuana and other drugs. The movie *Ray* about the life and times of the celebrated musician, Ray Charles, gave us some idea of that. But in the early 1930's the movie *Reefer Madness* was also conditioning

Americans to believe that marijuana was addictive and dangerous. By 1970, it was considered to be a spoof. Yet police departments around the country were using that, and a documentary movie called *Scared Straight* to discourage young people from using drugs. *Scared Straight* consisted of interviews with young people either in jail or in rehab centers for drug use.

Police departments would actually give a show and tell of how drugs were used and the paraphernalia for doing so. Their approach made no sense. They were not necessarily scaring people into not using—instead they were creating curiosity and showing them how to use. If the end goal was to stop people from using or abusing drugs and alcohol, their approach was obviously failing.

Edwards was a pioneer exploring the root causes of why young people were turning to drugs and another reality. The other reality was that offered by psychedelics and the high priest of L.S.D., Dr. Timothy Leary. They combined with the new reality brought on by the politics of the era. In some ways the harsh realities of the old and the uncertainties of the new caused many to seek an escape through drugs or to use drugs to enhance their appreciation of the new reality brought about by the cultural revolution. Edwards' theory in part had to do with his notion that people were "turning on, tuning in and dropping out" because they detested the insensitivity of the World War II generation. The Now Generation wanted more from the Greatest Generation. They wanted peace whereas many viewed their parents as being in a mindless, lock-step lifestyle that was pro-work, pro-capitalism, anti-communist, pro-government, and pro-war. Edwards believed that the use of drugs was meant to change the outlooks of young people or to permit them to escape from the world that their parents had created for them. Edwards was not condoning the use of illicit drugs but through sensitivity training providing an alternative to them. But, just like the drugs, sensitivity training did not reach those who needed it most.

A good friend of mine in college and to this day is Dr. Susan Tendy. We were students together and her father, William Tendy, was a very tough, anti-drug prosecutor from New York's famous Southern District of New York. Then and now it is a mecca for the largest drug cases in the world. He later became the Acting United States Attorney.

Bill and Sue were usually in attendance when Edwards was speaking. They could be counted on for a lively debate. Essentially, Bill would say that Edwards' theories were all poppycock and Gerry would impliedly say that Bill was part of the problem.

Meanwhile young people seemed to be relating to Gerry's touchy, feely approach. They wanted to explore their human potential, the subconscious and this would enable them to do it. It was either an adjunct to drug usage or an alternative to it. At the same time, the psychedelic protagonists were now moving to still another reality, a national one first introduced globally by the Beatles with the Maharishi Mahesh Yogi and Transcendental Meditation. That coincided with Gerry's approach, but to explore the full potential of the human mind and spirit, some believed that you needed to do that without drugs of any kind. I was not a full blown disciple of Gerry's, but I believed he was onto something. I was offered a job as a Health Teacher in the Great Neck North Junior High School where I would attempt to use Gerry's methods in my classes.

While I am sure that Bill Tendy did not view it as a moderate approach, it was. Gerry never condoned the use of drugs and I had my own apprehensions about them. That was a by-product of the brainwashing which our generation endured. But by accepting Gerry's ideas and rejecting an experiment with drugs, I showed that I was still not radicalized and that I was still worrying too much about myself. After college and later, I experimented with marijuana, cocaine, LSD, hashish and peyote. My mom and dad did not know much about drugs or marijuana, but they were vociferous in their opposition during our household debates. Of course, I had to remind my father that until 1968 when he nearly went blind from using them, he smoked four packs of cigarettes a day.

Chapter XV

<u>After Sports—Segue To Reality</u>

In the spring of 1970 I was ready to engage politically. I started hanging out at Democratic Headquarters in Mineola. There I met Gary Post, a political genius. Democrats had no power or patronage. I had decided that I would run for the Westbury School Board. I had no money and the Democrats had none. But Gary allowed me to use a union bug to print flyers at Headquarters with the Party's paper. We were working on the campaign when a young man from Mineola walked in one day with two attractive young women on either side. They had their arms around each other. He was barefoot, eighteen, and a Mineola High School student. He wanted to run for the School Board in Mineola. Gary and I both decided to help him. His name was Thomas DiNapoli. Tom won and became the youngest person ever elected to a School Board in New York State and the nation. He served with distinction for more than ten years and became the President of the Board, later moving on to become a New York State Assemblyman for twenty two years and finally by acclamation he became New York State's Comptroller, administering to the largest State pension fund in the United States. He was elected in 2010. Tom is a wonderful person and political leader. He is one of the few people I know in public life with a genuine concern for people. He is well aware of how ruthless some can be, but he always tries to look for the very best in people.

Meanwhile, in my race there were six candidates and three could be elected. The President of the School Board was running for re-election. I ran fourth in a six person race, losing by forty votes, but I learned a few more lessons about dirty politics. One of the candidates who ran last put out a fictitious flyer stating that he, I and the President of the Board were running on the same ticket. The flyer hurt me because it caused me to be viewed as aligned with the Conservative Board President.

I was running with the support of the minority community and I was an officer in my local civic association, the Sherwood Civil Association, so I had the support of the Jewish voters, as always, the pro-budget, pro-education people. Again, I received a standing ovation on candidates' night. Another candidate did a direct mailing which I could not afford. My campaign was essentially door to door with me doing all the walking, usually alone, and handing out a flyer, my one piece of literature.

Newsday, our daily paper, did a feature story about me[18] comparing me with another young candidate for the School Board from a neighboring community. They ran my picture touting me as an SDS sympathizer and my personal hero being Justice William O. Douglas. That probably alienated a fair number of people but I decided not to mask my views as too many politicians do. Honesty begins by telling people what you really believe, not lying about it or being deceptive in order to be elected. No one is perfect and most people will be forgiving, or at least understand your frailties if you admit to them, because they have plenty of their own.

That race got me into the political mix and I next became a member of the N.D.C. (New Democratic Coalition), the left wing of the Democratic Party. Allard Lowenstein was one of its Founders. Al spent only one term in Congress (1968-1970) when he was gerrymandered out of his District by Nixon's supporters in Nassau. Lowenstein was number seven on Nixon's Enemies List. Al really deserved a higher rating. He was such a motivator and organizer that Nixon really should have given him the number one position on the Enemies List.

I then became a Democratic Committeeman and Zone Leader. Over the next two years I would help to purge the regular Democrats from the Party and replace them with supporters of Senator George McGovern. We ran primaries against all the regular Democrats forcing out those who were leftover Hubert Humphrey supporters and replacing them with McGovern and N.D.C. people. It was a blood bath within the Party.

My father worked hand in glove with me in the School Board race and became a Democratic Committeeman. So did I. I then became a Zone Leader with 30 committeemen and committeewomen working under me. My dad was not interested in the ideological warfare. He was more interested in the pragmatics of how this would affect my own political career.

In 1970, President Nixon appointed William W. Scranton, the former Governor of Pennsylvania, to Chair the President's Commission on Campus Unrest. The report of the Commission[19] issued in 1971 was in many ways a disgrace. It completely missed the point of the causes for campus unrest. That had already been described in Reich's best seller *The Greening of America*. The report should have been a grand jury proceeding where the National Guard of Ohio and the police of Mississippi were indicted for the killing of innocent students at Kent and Jackson State Universities. The report was a cop-out. The Commission was a subterfuge created by Richard Nixon and his fascist Attorney General John Mitchell. The Report pointed to problems rather than the crimes that were committed. Students died. No National Guard or police died. It was a truly terrifying time in American life where the President of the United States would do just about anything to be re-elected and side with a police state. "These times [may have been] a changin'" for Bob Dylan, but for Nixon and his fellow fascists, they were nothing more than a continuation of the Red Scare of the McCarthy era.

Similarly, the Attica State Prison revolt of 1971 pointed to the class struggles and revolution taking place. Governor Rockefeller ordered the taking back of the prison by guards and State Troopers. Forty-three inmates were killed.[20]

In the summer of 1970 I helped Irwin coach the Manhasset Swim Club at the Garden City Pool and I took courses in Micro and Macro Economics in Adelphi's Master of Business Administration program. I thought that I might go for an M.B.A., but I was still more interested in politics and public service. Also, I had a teaching degree and a job in the Great Neck North School District that would begin in September. In addition, I had a second job. I was named as the Head Coach at the United States Merchant Marine Academy at Kings Point, a short distance from the Great Neck North Junior High School where I was teaching.

In 1970 I served as the Campaign Manager for Kenneth Rubinstein, a Democratic candidate for State Senator who ran against the incumbent, John Caemmerer. Ken was a smart, young, personal injury lawyer who taught me a good deal about politics. I learned of some of the practical aspects of running a campaign. Ken lived in Westbury and taught me the ropes. He was a regular Democrat. He lost.

In the Spring of 1970 my dad sat me down at Adelphi and wanted to know what I wanted to do with my life or at least what I wanted to do next. He was not pushing me in any particular direction, just acting as a sounding board. I had a desire to be in politics, but law seemed to be in my genes somewhere. It had my interest. Hofstra University School of Law was opening at that point. It was a new school. I scheduled an interview with its first Dean. I was a little late in applying. That was also true of St. John's University School of Law, which was next closest to me in Queens. That summer I applied to the Graduate Schools of the City University of New York, Bernard M. Baruch Graduate School of Business and Public Administration and New York University. I was applying to their programs in Government and Public Administration. New York University was private, more expensive and required forty-eight credits. The City University's facilities were not as nice but it too had a superb, highly paid faculty and was also located in downtown New York. As a public University, City cost a lot less per credit and the program was thirty credits plus a thesis. It was also located at 23rd Street and Lexington Avenue. I could walk there from Pennsylvania Station.

My thinking at the time was that I would work, coach, save some money, and keep my interest in politics, government, and law alive. I would get a Master's and better credentials for myself and for what might come next. I was, as they say, "burning the candle at both ends." But, I was also looking ahead to a career as a social reformer, possibly a politician or a lawyer. My models were the Kennedys, Ralph Nader, Al Lowenstein and Martin Luther King, Jr.

Unfortunately, during the summer, Deborah Allen returned to Alexandria and met someone. She came back to New York to tell me that she was leaving Adelphi and returning home. I was emotionally devastated. I was overwhelmed with the sorrow of losing her. I thought we had an ideal, perfect relationship. My perception of her was wrong, but now I really had no social life. I would occasionally return to Adelphi or meet women elsewhere, but I had no time for a social life. When I was not working, I was studying or politicking. My parents could not be happier. They wondered what would be next and so did I.

In the summer of 1970 I received B's in both of my graduate school economics courses. In the Fall I took six credits at Baruch. I had five years to get a Master's in some education—related subject if I wanted to continue to be certified, so I figured I had plenty of time. Although teaching was something I could do, I was not whetted to it. I was moving away from it. I loved teaching and teachers, but I wanted something more dynamic. I could not see myself teaching for thirty years.

My schedule was insane. I was running double workouts at the Academy. So every morning I ran a practice from 6 a.m. to 8 a.m. Then I would have the Merchant Marines back in the afternoon from 4-6 p.m. During the day, I would teach. Then I would drive to the Great Neck railroad station for the train to Penn Station. Then I would walk from 34th Street and 7th Avenue to 23rd Street and Lexington (about 15 city blocks). Dinner usually consisted of a sandwich and a beer at Blarney Stone, an Irish bar with outlets all over New York. I did this three nights a week. I would attend class for two hours, then head back to Long Island and my car. I would get home at 11:30 and study until 1 a.m. Then I was up at 5 a.m. to do it all over again.

Jim Bedell and Irwin had gotten me a full scholarship at Adelphi, but since graduating I was paying for my own education. I was still living at home rent-free and Mom was cooking some of my meals and taking care of my laundry.

New York University is a private school without a thesis requirement for a Master's Degree (at that time). I chose Baruch because it required eighteen less credits, it was far less expensive, and because the faculty was the second-highest-paid in the nation, just behind Harvard. Open admissions during Mayor John Lindsay's administration had devalued undergraduate degrees at the time, but graduate programs were unaffected. Baruch had a thesis requirement and my thesis advisor was Dr. Arthur Levine, whom I also had as a professor and who was the head of the National Aeronautics and Space Administration (NASA) Office in New York. He was a wonderful teacher and thesis advisor. He had a Ph.D. in Public Administration.

Since 1965 when Ralph Nader published his book *Unsafe At Any Speed*, I had admired his Spartan dedication to law and how he had been able to use it to enlighten us about dishonesty and corruption in both government and the corporate world. I admired his type of practice and public service. To me it exemplified the ideals of the 1960's. Nader's work was prodigious. He was churning out reports and books by the truckload. His output seemed comparable to my own in sports. I identified with his work ethic. Nader's books and reports about General Motors, DuPont, and others were revealing, but at the same time showed what could be done to make corporations more responsible. To me it was a question of how

David was slaying Goliath. He was doing it with energy and intelligence. He was speaking truth to power and money.

Nader created a consciousness among consumers that made them more aware of what they were buying. He told us of "planned obsolescence," whereby manufacturers would literally create markets for certain products such as automobiles by planning a vehicle's demise after three-to-five years so that customers would then have to return to buy a new car. It was ingenious but not known until Nader told us in a series of well-written, thoroughly-researched books with, among others, Mark Green, later a co-author. Both were graduates of the Harvard Law School. This told me that if I was going to be a prominent social reformer and I wanted to change the establishment and *status quo* or continue the 60's student revolution to bring it to society as a whole that I would have to credential myself, study hard, organize, speak out and publish. I would use the means available to me to continue to fight for change. I would further my education so that when I spoke people might be more inclined to listen. This is what motivated me and I wanted to motivate others to do likewise.

In any event, I chose as my thesis topic: *Ralph Naders's Impact On Governmental Action For Consumer Protection.* After two years of working on it, and thanks to Dr. Levine's help, my thesis was approved by the faculty and remains on file at the City University of New York.

I cannot say enough about the brilliant faculty that I was blessed to have at Baruch. Dr. Levine, who spent untold hours with me at his home on the South Shore of Long Island working on the thesis or at his impressive office in New York, was one. Dr. Donna Shalala, a graduate of the Maxwell School at Syracuse University was a high-energy person who was clearly destined to further an already distinguished academic career. She became a member of President Clinton's cabinet as Secretary of Health and Human Services. After leaving Washington at the close of the Clinton Administration, she became the President of the University of Miami.

I spent two years working on my Master's, taking classes every semester, including summers and always at night. In August, 1972 I received my Master's in Public Administration. I had thirty credits, plus the six in economics from Adelphi, which I felt made me better suited for public service.

I had kept my political involvement during that whole time, and through hard work managed to produce five All American swimmers in two years at the Academy. I was voted the Outstanding Coach at the Academy and in the Metropolitan area. I loved my athletes and they loved me. The Academy was cooperating with me and the rigors of training that I had established. One of my athletes was going to be thrown out of the school due to failing grades. The Academy had a trial and I was his advocate. I convinced the Administration that it had failed him. He stayed in school and won the Metropolitan Championship that year. The Academy had never had All-Americans in swimming before that, so I established a new tradition. The Superintendent, Admiral Arthur Engels, became a great supporter and friend. He offered me a job as a Commissioned Officer and his Chief of Staff. I turned him down.

At Great Neck, I resigned after six months and decided to substitute teach instead. I was all over the place with that including the Westbury Junior High School and other Districts. There was no permanency and I was not seeking any. At one point to make extra money, I went for a union "show up" at a soda distribution plant, but I was never picked. My primary mission was coaching, finishing my Master's and working in politics.

In 1972 I was heavily involved in reform politics and George McGovern's Presidential campaign. McGovern was a liberal, with a Ph.D. in history. He was from the Dakotas. He spoke slowly but with commitment. He exuded heart and compassion, the same qualities that drew me to politics in the first place in the 1960s.

All the while during this tumultuous time in my life, my parents were unfailing in their support. In the summer of 1971 I worked as the Pool and Beach Director of the Sands Point Bath and Tennis Club. It was a run down Club that had not been renovated since the 1920s when F. Scott Fitzgerald and John Philip Sousa had both been members. Many speculated that the Great Gatsby was conceived at the Club.

It was horrendous, the wealthy people of Sands Point simply used it as a place to get drunk. One nutty woman needed her precious Azaleas around the pool watered each day. At least once each year brown tide would come and wash up thousands of dead fish. We had a launch boy who took a few of our members by a small outboard power boat to the one or two sailboats moored off our coast in Manhasset Bay's north end. The pool had to be filled by a fire hose from an adjacent snack bar. The chlorine was fed to the pool by hand. If we fed it in the morning before the sun had a chance to burn it off, it was dangerous. One Saturday morning before we were open, a member jumped in. We saw as he exited the pool that he was nearly blinded. The pool became like a vat of sulfuric acid.

The pump room was dysfunctional and had not been upgraded in thirty years. The wooden deck was dilapidated. At the start of the season I took a hammer to at least fifty boards which had to be replaced.

There was a slew of students from China and Taiwan working as bus boys, waiters and maintenance men. They lived in illegal shacks at the back of the Club. They were all Ph.D. students in physics, science and math at StonyBrook State University. They got the worst jobs for the least pay.

When the Health Department came for their periodic inspections, I was told to keep the inspectors at the front gate and guardhouse for as long as possible while we attempted to get things into order. The Manager of the Club would then bribe the Inspector with a case of scotch. This happened at least once a month.

The place was like a chamber of horrors, a veritable "House on Haunted Hill," except it was on a pristine part of the North Shore Gold Coast. The place was closed down some years later and sold to residential developers.

By the end of the summer, the terrific people I had working for me were getting fed up with the conditions. We had developed a good swimming and diving team, the kids were happy, as were their parents, but the older members who were clinging to the past were all upset that we did not appreciate our wonderful conditions. Several of the women reminded me of Mrs. Haversham, the character from the novel *Great Expectations* where she and everything around her were decaying, collecting dust and rotting.

Most of the lifeguards I hired went on to become prestigious lawyers, doctors, psychologists and scientists. The older members decided to fire me and my fellow workers then had a walk-out which they initiated without any prodding from me. Among those walking out were Susan Buckley, a student at Mount Holyoke, later an Editor of the Fordham Law Review and an expert on the First Amendment's freedom of religion clause as a partner in New York's Cahill, Gordon & Reindel, where she works alongside of Floyd Abrams, the famous First Amendment expert who was, among other things, counsel to the *New York Times* in the Pentagon Papers case.

Artie Lynch was a lifeguard and also a diving coach. He attended Adelphi and later received a Doctorate in Psychology from Columbia University. At the end of that summer Artie and I decided to drive Susan

Buckley back to school at Mount Holyoke. We did that, said goodbye to Sue and detoured through Cambridge where the S.D.S. was holding a convention at Harvard. We slept on the floor in a dorm at Boston University and later marched with the S.D.S. against the R.O.T.C. at that University. We had about 20,000 marchers at that time. Others I hired were Ed Weiland who went to the University of Michigan, later becoming a Medical Doctor and Lindsay Gillies who went to Harvard and his brother Ewen who was a chemistry major at City University of New York. Also Mark Donovan and others were with us. Mark's dad was the Editor of Time Magazine. We held our breakout, strike party at his home. The solidarity with my co-workers was gratifying.

I returned to New York, resumed coaching at the Academy and continued substitute teaching. I wrote an article for the *Delphian*, Adelphi's student paper, about the S.D.S. convention. In doing so, I met the Editor of the *Delphian*, Debora Pitman—a bright, vivacious, beautiful girl with an acerbic, cutting wit that could easily make grown men both cry and then submit to her power. She was awesome. Despite my overtures she at first was more attracted to my friend, Artie Lynch, so I did what I could to help that relationship along. I think that because I did that she dropped her interest in Artie before it started. I asked Debbie out. The first time I did, Debbie's mom told me to put on a suit. She also told me to bring back flowers and candy. She was right. That is what a gentleman should do. While I was a bit put off, I went home and changed. I lived about a half hour away. We could not leave until I wrote down where we were going and what time we would return. We soon became devoted to each other spending all of our free time together. But, I was not giving Debbie the attention she deserved. I was too self-absorbed in graduate school and coaching.

Debbie did not know how to swim so after meets and practices, I taught her how. I was in a fugue like state with my only reprise being the time I spent with Debora. She was very good to me. She was working at Antun's catering hall in Queens Village; going to school full time and was Editor of the school paper. She would bring me lunch and dinner; made arts and crafts for me and left me love notes on the windshield of my car when I returned home late at night from the City. I am sure I did not fully show my appreciation for all of her love and kindness.

By the end of the swim season and after being named the Outstanding Coach at the Academy and in the Metropolitan area, Debbie had other relationships, particularly with a guy by the name of Richard who was more or less a political figure on the Adelphi campus and someone who organized the Speakers' Program for the University. I did not like him. He was a sleeze bag and later that perception proved to be more than accurate. Years later when he ran for office and touted himself as a "family man," I was able to show, as a spokesperson for his rival, that he was estranged from his wife and did not have any children. Then, in a national television broadcast, I showed that he was a gigolo, shaking down older women for money. It took a little while but he got what he deserved. His political career is forever over.

By the summer of 1972 Debbie had set up an arts and crafts store in Queens called All Thumbs. She was still working at Antuns and I was trying to finish my Master's, but because it was an Olympic year, Bill Irwin and I organized a nationally recognized Olympic Development Training Camp at the Christopher Morley Park Pool in Manhasset. I had no money. I was hitching rides to practices or riding a bicycle. I did not have a car. That summer I must have come down with depression, mononucleosis, or a radical change in metabolism because I could not stop sleeping during the day. I was exhausted. The only time I could wake up was for practices or if Debbie came over for a visit, which she did on most days. What a good woman—no, a spectacular woman. I respected and loved her. She was a challenge to my heart and mind. She and Irwin will forever remain my very best friends in this life.

Chapter XVI

The Tools For Reform

During the spring and summer of 1972, I had finished my course-work and my thesis was approved. It was entitled: *Ralph Nader's Impact On Governmental Action For Consumer Protection*.

My father taught me in baseball that follow through is most important. I admired Nader because he had follow through. He was making corporate America responsible to consumers. He was getting legislation passed. He was not just a rebel rouser although they too have their place in political change.

That summer we produced a Junior Olympic Champion and took another swimmer, Laura Smith, to the Olympic Trials in Cincinnati, Ohio. She did not make the team. I finished my Master's in August and had to decide what to do next. I was at a crossroads of whether I would continue in coaching or go into politics, government and possibly law. I was also thinking of pursuing a Ph.D. in Public Administration. I was looking seriously at the JFK School of Government at Harvard.

J. Edgar Hoover had died and the skullduggery of his long reign of terror was beginning to be aired. His F.B.I. secret called COINTELPRO (Counter Intelligence Program) allowed his Agents for more than twenty years to break into the homes and offices of political dissidents and plant evidence against them. There were thousands of these illegal actions, arrests and even convictions on the basis of Hoover's fabricated evidence. Nixon learned his dirty tricks from the master, Hoover. It was said that Hoover had damaging evidence stored against every leading political figure except Nixon who may have had the goods on Hoover. Certainly Watergate and "The Plumbers" may be *sui genesis*, but who is to say if Nixon used the practiced *modis operandi* of Hoover. Both were dangerous and deceptive men in so many ways.

During the summer of 1972 I had to start planning my next move. It was too late to apply to law schools, but my dad had seen an advertisement in The New York Times concerning a new law school that was just opening in the State of Delaware. It was founded in 1971 by Alfred Avins, its Dean. Interestingly, Vermont Law School was also started at that time. It too was the only law school in that state. Delaware was incorporated and chartered in the State of Delaware so that graduates could take the Bar in that jurisdiction and others by permission of the High Courts in each state. Those applications were liberally granted. The school was seeking the provisional approval of the American Bar Association, a first step before final approval. With provisional approval graduates could take the Bar in any jurisdiction without having to ask for permission first. I did not know anything about all these nuances at the time. All I knew was that I was late and it was a law school. I sent in my application and I was accepted.

Before leaving for law school I went to see Debbie at her store in Queens. She was still a full-time student, Editor of the school paper, and running a new business. She had met someone else. Undaunted, I proposed marriage, but it was either too late or too early for that. It was not the right time for it. I had not decided to give up law school to marry Debbie and stay in New York. While I did not have a plan, I asked Debbie to come with me. Clearly, that was bad timing, but of course, I was not exactly Prince Charming or a knight in shining armor sweeping her off her feet on horseback while riding off into the sunset.

Debbie is an extraordinary woman with immense courage. She graduated with one Master's Degree, taught mathematics in the Rudolph Steiner High School in Manhattan, and later put herself through law school at night. To this day, I consider her and Irwin to be my best friends. They are both people of character, a quality that I have learned to appreciate in others. To me it means strength, wisdom, compassion and joy—all the noble qualities that people should strive to possess.

I had the attitude that you must do something each day to improve yourself. Debbie was the personification of that with humble beginnings but high achievement in her veins and an incomparable world view. She was destined to be a big player in this life, so I believed at the time and still do. For the time being she is a practicing attorney raising a family in New Jersey.

Delaware Law School was founded as a private law school, much like Brooklyn Law School or New York Law School. It was not affiliated with any university and the brainchild of Dean Alfred Avins, an eccentric genius with seven degrees by the time he was 35 years of age. Avins graduated from the City University of New York at Hunter College and the Columbia Law School from which he graduated in two years. He then worked as an Assistant District Attorney in Manhattan while he secured a Master's in Law at night from the New York University School of Law. He then secured another Master's in Law from the University of Chicago and then a Doctorate in Juridical Science (J.S.D.) from the University of Chicago and a Ph.D. in Law from Cambridge University. Also by the time he was thirty five he had published four books and eighty seven articles. He had also argued a half dozen cases before the Supreme Court of the United States.

Dean Avins greatest achievement would be the founding of the law school if he could gain its ABA accreditation. Most people who knew Avins at the time believed that he might be destined to be an ultra conservative Associate Justice of the Supreme Court of the United States.

Avins' idea to establish a law school in a state that did not have one was smart enough but he also recognized that the Baby Boomers were graduating from college and more law schools would be needed. He foresaw the market and the demand.

In the first year of its operation, Avins ran the law school at night in rented space of the Wilmington, Delaware Y.M.C.A. After the first year he looked for a building and purchased a church, a parsonage and two residential buildings near downtown Wilmington. The church also had a parking lot. During the summer of 1972 Avins was busy trying to renovate the church to turn it into a law school.

The school was in an ideal location-at the Mason Dixon line, three hours by car from New York, thirty minutes from Philadelphia, and two hours from Washington, D.C. Its Bar was comprised of lawyers who for the most part, had graduated from the University of Pennsylvania, Temple University School of Law, or the University of Virginia. It had a small but very distinguished Bar. It had a low passage rate on its Bar Exam—under fifty percent. It did not want outsiders.

Most of the students came from Philadelphia, Delaware, South Jersey, Maryland and New York. The two main companies there were DuPont and Hercules. Both companies, together with the fact that Delaware was known as the "Corporate State" (due to its liberal corporate laws) made the Law School a perfect match for well-credentialed business-people and scientists who wanted second careers. Delaware had a Court of Chancery which attracted patent, commercial, stock and corporate lawsuits of various kinds that often resulted in favorable treatment for businesses. As a result, Delaware had a highly-regarded corporate Bar and it was not long before its members were offered faculty positions at the Law School and membership on our Board of Trustees. Avins was a thoroughly obnoxious individual, but one who also understood that if his law school was to succeed he would have to attract the rich and powerful to it, especially influential politicians and the Brahmans of the Bar. While I detected a tinge of anti-Semitism in the air because Avins was from New York and an outsider, I also saw a begrudging respect for his overpowering intellect.

Soon after receiving my acceptance I received a phone call from the school asking if I would help with a move of law books from the Pennsylvania Central Law Library in New York. Avins was a used book collector. He had purchased the books from the library because it was closing down. He wanted the books for the law school and what he could not use he would sell to other schools and libraries in need of law books. At the time the American Bar Association required that all of the approximately 170 law schools around the country have at least two sets of multi-volume texts such as the National Reporter System, the official repository for all cases officially reported in the United States. At the time I believe the Harvard Law School had over one million volumes of books in its library, whereas we were starting with zero. Today most legal research is done by computer. That has eliminated the need to compete for more law books.

I went to the Penn Central Library and helped to load at least thirty thousand pounds of books onto a meat truck borrowed from a student who owned a slaughterhouse in Lancaster, Pennsylvania. While I was surprised by what was entailed in the founding of a law school, I was impressed by the entrepreneurship of Avins in securing the books. At least fifty students helped with the move.

Soon thereafter my dad and I drove to Delaware for the start of school. I had applied as a part-time evening student since I figured it might be easier to secure a late admission on that basis and because I figured that I would have to work during the day. Once we arrived in Wilmington we could not find the school. We drove past it several times not realizing it was in a church in the process of being converted to a law school. It had a

marquis outside, and we saw in tiny letters, "The Delaware Law School."
It was late August—a hot, sunny day. No one was around. I needed to buy
books and find an apartment. I went up to the side door and knocked on
it. Avins came to the door. He was wearing a tee shirt and working. He
was alone. The building did not have air conditioning. My father stood
next to me. Avins opened the door. I was not sure he was the Dean. I
introduced myself and inquired as to whether this was the law school.
Avins looked over his wire rim glasses saying: "Yes, yes Mr. Liotti, we're
not open yet, it's too early." He knew my name probably from my picture
but had never met me. I asked if we could come in and look around. He
allowed us a peek but then said: "Be careful, we are still in disarray." That
was an understatement. Classes were starting in two weeks. It was difficult
to conceive of how he could possibly be ready. But Avins was a man
accustomed to dealing with challenges, nothing ever stopped him. He
was an optimist who took setbacks in stride. He was unflappable, never
showed a glass jaw, he was always confident and ready with a comment. My
father too was impressed by Avins' bearing. Avins had a way of instilling
confidence in people. My dad gave me his approval on the school. He
believed that Avins' intelligence, ingenuity, and diligence would carry the
day. My dad was right, but it took years to reach that objective and Avins
had to be purged because he was standing in the way of it. He was though,
the epitome of a lawyer—well schooled and highly educated. You could
just feel the law coming off of him. He had argued several cases before
the Supreme Court of the United States and picked Delaware because of
one of them. He was indeed a Constitutional scholar, but his opinions
were far right of the mainstream. His achievements made him into a role
model. I never accepted his ideas or philosophy, but I respected what he
had accomplished through hard work and ingenuity. Avins took great care
in preparing for his classes. You could see it, feel it. I remember the movie
The Paper Chase with Professor Kingfield, played by John Hausman, Avins
had that kind of aura about him.

I found a one-bedroom apartment for about one hundred dollars a
month. At first, I did not have a car so I had to ride a bike. I joined the
Wilmington YMCA for forty dollars a year. There I swam almost every
day, ran, lifted weights, and played either racquetball or handball. I put my
name on the substitute teachers' list for the Wilmington Public Schools.
My parents came just about every two weeks or so, my mom bringing

food and other care packages, as needed. They would usually stay the weekend.

My father and mother believed in me. They wanted me to have a good life. I think that my father also believed that I was headed for a career in politics and law that had eluded him. I think he also felt that the values he had instilled in me would allow me to help many others, the underdogs in our society. Years later, when I was being recommended for a federal judgeship, he wrote the following to the President of the United States, George W. Bush:

Dear Mr. President; Governor Pataki and Senator Schumer:

I am 88 and not in good health. My wife Eileen, 85, has Alzheimer's disease. I am writing this letter on behalf of our son Tom who has been recommended to you for a federal judgeship on the Second Circuit Court of Appeals or on the United States District Courts for the Eastern or Southern Districts of New York. Prior to my retiring, nearly 25 years ago, I worked for Western Electric Company and AT & T for 42 years. I served as a Local President of the Communication Workers of America (C.W.A) in the 1940's and before that served in the United States Army during World War II participating in the Normandy invasion. After returning from the War, I moved my family to a Levitt home on Long Island where I became President of the Little League and Boy Scouts. My wife worked as a key punch operator for the County and I have the distinction of having served as both a Democratic and Republican Committeeman. We now reside with our son and his family.

Our son was raised in a middle class household, attending both public and private parochial schools. In his early years he established himself as an extremely hard worker with an interest in sports. He became a County, State and Eastern Interscholastic Champion and record holder. He won a full athletic scholarship to Ohio State University and then Adelphi University, where he became an NAIA Champion; NCAA All-American and Olympic Trials participant. During college he began to excel academically. He became involved in politics and was Co-President of the Student Body with a young woman who has since gone on to become a United States District Court Judge in Philadelphia. After graduating from college he became a teacher and the Head Swimming Coach at the United States Merchant Marine Academy where in two years he produced five All Americans and was voted the Outstanding Coach at the Academy and in the Metropolitan area. He then obtained his Master's Degree in Public Administration, maintaining his interest in politics and writing his thesis on: "*Ralph Nader's Impact On Governmental Action For Consumer Protection.*" He then went to law school in order to achieve through politics, public service, government and the law that which we instilled in him and what he has acquired on his own, namely a fierce independence; loyalty; integrity and an unrivaled work ethic.

What I have come to realize and respect about my son is something that many others have said to me about him, namely that he has a natural talent for the law. I never called my son a genius because we endeavored to engender in him qualities of being humble and a gentleman. But I have heard many others refer to my son as a legal genius. What I do know for sure is that he is a very strong advocate for his clients and the positions which he supports. He is a fighter for the underdog.

I understand that you receive letters like this everyday and that you may never see this or that even your staff may be too busy to read it. I also know that all parents feel strongly about their children. I am no different than you in that respect but I would like you to know what kind of a federal judge my son would be if given that opportunity. First, he will remember the high ideals and values which we have instilled in him. I believe that he will always remember and honor us by striving to fulfill those ideals and values. Second, he will always treat everyone who comes before him with the utmost respect; cordiality and fairness. Third, he will listen, ask probing questions, thoroughly research the law and write decisions which will make sense by defining a path in the law for others to follow. In May, 2004 my son wrote a 109 page decision (the largest one ever written by a Village or Town Justice in New York) on search and seizure. The decision was controversial but it also served to focus attention on immigration policies and the lack of affordable housing for migrant workers and the poor. This has caused other public officials to focus on these and other problems.

Fourth, my son is well known and so are his views. My granddaughter tells me that there are over 40,000 references to his name on www.google.com. If there is one quality that comes through in these references, it is that he is an unrelenting warrior for justice and equality. Tom has told me that his model jurist is Hon. Jack B. Weinstein, our neighbor from Great Neck who is a United States District Court Judge for the Eastern District of New York. Judge Weinstein has published over 2,000 opinions and several treatises in the law.

Fifth, Tom's energy level will allow him to produce incredible volumes of work. I have seen him train 16 hours a day, 6 and even 7 days a week. I have seen him swim 10 miles a day. Nothing stops him. He once swam across Long Island Sound, without a pilot boat, a distance of 9 miles. Tom has tried all types of cases, complex and simple, civil and criminal. He will be able to handle any type of case that comes before him.

Sixth, Tom is very loyal. He will never embarrass attorneys or litigants. He will uphold his oath of office to the ninth degree. You will be proud of him. He understands and appreciates the balance of power, judicial review and his role as an Article III Judge. He will not be afraid to make decisions, however unpopular they may be.

Seventh, he does not need this job. He has been a successful attorney. It will be a personal sacrifice but one which he wants because he believes in public service. He is totally dedicated to helping the poor and disadvantaged. He believes in the pursuit of excellence and in enabling everyone to reach their highest levels of achievement.

Eighth, Tom will not be laid back at all. He will be proactive. He will teach and write extensively. He will volunteer his time in the ghetto and for charitable pursuits. He will encourage corporate America to achieve the highest standards of ethics and corporate responsibility.

Ninth, he is a proponent of the Warren Court and believes firmly in what President Kennedy said during his inaugural speech in 1961: "Ask not what your country can do for you, ask what you can do for your country." Tom has been the President of Kiwanis. He believes that each of us should be a positive and effective force for social change. From the time he was in college and became politically aware, he volunteered his time as a Board member in the Martin Luther King, Jr. Youth Center and later in the Three Communities Action Program (TRI-CAP) an anti-poverty agency. In law school he volunteered his time to work for the Legal Aid Society on landlord/tenant matters and in the Delaware State Legislature as an aid there. In law school he published a Student Note entitled: "*A Historical Survey Of Federal Incorporation.*" It became the definitive work on the subject and was reprinted in the Congressional Record of the United States.

Tenth, others may dance around a point, they may try to hide their views for political expediency. Not my son. He is opposed to the death penalty and supports <u>Roe V. Wade.</u> He will respectfully listen to countervailing arguments, but I do not believe that his views on those subjects will ever change. He believes in separation between church and state. He has a tolerance for free speech to the degree expressed by former President George H. W. Bush in his 1991 address at the University of Michigan. Similarly, he does not believe in undeclared wars; the needless expansion of what President Dwight Eisenhower referred to as the "military industrial complex" and he believes that everyone charged with a crime, including alleged terrorists, should have the right to effective legal representation. My son has been a registered Republican for 27 years. He formerly served as a Committeeman and Zone Leader in the Democratic Party; as a candidate for Supervisor; a judicial and national convention delegate. He changed his registration to the Republican Party in 1978[21] and did so at the time because he felt that by doing so he would have more of an opportunity to effect social change. At that time Democrats could not get elected in our County. Tom changed parties but kept his ideals. At the time he reconciled his views with those of the G.O.P. because the leaders in our Party, Governor Nelson Rockefeller; Senator Jacob Javits and

Attorney General Lewis Lefkowitz were all liberal Republicans. My son headed up the Nationalities Committee for Ronald Reagan's first campaign and attended his inauguration. He was offered a ranking position in the Civil Rights Division at the Department of Justice but turned it down due to the demands of his burgeoning law practice and because he and my daughter-in-law were starting a family. Incidentally Tom and Wendy are married for 28 years and they have three children, twins that are age 20 and a younger daughter, age 16. My daughter-in-law, Wendy, is an honors graduate from Duke University with a Master's Degree from the Pratt Institute in Brooklyn, New York. She is an extraordinary artist, teacher and currently works as a real estate salesperson. My grandson Louis has won a full hockey scholarship to Northeastern University. His sister Carole is a student at Nassau Community College and Francesca, 16, is a student at Pomfret Prep School in Connecticut. Wendy and Tom have passed along their strong work ethics and values to their children. Obviously that seems to be working as each of them have shown an interest in the pursuit of high achievement.

Eleventh, Tom has courage. He greatly admires the late District Court Judge John Sirica who, among other things, commanded the President of the United States to turnover the White House tapes during the Watergate case. A few years ago Tom and his family were stalked by a former Judge. The Judge did everything he could to destroy Tom and his practice. Tom stood up to him and became the main complaining witness against him. The Judge was removed from the Bench and disbarred on the strength of Tom's complaints. Tom is true patriot. He is fond of quoting Patrick Henry's: "Give me liberty or give me death." There is much more to say but I am sure that I have already tested your patience. I may not have much time left, but I wanted you to hear from me and to know that my greatest asset and legacy has been and forever will be, my son Tom.

Sincerely,
Louis J. Liotti

162

He heard back from Harriet Miers, Counsel to the President and later, albeit briefly, his nominee to the Supreme Court. She wrote the following to my dad (see copy of original letter in Appendix):

Dear Mr. Liotti:

Thank you for your recommendation of your son Tom for a Federal judgeship. Please be assured that he, and your views, are being given appropriate consideration.

In the event that additional information from you would be helpful to the selection process, we will contact you directly. In the meantime, please accept my thanks for your input.

Sincerely,

Harriet Miers
Counsel to the President

The first day I arrived at my apartment to move in, I had a U-Haul trailer. My parents were in the car. We arrived late and could not get into the apartment. It was a large complex. We located the Superintendent but he would not let us in because it was after hours. I managed to break into the apartment, moving my furniture in with the aid of my father. Our car had over heated. I do not think we had money for a hotel so we spent the night in the apartment. It is ironic but I started law school by breaking and entering.

The law is a reading, writing, and speaking business. If the function of a university education is to teach critical thinking and to develop a broad array of knowledge, then in law school you are taken to the next highest level. Learning to think like a lawyer generally comes to law students in their first year. The critical thinking and knowledge that they learned as undergraduates is now applied to problem solving. That is what practicing lawyers do all day, everyday—they endeavor to solve problems. One of my professors confounded the eagerness of students to solve problems by telling the class that there is one solution that they could consider in every case. He encouraged us to write down the solution. He said its proper application would make us very rich. The students leaned in and then he said: "Do nothing." This is not a multiple choice answer that you will find on any aptitude test but I thought that its expression reflected great wisdom and maturity on the part of the professor.

So much of law school is memorization and familiarity with legal terms. What is not taught and what differentiates law school from practice, is strategy. The law is only as good as your deployment of it. Later I learned that this is where my true talent lay.

The law is logical and really quite simple. Lectures are often superfluous. Indeed, the Founders of our country, many of whom were lawyers, became attorneys by"reading." They did not attend law schools. Abraham Lincoln did not attend law school and Clarence Darrow (1857-1936) briefly attended an undergraduate school and one year at the University of Michigan School of Law. Even while I was attending law school you could still become a lawyer without attending law school by merely clerking in a law office. The difficulty is that those who strive to become attorneys using this method miss out on a legal education that is geared to teach you to think like a lawyer. Their passage rate on bar examinations is historically under twenty percent. The legal education depends on the nature of the law practice where they are clerking and the mentoring that they receive. As Professor Kingsfield (John Hausman) noted in the movie *The Paper Chase*, the purpose of a legal education is to "Turn your minds from mush into finely tuned machines." Unfortunately, the process of learning to think like a lawyer can be very destructive for attorneys who cannot separate their personal demeanor (which may apply in a family setting) versus the game face that they must deploy in the courtroom. It is also true that many lawyers are sensitive to this dichotomy in their personas. They are humanistic and sensitive but some of the public view them as annihilistic nerds. Part of what I was striving to do as a law student was to maintain my humanity. This then put me into a philosophical conflict with Avins and his fellow conservatives who were all about business.

I was so in love with the sport of competitive swimming that I thought that I might be the Olympic coach. Just prior to deciding to go to law school, I had applied and been accepted for the Olympic Coaching position in Hong Kong. Ironically today, all these years later, Asia has developed into a sports mecca, particularly in swimming and diving. At the time I did not see the potential of Asian athletes but I believed that by coaching a national team that it would be a stepping stone for me to better coaching positions in the United States or abroad. I believed without a doubt that I could become the best coach in the United States.

In going to law school I had to go "cold turkey." I was offered an assistant swimming coach position at the Wilmington Swim School and there was also some talk about me becoming a coach at the University of Pennsylvania. But I just could not do it. I knew what would happen. I would not be focused on the law. I had decided that my future would be in reforming politics and the law. Much as Barack Obama has today set his course on the politics of change, I was then pursuing a similar genre.

I was immersed in my studies from the beginning. Like most law students I was terrified. Everyone was smart and working hard. They all wanted to be lawyers. From the beginning the curriculum was rigorous. We used the Foundation Press *Cases and Materials* texts which law students everywhere used. In the first quarter, my classes included Torts, Contracts and Legal Methods and at least one other course which I do not recall.

I learned quickly to brief cases. In the beginning I kept elaborate notes on the cases: titles, citations, facts, questions, holdings, point of the cases, and dicta. Later I learned to book brief instead of writing out the briefs. This involved making notes in the margins of the books. I also paid more attention to the questions presented by the authors at the end of each case. I purchased outlines such as Gilbert's and then Hornbooks or scholarly treatises on the law much like single volume encyclopedias, but on a particular subject. I am sure that I was overcompensating and studying too much or at least reading too much legal theory and not enough black letter law. Theory is good because it makes you think with more flexibility, more creativity. That is the purpose of the Socratic method used in law school, to raise legal questions and attempt to answer them. However, it is not what gets you through the Bar Exam, which is all nuts and bolts, pure regurgitation of law. I detested memorizing, but some concepts in the law require precisely that. In my law school, final exams were essays which lent themselves to spotting legal issues, problems and solutions. That first quarter I did well. I was in the upper twenty five percent of the class. This was my niche. I did not miss a class and I was studying all the time. It was my life, everyday. I found different places to study to break up the monotony. Some days I would stay in my apartment but more often I would drive thirty minutes south to Newark and the University of Delaware undergraduate library or thirty minutes north to the Biddle Library at the University of Pennsylvania Law School or at the

Brandywine Community College or very often the Wilmington City Law Library located in a downtown courthouse and open twenty four hours a day. Law students could be found there at all hours of the night. Our library was under construction and not an ideal place for studying. In law school you are in a holding pattern, you crave a real life, but you live like a monk. You want to be around people, but the discipline of studying law does not allow for it.

I really had no social life. I was pretty much on my own except for a few male friends. I was not really dating, I was too busy studying, even when my parents came to town. While they watched television I would go into another room and read. Even on a Saturday night, I might go to the YMCA and workout. My dad would usually come along to watch. We would chat. He and my mother devoted all of their time to my development and well being. I was out of touch with New York politics and the legal community, but would occasionally buy *The New York Times* when I could afford it and when it was available.

While Nader called it the "Corporate State," and in going over the Delaware Memorial Bridge on I-95, you may think that all of Delaware is like the oil tank area of Elizabeth, New Jersey, that is not the case. In fact, there are a great many truly beautiful parts of Delaware. For example, just over the line in Pennsylvania is Longwood Gardens, one of the prettiest arboretums anywhere. In Delaware just off Route 202, I would also occasionally visit the Brandywine Art Museum, home to a great many Wyeth family paintings. When my parents were in town, I would take them to these places. When you are a law student without much money, the simplest pleasures count for a lot. They are a diversion from the drudgery of studying.

The first class of the law school was due to graduate in 1975. We wanted to secure provisional accreditation by then so that they might take the Bar Exams in any state. As a part-time student, I would not be graduating until 1976. If I sped that up by going full-time or attending the summer sessions, then I could graduate earlier.

The students were concerned about the school's progress. We learned during that first year that while the school was progressing very rapidly, Avins wanted to establish a conservative law school. He wanted it to remain independent and not affiliated with any university because he felt that law schools are profitable, that universities skim money from law schools and as a result, most of their other programs are not profitable.

Avins did not want the American Bar Association and its Legal Education Committee, headed by James White, to dictate to him on anything. This put us at logger heads with the ABA. Avins was building a conservative law school. He was attracting conservative faculty members and Board members. One of his faculty members had commenced a lawsuit to get the United Nations out of New York; another did not believe that income taxes are constitutional and Avins himself believed that the 13th, 14th and 15th Amendments should not apply to the states. That being the case then, segregation and slavery would be legal.

In the summer of 1973 I worked as the Pool and Beach Director of the Creek Club in Locust Valley, New York. The Creek Club is one of the most prestigious, elitist, exclusive clubs in the nation without minorities of any kind as members. It had about four hundred members; a sixty five hundred yard golf course overlooking Long Island Sound; a bowling alley; tennis courts; clubhouse and golf lockers dating back generations; indoor and outdoor dining facilities; cabanas; an outdoor pool and beachfront.

The Creek was really the home of old money even more so than its companion club, the Piping Rock with over eight hundred families as members. The Creek had one campus whereas the Piping Rock had two. Piping had an outdoor pool and beach house with a bar just north and within walking distance of the Creek. The main campus for Piping with a formidable golf course, horseback riding and clubhouse is inland. Both clubs are magnificent and include some of the prime real estate on the North Shore.

President Richard Nixon and Nelson Rockefeller, when he was Governor, both stayed at the Creek Club. Joseph C. Dey, the head of the P.G.A. was a member as was John Pickett, the owner of the Islanders Hockey Team. The Founders of Alcoholics Anonymous and numerous major banks including the J.P. Morgan family, were members. I spent much of my time coaching the swimming team and giving swim lessons to children. I taught the children of Anthony Bliss, the Director of the Metropolitan Opera and a partner at the law firm of Mudge, Rose, Guthrie and Alexander. Mr. Bliss' mother was the Founder of the New York Museum of Modern Art (MOMA). I taught President Franklin Delano Roosevelt's great granddaughter to swim. She was walked over to the pool each morning by her nanny to be taught how to swim. She and her nanny lived just down the beach, by the Piping Rock beach facilities.

Except for her nanny, she was alone in a magnificent beach house. She was seven years of age at the time.

The lives of nannies on the north shore are unique. I got to know a great many of them. All day long they would look after children. At night they needed an escape. Most had beautiful living accommodations on the estates of the wealthy of the north shore.

The President of the German Bank took a liking to me. His wife was a gorgeous fashion model in Europe. I taught her two sons to swim. They were so young that she would get in the pool with them. She really was beautiful, although not much of a personality and a snob. I was invited to dinner at their summer home in Syosset. After the Mrs. and children went off to bed, her husband and I continued to hammer ourselves with cigars and cognac. Then he started to take out Nazi memorabilia and showed me a picture of his father with Adolf Hitler. His father was the Minister of Foreign Affairs in Hitler's army. He was the number two in command. His name was Joachim von Ribbentrop.[22] I was horrified. I felt that I was viewing classified documents of war crimes. I left, politely but abruptly. I was feeling sick to my stomach over the photos I had seen and the cavalier way in which they were shown to me.

I also taught David Boyce Garvan to swim and to scuba dive. I had become a licensed YMCA scuba diver in 1972 and at Adelphi became a Water Safety Instructor. David's grandfather had been a member of Franklin Roosevelt's cabinet. When Robert Moses was attempting to construct Northern State Parkway parallel to the Long Island Expressway, the Garvan's did not want it to run through Old Westbury and had the Parkway diverted five miles to the south. They also did not want entrances or exits onto or off of the Long Island Expressway in Old Westbury from Glen Cove Road to Jericho, a distance of five miles, there are no entrances or exits along the L.I.E. That was the affect of power and money. [23]

In the early 1970's Governor Rockefeller wanted to put a bridge across Long Island Sound from Connecticut. The Creek Club membership did not want it. Tom Hogan, a Councilman from Oyster Bay and a wealthy landowner at the Creek Club, together with other powerful members, killed the deal. I was witnessing the power of money, law and politics first-hand. What I saw confirmed any rationale for going into law. I could never be a part of this upper class elite, the landed gentry. I would have to start from the bottom up, making my way against the odds, helping to level the playing field for myself and others as I made my way.

I am reminded of a quote from Clarence Darrow which has been inspirational to me and by which I have lived:

"I have lived my life, and I have fought my battles, not against the weak and the poor—anyone can do that—but against power, against injustice, against oppression, and I have asked no odds from them and I never shall." Clarence Darrow

After leaving the Creek I would generally head to private estates where I would give swim lessons in the evening. One such estate was that of Richard Storr in Oyster Bay. Mr. Storr was a Senior Partner at the prestigious New York law firm of Sullivan & Cromwell. His family had been a fixture on the Gold Coast and he had a Yale/Harvard pedigree. Mr. Storr was a very nice man. The entrance to his home was magnificent. The property was a compound. He would usually sit nearby sipping a gin and tonic, still dressed in a business suit from his ride back from the City by train or chauffeur, I am not sure, but he was always there watching me teach his three grandchildren how to swim.

I admired and I am sure envied the people I met at the Creek and on the Gold Coast. I was struggling and most of them found their way to good schools and easy money such as trust funds due to family ties or simply marrying well. It is one thing to hear or read about it but quite another to observe it up close as I did. They were lucky and I was not as lucky. I still did not understand the exclusionary practices in the legal profession or in their society but looking around you could see that minorities were not welcome. It was clear to me that someone with an ethnic or Italian last name such as mine, would never be a welcome member of this closed knit world. There were no Jews, African Americans, Asians or Hispanics.

Although I had a bedroom that I could use at the Creek in the back of the cabanas, I never used it. I always went home at night. I was getting by on a few hours of sleep each night because I was "partying" every night, usually with my fellow workers from the Creek or the nannies. My father had suggested that I take a speed reading course at Columbia University that summer. I did that too and perfected my reading to 1,200 words per minute with a comprehension level of fifty seven percent. I was told that this brought me near the one-hundredth percentile.

It was a good summer. I survived it, making my way back to Wilmington for my second year where Constitutional Law with Dean Avins awaited me together with Criminal Law and Procedure, Commercial Transactions, and Property.

The students and parents were becoming more involved in the accreditation process. The students had a Student Bar Association, the *Delaware Law Forum* (the student newspaper), and the Journal of Corporate Law, its Law Review. I was attending all of the meetings about the school. Inspections by the ABA were periodically made and we would have to get ready for them. That was the plan—to get the school ready to be approved by the ABA's accreditation team.

Avins had raised a great deal of money through tuition and by selling law books, but he was fiscally conservative and did not want to be dictated to by the ABA. The students eventually hired a lawyer to make sure that their interests were being protected. The students started to run the school. In doing so, they learned that one member of the Board of Trustees was a member of the John Birch Society in New Jersey. Another Board member was United States Senator Jesse Helms (R-C, North Carolina). The students were working hard at school work and in organizing to get accredited.

As time wore on it appeared that Avins and the ABA would never get along. While the students were blindly loyal to Avins, they were not about to sacrifice themselves or their careers for him. One evening I went back to Avins' office with fellow students, Jon Fox (later a distinguished Congressman from Pennsylvania) and Richard Hoy, a rising star among student leaders. We listened to Avins and his Assistant Dean, John Tovey, until I finally put a question to them which was: "If it comes down to sacrificing the lives and careers of five hundred students or you having your way with the ABA, what do you do?" They understood the question. Avins hesitated and Tovey said: "We will sacrifice the students." Avins did not disagree.

For me that was the line in the sand and they went over it. What I learned from my father as an organizer, at Adelphi and City University would now be used to get the school ABA approval. My first objective was to purge the school of conservative ideologues. This had to be maneuvered carefully, because the conservatives who ran the place might retaliate by finding a way of getting rid of me.

I stayed in the background for awhile but became friendly with Rich Nidel, the Editor of the school paper, and Steve Harz, the Editor of the Law Review. The students had budgets for two publications plus the Student Bar Association. Now when we held meetings they were official and the minutes of those meetings would be made public. If Avins did not do the right thing in terms of following ABA guidelines and recommendations for approval, then he would be criticized. We had the ABA on our side. They knew that the students just wanted to be lawyers, they did not want to spearhead Avins' idea to establish an arch conservative, right wing law school, the only alternative as he called it, to liberal schools such as Yale and Harvard. Of course, it was ridiculous for Avins to compare his neophyte ambitions to the traditions of such venerated institutions but that is what made Avins even more dangerous and, at the same time, respected for his *gravitas*. He was a throw back to Senator Joe McCarthy, except he had a big brain and a stubborn intellect. His faculty and Board were anticommunists who hated the Kennedys, opposed desegregation, supported the Vietnam War, Richard Nixon, Chief Justice Burger and Chief Justice Rehnquist. They were against abortion and *Roe v. Wade* when Justice Blackmun authored that opinion in 1974.

We were doing research on faculty members and trustees. We came across an article in *The New York Times* about a meeting of the John Birch Society in New Jersey. A member of our Board was quoted in the article. The rhetoric was clearly racist and out of step with reality. We posted it on the bulletin board of the school for all the students to see. The students were beginning to rebel and I was acting as a catalyst for that.

Avins was dogmatic and autocratic but I cannot say that he was intolerant of free speech. He was not persuaded by students but he was being out-maneuvered by us. The odds were not in his favor. Although none of us could match him academically, he underestimated our street smarts and our motivation to become lawyers. No matter where the students sat politically, the overriding concern was to accredit the school. It was equally important for us to demonstrate to the ABA that we were a politically diverse student body. If the ABA believed that we were no more than clones of Avins, then all would have been lost. As future lawyers we had to show our courage in advocating and standing up to institutions and to not only question authority but to take it down when it was clearly not doing the right thing.

I would give my dad daily reports, but we both believed that the hurdles would be overcome. The parents involved at the school were mostly prominent judges and attorneys from the Philadelphia area. One such judge was Hon. G. Fred DiBona, a Common Pleas Court Judge in Philadelphia. His son, my classmate, would later become the CEO of the largest health care provider in the nation, but at the time the Judge was in the front lines, meeting with the ABA and attending their conventions. He was all for the students. No one really wanted to push out Avins, but his inflexibility was really becoming a problem. Senator Helms resigned from the Board and he was replaced by prominent attorneys and corporate executives mostly from the Wilmington area.

Through student pressure, Avins was forced to relent. Finally a new dean was brought in, Arthur Weeks, the former Dean of the Cumberland Law School in Alabama who had guided them to ABA approval. Avins was pushed out on a promise that we might name a building after him. Weeks was just what we needed. He was from the South, so he could cool down the Avins people by masquerading as one of them. In fact, he was brought in because they thought that he was one of them. Weeks was not a stupid man[24] and he realized that the students were emerging as the stronger force to be reckoned with but not yet at the "tipping point." He quickly realized that Avins needed to be placated, but he also had a working relationship with the ABA. He was open with the students and friendly toward us. He once told me that he thought that I would be a great success as an attorney. I thanked him for that, but it was important for the students, at least initially, to have an uneasy yet symbiotic relationship with him. We could not allow him to lapse back into a relationship with the Avins camp although he was brought to the school by them.

In the '73-'74 year, the first quarter with Avins was insane. One of his books had to do with the history of the 14th Amendment. He had reprinted the Congressional Debates from the 1840's through the 1870's, which we were compelled to read. In order to do that, linear magnifying glasses were sold in the school book store. Most courses involved a minimum of two hours of studying outside of class for every hour in class. Each class ordinarily covered fifty pages of text. With Avins, the tedium or reading of the debates drove most of us to the brink of madness. I was trying to show a tolerance for the ideas of someone who we believed was in a minority of one as a Constitutional scholar. Teaching us why *Brown v. Board of Education* was wrongly decided, caused many of my classmates to feel an animosity for the man. His classes only served to confirm my feelings that he not only had to go, but that any vestige of him had to go as well. It would be a matter of time. I watched as he metaphorically proceeded to cut his own throat, slowly but surely.

I felt like I was being taught by an educated Klansman in a suit. My rage was building but, at the same time, I had to respect his intellect and foresight in founding the school. Once Avins screamed at a flustered student: "The Constitution is not an impressionist painting" and to another who muttered to the Dean: "If you read between the lines . . . ", the Dean replied: "If I read between the lines, all I see is white paper."

I was getting a great legal education because I had to fight for it. The students had to study but they also had the opportunity to watch the machinations of Avins. We were involved in a sophisticated, massive chess game with many players. Our job was to checkmate the master who brought us there in the first place. He was teaching us both inside and outside the classroom.

In 1973-74, I was offered a job teaching economics at Delaware Technical Community College. Today, Vice President Biden's wife teaches at that institution. It was terrific teaching on a college level and it helped a lot financially. I was used to saving my money from the summer, but I could not just cruise all year on that alone.

A college friend from New York, Rick Handler, had enrolled in the law school. I needed a little extra time to study for my law school classes and asked Rick to come into my class as a guest lecturer. We decided to have a little fun, so I embellished his credentials. I introduced him to the class as the Wright Pembroke Memorial Fellow from Harvard University, a Ph.D, and Professor at Harvard who had just returned from the Middle East after discussing peace accords with Henry Kissinger and Golda Meir. Coincidentally, I added that he was also an Olympic Tower Diving Champion. The shock value alone got the students to sit up and pay close attention.

Rick showed up with a briefcase filled with obsolete newspapers, a cup of coffee, and a lit cigarette as props to add to the distinguished image which I had created for him in my introduction. He was also wearing a corduroy sport jacket torn on the shoulder seam and jeans. My introduction of him took at least ten minutes. My goal was to use up the hour of class time. There were between 20-30 students in the class. Rick ran out of material in ten minutes. He then took questions for another thirty minutes. Most of my questions were longer than his answers. We filled the remaining time, a few students seeking autographs with Rick writing obscurely so as to disguise his true identity. All went well until the last student came over and said to Rick: "Didn't I see you playing racquetball at the YMCA last week?" Handler cleared his throat, coughed a few times, shook his head and said: "No, that was not me, I was with Henry in the Middle East."

The student walked away looking somewhat unsatisfied by the answer, but nonetheless the lesson was a resounding success. I do not believe that any of the students believed my introduction but most came back in the next class to tell me how entertaining and informative it was. Rick is a historian so he easily filled his talk with anecdotes from history. Even if a simulation, it clearly was beneficial to the students. It kept their attention and it was informative. I never admitted to Rick's true identity, but I am sure that too was thought provoking for the students. Rick has since earned a Ph.D. in Architectural History from Columbia University. He is also a New York attorney.

I had gotten over some of my fear of law school and started dating a bit. I either met the women at the YMCA, which was co-ed and a convenient place to workout in downtown Wilmington or at the law school or at the College where I was teaching. I dated a few students, none in my classes. They were adults, or older. I was not taking anyone out to dinner. I could not afford it. It was either their apartment or mine. Wilmington did not really have much in the way of entertainment. There were no clubs or shows except for what you might catch at the DuPont Hotel, an off-Broadway production without the elaborate stage and other accoutrements that you find on Broadway.

One of my girlfriends, I found out later, was an alcoholic. She was arrested in Pennsylvania and called me for help on a D.W.I. charge. I, of course, was not a lawyer. I called her father and we both drove to Pennsylvania to bail her out. In gratitude she took me to a Joni Mitchell concert at the Philadelphia Academy of Music. I became a fan of her music and the reggae music and movie of Jimmy Cliff, *The Harder They Come*. Both were anti-establishment heroes from that era, celebrated by the young, but not recognized by mainstream America.

I got my lowest grades in law school that year primarily because I tried to implement the speed reading course from the previous summer. My second year was still filled with politics and getting to know the students; the dynamics of the accreditation and the nuances of Avins.

Handler had not yet become a full-fledged roommate. He was still in New York and working with a law firm there. He was not sure that he wanted to stay and commuted to and from New York. My parents were still coming up every second or third weekend. Delaware was more my home at this point than New York. I was really starting to feel comfortable there.

In the summer I was back at the Creek with my usual routine. I would continue my reading during the summers. The previous year I read the Hornbooks, Corbin on Contracts and Prosser on Torts, cover to cover. These are both mini encyclopedias on the law comprised of about 500 to 1000 pages each together with extensive footnotes. My thought was that if my legal education was deficient at a fledgling school that I should make up for that with a lot of independent study. In the summer of '73 I was reading more generalized books on the law and took my father's advice of reading the newspapers each day. In law, you must know the players, that means anyone who can move and shake, anyone who can push the right buttons for you or your clients.

I had a feeling from the moment I entered law school that I would be working with the poor once I became a lawyer. So from the very beginning and into my second year I worked as a volunteer at the downtown Wilmington Legal Aid Office. I worked on civil cases, mostly landlord tenant matters. I would go into the poorest neighborhoods and report back on conditions. In one of my first times out, I went to a walk-up apartment building, four stories, an old building in the heart of the City. When I got to the front door I noticed that all the doors were set about three or more inches off the ground. As I walked into the vestibule I saw large rats at my feet. I had never before seen a rat. They were feasting on a piece of bread. I freaked out. Luckily I had boots on and shouted "Oh my god," and stamped my feet. They finally scattered. Now I was afraid to go any further for fear of what I might find. I walked up to the third floor and knocked at the door. I was told to come in. There was an unmarried couple there, in their 50's. They were both in bed covered with used clothing that they would stack on themselves for warmth. They did not have heat. The few groceries that they had were kept up against the windows so that the cold winter air would protect their food. Like a lot of the poor people I was meeting without health or dental benefits, both of them were missing teeth. I saw soggy white bread on plates with baked beans on top. That was their main meal.

In my second year of law school I had done well enough to feel confident. When you first go to law school you are exposed to a lot of law but usually not legal research and writing which I called "the secret." Knowing the law and how to solve legal problems is the first part of what you learn, but no one can learn all of the law. You begin to understand the logic of it but you must always have cases and statutes to support your points. Learning how to do that required a course in research and writing. Today it is all done by computers, but then it was all book work. I took Legal Research and Writing and now I had "the secret" of how to find the law, the legal solutions to the problems once you have decided what the issues are. This, I realized, is how lawyers made money, by having this "secret." It was perhaps the most important course in law school once you have learned how to think like a lawyer. Even though I was not yet an attorney, I thought I could almost function like one (I was wrong). I had not quite figured out yet that to be a success as a lawyer you must have contacts and clients, otherwise you will spend your career waiting for the phone to ring. Law Schools teach you how to be interviewed and work for others. I had a feeling, given my background that I would have to make my own way. The establishment had their vested financial interests for keeping outsiders like me down. My mission had to do with assembling enough credentials, contacts, and resources to put them in check or take them down, as needed. I was an outsider and it was a class struggle. The United States might be a land of equality and opportunity, but you had to fight for both.

The next summer, I made my way back to the Creek and continued to live at home and followed my usual routine except I started seeing several women on the North Shore, some members, some nannies, some fellow students. All of us were finding ourselves as young people, experimenting with sex and drugs, all in plentiful supply. One time in particular I remember overdoing it. My girlfriend Kathy, whom I was seeing almost every night, introduced me to mushrooms. After we removed the strychnine, a poison, from them, we chopped them up and mixed them with a thick shake type drink which almost made them palatable. But it made me really sick. I mixed it with alcohol. I was not hallucinating, but I thought that I would die. I can remember going back to my room at The Creek and praying to God that if he just let me get through the night, I would never do anything like that again. I lived through the night and never again did mushrooms.

It was that summer that an older member of the Creek had said that his son swam across Long Island Sound in 1936 and no one else had ever done it. So I decided to do that, not to show up the old man, but because like Mount Everest, "it was there." I borrowed a member's boat and we took it across the sound from The Creek to Greenwich, Connecticut, a distance of nine miles across the water. When we got to Greenwich the boat broke down. We told our boat people that we were starting and once they got the boat repaired they could catch up to us and continue with us as our pilot boat. Terry Laughlin, my partner and I started the swim from Greenwich. The boat came by and it was being towed. They had not been able to fix it. Laughlin wanted to ride back. I told him no way, we would make the swim without a pilot boat to watch over us. It would be just he and I out there in the open water swimming across the sound.

Along the way we were met by drunks in a powerboat who circled us and threw cans of beer at us. But perhaps the single most frightening event came when we were out in the middle of the sound. Off in the distance you could see on the horizon the outline of a very large boat. It was coming directly at us. We started swimming faster and faster, each time we picked up our heads to look for the boat, it appeared to be right on us. We sprinted for our lives and at the last minute the tanker turned from us, the Captain blew his horn, laughed and barely missed us by twenty yards. The wake from his ship was about three feet.

I was really starting to get sick from exposure to salt water. In August you have to watch out for seagulls because they follow the schools of blue fish, which are big and eat like piranhas. If you get caught in one of those schools you can become instant caviar. August is also brown shark season so as we approached the shore, the sun was down but it was still light out. Oyster Bay, Town of Huntington, Nassau County and the City of Glen Cove had their rescue, marine, and police boats there for us. The crews had shotguns out to ward off a shark attack. We made it across without a pilot boat, three hours and forty five minutes later. Laughlin was fine. I again thought I was going to die. I said more prayers. I lived but I never again swam that far across the sound without a pilot boat. In swimming across the sound I was testing myself, but also in a way saying to the members of the Creek that I was doing something that none of them could do, not with all their money and power, not in their dreams. I suppose that they might say in response that it was pointless and that they had no interest in it.

During that summer my swim team was not doing well. I could not get the kids at The Creek to consistently train. Many were not even around the entire summer. They would go to the Hamptons, Block Island, Nantucket, Cape Cod or Martha's Vineyard (the Vineyard as they called it) or Fisher's Island. It was just a little country club team but they expected to win. The kids had too many competing influences, golf, sailing, tennis, horseback riding. My practices were in the morning but they could not get up for them even though I would run them for just an hour between 9-10 a.m. I even tried afternoon workouts but nothing worked. The kids were just not into the hard work that any level of competitive swimming required. It was the first time that I was not able to ignite an interest in something and we lost to teams we should not have.

At the end of the summer it was customary to have an awards ceremony and dinner, which we held down at the beach. The parents were all invited and every child got a trophy, but I just could not give them the "Rah-rah" speech which they expected. My heart was not in it. I think I had some resentment for the lifestyles into which those people were born. It was not their fault and most were nice, wonderful people, but my attitude may have showed.

I do know that I taught a lot of the kids to swim. Many developed a sense of accomplishment and confidence by that act alone. Nonetheless, I knew I would not be invited back the next summer.

By my third year at Delaware we still had not been approved by the ABA and now the students were getting nervous. A lot of money was being spent, renovations were made but because of Avins' influence they wanted us to affiliate with a university. I was now very active in the Student Bar Association although I was not an officer. I had taken to writing in the *Delaware Law Forum* and meeting with Trustees. I had developed a relationship with Charles Maddox, the head of Hercules Corporation and the Chairman of our Board.

The Student Bar Association election was held and I ran for the Presidency, which I won. It was an honor because we still had not received accreditation and the new Student Bar leadership was expected to continue with its tradition of organizing and fighting for final approval. There was much at stake. The students entrusted me with that responsibility. I endeavored to live up to it. As the first class approached graduation, it was decided that instead of having the graduation then, it would be deferred until after the ABA met in August. At some point the ABA told us that affiliation was necessary. Avins and the Board wanted to maintain independence but Mr. Maddox and the others had been convinced by us that they had to vote to affiliate. If they did not, then they might have been sued for breach of their fiduciary duties. In any event, Mr. Maddox told me of his plans to push for affiliation with the University of Delaware but said to keep it under my hat. I did. The University of Delaware turned us down but an enterprising President from Widener College, just over the boarder in Pennsylvania, Clarence Moll, was pushing his Board to acquire us. Widener had been a military college and in 1975 it had a Board that wanted to build that school. They also had a lot of money. For example, the undergraduate library at Harvard is named after the Widener family. Our Board then voted to affiliate with Widener. Five hundred students were milling about in front of the school. It was summer. The ABA was in session. Our delegation was there. I was waiting with Dean Weeks in his office. The call came through. It was for me from Mr. Maddox. I was the first to know that the Board voted to affiliate with Widener. Word was sent to the ABA and their House of Delegates voted to give us provisional ABA approval. I told Dean Weeks and then walked outside to tell the students. All hell broke loose with jubilation. The students graduated and got to take their bar exams. The ordeal for accreditation was over but Avins was not going without a fight.

Avins sued me. I was the only student sued. He took my deposition, an examination before trial. He did not know how to ask questions. He was a scholar, not a litigator. He was trying to claim that I was involved in a grand conspiracy with the ABA to dethrone him. His lawsuit failed.

The summer of 1975 was a year when I no longer had the easy money of The Creek Club, but managed to get some money by working four jobs. I was coaching with Irwin in the morning and then I worked as a Law Clerk for Connally, Sullivan & McCarthy, a three-man litigation firm in Garden City until about 3 p.m. each day. All three were heavy drinkers and their behavior a bit unpredictable. Tim Sullivan was my Assembly District Leader and a trial lawyer. Because of the alcohol, he had a mean streak. Tim is now in his 70s and has been a reformed alcoholic for more than thirty years. Today he is a compassionate sponsor for people in AA, mostly lawyers. He is still an excellent trial lawyer, but his passion, aside from work, family and his faith, is what he does to help people overcome alcohol addiction. He has saved so many lives and with his insight, he has become a kind and wonderful human being. Tim knew that I needed a legal job because my father approached him. Tim gave me my first legal job, became a mentor and got me started in my study of New York law. I shall always be grateful.

I drafted legal papers for the law firm that summer-boring work but something you had to learn. I reported to Jack McCarthy. He was the inside partner. Connally was never around. He was always out socializing, networking and drinking. Tim was in the courthouse trying cases everyday. Jack was what lawyers call the" back office guy," moving the paper. The firm represented Allstate Insurance Company and did a great deal of insurance company defense work. Once I came across a file where we were representing a plaintiff in an action where Allstate was the carrier for the defendant. We were not representing the carrier in that particular case, but I reported to the firm that this was a conflict of interest. I learned something about the practicalities of such situations when Tim said that we will settle the case and if it does not settle, we will then refer it out. Tim's view was that the conflict had not yet ripened. We later settled the case.

I would do most of my work for the firm at the Supreme Court Library in Mineola, handwrite my pleadings and research and report back to Jack. I billed them on an hourly basis. I think it was probably minimum wage, but I felt honored and grateful to Tim for the chance.

At 3 p.m. I would head to the Garden City Community Pool where Irwin had arranged for me to be a lifeguard and my last job of the day was to teach an adult swim class. That was really the most fun because I had adults who had never learned to swim at all, had a tremendous fear of water, but really wanted to learn how to swim. In a class of thirty I taught them all to swim, even 87-year old Hank, who I taught to float on his back and paddle. That was really very satisfying because I had given them something that they would receive enjoyment from for the rest of their lives. It also allowed them to overcome their life-long fear of the water. They loved the classes and were very proud. I was proud of them and myself.

I had developed a teaching technique that summer whereby I could teach anyone to swim. First, I taught them to overcome their fear of water. They walked across the pool in four feet of water, then they would hop using their hands to press down and keep their heads above the water. They then transitioned this into dog paddle and breaststroke. It works every time. Freestyle or crawl came next and I had my own exercise for that. The students would come to class early and stay late just to practice and enjoy their swimming. Lifelong fears were overcome. There is always a way to overcome fear if you recognize it and choose to deal with it.

On Mondays I was off so I decided to volunteer my time at the Nassau County Jail. I wanted to be around prisoners because I felt that I wanted to work with them but also to get over whatever fear I might have of them.

I volunteered to work in the school, library and recreation yard. What I found there was frightening. An educator from East Meadow High School was supposed to come over to teach reading and writing, but never showed. The psychologist never showed. The law books were all outdated and prisoners had almost no access to them. In the recreation yard the guard on duty had no medical training. A prisoner had an epileptic seizure in the yard and nearly choked to death until I managed to insert my belt buckle between his teeth and turn his head to the side.

I wrote a lengthy report of my observations. It was really an indictment of the abysmal conditions at the jail. I forwarded it to the District Attorney. That Fall, nineteen Correctional Officers were charged and convicted. My report precipitated an investigation by Internal Affairs which led to a partial clean up of the jail and the prosecutions. For a long time the jail had a KKK chapter within it. Thankfully that has changed but there was a time on Long Island and in most other American cities where the Klan was very active. In the Freeport, Long Island Recreation Center, the home of a mixed community, there remains in the trophy case an award donated by the Klan.

In my final year of law school, I could have graduated early but instead chose to complete my term as President of the Student Bar and graduate with my classmates. Widener was already making plans to sell our downtown campus and buy the Brandywine Community College campus in north Delaware, which is what they did. They built a new law school building and a second one in Harrisburg, Pennsylvania, that state's capitol. They obtained final or permanent approval from the ABA and also received accreditation from an even more prestigious accrediting body, in fact the only other one after the ABA, the American Association of Law Schools (A.A.L.S.). Today Widener University School of Law has graduate programs in law, business and paralegal studies. It is dominant in Delaware, south Pennsylvania and south New Jersey.

Avins was eventually pushed out. He went on to found other independent law schools but eventually died of brain cancer twenty five years later. I wrote an article about him after his death for the Delaware Law Forum, the student newspaper, entitled: "The Smartest and Dumbest Person I Have Ever Known."

My last year in Delaware was marked by my work as President of the Student Bar. At the end of my term students gave me a plaque and standing ovation. I was continuing to workout and while at Delaware, had become a vegetarian. I ate some tuna fish but mostly I ate health foods. I was continuing to have relationships with many different women, one married to a fellow law student. In the second part of that final year I was living with a part-time law student, Barbara. I kept my apartment but lived in her home. We both liked the same things: law, politics and sex, lots of it. She was a wonderful, uninhibited and some might say, a promiscuous companion. She was very supportive of me. She attended my graduation but my parents, on my invitation, also brought Debora with them. We had been communicating for a year before that, rekindling our relationship. I felt a great loyalty, love and friendship for Debora. Debora was an exceptional person but my college coach described our relationship as "nuclear fission." I admired Debora because she came from very humble beginnings, Queens Village, a blue collar neighborhood, known as the home of Archie Bunker, the television character. Her dad was disabled and Debora had a love of life, a great intellect. She was on the edge, very refined, worldly and cultured. She was uplifting me, teaching me a better way to live. Debora was also a favorite of my parents. They loved her, especially my father. My parents had regrets that we never married. My father once said to her: "You could have been married to Tom." With Barbara it was mostly lust, a terrific lust but neither one of us seemed sure of any commitments. Barbara was also a successful business woman with political contacts everywhere. She was ambitious and wanted to help me succeed politically. I think that she thought that we would conquer politics together as husband and wife. Years later I learned that Barbara had died in 1981. I do not know how or why.

Barbara was tall, slim and attractive, but she was a hard liver. She worked full-time and was a law student. She had done a lot of drugs and burned the candle at both ends for a long time. It seemed that her entire life was a near-death experience. Each day she acted on impulses, living her life to the fullest with the prospect of dangerous consequences. She showed me her ear which had been sown back on after she and her South American, drug smuggling boyfriend had a tussle. In the home which she owned she had cigarette holders everywhere.

In my final year of law school I took a course on Legislation and also clerked or interned in the Delaware State Senate, nearly two hours south of Wilmington in Dover, Delaware. That was a round trip that Rick Handler and I made once a week. Again, I needed to know how the establishment functioned in order to beat them at their own game.

I was one of three students to receive awards at graduation. I could have given the commencement address but chose not to push the issue. It was a spectacular weekend. My parents were naturally very proud. I had made Law Review and co-authored, with Rick Handler, a Student Note (a legal article) entitled: *An Historical Survey Of Federal Incorporation.* It was printed in the second issue of the Law Review, The Delaware Journal of Corporate Law and it was reprinted in the Congressional Record of the United States by Congressman James V. Stanton, (D-Ohio), one of the co-sponsors of a Bill on federal incorporation at the time.[25]

Federal incorporation was first introduced in the early 1900's during the anti-monopoly, trust busting, muckraking days of President Teddy Roosevelt, Ida Tarbell, Upton Sinclair and others. Its purpose was to have one national incorporation statute instead of allowing corporations to incorporate in any state they chose. Many chose New Jersey, Delaware or North Carolina because those states had the least restrictive laws concerning the governance of corporations. My primary purpose in writing the article was to espouse an idea that would show the ABA and others that the law school was not going to be a tool for the "Corporate State" and Bar of Delaware. The article was also consistent with my personal agenda as well as my mission for social reform.

Federal incorporation in the 1970's had been recreated as an idea by Ralph Nader. He was pushing the idea in Congress in order to improve the governance and oversight of corporations that were running amok of the environment and consumer protection.[26] In addition to our article I managed to obtain an article for the *Journal* written by a Nader protégée, Joel Seligman, Esq. It too, was a highly acclaimed, scholarly work. Both articles demonstrated that the law school's Law Review would be a forum for ideas, both liberal and conservative. It would not adhere to the conservative vision that Avins and his disciples had planned. This too was another subtle breakthrough point. Changing ideology is never easy. Some students retained a loyalty to Avins. Unlike me, many simply saw the law as an occupation, a title and a way to make money. Yes, it might allow them to run for office or become judges, all of which they have, for the most part, commendably done, but few saw the law and their role in it as a means for ideological change. I did, but while I was at Delaware I was determined to stop the school from being a conservative haven because I believed and still do, that that would be counterproductive to the school's reputation. I was determined to purge the school of as many "wacko" conservatives as I could, but also to put into place a structure that in the long term would show a tolerance for ideas and a balanced, if not liberal approach to the study of law.

I believe that I achieved a total victory at the Law School, not alone but with a great many fellow students and parents. None of that would have been possible without the guiding hand of my father who taught me everything about democracy and organizing. I was his pupil and in this course I received an A+.

There is another point worth mentioning. For four years of law school I dressed in jeans, usually torn. I had long hair and a mustache. I deliberately dressed this way because when I first came to the school a real property professor told the students that they had to wear jackets and ties in his classes or they would have to sit in what he called the "row of shame." This was the same nut who wanted the United Nations out of the United States. While he may have thought that this sort of corporate apparel would show the seriousness of our students and make them more readily accepted by the "Corporate State" or law firms in general, I saw it as a lack of diversity which would not convey the right image to the ABA and others. I made a point of dressing like that even during ABA inspections and to be conspicuous. I also wrote and published a number of left-leaning articles in the law school paper which was distributed to the organized Bar of Delaware. Again Avins had come up with a brilliant idea and that was to report in the school paper the unreported corporate decisions from the Chancery and other courts of Delaware. This was ingenious because now the Bar had to read our paper and it was being cited by them. As a result they could also see the articles in the paper showing that the students were providing a check and balance to the school's original, conservative mission. This provided a healthy perspective of the law school.

Avins also came up with the idea of naming our Law Review, *The Delaware Journal of Corporate Law*. This too was ingenious. We were in the Corporate State and he believed that that connection could be exploited and marketed. Instead of competing with other law schools around the country which published articles on a great variety of subjects, usually unread, we focused on corporate law alone. It was brilliant, timely and gave our Law Review instant credibility. The Bar was dependent upon both our paper and our Law Review because they did not have any publications of their own. We reported Chancery and other state court decisions in those publications. We had a monopoly on that. The local bar had to read and subscribe to our publication if they wanted to regularly read reported cases from the Delaware State Courts.

With law school behind me, I was filled with a sense of pride, accomplishment and empowerment. A law degree gave me the feeling that anything was possible, that the world could be conquered, and that it lay at my feet. Barbara had gotten me a job with the Legal Services Corporation in Washington, DC and my old coach, Bill Irwin, had managed to get me a position at the Legal Aid Society of the City of New York in the Criminal Law Division. I received an offer to become an Assistant District Attorney in Orange County, New York. I was also offered a position as legal counsel to the Grievance Committee in Nassau and Suffolk Counties.

But in coming home from Delaware, I decided to devote myself to preparing for the Bar Exam which was offered at the end of July. I had decided to take the New York Bar. I was the representative for the Practicing Law Institute at Delaware, thus, I took the course for free. It was a mistake.

The New York Bar tested in forty different areas at the time. The test lasted two days with twelve essays; multiple choice and other short answers. The New York Bar concentrated on the Civil Practice Law and Rules of New York and Evidence. Delaware was a national school, which taught national law, common law and lots of theory, and at the time students from national law schools were not geared for the localized New York Bar Exam, which was all about the unique and complex "nuts and bolts" of New York statutory and case law. Schools like St. John's fared far better on the exam than Harvard and Yale grads did.

That summer from the end of May until the end of July, I worked like a dog. Each morning, Monday through Saturday, I took a three or four hour taped lecture at Hofstra Law School. Then I would study there in the afternoon or at home. At night I was studying at C.W. Post College or at home. Neither had air conditioning.

I had told Debora at the start of the summer that I would not be able to see her for two months. She was understandably angry and did not speak to me again for several years. She was giving me an ultimatum and I do not relate well to people when they give me orders. I fought too hard to get to where I was and I did not go to law school so that others would tell me what to do. I did it to be my own person; to determine my own course and decide my own fate. I was also reverting back to my training as an athlete and what had allowed me to persevere through law school. It was about hard work, self-sacrifice and my autonomy. I disliked the corporate mentality which required strict obedience and the following of orders. That was not for me. The reality was that I could have been kinder to myself and Debora but I was twenty nine and the world needed changing. I was back to buckling down. I should have listened to Debora. I had taken her to my law school graduation and I had figured that we would inevitably marry. We both should have been thinking more about the future together and less about the moment. It was an unfortunate end to the boyfriend/girlfriend relationship that had begun five and one half years earlier. Our adamancy and severance made no sense. We were thinking like young lovers instead of mature adults. I could not take the distraction. I thought that I had to go "cold turkey" on the relationship. I was too hard on her and me. But that is the mentality of some Spartan athletes.

On Sundays in New York I would take the Kass writing class. Lou Kass had been running his writing class for decades. Every Sunday we would be there to listen to his lectures. Frankly, I was in awe of just being back in New York. Everything about it was a distraction for me.

I studied hard but too expansively. I should have just stayed with a few areas but I read all the outlines on every subject. My parents stayed out of my way, helped me with meals, lodging, a car, and anything else I needed. They too saw the importance of achieving the goal. While they could not make my life perfect, they wanted it to be better than theirs' had been.

I had collected rejection letters from every "white shoe" law firm in New York. The big shots at The Creek Club who had promised me a job did not come through.

As a graduation present, Barbara purchased an entire set of McKinney's Laws of New York for me. It was about one hundred and seventy volumes. That in itself was amazing, but she also paid the subscriptions on them for two years, which meant that she was paying off the books on an installment basis. At the same time she was paying for me to get updates on the books on a monthly and annual basis. That was surprising in itself and then she came to New York to visit with me during the Bar exam preparation. It was a relief. All we did was study together and have sex.

After the Bar exam Barbara invited me to meet her parents at their summer home in Atlantic City, a few blocks from the beach. Her parents seemed uptight about me, a Catholic boy about whom their renegade, rebellious daughter might be serious.

Barbara had some family money but she also worked full time and was very involved politically. She knew a great many people in Delaware State politics. Her brother Jeff was a highly regarded lawyer in Delaware who was no doubt concerned for his sister. I have never spoken with Jeff about Barbara.

Barbara had an impulse-control disorder. For example, everywhere in her home she had cigarette holders. She chain-smoked. She liked drugs and sex. I was not her only boyfriend. She wanted me to know that. She once had a State Senator call me from Dover after she had spent the weekend with him to tell me we should all get together. I can recall phone calls which I answered at her home from her law professors whom were no doubt interested in a liaison with her or who already had one with her, unbeknownst to me. At the time I could not discern whether Barbara was doing this in order to make me jealous or to act on her own sexual impulses or to show me her liberated sexual state so that I might find her more appealing because she was open to any kind of a sexual relationship including threesomes or whatever combination of people and ideas you can imagine. Probably it was all of these factors that kept me interested in Barbara. I was curious about how my fantasies would evolve but again, wary of them because Barbara had a propensity for going too far. It was for me to decide how far along this journey I would travel. There were some danger signs or at least what I interpreted as that. It may have been my father's voice telling me throughout my life to "be careful" but I chose not to take advantage of these endless possibilities which sometimes present themselves once in a lifetime or not at all. We meet few truly uninhibited people or those willing to aggressively pursue their sexual desires. It is a bright light, but also a scary one because we are so accustomed to people who are guarded when it comes to expressing and acting upon their sexual desires. I have some regrets about not taking full advantage of acting on Barbara's sexual smorgasbord, but I am alive and she is unfortunately dead. I was still free to act on my fantasies.

Barbara was a good person who needed and gave lots of love. She was too much though, although she had enormous sex appeal and was an incredible romantic, her extreme conduct was scary and turned serious suitors such as myself away. You did not want to join in her self-destructive, death-wish behavior. To a point it was fun, new and experimental, but there was also a dangerous side and Barbara was usually at or over the line, into the zone of danger.

Once while I was still in Delaware she was admitted to the hospital with a high fever and who knows what else. She called me and wanted me to come and see her. I did not go because I felt that I would be catering to her excessive, self-destructive behavior. I did not want to reinforce that or create the impression in her mind that my appearance at the hospital would make for a stronger bond between us. I felt at the time that she was not that sick and trying to manipulate me. I may have been wrong about that. Probably I should have just gone to the hospital.

While in Atlantic City after the Bar exam, we fought and I went home. Barbara had already decided that she wanted to take me on a "Jamaican Holiday." She was paying for both of us to go to Jamaica. After the fight, I left and came back to New York. As soon as I arrived, she was calling and crying, begging me to return. She had not cried during the fight, but now she was. In leaving Atlantic City abruptly I had also told her that I was not going to accompany her to Jamaica. We were already booked for flights and a hotel. Barbara was a tough woman but now I was seeing her sensitive side. Her demonstrated weakness caused me to relent. Almost as soon as I arrived home I spoke to my dad and told him that I wanted to go back to Delaware and go to Jamaica with Barbara. I am sure that he must have been perplexed by my on-again/off—again actions. He gave me a few dollars and I was on a train back to Wilmington. In a few days we arrived in Montego Bay. It was August. The airport was filled with Americans.

While I was very close to my parents, it may have been their thought at the time that I should go my own way to independence. They had me but in their minds they may have considered me to be a free agent, unattached to them except emotionally. They knew that there was no blood connection to me but I was unaware. Had I known this sooner I might have stopped my dependence upon them. It may have also stopped my will to achieve.

Barbara asked me to drive the red rental car which, of course, was an English model with the steering wheel on the right and a stick shift. I knew a little something of how to drive a stick shift but had never before driven on the right. The airport parking lot was under construction—essentially a bumpy, cratered road filled with water.

Near the end of the road, a friendly black face appeared, waving me to come toward him. I did. I thought that he was employed by the airport or rental car company. He jumped into the back of the car and needed a ride into Montego Bay. Along the way I was driving on the cliffs overlooking the majestic Montego Bay, one of the most beautiful places in the world. As we drove by the rich mansions on the Bay, I looked at the whites of his eyes which were not white at all. They were completely red and I figured that he had a rare eye disease or was consuming a lot of cocaine. Barbara kept her cool—nothing bothered her on the outside.

Our passenger opened his coat and inside he had a veritable drug store of anything an American tourist might want; from marijuana to hashish, cocaine to anything. I chose not to take him up on his bargain. I pulled up next to a policeman and told him to get out.

We drove on to Negril, over an hour from Montego Bay. It was not very developed. You could buy an acre on the water for thirty thousand dollars. We had just settled into a beautiful cottage when Barbara said that we had to leave. She had met a "connection" at the place where we were staying. We put our bags down and got into our car. I drove with Barbara in front and a Jamaican man in the back.

Jamaica had eighty percent unemployment at the time and little in the way of natural resources, except marijuana, a/k/a "ganja", a/k/a "hooch". Hitchhikers along the road were looking for rides but also looking to sell you marijuana which was available everywhere in plentiful supply. The police could hardly be seen; the D.E.A. was non-existent and the Island was relatively safe so Americans came in droves for week long vacations to smoke "weed" and get stoned on the high quality Jamaican pot. They did not bother anyone. They would just stay by themselves, have a good time and go home.

Going to law school was breaking away from the hum-drum existence that is lived by most athletes, doing the same routines each day. This was an extension of that and perhaps an over compensation for the good times I missed as a struggling athlete. It was also anathema to how I was raised.

But here we were in Jamaica, taking a long ride of at least a half hour when I was told to pull over by a shack on the side of the road. The red rental car stood out on the long stretch of highway on either side of us. We were led through the shack which had a menagerie of animals milling around—chickens, hens, goats, donkeys, cats and dogs. There were men standing by an open fire contained in a large metal barrel, unphased by the summer heat and all were Rastafarians. I did not know much about Rastafarians, indigenous people of Jamaica. They are a religious group where the men grow their hair in very long dreadlocks and members smoke marijuana everyday. Some were followers of the Ethiopian Emperor

Haile Selassie. They were friendly but also had a reputation for political militancy, particularly in Kingston.

We were led back into a marsh area. I was wearing a bathing suit and Barbara had on a bikini and cowboy hat. I was deferring to her since she made"the connection"and had obviously done this before. Men wearing gun belts gathered around. They were smiling and engaged in small talk asking where we were from. One of the men broke off and ran into the marshes. We could see him through the reeds. He came back carrying a large brick over his head. He threw it down on a piece of cardboard. The men did not have rolling paper. Instead they had hero bags, ordinarily used to hold long French bread. One man broke off a large piece of marijuana from the brick. He pulled off a few twigs and then poured it into a sack, the hero bag, which he called a "spliff." It was like an oversized Churchill cigar, perhaps two inches in diameter and rolled at both ends. He held it like a giant Genoa salami while another man lit it with his lighter. It caught fire like a torch in a cave but quickly began to smolder. Now they passed it around but did not put it to their lips. They held it at arms length and just breathed in the smoke. One "toke"or "hit" and you were in La La Land. It was nirvana.

Now it was time to do business. The men having given us a sample of their product wanted to know what we wanted to buy. Since the sample itself was probably an ounce, I think that they figured that we wanted a lot, maybe to ship into the United States. When Barbara told them an ounce, they broke into laughter. I thought we were going to be killed. One of the men took off Barbara's cowboy hat and filled it with pot. It was overflowing and appeared to be more like a pound. The price was an unbelievable twenty dollars. We were led back to our car and drove back to the cottage. I was thankful that we had not been arrested and that our lives were spared.

I did not know it at the time, but Barbara's version of a "Jamaican holiday" was to smoke reefer all day, interrupted only by sex, food, more sex and sun. It was one of the best vacations ever and a far cry from anything that I had done in my youth.

Two mild disappointments occurred during the trip. One was that we drank the local water when we first got there, and as a result both suffered from the effects of it. Barbara met a guy who was there with some of his friends. They had a room next to ours. One night she was missing for awhile. We were arguing about something ridiculous and she went off and had sex with him down on the beach. I never tried to control Barbara. She was too liberated for that but dangerously so, in her own world of needs and wants. The "Jamaica holiday" ended with our return to Delaware and my departure for New York. I had little contact with Barbara after that and we drifted apart. While Barbara presented some enticing options, I viewed our relationship as a mysterious phase that I was passing through and that other experiences and relationships awaited me. The law provided stability and uncertainty. I was moving in a direction that was more grounded.

After the Bar Exam I waited impatiently for the results, which did not arrive until December. The results were published in The New York Times, and you could get them in the early edition if you went to Times Square. My mother and I drove there to get the results. Law students were everywhere. It was midnight. I did not pass. I had to go home and tell my father. My parents took it in stride. They wanted to know my next move.

Chapter XVII

<u>Down But Never Out—Stepping Up</u>

A professor friend from Delaware, Judith Teitelbaum, was getting advanced degrees in law from New York University and had a room in one of its dormitories when she was in town. Judy urged me to enroll in the Master's in Law Program at New York University; to secure a dormitory room at the University; to take a bar review course in the City and to study at N.Y.U. I followed her advice and enrolled in the Master's in Tax Law program. This was a program for serious tax law students, most with accounting degrees who planned on careers in tax law. I did not. Most of the students in the program, which consisted of twenty-four credits, were in it full time. I was taking one course so I could get a cheap room in the City where I would have a place to study. I probably should have enrolled in the General Law Master's program, but the Tax Law program was prestigious.

Hayden Hall was a great spot. It had a pool and steam room in the basement which I used everyday. It was just off of Washington Square Park, so I would run around the park each day. I continued to live my monastic existence. My meals usually consisted of a quiet lunch each day at a restaurant on West Broadway where I could get a simple meal with pecan pie as a desert for under ten dollars. Later I would grab a meal at a hole-in-the-wall falafel stand on MacDougal Street. In the morning my breakfast was on the run at a deli. I would usually head uptown by subway to a hotel and take the bar review lecture live from Joe Marino.

Before enrolling in the course I met with Joe Marino personally in his office in Garden City, New York. He was a legend. I went there with my father. They spoke in Italian. Marino assured us that I would pass the Bar if I just took copious notes on the lectures and read them over and over. The reason for this was that he had one employee whom he paid to fail the Bar Exam. As of 1976, he had failed it fifty seven times. Each time he would go to Albany to review his exam and copy down all the correct answers. He would bring those back and incorporate them into the lectures. The questions on the Bar Exams tended to be repeated so his lectures focused on questions from the exam, given over the past five years. There was no questioning the instructors at Marino. You just wrote for four hours everyday. I had over five thousand pages of notes at the end of Marino's review course. I had read them cover to cover four times. I was becoming more utilitarian, more pragmatic. Marino was all about New York Law. At my table in the hotel there were nine other law school graduates from the leading law schools in the country. They were all working for major law firms. They had all failed their first time.

I was petrified of the February Bar because it had a low pass rate of less than sixty percent, but Marino explained why. If you failed the Bar twice you could only retake it in February, once a year. There were many foreign students with language and other issues who were repeat takers, which accounted for the low pass rate.

While I was at N.Y.U. just like Delaware, I was constantly in search of quiet, nice places to study where the ambiance was pleasant but not too congested or exciting. So I studied in the dorm conference room; in the lower level of the law school library, ("the dungeon," as I called it); or at Bobst Library, the undergraduate library on the park. Bobst was about ten stories with a magnificent open cavern in the center. It had study corals everywhere. N.Y.U. had fifty thousand students but I could usually find a quiet place to study. All this isolation though was driving me a little mad. I was not attending the tax classes regularly or studying tax law. I was too busy studying for the Bar Exam.

I met my wife, Wendy, at N.Y.U. She had just graduated from Duke University with honors. Her degree was in Fine Arts. She was and is an exceptional artist. She was back in New York. She had been a competitive swimmer, a butterflier, and I had briefly coached her when she was sixteen and I was twenty three. She had also been the Salutarian of her Carle Place, Long Island high school class. As number two in that class, her average was ninety nine. She only applied to two universities. She was accepted at Cornell and elected to attend Duke.

During the break after the July Bar, and while I was awaiting the results, I had gotten reacquainted with Wendy—I was friendly with her brother, Eddie, also a former competitive swimmer, who was living next to a rock 'n roll concert hall in Roslyn, New York, called My Father's Place. At the time it was famous. Eddie invited me to a few parties and I got reacquainted with Wendy. Years earlier I had coached her when she was a competitive swimmer.

I was reluctant to ask her out because she was seven years younger than I. But at N.Y.U. one night, I was just walking near the law school when I saw Wendy. Her car had a flat tire. We were trying to get the firemen at the local firehouse to help us, which they did. We got it changed. Wendy was taking a course in retail at N.Y.U. and we started seeing each other. It really was not much fun because I did not have any money, but Wendy was in the City two nights a week and she would usually find me. The girl was tenacious. No matter what remote hideaway I was in, she would find me. We would either grab a falafel or coffee and cake at Le Figaro Café, a well known coffeehouse at the corner of Bleeker and MacDougal Streets in Greenwich Village.

I was reluctant to take time away from my studies but thankfully, Wendy persisted. She was a relief and one of the few contacts I had with real people outside the law. I was living like a hermit—law, law, just law and more law. The Bar exam took place in February and this time I was ready. Marino had accurately predicted at least eight out of the twelve essay questions and by this time as soon as I spotted the issues all I had to do was regurgitate the answers which I had nearly memorized from going over the notes again and again, a total of four times plus other reading.

I was tired of N.Y.U. and needed to get on with my life but I was not yet a lawyer. My choices were limited. Wendy and I were still together. Wendy has a sister and two brothers. She was twenty three and I was almost thirty. Even though I felt embarrassed that I was robbing her from the cradle, I had gotten the courage to ask her out and meet her parents, Edward and Carole Zeilman. Edward was a Captain, Stevedore and President of Northeast Terminal Corporation, a long shore firm on the Brooklyn piers. Carole was a successful real estate salesperson in Carle Place, Long Island.

I did not go to work for Legal Aid or anywhere else where I had received real legal job offers because I had failed the Bar exam. I felt that it was unfair to those prospective employers even though they would have taken me on. I took a low-paying job as a law librarian and junior Associate at a downtown New York law firm at 120 Broadway, a landmark in New York City. The firm was a defense firm which received much of its business from an old line firm, White and Case.

A senior, named partner, was in his eighties. He was a Knight of the British Empire, with homes on Park Avenue and in France, where he spent six months out of the year. He was, to say the least, eccentric. His chauffeur would pick him up each day and drive him downtown. He would arrive late. The firm maintained a kitchen and a chef just for him. He would have his breakfast served to him at his desk with the Wall Street Journal and The New York Times. In the early afternoon he was taken to the Wall Street Club for lunch and then he would go directly home, usually without doing any actual legal work during the course of the day. The firm had about 30 lawyers and he had his rules. One rule was that you were not permitted to take off your suit jacket in the common areas of the firm or in the presence of clients. The other rule was that you had to re-shelve your law books.

We had been working on a research project for the Nigerian government. I was getting about four hours of sleep a night and living at the downtown New York Athletic Club. The project was ongoing for about a month and our research was piled on conference room tables in the library. All of the books were left open to specific pages. The partner had been in France. We were unaware of his return. Four of us had been working on the project. We completed our research and went to lunch to celebrate. We figured that we had accumulated more than one hundred thousand dollars in billable time on that project. When we came back from lunch, all the books had been shelved by the partner. I could not believe it. I hand-wrote a letter of resignation, put it on another partner's desk and walked out without saying a word to anyone. I was unemployed.

At home in Westbury I was starting to talk about my options. I did not have a real job and I was not a lawyer. I started to look at the local political scene and talk of politics. At that time the Republicans controlled my town of North Hempstead, so any Democrat running was a sacrificial lamb. The Democratic Party had no money and the Republicans had the best political machine in the country, run by the "Boss of Bosses," Joseph

Margiotta, a powerful figure who controlled everything in Nassau and statewide politics. He was also a National Republican Committeeman.

Running against the machine was an impossible task but after talking it out with my dad, I determined that I had nothing to lose. I would endeavor to return to the Democratic Party and secure their nomination to run for Supervisor in the Town of North Hempstead, a community with about 250,000 people residing in it. I quickly garnered the support of two fine friends from my former days in politics, Ted Miller, an African American with a heart of gold, and Bill Kenneally, an engineer, labor organizer and my Assembly District Leader. Also on board with me was Ann Weiland, the other Assembly District Leader whose son, Eddie, had worked for me at Sands Point. Eddie and his sister swam with us at Renaissance and Ed's dad was a lawyer. He too was active in the Democratic Party.

There were three candidates at the convention and I won the nomination to run for Supervisor. On that same ticket were Barbara Blumberg and Dick Paige for Town Council. Dick was an incumbent who squeezed into office just after Watergate. Tom DeJesus, a young Hofstra University School of Law grad, also awaiting the Bar results, was running for Town Clerk.

Great Neck, New York, 1977, starting the campaign for Supervisor with a kick off breakfast. Tom is endorsed by former Congressman and Ambassador Allard Lowenstein. Wendy Liotti on left drew and made the lithograph of former Senator Robert Kennedy which was presented to Ambassador Lowenstein. Other candidates, left to right: Barbara Blumberg for Town Council; Thomas DeJesus for Town Clerk and Councilman Dick Paige

Since the Party had no money, they wanted candidates to pledge to put up money. I had planned to run without it, but my dad handled those negotiations. He was a man of honor, but of modest means. He pledged $15,000.00—a generally small sum but unlike others he kept his commitment and paid it during the campaign. It was not a small sum for him.

Outside of what my dad contributed, we did not raise much. A friend gave us a storefront. We had limited money and literature. I walked through some of the worst neighborhoods by myself everyday, knocking on doors. I was not working, just campaigning. I would start in the morning and finish late at night. It was grinding, but my name was getting around.

I ran into an old friend, Neal Belmuth. He was a genius. Wendy, my father and Neal were the mainstays of the campaign. As fast as I could put up posters, the Republicans would take them down.

Early one morning we were greeting commuters at the Port Washington railroad station. Neal had designed a briefcase that when it was opened, would loudly play John Philip Sousa music. Wendy and my father wore straw hats with my name on them. Wendy had made a banner and because we did not have enough literature, I would literally go up to the garbage cans between trains and pick out any literature which had been discarded and we then gave it out to the next wave of commuters.

In the early stages of the campaign, I appeared before the Liberal Party for their screening to determine whether I would receive their endorsement and nomination. Idealistically I arrived for my interview with my liberal credentials and those of my family, including medals my father had received from the AFL-CIO.

They did not care about any of that. They were patronage hounds and political whores. The Chairman of the Party stopped my presentation and said:"We do not care about any of that. We just want to know if your Party will endorse our candidate for Town Clerk." I explained that it seemed like a reasonable request but I had nothing to do with that and we already had a Town Clerk candidate. The Liberal Party already had their minds made up. They would put up a candidate who did not campaign and who had no real interest in politics. He was put up, as is nearly always the case with minor political parties, to be a spoiler and to remind the major political parties that they must deal with them or be denied nominations in the future. The Chairman of the Liberal Party later became a State Supreme Court Justice. That was his payback. Another of their officers was a token

Deputy County Attorney for thirty years. He did not care that he was a political prostitute. He needed a job and got one.

In the middle of the campaign I got word that I had passed the Bar. A great weight had been lifted from my shoulders. I was campaigning as aggressively as I could with no money. North Hempstead is the smallest of three towns in Nassau County. Nassau also has two cities, Glen Cove and Long Beach. But North Hempstead is considered to be the jewel of the Gold Coast because it is closer to the City than Glen Cove or parts of Oyster Bay. Some of the wealthiest communities in the world are in North Hempstead. Old Westbury, Roslyn Harbor, Manhasset, Plandome, Sands Point, Great Neck and Kings Point are all part of the Town. The real estate is expensive and the *per capita* income is very high. I was from the southern part of the Town, which was considered more middle class with some blue collar people and a few small pockets of the poor as well.

I became a campaigning machine. I was at it sixteen hours a day. We had a paid campaign coordinator who organized our walk throughs, coffee klatches and speaking engagements. My opponent, Mike Tully, was a savvy politician and attorney who had name recognition, money, and a machine behind him. Later, Mike's life was marked by personal tragedies and a premature death, but during the campaign, he was considered invincible. The Republicans had controlled all three towns for more than seventy-five years.

It was exhausting, but just like competitive swimming, I brought a new verve and energy level to politics. At my first fundraiser and kick-off, former Congressman, and later Ambassador, Allard Lowenstein, was my guest of honor. Al was assassinated in his law office in 1980. Later I secured the endorsement of Congressman Peter Rodino, the famous Democrat from New Jersey who Chaired the House of Representatives Judiciary Committee and consequently the Watergate impeachment hearings of Richard Nixon. Another avid supporter was former Congressman Tom Downey, the youngest person ever elected to Congress, at age 25. Tom suggested that I have a "pig party." It was something he did in Washington. He would invite lobbyists and they would contribute to his campaign. I did not know any lobbyists or even big money donors who would give me lots of money. Tom is a lobbyist today in Washington in partnership with a former Republican Congressman from Long Island.

Newark, New Jersey, 1977, Tom is endorsed by former Congressman and Chair of the House of Representatives Judiciary Committee, Peter Rodino ("The Watergate Committee") which voted to impeach President Nixon.

Heading the top of our ticket that year was Assemblyman Irwin Landes, a Harvard Law School graduate, a brilliant lawyer, and highly respected politician. Irwin was from North Hempstead and had been in the Assembly for seven years. He was our County Executive candidate while the Republicans were enmeshed in a bitter primary battle. Up until five weeks before Election Day we were closing with some polls showing us just two percentage points behind. All I had to do was stay clean, keep going and ride Irwin's coattails.

I was looked upon that year as the only Democratic, Independent Town Supervisor candidate with a shot at victory. The Democrats decided to showcase me by allowing me to give the keynote speech and introduction of Irwin Landes at our County dinner. Aside from Commencement, it was my first time speaking before a large group. They were mesmerized and gave me a standing ovation. There is a magic or gift of great oratory either in the courtroom or on the campaign trail and I apparently have it. I was a no-holds-barred speaker to whom people wanted to listen. I was not hedging and I was an outspoken critic of Nixon, Watergate, and the local political machine for siding with Nixon. I called them out on corruption and kickbacks. I was the future and Irwin was the present. My father and mother were at every event, applauding, encouraging, financing, and glowing with pride. I was a "comer" but I had not yet come, at least not into elective office which was my burning ambition, to be like Bobby Kennedy and Allard Lowenstein (although not dead), to be a leader of public opinion, to set political trends and oppose the forces of evil. I wanted to be a spokesperson for civil and human rights.

Five weeks before Election Day it was revealed in the media that Irwin had not filed personal tax returns for several years. It was a crime and Irwin's campaign started to plummet. All the money raised and time spent were going down the tubes. As a result my own quest would be imperiled because I was tied to Irwin and trying to ride his coattails or what was now left of them.

Irwin would not even get out of bed to campaign. All of his brilliance and promise would now be taken from us. I felt that the voters were being deprived of a great leader who had already made, but could make an even bigger difference in their lives. But Irwin's honesty and integrity were now in question and therefore, so was mine and every other Democratic candidate's.

Within a couple of weeks of Election Day we were scrambling to keep the campaign afloat, effectively without a County Executive candidate. Then the second shoe fell. Irwin had been practicing law without a license for twenty-four years. He had indeed graduated from Harvard College and Harvard Law School, had passed the Bar exam but had never completed the Character and Fitness application and review, the last steps before being sworn in and signing the Roll of Attorneys.

Naturally these revelations were set backs. Irwin was accused of multiple misdemeanors, retained the former New York City Police Commissioner as his counsel and was to be arraigned just after Election Day.

I was seeing the underbelly of politics. Through no fault of my own I would be deprived of my dream. I lost, but so did an incumbent Councilman, Dick Paige. Barbara Blumberg won by one hundred votes. Now I had to decide what to do next.

After the election, even though I had lost, I figured that my efforts would garner a position in government. The District Attorney was a Democrat and he had just been re-elected. Also, my Assemblyman was a Democrat. Both turned me down. I was on my own, no job, no clients.

After the campaign I thought that I would probably be hired as an Assistant District Attorney in Nassau or receive a part-time position in the

Albany State Legislature where I would start my career in public service, begin to build any credentials and gear up for future runs for office. I had lost the School Board and Town Supervisor's race, but won my college and law school elections. That inspired me to continue, to strive to be a candidate for change, equality and freedom. The people I admired most—the Kennedys, Martin Luther King, Jr. and Allard Lowenstein, all had their share of defeats. I felt confident that I could make a difference, but I still had to survive financially, get a job and keep going. While those things were important to me, I could not give up my ideals. I could not forsake those beliefs for political expediency. They were too much a part of me. Too many had died for those beliefs. Memories of them were seared into my brain. I had to go on for them. I had to do my part. I had to pick up the cudgels of those who had fallen. At the same time, I had no money, no mentors. The political causes were important to me but I was also faced with a dominant Republican machine whose ideals were not mine. The machine really had no ideals. It lived for patronage alone. Without a higher purpose, I knew that that could not last forever but there it was for the time being—a monolith, capable of crushing all opposition and not caring about the goodness of a person running against them or the rightness of a cause championed by others. The machine wanted so-called conservatives, members who would not rock the boat or question the *status quo*.[27] They had to cater to the senior citizens and an older population that had controlled Nassau County politics for years. I had to get a start politically and make money. Money and power go hand-in-hand. Politics and law were my vehicles for social change.

Some needed jobs or titles. Many were impressed by those things. I was not except that I knew that they could empower me to help others. That was what I cared about, not being called Senator, Congressman or Judge or being in a pension system or having a guaranteed salary. Those were the wrong reasons for being involved in public service. The machine wanted malleable, uncommitted persons to do its bidding. They were comfortable with whites over blacks and minorities, older people over younger ones, segregation in schools, and the proliferation of a government bureaucracy giving them more jobs and patronage. They wanted a system which furthered their own financial ends. For example, in the early 1980's Joseph Margiotta, the Republican County Leader, was indicted and charged with a violation of the Hobbs Act, a federal extortion statute. He was ultimately convicted and went to jail. His alleged violation of the law occurred when he divvied up the insurance premiums paid by municipalities among his fellow political leaders and himself. This practice existed long before his arrival on the scene and occurred even during the brief tenure of Democratic County Executive in Nassau from 1961-1970 when Hon. Eugene Nickerson, later a federal District Court Judge, served in that capacity. Margiotta did not intend to violate the law and the application of a 1941 Labor Racketeering law to him was really a reach, but the questionable practices were simply the way things went at that time.

Margiotta was a brilliant leader and a General who presided over an unrivaled, enormous political machine with tentacles extending and reaching into every aspect of government, locally, statewide and nationally. I did not receive any appointments from the Democrats, only lip service. I began to think that I might have few choices but to consider a change in my political registration if I wanted to move forward in politics. The extent to which I might have to prostitute myself or compromise my political beliefs in order to do that was still an open question. I suspected that I might conceal my true reformist beliefs to a point, but if push came to shove, I would never be involved in questionable or illicit activities or policies not representing my core beliefs. Yet, I also believed that if I changed my political registration that I could be a liberal, maverick Republican like Nelson Rockefeller, Senator Jacob Javits or Attorney General Louis Lefkowitz. I thought I could change the ideology of the Republican Party. That was naive but I believed in my ability to lead if given the opportunity. I thought that I could show them a better way.

The Democratic National Convention in 2008 produced a phenomenal, unprecedented political rally where Presidential nominee Barack Obama spoke to an audience of over 80,000 people at the Mile High Stadium in Denver, Colorado. While this political event could not be foreseen by me in the late 60's and 70's, it was the kind of activism on the part of all people that we were trying to generate.

My points of reference were Martin Luther King, Jr.'s 1963 March on Washington, "I Have A Dream" speech, and the political and anti-war rallies of the 1960's. I knew that if such political excitement could be stirred, that corrupt politicians and institutions could be toppled. I was locked into a Heartland where mediocrity and survival were the order of the day. The concerns were day-to-day, not the future.

My view did not fall into the category of delusions of grandeur. Instead, I saw myself as a vehicle for social change. My role was instilled in me as a child—stand up, stand out, take hold. To me that was a personal matter which had little significance if I could be the instrument to help others. In my lifetime I had seen an undeclared war in Southeast Asia stopped by a well-organized anti-war movement. I had seen a President of the United States impeached. But there was still so much work to do. Aside from rampant political and corporate corruption at home, *de facto* segregation in our schools, and the onset of political malaise signaling an end to massive political protests, we still had the Cold War; the threat of the Nuclear Age, huge environmental problems and Apartheid in South Africa. While many of the activists from the 1960's and early 1970's had mainstreamed or were in hiding or jail, I was biding my time, waiting to make my move, hoping to get the opportunity to advance in public service so that I might help others. If not, then I would do it on my own, more slowly perhaps, but I was determined to fight against the forces of evil so that no one and nothing could stand in my way. In my own way, on an emotional and political level, I was an assassin. If you were a corrupt politician or businessman, you had much to fear from me because I would do all that I could to take you out. Often I was a voice of one, alone on the battlefield of social change.

I cared, but it made the struggle more difficult. The worshipers of "supply-side economics" and the "trickle-down effect" were taking a foothold. The economic prosperity of a few tended to obscure if not obliterate, the political consciousness that had been prevalent in the1960's. I listened to voices like Bob Dylan's "Blowin' In The Wind," but either they were silent or the children of the 1960's were now deaf, or maybe both. The times were not changin' anymore, except for the worse.

By 1978 I was practicing law full time, a local practice of real estate, wills, and separation agreements. But I also took just about any case that walked in the door. Out of economic necessity, perhaps, I was transitioning somewhat out of institutional politics and gravitating to the law where I would proffer my message of social change, slowly and on a small scale, but always pointedly. Jimmy Carter was in the White House and Democrats controlled both houses of Congress. Inflation was rising together with interest rates. My real estate practice was being hurt by these events and others. In 1978 the Carter Administration had established the first bi-annual National Democratic Convention and I was elected in a contested election, as a delegate to that from Nassau County. I was a populist with all the rhetoric to go with it, never flinching from what I had learned in the 1960's.

Along the way I was always using the media to further the cause of justice. There was a lot of publicity, sometimes just local and sometimes national, mostly positive but sometimes negative. Many I am sure believed that I was simply egotistical but that was not correct. I was building a law practice and using it to take on the issues of the day. People came to me for routine matters as well as political or social concerns. If I was paid on a real estate matter some portion of my fee allowed me to become more active in political and social venues.

I had started to make campaign contributions to elected officials and judges. I signed up to become a member of the Assigned Counsel Defender Plan and Family Court Law Guardian panels to represent the poor. The legal fees that you could generate in these cases were minimal but judges started assigning them to me. I was becoming one of the regulars around the courthouses, but did not have a teacher or a mentor.

One of the judges I had come in contact with was Robert Roberto, a Republican/ Conservative from North Hempstead. He was a candidate for the Nassau County State District Court Bench. I was invited to a fundraiser for him at the Strathmore Vanderbilt Country Club, an enclave for Republicans in Manhasset. At the time it was considered sacrilegious to attend a fundraiser for a member of a rival Party. I was mindful of that and felt odd in attending but there I was, amidst the "hangers-on," the parasites, the establishment of the Republican Party. I went unnoticed except by Bob Roberto. I made my obligatory salutations and began to feel somewhat disenchanted with myself, deciding to make an early exit. On my way out Bob could see that I was leaving and he came over to me. He had been a Deputy Attorney General in New York State; a Law Secretary to a County Court and Supreme Court Justice and a Chief Assistant District Attorney. He greeted me and thanked me for coming. My reservations in going were assuaged by Bob's personal touch. There was a human side to the political machine after all or so I thought at the time.

Assemblyman Angelo Orazio, a Democrat/Liberal engineer from North Hempstead, was my Assemblyman, but had not offered me a position on his staff. I had always supported him so this lack of reciprocation irritated me, to say the least. At the same time a very popular Town Clerk from North Hempstead, John DaVanzo, a Republican/Conservative, was nominated by his party to be Angelo's opponent. I had met John on the campaign circuit. He was always affable and gracious. He began to talk with me about how I should make a change in my political registration to become a Republican. Every time I saw him, which was often, he would say something about it. He was from the neighboring community of Mineola.

I was still a Democrat and the potential or actual threat of me endorsing a Republican like Davanzo in a close Assembly race could cause Orazio to lose. It was the last chance for the Democrats to hold onto me. One Party Democratic rule in Washington had pushed the country into recession helped by high gas prices and the Iran hostage crisis. Still the Democrats were not offering me anything in the way of a position in government. At the same time there was little patronage among Democrats in Nassau. The Democratic County Leader, Stanley Harwood, a former Assemblyman, was greedy. He had hogged for himself a well-paid Commissioner of Elections job; served on the State Assembly staff for Brooklyn powerhouse Speaker of the Assembly, Stanley Steingut; served as County Leader, and was a partner at a prominent Nassau County law firm. The Democrats were failing, having great difficulty in getting anyone elected. The Democrats, at that time, were not a beacon of honesty in government. There were plenty of examples of corruption in New York City where political leaders were even more avarice than Joe Margiotta and where the large public trough provided even more opportunities for fat cats to feed.

DaVanzo made arrangements for me to meet with Margiotta. I went to their opulent headquarters in Hempstead where I was ushered into Margiotta's office. Also present were DaVanzo, "Buddy" Pierce, the Town of North Hempstead Republican Leader, Supervisor Michael Tully, my former opponent and Town Councilman Charles Fuschillo, my local Republican Leader.

I was there to talk about a possible change in my political registration and to determine how warmly I might be received within the Party. Margiotta kept some distance between us—he did not offer me anything but simply said that I would be embraced and given a fair shot to prove myself. He said that his Party was built from the ground up by its "soldiers," his Committeemen and women. He said some distinguished themselves in five years and some took longer and some never made the grade. A fair shot was all that I was looking for. The other leaders agreed. I left to talk it over with my family. Wendy and my mother were both Republicans. My father was still a devout Democrat and former Committeeman.

Unbeknownst to me at the time was the animosity Fuschillo held for me. Sometime after I had graduated from law school he had called me at home to invite me into the Republican Party. At the time I did not know much about him. I was already embarking on my renewed efforts in the Democratic Party. Fuschillo was angry with me for running against his friend Mike Tully. Tully was very gracious and friendly toward me but Fuschillo held a grudge. He also viewed me as a threat to his leadership. I was not aware of any of this and, based upon this agreement with Margiotta and Pierce at the meeting, I thought I would be given a fair shot. But Fuschillo was not honest at that meeting. He had other plans. He kept his foot on my neck for more than ten years, never fully embracing me, never giving me a fair shot as he and Margiotta had promised, never giving me a position in government, and never even making me a Committeeman. Politics is a very tough business. Loyalties and special interests change by the nanosecond.

Right after Election Day, Wendy and I decided to get married. It was scheduled for December 17, 1977. It was a beautiful day. I had made arrangements with the Merchant Marine Academy to use their chapel for the ceremony. Bill Irwin was my Best Man. We had fifty children from the Manhasset String Ensemble playing violins and all dressed in red vests and white turtlenecks. Edgar Kendricks, a gospel singer from Harlem and a former star of the television show "Sesame Street", sang for us. He was magnificent. His voice filled the room.

Prior to the wedding, I had decided that I wanted my friend Arthur Dobrin, the leader of the Ethical Humanist Society of Long Island to conduct the ceremony. My father resisted and said that he would not attend unless a priest performed the ceremony. I was prepared to go on without him, but my mother-in-law, Carole Zeilman, convinced me that I must have my father there. So I relented. We had a Roman Catholic priest assisting Arthur Dobrin in the performance of the ceremony. I felt that it was a bit of an insult to Arthur, but he was okay with it, which made it easier for me to accept.

My parents held a rehearsal dinner the night before the wedding at the Piping Rock Restaurant in Westbury. We had over three hundred people at the wedding ceremony. Two hundred joined us for a reception at the Plandome Country Club. Our wedding song was the theme from the movie *The Godfather*.

Just prior to the wedding there was a Special Water District Election in Westbury. I was living at home and not a property owner. I showed up to vote but they would not let me vote because I did not own real property. Naturally this Town Law which ostensibly allowed them to exclude me, was an outgrowth of Jim Crow and meant to preclude the poor from voting. I used the same water as everyone else and so did the sizable number of apartment dwellers living in the District. I promised myself that I would sue the District upon my return from my honeymoon and that is exactly what I did. It was my first lawsuit and the District capitulated, all residents of the District would be allowed to vote in all future elections and a Democratic Assemblyman, Lewis Yevoli, introduced state legislation at my request which brought about a change in the Town Law eliminating the disenfranchising provisions therein.

We had hastily organized the honeymoon through a local travel agency. We went to Eleuthra in the Bahamas in December. The weather was not terrific and the hotel was called the Current Club. Wendy and I went there so we could scuba dive. We renamed the place the Past Club because it was falling apart. The boat which was supposed to take us scuba diving never left the dock. The ping pong table had only three legs and the conch was wonderful the first night for dinner, but it was served at every meal thereafter.

Desperate to find a place where Wendy might learn to scuba dive, we retained the services of a local fisherman who apparently had no license and did not scuba dive himself. He did, however, have scuba tanks and drove us out to a reef. I was a certified YMCA scuba diver so I could teach Wendy but my prerequisites to our guide were to bring us to shallow water and to an area where there were no barracuda. Unfortunately, he violated both of those requests. As we hung on the side of the boat the harness used to mount the tanks was rusted. Wendy's tank fell off her back and went down to the bottom. I dove down, without a tank, to retrieve it. We were now both in tanks and swimming around when we noticed that the area was infested with barracuda, mostly small fish, a foot or so long, but one really big boy, whose size I estimated at six feet. I bobbed up to the surface to get us out of there. Our guide had left us. We were in open water by ourselves. We kept swimming around, avoiding the barracuda and eventually about a half hour later, our man came back and took us into shore.

Chapter XVIII

<u>No Office, No Clients,</u>
<u>No Money But An Attorney</u>

Upon returning home we needed a place to stay. We had used some of the wedding money for our honeymoon and Wendy decided that the most essential purchase that we simply had to make was a good stereo system for our new apartment. The only trick being that the apartment was not so new. After we returned home from the honeymoon we were staying at my folk's house until I got my first client, a small construction company with an office in a house on a main street in my Village. The company's name was New Again Construction Company and I called them Sued Again Construction Company. They were good guys, doing fine work but their industry was prone to litigation. The partners were Nino Luciano, a former opera singer and his partner, Charles Givens, a Physical Engineer. The company specialized in historic renovation and preservation. While those terms may seem contradictory, Nino and Charles did unique work all over New York. They asked me to be their lawyer. I worked cheap and at first they were my only clients. I billed and they paid. I was able to win or settle most of their cases "on papers," as we often say in the legal business.

But we needed a place to live so by January my clients gave me a four room apartment on the second floor of the house that they were using as a business. We did not have any furniture so we bought a king size bed. We did not have a dining room or even a kitchen table, so if we had friends or family over for dinner we ate picnic-style on the floor. I borrowed a desk and chair from my clients. I bought a used IBM Selectric typewriter for fifty dollars. I would hunt and peck my work because I could not type.

I used one of the rooms as an office to work in, but I never saw clients there. Instead, I used the back of my mother-in-law's real estate office to see clients. Aside from New Again, my main clients were those sent to me by my mother-in-law, Carole Zeilman. Carole knew everyone, especially the people in the local Italian community. She was in the real estate business for many years and one of the most successful residential sales people on the Island. With New Again, I was doing civil work and Carole was feeding me clients. Once I did a client's closing, I would get their wills, their divorces, and whatever other legal problems they had. Word spread and I turned almost no one away. I would go to the worst neighborhoods or they would come to me.

The house I was living in was being used illegally at the time, as Nino was not living in it and it was not owner-occupied. He had some construction material on the first floor, but it had fallen into some disrepair. I nicknamed Wendy "The Hunter" because while painting each night, she would capture or kill mice which unfortunately inhabited the building.

We stayed for seven months in Nino's house. I told my mother-in-law that I wanted the ground floor of a building which she owned with her sister, next to their real estate office. She had a tenant there who was not paying his rent. I effectively moved him out without an eviction. He left quietly. It was five rooms in a railroad-style row house. By August, 1978 we had moved in. I had a big wooden sign made for the front of the building. Another good friend and client who had sued Nino was Jerry Bruckner. He took care of the electrical work. The building had pull lights. These were lights with no light switches, but lights with cords hanging down. With friends and family helping, I was starting to build a practice.

The apartment was in a small, narrow building. It had a porch in front. There was a tenant upstairs. We paid rent to my mother-in-law and her sister. The building was built in the early 1900's and was in disrepair but in a good location for a law office. As you walked in the front door there was a door to your immediate left which let you into the apartment. We sealed that door and used the first room as a bedroom which then faced the street. As you walked into the building where the front door was left open, all the time you faced a staircase leading to an upstairs apartment and to the left of that was a narrow corridor with a door at the end of it. I put a sign on that as well indicating law office. Through that door you walked into the reception area to the law office where I did not have a secretary but instead had props which I thought looked like a secretarial area. It had a desk; a typewriter table, my IBM Selectric, two ugly wing chairs which we purchased from a furniture dealer in Queens whom my mother knew. The apartment was set up front-to-rear as a bedroom, then my law office, a reception area, a small room behind that which Wendy used as an art studio and at the very rear we had a kitchen and bathroom. It was unconventional and disgusting, but we lived in those conditions for another year and a half. Wendy deserves a lot of credit for putting up with this madness. To say that I began with humble beginnings would be an understatement.

Wendy graduated from Duke University in 1976. She continued painting. When we first got married our only vehicle was the one which she purchased, a four-on-the-floor, B210 Datsun. Wendy was not yet a full fledged faculty member in Carle Place but she was teaching Calculus there. She had high energy, drive, ambition and required almost no sleep. She is an extremely talented artist and very cultured. She did not come from a family that cultivated those attributes; she developed them on her own. In high school she would get up in the middle of the night to do her homework, always drawing an A+ in every class and becoming Salutatorian, graduating ahead of a number of very talented people. Wendy is a well-deserved perfectionist.

Wendy was painting and decided to study Chinese painting on silk and rice paper, a highly disciplined art form which generally requires some knowledge of the landscapes of China. She took lessons from Mr. Hu, who had been renowned in the Chinese mainland prior to the cultural revolution there and who later migrated to Taiwan where he was also a national, cultural hero. He then migrated to Forest Hills, Queens where he continued to teach privately and paint.

We were invited to attend an art show opening of Mr. Hu's work in Chinatown. Hordes of people were milling out in front of the gallery. We gradually made our way to the front. The people parted and we approached Mr. Hu. He bowed and in doing so said: "Number one student." The people on either side of Mr. Hu had also formed greeting lines of sorts and they too then bowed repeating: "Number one student." My wife was the only American. We did not know what to say, but we both bowed and smiled.

A friend of ours managed a gallery in the Roosevelt Field Shopping Mall. A customer had come to the store to commission a hand painted Japanese screen for his home in the Caribbean. He gave the job to Wendy, an incredible task as we soon learned. The scene which he wanted to be painted was from the Ming Dynasty. The screen which had to be made by hand would stand six feet high and ten feet long. The wooden screen had special hinges between the panels of gold leaf paper on which the scene was painted. It was surrounded by special embroidery. When the screen was opened and flat, the entire colorful scene was cohesively exhibited. It was not a landscape but showed various people at work and play. It was to be done in acrylic paints, requiring Wendy's fine hands and eyes to produce a meticulously prepared work of art. This was not creative art—it was replicating a picture with incredible precision.

Wendy had never made a screen before but knew someone who had. That part of the job had to be subcontracted out. The end product was phenomenal, a beautiful, handcrafted work of art sitting in someone's living room in the Caribbean. While I might be tempted to say it was priceless, to put a dollar value on it really almost does it a disservice. From my layman's perspective I would say that it was worth twenty five to one hundred thousand 1978 dollars in an open market. But Wendy had agreed for her many hours of work to a fee of $1,600.00 including materials such as gold leaf papers. Of that she gave $600.00 to her friend for the production of the screen. We hated to let that screen go for such a ridiculously low price, but we stuck to the bargain Wendy's naiveté had made. It was very unfair, but Wendy was a trooper and let it go. I was angry that someone had taken advantage of her.

I had not yet changed my registration, but I had endorsed DaVanzo when some Democrats realizing the closeness of the Orazio race started to retaliate. Stanley Harwood, the County Chairman, alleged that I had sought a "no show job" and been turned down for it. He lied. I called all the political leaders and tape recorded my discussions with them about whether I had sought a "no show job." They all denied that I had except for Harwood. When I called him to confront him, I accused him of lying. I said: "You know I never sought a no show job. That was a lie." He said that he would not discuss it. I took my tape to Shirley Perlman at *Newsday* and Pat Weiner at *Community Newspapers* and they reported Harwood's lie. Up until then I believed that the Democrats were better than that. I was wrong.

I had been asked by Arthur Spatt to deliver his nomination speech in 1978. He was running for office in order to become a Justice of the New York Supreme Court, the Trial Court. Arthur was a Democrat who had a chance to win that year because the Conservatives were endorsing him. Arthur, a good friend, called me and told me that I could not give the speech. I understood. Arthur had the guts to tell me directly. I was sorry because I really loved Arthur and he deserved to win, having run four times for the State District Court from the Town of Hempstead and losing each time. He was a great trial lawyer who had paid his dues. Later that year he won and went on to become the Chief Administrative Judge on the Supreme Court and then Associate Justice of the Appellate Division and then a United States District Court Judge, where he still deservedly sits with distinction.

Harwood was also threatening to challenge my election to the national convention. I withdrew before he could do that. The combination of the Democrats' actions, Harwood's lies and what was happening in Washington, really pushed me over the edge. I was campaigning hard for DaVanzo but John really did not want to go to Albany. He was happy staying in the Town of North Hempstead. In supporting DaVanzo, I did, in essence, betray some of my long-held political beliefs. While I later returned to them, DaVanzo was a right-to-life and pro death penalty candidate.

The local papers started to carry headlines: "Is It DaVanzo or Liotti Running Against Orazio?" I changed my registration to the Republican Party. DaVanzo lost his race by 29 votes. There was no turning back but it looked like I would be the Republican candidate in 1980 to run against Orazio.

In the meantime, I was practicing law and involving myself in community affairs. I became a member of all the bar associations and kept contributing to candidates, especially judicial candidates. Fuschillo was still my leader and he had not made me a Committeeman, the usual prerequisite or starting point for being involved in organizational politics. I became a member of the local anti-poverty agency board, the only Caucasian member. I joined Kiwanis International, championing their scholarship committee and anti-vandalism campaign. I then became their President for the Westbury/Carle Place/Old Westbury Chapter. Women were not members at the time in any of the service clubs, such as Kiwanis, Lions, and Rotary. I wrote an Op-Ed piece in *The New York Times*[28] which later helped to change those rules.

Wendy had gotten a job as a full-time art teacher at the Cathedral School of St. Mary's in Garden City, an Episcopalian School for the well-to-do. She founded the after-school Art Academy, which became a huge success. She also became the President of the League of Women Voters and a writer for the *Westbury Times*. She was showing and donating her artwork to the American Cancer Society and other groups. She began to pursue her Master's Degree in Fine Arts at Pratt Institute in Brooklyn and she was painting privately in the little spare time that she had. Our pace was frenetic. My parents had not yet retired. Wendy's mother was still selling real estate and her father was a Captain/Stevedore and President of the Northeast Terminal Corporation, a large international shipping company with headquarters on the piers of Brooklyn Heights.

Ernest Chester, a local insurance agent and member of the "Hump Pilots Association," perhaps World War II's most famous bombardiers group, recruited me to become a member of the Republican Party Chairman's Club, the fat cats of the Republican Party. I started giving even more money to the Republicans because I was told that advancing in the Party had everything to do with how much money you raised or contributed. I was giving at least five thousand dollars a year to Republican candidates and raising even more. I never asked for anything and I never got anything. It was clear that Charlie Fuschillo was my nemesis. He was getting credit for the money I raised or contributed but he would not give me the time of day.

This was bad leadership. I was brought up differently. My father told me about Tammany Hall when he was growing up and how things got done at the local clubhouse. My grandfather, after whom I am named, was a District Leader. My father spoke about how he would accompany his father to the homes of the poor in his district to bring them groceries. My father told me that good political leaders find out what people need first and you try to get it for them. My father's motto was "help those who cannot help themselves first." He told me to remember who I owed and who owed me. He said that you should never have to call in a marker. People should know when they owe. If they cannot deliver or pay back, that is excusable as long as they try. This just means one hand washes the other as long as moral and ethical principles are not forsaken and as long as nothing illegal transpires. My father said that as you advance, remember where you came from, help the little guy, help those left behind. Everyone has dreams. Society as a whole benefits when you help others to realize their dreams. They, in turn, will help you to realize your own. But, it should never be a *quid pro quo*. It is never based upon "I will do for you if you kick back to me." No, it has to do with providing access and giving qualified people a chance to succeed or an opportunity to earn their chance. Everything is possible if you are willing to work for it. My father taught me to keep all the doors open for everyone. To give everyone a fair chance. At the same time he also knew that there are some who maybe unqualified but who look to government for help, jobs and the like. Our first priority had to do with trying to help those people. Whether they were qualified or not, it was your job and the government's job to help them if we could do so. This was not viewed as a handout or welfare. Those provided for had to earn what was given to them or at least try to do so.

My father knew that you had to have money to get ahead in politics. Very few people could just come on the political scene and generate the kind of popularity that the Kennedys or more recently Barack Obama created without raising huge sums of money. While I certainly understood the reality of what my father was saying, I disliked the idea of political and judicial candidates raising money to get elected. I had read Joe Ginnis' book "The Selling Of The President, 1968". On the cover was a photo of Richard Nixon on a package of cigarettes conveying the message that even cancer can be sold if properly marketed. I always believed that your identity and skill should be well-known to the voters before you run. With the help of the media providing free press coverage, you should be able to run on your laurels or to create a popular movement which would cause others to rally around you. That is what President Obama has. It explains how he was able to attract over 80,000 people to Mile High Stadium during the 2008 Democratic National Convention. While touring Europe, and during a rally in Germany before the election, he had over 200,000 enthusiastic listeners in attendance.

My father was correct, though I was still an idealist believing in the power of ideas and honesty. But I also realized that while you might be lucky enough to create a movement, you had to work in the trenches along the way. If you did not have the name recognition or the ability to mass-market yourself, then you had to start one on one, with community organizations, exactly as President Obama did. He obviously understood that better than his rivals did.

In 1979, I was asked by the Sons of Italy to represent a World War II veteran, Tony Casamento. Mr. Casamento was permanently disabled but had been turned down for the Congressional Medal of Honor, receiving instead the Navy Cross. My father and I went out to Suffolk County, first to the Sons of Italy Lodge where I agreed to take the case, and then to Mr. Casamento's home in West Islip. The home, a small cape, was inconspicuous until you entered. Greeting us at the door was Olivia, Tony's wife. They lived on Tony's disability income. They had a grown daughter. Tony had a young Democratic Congressman trying to help him, Tom Downey. The Navy Department and President Carter had turned Casamento down for the medal. The medal would mean more pension money for Tony and for Olivia once Tony passed away.

As I stepped into the Casamento living room, my father was at my side. I could feel an aura of greatness though Mr. Casamento was not yet in view. The living room was covered with medals, plaques and awards, all with Mr. Casamento's name on them. The Navy Cross was mounted on one wall standing out from the other awards. A glow seemed to be emanating from around the corner, when suddenly he was there.

While defending his fellow Marines in Guadalcanal, he was shot in the throat and elsewhere. He had difficulty speaking and was confined to a wheelchair. He spent most of the 1940's in a military hospital. As my father and I approached, quietly and very respectfully, Mr. Casamento smiled. To me, he seemed like an icon. I bowed and extended my hand, when suddenly Mr. Casamento tried to stand. I pleaded with him not to try and he relented. He already knew our names. He and Olivia told us their story. Casamento was a hero and in fact, so renowned, that even Japanese Generals had signed affidavits attesting to his gallantry. The Sons of Italy believed that he was being denied the medal because he was of Italian descent. Frankly, as my father and I heard the story, we could think of no other reason to explain the denial. I agreed to represent Tony. Every Sons of Italy chapter in the United States was behind him.

My first order of business was to arrange for a parade permit in Washington for Tony and his supporters to picket outside the White House. We received that from Congressman Norman Lent, a Long Island Congressman. We brought a thousand supporters to Washington by bus for Tony. My father was with me.

As we left, Tony stayed behind for another month by himself, in his wheelchair, with signs around him saying "Carter Justice." He stayed there over the holidays, in front of the White House, in the bitter cold, as the limousines passed. Tony had heart. He was an inspiration to many.

In the later part of 1979, my friend Robert D'Agostino, a Professor at Delaware, had gotten very involved in Ronald Reagan's campaign.

215

He called me and asked me to head up the Nationalities Committee for Reagan, which I did. Bob wanted to know if anything could be done to get Italian Americans to vote for Reagan. I called him back with an idea. If Reagan would announce that if elected, he would give the Congressional Medal of Honor to Casamento, every Italian American in the country would vote for Reagan. Bob thought it was brilliant. "I'll get back to you." A few days later he got back to me. It was the summer of 1980. He had checked with Reagan. Reagan would hold a press conference in New York City with Tony at his side and make the announcement.

I called Olivia. She wanted me to hold off until she spoke to Representative Downey, a Democrat. We then learned that Carter had given in and decided to give Tony the Congressional Medal. In September, 1980, two months before Election Day, Tony was awarded the Congressional Medal of Honor. Olivia, Downey and others told me that the threat of Reagan's press conference, is what got it for him. We were not invited to the ceremony. Reagan never had his press conference but he was elected. Wendy and I attended his inauguration in January, 1981 with the Chairman's Club and attended the New York State Ball, greeting Nancy and Ronald Reagan personally. They were gracious. Reagan remembered the story and he told me that if Carter had not given the Medal, he would have done it anyway as one of his first acts as President because he said, "it [was] the right thing to do." Nancy nodded, touched my arms and both thanked me as Reagan shook my hand. They left my side saying they would see us soon at the White House. I never got there, but Reagan was a gentleman and Nancy was a very classy lady.

I organized a dinner through Long Island Kiwanis for Anthony Casamento, my client and a Congressional Medal of Honor winner. (l to r) Dan Fisher, former Town of Hempstead Clerk and Town Supervisor Thomas Gulotta presenting a Citation to Mr. Casamento and Olivia, his wife, as I look on.

Chapter XIX

<u>Battling At The Bar</u>

Another life-changing event occurred in 1979. I was sitting in my office one day when the phone rang. It was my father. He knew someone who knew someone whose son was in trouble. As he told me a little of the facts, I recalled similar events from a case that I had recently read about on the front page of the *New York Law Journal*. A rape conviction had been reversed by the New York Court of Appeals and an indictment dismissed on double jeopardy grounds. The name of the case was *People v. Eric Michael*. It had been a state case out of Manhattan but after the reversal, Robert Morgenthau, the venerated District Attorney and former United States Attorney, called upon Robert Fiske, then the United States Attorney in the Southern District of New York to initiate a federal prosecution against Eric Michael, stating that: "This was one of the most heinous crimes ever committed in the Southern District of New York."

In rendering its decision the New York Court of Appeals, for just the second time in its history, admonished a sitting judge, Hon. Arnold Fraiman, a former Assistant United States Attorney in the Southern District of New York and the Supreme Court Justice presiding over the Eric Michael trial in state court. The rebuke by the Court of Appeals was so significant that the Association of the Bar of the City of New York appointed a special committee headed up by Whitney North Seymour, Jr., another former United States Attorney, to review the decision and conduct of Justice Fraiman. The decision had effectively put an end to Justice Fraiman's career.

The legal basis for the Court of Appeals ruling had to do with Eric Michael and his co-defendants being accused of the violent rape and sodomy of two graduate students from Columbia University who lived on the West Side of Manhattan around 78th Street. They were boyfriend and girlfriend. During his trial, Michael's attorney had disappeared, his father had died and he was somewhere on his way to upstate New York to sit Shiva, not leaving word as to his whereabouts or how he might be reached. Justice Fraiman declared a mistrial over the prosecutor's objection, but at the same time, said that the case could not be adjourned because he and several jurors had vacation plans. The jury had been sworn, so this created a double jeopardy problem. This statement and action by Fraiman is what got him into trouble with the New York Court of Appeals.

Eric Michael was retried and convicted, receiving a sentence of 21 years. The Appellate Division let the conviction and sentence stand but by the time New York's highest court reversed it, Michael had been in jail for nearly seven years. The federal government had decided to prosecute Michael and he was taken from state custody to detention facilities at the Brooklyn Navy Yard. While he was incarcerated Michael had failed to report his whereabouts to state authorities so he also had an immigration problem. He was from Haiti, speaking a hybrid of Patois and English.

My father made arrangements for me to meet Michael's mother. I had not been to federal court before except when I was sworn in, and I had never tried a case of any kind except for possibly a Small Claims Court case and one small marijuana case in the state District Court.

I met with Eric's mother and aunt in uptown New York. My college swim coach, Bill Irwin had by then left Adelphi and was the Head of Buildings at Columbia University. He had an apartment there and I used it to meet Eric's mother and aunt. They lived more toward the East Side in uptown New York, a very poor neighborhood. Mrs. Michael and her sister had little command of the English language and I had none of Patois, but we managed.

I had no idea what legal fees to charge or why to charge them except that I sensed that I had a big case. I was not sure if it would last a day, a week or a month and what would have to be done to get to that point.

I did not know it at the time, but Eric was represented by one of the finest lawyers in the country, Roland Thau, a Federal Defender in Manhattan. I had never taken over a case from another lawyer before so I was not quite sure what to do, but first I had to get retained. I am sure that in referring the case to me my father never gave a thought to what the legal fees might be or whether Eric or his family could pay them. My father was more interested in just getting cases and people to me. He bragged about me to everyone. He never did that around me although his support was obvious. I heard from others how he often expressed his pride in me to them. My father was building for the future, trying to help humankind through me. My parents had decided not merely to nurture me, but I believe that they were determined that the best way to help humanity was through me. My father was a very religious man, the sacrifices that he and my mother made for me can best be understood in a religious sense. This is what he taught himself about Christianity. He devoted himself to his church and his family first. In 2008, the Republicans had a slogan—"Country First." That was not my father. With him it was family first. He had pride in his name and heritage.

When I met Mrs. Michael I quoted her fifty thousand dollars for a fee. She had no concept of what I was saying. I wound up receiving one thousand dollars which I split with a friend who I brought into the case to help me, Roger Regenbogen, Esq. I had one of the biggest cases in New York for one thousand dollars.

The case[29] was prosecuted by Don Buchwald, Esq., the Deputy Chief of the Criminal Division in the United States Attorney's Office. The Judge assigned was Thomas Griesa, formerly a partner at Davis, Polk and Wardwell. I first encountered Judge Griesa on the third floor of the old federal courthouse, now known as the Justice Thurgood Marshall Courthouse at 40 Centre Street. We were waiting outside the courtroom. Off in the distance you could see the Judge walking toward us with his Courtroom Deputy in front of him and Law Clerks on either side. As he walked by us I said good afternoon. He kept walking and paid no attention to me. The Judge reached his robing room door first. He stopped and stood at attention, not reaching for the door, just waiting. Then his Deputy opened the door and stopped it with his back, standing at attention with his jacket firmly buttoned. The Judge then walked forward, his Law Clerks followed and then the Deputy. Roger turned to me and said: "You've just seen your first federal judge." The pomp and circumstance seemed overwhelming.

Moments later we were invited into the robing room. The Judge sat a short distance across from me with Law Clerks on either side of him and a court reporter taking it all down. The Judge never made eye contact with me. He turned to the prosecutor and inquired as to what the case was all about. I had filed motions and indicated the state court proceedings should be explained to the jurors. The Judge finally looked at me, sternly saying: "If you can't try this case, we'll get someone who can." It was like a knife through my heart, but I replied: "I'll try the case." The Judge then said: "that's all, you're dismissed." This was not a warm and friendly place. Federal courts are terrifying enough, but then Judges like this make it even more frightening. Of course, it discourages people from having access to the federal courts because so many federal judges intimidate people instead of welcoming them. Griesa's disdain for me, an outsider with an Italian last name, was palpable. For me, I viewed him as a mean, pompous, elitist snob. If he had redeeming qualities I could not determine what they might be.

I had no money, no experience, no mentor except for Roger, a hostile judge, an experienced prosecutor, a big case, a Haitian client with white victims, a Manhattan jury and a client who understood little of what I had to say. Eric was six feet, six inches. His arms were the size of tree trunks. He wore a Star of David and a cross. He made no sense and his English was extremely poor. He had no concept of why he was in federal court. The evidence clearly showed that seemingly without any doubt, he had committed the underlying acts of rape and sodomy. He had beaten his state case on a technicality. I was walking into a mine field without any armor. The case was a dead-in-the-water loser, but I was in Manhattan and trying a big case. I had to believe in fate and to a certain extent my father's prayers and my own positive thinking. It was ironic. This is what I wanted to do, but I was stuck in the suburbs, removed from where the real action was, the center of the universe, the City. Like my ancestors, I thought New York City was giving me a shot, my first opportunity. It was coming to me not in the suburbs, but in federal court in Manhattan where the Brahmans of the Bar made their home, where the wealthiest and best-educated lawyers practiced. I was not one of them. I was an outsider but I was suddenly in their world, clashing with the great institutions and attorneys in New York. They were legends, I was nobody except something told me I deserved to be there. My father had his obvious trepidations but he encouraged me to go forward. He was so New York. He knew that representing the underdog was never easy but aside from being born into fame and fortune, there were other ways to make it to the top. You had to realize those opportunities and not be afraid to take on the large institutions and the members of the upper class. It was a gamble but life and law can be about taking chances. My father's models were the Jewish lawyers from Manhattan, the scrappers who rose to the top as trial lawyers, organizers and labor leaders. He also admired the Irish politicians of New York like Paul O'Dwyer who identified with the poor and middle class. Like the Italians, they had been discriminated against but made their way against all odds. I had no choice that was the path that I had to follow or be condemned to a life of mediocrity.

My father was never one to dwell on discrimination. He was well aware of its existence but he was eager for a fight even against impossible odds. In a sense he knew that he was not alone, the spirits of all those underdogs who had advocated before him, were there. You could not feel alone with that force of history beside you. Also, when no one and I do mean no one expects you to win and you do, the victory is always sweeter. That is one of the real pleasures in representing the underdog or being one yourself. The establishment may win ninety percent of the time but then there is always that ten percent chance of a miracle. To take on the Michael case I had to take a big risk but believe in miracles.

Walking into Griesa's courtroom was an intimidating experience. I did not know at which table to sit. The Judge had already precluded me from saying anything about what had happened in the state courts. He was going to allow the prosecutor to bring out the gruesome details of the rapes and sodomies. I figured that once a jury heard that, it would be all over.

In federal court, the Judge picks the jury and Griesa did that very quickly. I do not remember Griesa entertaining any challenges. Our jury was all white. Our ship was quickly going down. I did not want to speak to Eric during the trial because he had nothing to offer and I was afraid that he might act up and seal his own fate. I kept Roger between us. I kept Eric way off to one side of our table so that jurors would not feel his presence. Eric was still incarcerated so a U.S. Marshall sat near him.

Don Buchwald gave his opening statement. There were few spectators in the courtroom. My father was there, having walked over from his office in lower Manhattan. He spent more time with me than he did on his job. Also present were Naomi Rice Buchwald, then the head of the Civil Division of the United States Attorney's Office and later a brilliant federal Magistrate and a United States District Court Judge in the Southern District of New York where she still sits.

Don made no mistakes, but I have an internal sensory system that tells me when adversaries have really hurt my case. It is like chills up and down my spine, the kind I get when I happen to hear a terrific Frank Sinatra song. It tells me how persuasive and powerful my opponent is. I did not get the chills after Don spoke. Now it was my turn.

Just prior to trial Don offered us an unprecedented agreement. It was the first one of its kind and it was approved by the Department of Justice just as they had approved this second prosecution of Eric. In federal court, Judges are never involved in plea negotiations the way they are in state court. By this agreement the Judge would be asked to take a plea of guilty and Eric would be given a sentence of less then what he got in state court, possibly as little as time served. Of course, once pleading guilty, he would be deported. The agreement was rejected by Eric.

As I nervously stepped to the podium, I wished that I did not have any notes with me but I could not do without them. With Roger's help I had written out my whole opening statement. If I had been interrupted by Don or the Judge, I do not know what I would have done because I scripted everything. I had practiced reading it over at least five times so that I would have as much eye contact with the jurors as possible.

I did not want to use a podium but I had to rest my papers on something. My opening lasted about twenty minutes. It was longer than Don's. While I could not refer to the state court proceedings for fear that Judge Griesa would be all over me, I had emotion and fire in my voice. The jurors were paying attention. They were not bored by my reading. Of course you never really know how these things are going, but I got through it uninterrupted.

The Government's main witnesses were the victims, the two white graduate students. All the details came out, but we tripped up the young man on one detail. The Government had to have a basis for federal jurisdiction. He claimed that he had five hundred dollars in cash for the payment of taxes in New Jersey and that Eric stole that money. That was the Government's tenuous interstate commerce connection. There was one additional hitch, he had a business in Jersey and was collecting unemployment insurance. While it was a home run for us, given the graphic details of the crime itself, it was hard to believe that it had much significance. Indeed, Judge Griesa was letting the case go to the jury no matter what. He was not agreeing to any jurisdictional or any other objections that we might have. I stayed up most of the night writing out the summation. While I was working Eric's mother called. She wanted me to stop working because her son was guilty. She did not come to the trial. I was cordial, thanked her and said good night.

We had no witnesses and did not dare to put Eric on the stand. His presence alone would scare them into a conviction or so we thought at the time. I stood for summation. The Government goes last. Again, I was petrified and had written out my entire closing argument. Once again it was filled with fire and I was later complimented by among others, Don and Naomi. They acted like true professionals. Also, assisting Don at the time was AUSA Peter Romatowski, a brilliant young prosecutor who was learning at the feet of Don, the master. A few years later he and Don would face off against each other in *U.S. v. Winans*, 484 US 19, 108 S.Ct. 316 (1987), the famous Wall Street Journal reporter allegedly selling news stories for stock tips. The case went to the Supreme Court of the United States with Don losing and Peter winning. However, Don's star has continued to rise. He is now a partner at a major firm in New York and most recently, the attorney for Ashley Dupree, the alleged prostitute at the center of the former Governor, Eliot Spitzer, fiasco.

Don gave his closing remarks. My sense of Don was that he did not have conviction in his voice and understandably so. He was carrying water for others and being a loyal soldier, but it was also his last case before going into private practice with Alan Kaufman, twice the Head of the Criminal Division in the S.D.N.Y. United States Attorney's Office, a brilliant lawyer and essentially the number two prosecutor under Bob Fiske in the most important prosecutor's office in the country.

Griesa gave his charge on the law to the jury. I was too nervous to pay much attention to it although I should have. He was clearly trying, as lawyers say, to "charge us out of the case." A judge's explanation of the law can basically make or break a case, depending on the emphasis. The jury went into deliberations. A short while later they came back with their verdict. I expected a resounding defeat. They said, "Not guilty on all counts." The courtroom was deadly silent. I was in shock. The Judge asked them three more times as if not hearing them, "Not guilty?" Each time the foreman said "Yes, not guilty." My father was beaming in the back, Naomi was serious. The Judge spoke to the jurors privately and then discharged them. At the back of the courtroom I tried to speak with them, but they just walked past me, stone faced.

Now I knew for sure what I wanted to do. I had the taste of victory. I wanted to be not just a lawyer, but a courtroom lawyer, a trial lawyer like Perry Mason, like Clarence Darrow, like Buckbinder. My father had launched my career as a trial lawyer with this one case.[30] The New York

Times wrote an Editorial about the case at its conclusion. It decried the attempted cover-up of Fraiman by the Association of the Bar and the Dual Sovereignty prosecution of Michael.

I learned during the trial from Don, who urged me to do two things. He urged me to apply for membership on the Southern District of New York's Criminal Justice Act Panel, a select panel of attorneys who represent the poor in criminal cases. The Panel was limited to just one hundred members and some of the very best lawyers in New York were on it. Don was applying and as a former Assistant United States Attorney and Deputy Chief of the Criminal Division, he easily had the inside track. But Don put in the good word for me and when I was interviewed, I too was given the red carpet treatment, possibly because of my victory in the Michael case, which was considered a miracle. I got onto the Panel and stayed on it for the next seven years, trying some of the biggest cases in New York with some of the best lawyers in the country. I was always watching, learning and improving my craft thanks to them, and my father, who got me the Michael case. This was my big break, together with the business my mother-in-law sent to me. I was making a good living, working for myself and doing what I wanted to do. I was trying one major case after another, getting better and better. I was getting my ass kicked, but I was really learning to the point where I could try any type of case; white collar, complex, fraud, securities, murder, taxes—it did not matter, I was doing them all.

Don also encouraged me to join the Federal Bar Council, an elite legal organization in New York comprised of federal practitioners. I did. My practice was on a roll. My dad was in the audience for every trial, always commiserating with the court buffs, the lawyers and the defendants. We were making a lot of friends in the New York legal community and getting to know our way around the byzantine labyrinth of New York politics and law.

My wife and I were out every weekend to the best restaurants in New York. Wendy's personal shopper was the wife of a Federal Circuit Court Judge. We were still working long hours everyday.

In 1980 Wendy's mom found a house for us in the Carle Place School District. We moved out of our tiny apartment which I continued to keep as my law office and moved into a brick home built in 1936. It had four rooms on the first floor, an unfinished attic, basement, and a garage. It sat on a seventy-five-by-one-hundred foot lot. It was in the Village of Westbury,

Carle Place School District. We paid fifty nine thousand dollars for the house. The sellers' attorney was a terrific fellow, Bob Hall. I represented myself. That was a mistake. At the closing I was off in my adjustments by two thousand dollars. Bob and the sellers were good enough to let it close. I went to my parents and borrowed two thousand dollars. I sheepishly paid it the next day. We now owned a home.

In 1981, I became involved in Westbury Village politics. I co-authored my first book with Lynn and Arthur Dobrin, entitled: Convictions: Political Prisoners, Their Stories (Maryknoll Press, N.Y., 1981). It was about international human rights. It was reviewed favorably by Amnesty International and other groups. My parents lived about one mile from us and a friend from my old neighborhood, David Resnick, an attorney and Trustee, was involved in a Village election. I wanted to help David. There was a contested election that year. My dad and I worked for Dave and the incumbent village party, the Action Party. My dad was there for every envelope I licked, every phone call I made, every door to door visit, every speech and every poster I put up.

Following the hard-fought campaign David and my new friend, the newly elected Mayor Ernest Strada, gave me my first political opportunity. They made me the Chair of the Code Review Commission for the Village. In short the Commission drafted the Village's Local Laws. I stayed in that position for another ten years. That's the way politics works—sometimes you have to seize an opportunity but most of the time you have to bide your time.

My practice was still growing but now I also got on the indigent defense panel for the Bronx where, at that time, blood was running in the streets. It was the inspiration for Tom Wolfe's famous book *The Bonfire of the Vanities*. I was trying cases there too and on Long Island. In fact, I was trying cases in every County and in both federal districts. I was a member of the prestigious Second Circuit Court of Appeals CJA Panel as well.

Once I started practicing I was taking on all sorts of cases, civil and criminal. I was on television and in the news often. I became a regular commentator on Court TV, but I had also been on Donahue, Mort Downey, Montel Williams, the Early Show with Bryant Gumbel, Lou Dobbs and every major television network. I took on popular and unpopular causes, usually winning. That led to more and more cases. I represented a little girl, Dina Cantone, who was misdiagnosed as a child as emotionally disturbed when in fact, she was profoundly deaf. That got us onto ABC's 20/20. My cases have since been on 60 Minutes. I was mentioned repeatedly by my good friend Ron Kuby on his former WABC Radio Show, Curtis & Kuby.

I successfully represented female lifeguards trying to become oceanfront guards; a woman forced to work on her Sabbath; a blind woman excluded from a movie theater because she had a seeing eye dog; a teacher-advisor to a student newspaper wrongfully terminated because she allowed stories to run that were critical of the school administration. I was chasing after slumlords and attending housing conferences in Indiana and Philadelphia. In Philadelphia, I met Dr. Kenneth Clark, the renowned psychologist from the City University of New York who assisted Thurgood Marshall in writing the first Brandeis brief in *Brown v. Board of Education*.

In 1985 our twins, Carole (named after my mother-in-law) and Louis (named after my father) were born at Columbia Presbyterian Hospital in New York City. Four years later in 1989, our daughter Francesca Eileen (named after my mother and Wendy's late grandmother) was born there. My parents were immersed in supporting the kids as all grandparents are, attending every soccer game and violin recital.

Chapter XX

To Judge

In 1991, I got another break. This time my good friend Mayor Strada came to me and asked me if I wanted to be the Village Justice. My distinguished predecessor, John L. Molloy, had been on the bench for more than forty-one years and had grown ill. The campaign was hotly contested. Our opponent tried to knock us off the ballot on an election law technicality. Nearly eighteen hundred people signed our petitions when we only needed one hundred signatures. It was a bitter fight. At first the Board of Elections knocked us off the ballot, then a Supreme Court Justice put us back on. The other side appealed and we won in the Appellate Division thanks to my former partner, Peter B. Skelos, now an Associate Justice on that same appellate bench, and Lawrence Boes, Esq., a former partner at one of the nation's most revered law firms, Fulbright & Jaworski. Larry is a friend, neighbor and we have since acted as each other's attorneys in cases in which we or members of our respective families have been involved.

The campaign for Village Justice, a part-time judicial post paying at the time just $14,000 *per annum*, was grueling. The Village of Westbury has about 15,000 people in it. Village Justice Court is a local criminal court where the judge presides over Vehicle and Traffic Law violations and alleged violations of the Village Code, usually involving Building Code cases of illegal occupancies.

My dad was with me every step of the way, going door to door and meeting the commuters at the railroad stations. The Mayor got us a storefront and my dad paid for the installation of our phone bank. My dad and mom had both retired in 1982. My father had been working everyday in my law office as a volunteer ever since.

We hit the campaign trails together, everyday. In the end we won. I was sworn in as a Village Justice in April, 1991. Since then I have published thirty-five reported cases and co-authored a book which has become the bible in New York State for all 2,300 Town, Village and District Court Judges.[31] While my decisions often address Constitutional rights, some have been extremely controversial. Westbury is a multi-ethnic community. In 2004, I wrote a 109-page opinion and one page of guidelines, the longest ever written by a Village or Town Justice in New York State.[32] I suppressed evidence in that case. In 2007, I wrote a decision[33] declaring New York State's laws on unlicensed operation of motor vehicles unconstitutional because non-citizens could not qualify for licenses.

The Community Newspapers of Long Island asked me to write a syndicated column for them which appeared in eighteen of their papers on Long Island. I wrote from a liberal perspective, but I was too liberal for them. After a year they discontinued my column and have never had that perspective since.

I had been involved in a litany of legal organizations and civic groups. One such group was the Criminal Courts Bar Association of Nassau County, started in 1953. They had become a Marching and Chowder Society but founded in 1953 with a noble purpose in mind, to preserve and protect the Constitution by standing up for defense lawyers and the individual rights of defendants and by educating the public and the profession about criminal law. When I first became involved in the group its membership had dwindled to almost nothing. They were meeting at the Island Inn's John Peel Room, but the usual attendance consisted of about ten defense lawyers. I got involved during the administration of Frank Dillon. Frank was the former head of the District Attorney's Homicide Bureau. Frank and his successor, Jack Lewis, asked me to get some speakers for the monthly meetings. I started to organize just as I had done in the past. I began to bring in one big name after another. Attendance grew and I became an Officer and eventually President. These were organizational skills which I first learned from my father by watching him.

I focused on involvement in legal organizations rather than other community-based organizations because lawyers are the true power brokers. Plus, I was spending a lot of time on the law anyway and legal organizations were a natural corollary for what I was doing with my practice. I liked being around lawyers and that seemed to be an avenue from which I could garner a platform and speak to the larger issues of social change. It was also a way to network with other lawyers and get business from them. Surprisingly though I found that the lawyers in Nassau were extremely conservative. Some defense lawyers favored the death penalty and spoke disparagingly of their clients. By this time I had been the President of the Columbian Lawyers' Association of Nassau County. I had helped to build them into one of the most popular and formidable bar associations in the State. Attendance had shot through the ceiling because of the speakers I brought in. Other bar groups were attempting to replicate that model. I was trying to do it with the Criminal Courts Bar Association, taking it from its moribund state to an exciting speakers' program. More and more members showed up for meetings and more people joined.

I had been a lifetime member of the National Association of Criminal Defense Lawyers since 1989 and a member of the New York State Association of Criminal Defense Lawyers (NYSACDL) since 1987. I would later become President of NYSACDL. I was active in the Federal Bar Council from the early 1980's, the Nassau Lawyers' Association where I would become Chairman of their Board; the Catholic Lawyers Guild; the New York State Trial Lawyers Association and the Criminal Justice Section of the New York State Bar Association, where I would later become Chair.

I invited Medical Examiners, prosecutors, defense lawyers, sentencing consultants and probation officers to speak. I did not care about their politics. What interested me was whether they had been in the news; had something to say that members might learn from and whether they could draw a crowd. I had gotten to know many of the big names in the legal profession and learned that even those you did not know would come and speak because it was their way of networking and generating more business for themselves, sometimes staying in the public eye with controversial statements. I had started a newsletter for many of these organizations so that too generated interest.

I invited Bill Kunstler to speak at the Criminal Courts Bar Association. Bill was one of the premier civil rights lawyers of the Twentieth Century, a highly controversial attorney who had represented Jerry Rubin in the Chicago Seven conspiracy trial, Jack Ruby, Martin Luther King, Jr., and many others. He was a brilliant lawyer and a spellbinding orator. After I had invited him, the President and Past Presidents of the Association cancelled his speech for political reasons.[34] That produced a major controversy and debate within the Association but it also stirred up a crazy, bi polar judge who was not taking his medication, B. Marc Mogil. He began to send me anonymous, threatening communications. He was a County Court Judge who was presiding over felony cases.

I filed a complaint against him with the Judicial Conduct Commission and others. After years of litigation, trials and appeals he was removed from the Bench and disbarred. I and others have written elsewhere about this episode.[35] By then Bill Kunstler had spoken to the Criminal Courts Bar Association and had received the Outstanding Practitioner Award from the New York State Association of Criminal Defense Lawyers, both of which I engineered during my Presidencies of those groups. Bill died on Labor Day, 1995. Over 5,000 people attended his funeral service at St. John the Divine Cathedral in Manhattan. I was there with my father and my son. I wrote an obituary column about Bill for the Community Newspapers of Long Island. It read in part:

WILLIAM KUNSTLER WAS A FRIEND

By: Thomas F. Liotti

William Kunstler was a friend of mine. I knew him well. I regret to say that I am no Bill Kunstler. But then again, no one is. If Clarence Darrow was the most noted lawyer from the first part of this century, then Bill was perhaps the most outstanding lawyer at this end of it. He was larger than life. A first class gentleman, a scholar and vibrant person with an indomitable courage that allowed him to survive innumerable controversies and cases. He was the conscience of a nation, of the world. He represented not just the outcasts and the underdogs. Kunstler took on nations. During the civil rights era he represented Dr. King. He challenged segregation and racism. He risked his life day after day for over 40 years. Kunstler had not just enemies, he had assassins in search of him. The KKK had a perpetual bounty on his head. Those accused of crime from judges to alleged Mafioso wanted him as their lawyer. He was not one in a million, he was one of a kind.

231

He was a man of great love and compassion. He truly did love his clients and empathized with them. Money was not important. The case was. The client was. He understood that he was more than just a vehicle of social change. He was history and change itself. When he died on Sept. 4. 1995, a part of this nation died. He was a national resource, a veritable icon. He challenged us to be better, to stand taller, to open our society, to be democratic and just. He believed in equality. He lived for his cases, his clients. He was larger than life. He was an alternate on the 1936 Olympic Swimming Team and served as an officer in the armed services.

I once introduced him and before doing so did a search of his reported cases. There were over 400 of them. He argued before the Supreme Court of the United States, twice successfully on issues involving freedom of expression. He was against bureaucracy, big government and ethnocentrism. He believed the people of the world were one. He specialized in turning institutions on their heads. Just when we thought we had it figured out, Bill would present another side of the story. Larry Davis, Jack Ruby, John Gotti, The Chicago Seven, Wounded Knee, Attica, Shabazz and the Black Rage defense of Colin Ferguson were among the clients and issues he championed. There were many, many others. He wrote poetry, books and legal articles. He appeared in movies and on television. He once said the measure of each of us is not the wealth and power we achieve but how we treat each other, one on one. Most of us, he said, will not be remembered a hundred years from now, so let us at least love each other. Two years ago, Bill received the Outstanding Practitioner Award from the New York State Association of Criminal Defense Lawyers. At that time he said his life was about challenging authority. He was independent. He stood alongside of people when no one else would. Now that he is gone, who will pick up the cudgels of dissent? A great leader in law and life is dead. It is an insult to his great memory to state the obvious, that he will live on in our hearts and souls. Of course he will. He will stand alongside of his clients for all of history.

Mogil was disbarred in 1998. After seven years he was permitted to file for readmission. His most recent application for readmission was denied in 2008 with a rebuke from the Appellate Division stating that he is "unfit for the practice of law." This should have precluded him from ever being re-admitted. The fight against Mogil was a difficult one where members of the judiciary retaliated against me to protect their own. Lawyers in my firm jumped ship and I suffered financial losses that nearly ruined me. Few thought that I could prevail against a sitting judge and most thought that they could easily destroy me, that I would never have the metal or courage to stay the course. But I did. I had some close friends who saw me through it but most importantly, my parents were with me for every single proceeding everyday on trial, during hearings and even when legal arguments were heard before the Judicial Conduct Commission and in the New York Court of Appeals, the State's highest court. In 1997 I received the Martin Luther King, Jr. Award from Nassau County and its Human Rights Commission based upon (they said), "over 30 years of extraordinary service as an attorney, judge, and community activist." I gave a speech which was not the standard fare for the occasion. It was rabble-rousing. Charles Brennan, a former Associate in my law firm, a veteran politician, attorney and with a Ph.D. in philosophy said that it was "the best speech [he] had ever heard." I received a standing ovation after asking the audience to join hands and say that if given the opportunity now, that they would take a bullet for Dr. King. The County League of Women Voters printed the speech in its entirety in their monthly newsletter.

The Town of Huntington had a huge ethical problem in the mid 1990s where a local car dealer had hired a politically-connected lawyer who then allegedly used his influence with the Town to win a favorable zoning ruling for his client. The Town Board was mixed between Democrats and Republicans. The Democrats wanted a prosecution of the lawyer, the client and all those connected to the lawyer including Town attorneys and members of the Planning Board and Board of Zoning and Appeals. It was a very delicate matter. The Supervisor at the time was a registered Republican. The Republicans on the Town Board reluctantly agreed to an in-house investigation and report by a non-partisan, outside counsel. The Town had about 230,000 people in it. I was chosen as the Special Counsel and Fact Finder, promising to act quickly.

Within 30 days I interviewed more than twenty witnesses on tape and then issued a one hundred-page report exonerating everyone. Several of those I investigated became judges. I recommended changes in the Town's Code of Ethics and they were adopted by the Town Board. I am sure that there were those who wanted heads to roll and people to be prosecuted but the objective evidence did not support making a referral to any prosecuting agency.

I had already served on my County Bar Association's Professional Ethics Committee but in 1997, Hon. Charles P. Sifton, Chief Judge of the United States District Court for the Eastern District of New York, appointed me to the "Panel of Attorneys who are members of the Bar of this Court to advise and assist the Committee on Grievances of the Board of Judges in connection with the discipline of attorneys pursuant to Rule 1.5(a) of the General Rules of the United States District Court for the Eastern District of New York."

Since I started practicing, I have published more than thirty five judicial opinions; over one hundred twenty five legal articles, Op-Ed pieces and other articles, five books, and I have more than four hundred reported cases which bear my name. This has always been my way of extending my reform message and generating more business. It is also what I really like to do. People have to know what you have done and what you are doing. An attorney who waits for his phone to ring will keep waiting. I never waited. Judges, courts and adversaries know when I am in a case. Having a big-name lawyer in the case generally helps the client—jurors pay attention, prosecutors give better plea bargains, adversaries are more conciliatory, insurance carriers pay more in settlement, and Judges give more favorable rulings. Being in the public eye as much as I have been helps the client. If the client has a small case and wants it to be a bigger one, I can do that. If publicity will help the case, I can generate it. After more than thirty-three years of handling tough, and at times, impossible cases, I can think outside of the box. I have been through so much that any fear that I might have is not just subdued, but usually is non-existent. I do what is best for the client—legally, morally, and ethically. But after I comply with the rules, anything goes. I am not hurtful or mean-spirited, but I will meet arrogance not with arrogance, but with the power of what is right. I have some adversaries with whom I will never again speak. If lawyers are nice to me, they will find me to be a perfect gentleman and accommodating in every way. But if they or a Judge are rude, nasty, unpleasant or mean spirited, then I may become their very worst nightmare. I do not pick fights but I will expose dishonesty and corruption in the system. When others pick fights with me, they will generally come to regret it.

One federal prosecutor claimed that my client was a mobster because his name ended in a vowel. She got my attention. I told her that she would come to regret her comments. She laughed until three weeks before trial when I put her in the hospital with a nervous breakdown. The Government had to try the case with a substitute prosecutor. My client was fully acquitted following a jury trial after his co-defendant pled guilty right before trial and went to jail for three years.

The Wyandanch Union Free School District in Suffolk County may be the poorest in New York State. It is all minorities and mostly African Americans. Due to its many problems it is constantly searching for new leaders, superintendents and principals to solve them. In 1997 they fired a good friend as their General Counsel and hired me. I was a white guy succeeding my friend, an African American. I did not like the fact that they were firing an African American, but I was honored to serve and I did for two and a half years. This is just a part-time position. When I came into office, there were at least one hundred fifty litigation files; another twenty tuition reimbursement cases and numerous other open files. I resolved all of them. School Board meetings which were often held once per week sometimes lasted from about 6 p.m. until sometimes 4 a.m. the next morning.

In June, 2000 I was appointed by Democrats and Republicans of the Town of North Hempstead to serve on a Councilmanic Commission. Our goal was to determine whether the Town Board should be expanded from four to six Council districts. As soon as I came onto the Commission I told them that we needed to expand the Commission to include more women (we had only one) and minorities. They did so. I was in the minority as a Republican, but I issued a report which recommended that we have six Council seats. That was submitted to the voters in a referendum which they overwhelmingly approved. But even better, I knew that if we had six districts, one would go to a minority population, and that is exactly what happened. There was an election held and a wonderful Democrat, Robert Troiano, was elected. Bob is part African American. My mission was accomplished. Out of the six seats, the Republicans did get one seat that they can call their own, so it is a bipartisan Town Board. I also became good friends with a conservative-turned-independent, Mike Camardie, an unsung hero.

In 1993 my father was diagnosed with severe coronary heart disease. He had not yet had a heart attack. He was seventy-seven and in a high risk category for open heart surgery. My father looked to me to investigate and to decide what should be done. He had tears in his eyes as he contemplated his choices and mortality. His cardiologist at Columbia Presbyterian Hospital in New York City would not make a recommendation, but merely gave us options. He recommended Dr. Eric Rose, the premier cardiac surgeon in the world, Bill Clinton's surgeon, and I have seen his name over the years acting as the surgeon for numerous celebrities. Dr. Rose was great. To help me make up my mind and help my dad make his decision, he took me through the whole process with models and films. He answered all of my questions, and gave me plenty of time. If successful, it was projected that it would give my father another five years of life. Not only did he survive the surgery, but it gave him nearly fifteen years of extra life. Of course, in later years, we explored additional heart surgery and he was turned down for that as too much of a risk. His doctors, Dr. DeLeon and Dr. Mark Adler were instrumental in keeping him alive by pharmacological means.

My father had three or four minor heart attacks prior to his death in April, 2008, at the age of 91. Somewhere around 2000 my mother was diagnosed with Alzheimer's disease. Her condition back then was not so noticeable. My parents still lived in their own home although they were having difficulty keeping it up. It was paid off and they were retired for eighteen years at that point. My father was still driving a 1987 Volvo, his pride and joy. They did not have a dog of their own but loved our dog, Duke, a black Labrador Retriever with an English head.

By 2002, it was obvious that they were having huge problems taking care of themselves. Without intruding into their lives or their privacy, I began to speak with them and my wife about options. We decided that they would sell their home and that we would use the proceeds from it to help us renovate and enlarge our home so that they could move in with us. The renovations lasted six months. The roof was taken off of our home and two stories were added. Our furniture and other belongings were kept in a giant trailer on our front lawn. Our kids had to sleep at Wendy's mother's home. Wendy and I slept in our dining room. One night during a rain storm, a hole broke through the temporary ceiling and water came gushing in. We called our contractor and he came to the rescue, but there were many tense moments like that.

We closed on their home in February, 2003 and they moved in with us into the small apartment that we built for them. They had the run of our home but never used it, except for the kitchen. We hired a live-in housekeeper to clean up and look after them five days a week.

My mom continued to deteriorate. On any question that tested her memory, she deferred to my dad: "Oh, I don't remember—Lou?" After each meal she would wash the dishes by hand, although we had a dishwasher. We asked her not to and showed her how to use the dishwasher. But, those with Alzheimer's often perform by rote. My mom may have thought that she was in her own home doing exactly what she had done for years—lovingly performing her duties as a homemaker by carefully and almost ceremoniously washing the dishes. In all the time I was growing up I never once saw a dirty cup, glass, plate or piece of cutlery in the sink. My father was a stickler for that and so was she.

My father would drive himself to church each morning, but the quality of his and my mother's lives were rapidly going downhill. Local police reported that my dad was driving the wrong way on a street. Finally, he had an accident with the car, causing irreparable damage to it. He and my mother both survived, and luckily no one was hurt. I called a client in the auto repair business and he took the car away. He got rid of it for us. He said my father had irreparably damaged the undercarriage, but frankly, probably got rid of the car because we could not convince my father to stop driving. It was his last vestige of independence. It was terrifying to watch him pull away from the curb each day. For a long time after that my father complained that the Mafia stole his car.

My father became increasingly negative and depressed. While my mother was taking some anti-depressant medication, my father refused to take anything or even to discuss it with a competent psychiatrist. He had been vibrant and was now just a shell of himself. Following his heart surgery, he had some strokes and additional surgery on his carotid artery. He suffered from dementia. He was angry about the turn his life had taken, my mother's condition, and the fact that more than anything else, he had lost his independence. That led to a sense of hopelessness, despair, and depression, the inevitability of death. He was taking up to sixteen pills a day under protest. When he took them, he was taking them for my mother—to be her protector, to watch out for her. When he had difficulty swallowing he was advised to take them with apple sauce. As of November 22, 2007, they were married for sixty six years.

My father had no teeth, and always had problems with his dentures, but now he was eating less and less. He was losing weight and once told me that he was going to starve himself to death. He was bitter about his situation, angry about how his money was being spent, but unwilling or unable to make decisions and appropriately take charge of his affairs. Many years before I had introduced my parents to two young female lawyers, Franchina & Giordano. They specialize in Elder Law, and were tenants of mine, and at onetime, clients. But I wanted them to draft my parents Last Wills and Testaments, health care proxies, living wills, and powers of attorney. Few elderly people take these precautions or do an appropriate inventory of their assets. Fortunately, we had done most of that and I had my parents' power of attorney. I never tried to find out what was in their wills. That was their prerogative. I kept my distance from what I considered to be the privacy of their decision making. They wanted me to have everything and to draft all of their papers and to be their lawyer. That could have easily been done, but as a lawyer I felt that there was a real conflict of interest, being I was an only child. I was their son. I would help them but they should still have the more objective hands of somewhat dispassionate lawyers helping them. Emily Franchina and Mary Giordano were also my lawyers, drafting wills for both my wife and myself.

After four and one half years of living with us, my parents had taken a turn for the worse. They were starting to fall with more frequency. My mother could not help my father get up and she was falling herself. They refused to use walkers. We had live-in help five days a week and a visiting nurse on weekends. We tried to make sure one of us was always around the house. They began leaving the stove gas on, thus, we did not want them cooking. My mother had gone from forgetfulness and asking my father to fill in the gaps of conversations to not recognizing who anyone was. She also started to wander, once leaving my father in a department store and aimlessly going for a stroll until she fell and the police found her. We confiscated car keys and locked doors. She had difficulty turning the simplest of locks, but if my father was in the hospital, she wanted to go to him. She would have no idea how to get there and if left to wander, there is no telling where she might have wound up.

We had to keep doors locked so that she would not just get up and start wandering in the middle of the night. Once, when my father was in the hospital, she attempted to get into their car and drive it, even though she had not driven in at least ten years. She would say that she wanted to go see my father. She did not know who the President of the United States was and intermittently thought that I was her husband. Her short term memory loss went first, followed by the deterioration of long-term memory loss.

My parents were in and out of hospitals and rehabs. Once my mother broke her knee cap in a fall. After speaking with Mary Giordano and my parents' physicians, we decided that we would have to move them to assisted living after they were discharged from Winthrop University Hospital. In 2006, my mother was taken to the hospital for dehydration. My father was often taken to the hospital for pains in his chest. He had become increasingly dependent upon nitroglycerine which, he carried on him at all times, secretly popping up to four tabs of it a day.

My father was always feisty. He would pull out intravenous leads in the hospital and fight with aides until they would either calm him down or subdue him. I tried never to argue with him. He would insult me, his doctors and everyone else. Sometimes he would be so verbally assaultive and belligerent that the hospital would put him in a hallway chair that had a hospital tray in front so that he could not get out of the chair. This was my father's bottom, his worst moment, when I felt most sorry for him. There he was, in his chair, restrained and fiddling with his hospital robe with nothing to say, quiet from his medication and the emotional strains that had sapped his strength. He did not have a glass to drink from, a newspaper to read or a television to watch. He was embarrassed and beaten, unable to even carry on a conversation with me. His anger and frustration were subdued by medication and restraints. The memory of that still haunts me.

Chapter XXI

<u>The Adoption Secret</u>

In August, 2007 he was at home and in one of his nasty moods. Later he would claim that the devil was in him when he acted like this. He still had most of his mental faculties but he would often lapse into anger, depression, and bitterness. In a way I could not blame him. His quality of life was close to zero. All he could do was watch television. When he got too upset, I would usually stop an argument or discussion before it escalated but this one day he said something he had never said before: "You're not my son." At the time he was upset, so I did not dwell on it. I also thought that he was just using it as a figure of speech to say that I was somehow not treating him right. I was sixty years of age at the time.

Later that August and early September, my father was once again admitted to the hospital and so was my mother. They were both in the hospital at the same time. We had decided that they should not return home to our house but should make arrangements to go directly into an assisted living facility. We moved them in September, 2007 by ambulette to Amber Court in Westbury, a facility which was recommended to us by Mary Giordano, Esq.

My parents had their own room and bathroom there. A Medical Doctor is in attendance daily, and staff to insure that residents are given assistance in getting dressed, taking their medication and getting to all meals. Over time we had to hire full-time aides, seven days a week. I would visit every Tuesday and Sunday, always bringing flowers and coffee. My wife and kids would also visit. It was costing in the neighborhood of fifteen thousand dollars a month for both of them. My parents' savings were dwindling. They were still being taken to the hospital on emergency visits—my father with chest pains, my mother from falls, low blood pressure, and, on

240

two occasions, being unable to open her eyes. She had been incontinent for sometime and wore diapers but now she was beginning to lose all voluntary functions. She had forgotten how to stand, walk, wave, hold a cup, use utensils and chew. She had no hearing loss, but if I said "Mom," she would not look in my direction. She mumbled but had no discernible speech. Even the words "yes" and "no" were gone. She was left to fidget, propped up in a chair each day. Her whole life was determined by aides and where they pushed her in her wheelchair. There was no cognition and she slept for longer and longer periods, up to sixteen hours a day.

On December 17, 2007, my thirtieth wedding anniversary, I spoke to my dad and asked if he remembered our earlier conversation in August. He said he did. I asked him if it was true, that I was not his son. He said it was. He told me that I was adopted right after my birth. I would have been a ward of the state. The legal papers were under seal in the Surrogate's Court in Nassau County. He knew little about my natural parents, except he thought my mother's last name was Smith. He said that she was married and had at least one child, a son. She had lived in Garden City with her husband and son. She was a nurse. He knew less about my natural father. He said only my aunt knew. My aunt told me that she thought that my natural father was an attorney in Manhattan. In 1947, all the big law firms were located in downtown New York.

My father told me this as my mother sat nearby, not grasping any aspect of the conversation. I asked him why he had not told me sooner and he replied, "We thought that you would deny us." He broke down in tears as he said it.

In later visits with him, I told him how grateful I was for all he had done for me and that I loved him and my mother, that they were the only parents I knew, needed or wanted. He asked me how I was doing. I told him fine, though the revelation was unsettling. Thereafter, he called me his son every chance he had. He was proud of me. I published a book in early 2008 and inscribed a copy for him. See Thomas F. Liotti, <u>Judge Mojo: The True Story of One Attorney's Fight against Judicial Terrorism</u> published through iUniverse. He showed it to his fellow residents. He was only able to read the first eighty pages of it but kept looking at the cover, with my name—his name—on it.

On March 22, 2008, we celebrated my father's 91st birthday by bringing two large cakes to Amber Court for everyone to enjoy. My son Louis came home from college to celebrate and my daughter Carole was there with

Wendy. It was a happy occasion. A few days later he was admitted to the hospital. I went to see him on a Sunday. I was on trial in Manhattan and staying at a hotel there, but came home for the weekend. It was my last visit. He was sitting up in a chair, unable to eat or drink. He could listen but barely speak. His kidneys were failing. I put my hand on his shoulder. We never hugged or kissed. The most we had ever done was shake hands. I could tell that he could feel my touch, receiving it with warmth and comfort, perhaps recognizing that it would be our last. He was bent over, in a drugged stupor. We could have sat there and cried, but it would serve no purpose and probably distract us, or at least me, from the deeper meaning of life and death at hand. All was well there. The message that I sought to convey is a reaffirmance of his faith that we would meet again in the afterlife, that we would be together with Mom. I needed to convey that Mom was okay, that she would always be taken care of and that he had provided well for us. Then he needed to know that I would be okay and Wendy and our children. I had said all of this to him in the months before his death.

I took my hand away from his shoulder. I said nothing. In the face of death, nothing can be said that has not already been conveyed. I turned around and walked out, tears were welling up in me but I shook them off, searching for a higher meaning, then and now. I could feel that he was listening to my walk as I left his side for the last time.

I was back in the city on trial in federal court before Judge Robert Sweet, a courteous gentleman of the highest order. I had these personal issues, but my father would have told me to take care of my clients, that was my first responsibility as a professional.

That Wednesday I was having dinner in the hotel's fancy restaurant with clients and co-counsel. I told them that I was expecting word at any time that my dad had died. Sure enough I returned to my room after dinner at 8 p.m. and received a call from Wendy. My father had passed away a short time earlier. She was with him when he died. They had had some rocky times together but in the end, Wendy was there for his final exit.

A few days later, I gave his eulogy at St. Brigid's Church, where he had served as an usher for so many years.

EULOGY OF LOUIS J. LIOTTI

BY THOMAS F. LIOTTI APRIL 7, 2008

Good morning. Not having much experience in delivering eulogies, I turned to my children and wife for advice. My daughter, Francesca, had received an impressive high school assignment to write her own eulogy placing within it what she believed others would say about her. My father was never analytical that way about his own life or any meaning to be derived from it. That formidable task has been left to me in these few words. So I am in search of the big picture—we always are—of the deepest meaning of life and death. We look to see whether we can examine the life of someone and then resolve whether they have given us answers to age old existential questions, imponderables, questions to which we have traditionally not had answers. What we seek is a resolution not merely as to how we can live better lives and inspire others to do likewise, but we seek a permanent connection to those who appear to have left our physical presence. Thus, many of us, particularly the faithful, reject the finality of death and believe that the spirit, human energy moves on to a connecting point in eternity. My father was someone who believed in his faith and eternal life, but humbly questioned his own worthiness before God. God was the only entity that could humble my father, no human was ever capable of that. Louis Joseph Liotti lived on this planet earth for 91 years and 11 days, from March 22, 1917 to April 2, 2008. He was a proud member of what Tom Brokaw has referred to as the "Greatest Generation," through 16 Presidents, the Great Depression, two World Wars, the Korean and Viet Nam conflicts, 9/11, Afghanistan and Iraq. He was, in Billy Joel's words, in a perpetual "New York State of Mind," feisty, scrappy and at times brutally candid in expressing his always independent views and lifestyle.

His background gives meaning to his existence and verification that it will carry on. It is a physical impossibility and I say this with a belief in the scientific certainty of it, for so much energy to suddenly subside or disappear. My father in so many words would tell you that death is an event in a grand continuum, that it does not exist, *per se*, that we will be reunited and that in the interim we should exude our energy, live our dreams, love our lives, each other and most importantly inspire others and help them to fulfill their dreams. To be or not to be is not the question. That has already been answered. My father's message is to live your life with verve, to be larger than life. In 1948, Claude Bristol published the *Magic of Believing*. It showed through scientific examples that by meditation, focus and prayer that energy is created that not only helps to accomplish your goals, but can literally change your life and the world. My father believed that.

From his days growing up in New York County where his father Tom had a barbershop on 9th Avenue, and where he later lived in Bayside, he learned to fight in the Golden Gloves and play sandlot baseball with the Queens Alliance and tried out for the New York Giants and Brooklyn Dodgers. He could field anything, always get a hit and like the great Jackie Robinson, liked the excitement of stealing home. His best plays in sports and life were to accomplish the unexpected, to ignite the dream each day.

I still remember a visit to Ebbetts Field meeting Emmet Kelly, the renowned clown; Gil Hodges; "Pee Wee" Reese; "the Duke" Snider and Roy Campanella in their locker room. They all knew my father. My father believed that to be great you should be around greatness, to see it, to feel it. I remember sitting on the bench during a little league game one day just daydreaming when my dad came over to say "watch those guys, watch what they do, you'll learn from them." So I watched and tried to replicate the best hitters, pitchers and ball players. I have incorporated that lesson into my life, trying to emulate and surpass the great trial lawyers, judges and statesmen. My father would tell you that anything is possible, pursue your dreams, stand up for your views, your independence. Have no fear, you are the equal of anyone. I can remember one day being in the street, confronted by some older stickball players who wanted to take me to task with bats. My father came out of the house and inquired of the young men whether they wished to fight. They said "yes." They were older and bigger. I was about 11. My father said: "O.K. he'll fight you, one at a time. Put down your bats and who is first." They left without a fight. My father had no tolerance for bullies or anyone who abused their power or authority. Public figures, servants, elected officials, lawyers and judges have but one mission and that is to help others. It is never about ego, self-aggrandizement and the acquisition of wealth for their own ends. It is about using yourself as a force of social change and improvement. My father admired Fiorello LaGuardia; Franklin Delano Roosevelt; John F. Kennedy; Robert Kennedy and Martin Luther King, Jr. because they all believed in equality, justice and being all that you can.

My father was a union guy, rising to the level of President of the CWA in the 1940's, during the bare knuckle days of that movement. He favored the underdog, the common man, the middle class and minorities. He admired the courage of his own father who held a straight edge razor to the throat of a member of the Black Hand, to avoid being shaken down for protection money.

My father spoke fluent Italian, studied the violin and opera in his youth. He attended Stuyvesant High School, one of the three exclusive, special admission schools in New York City. He was a combat infantryman in the U.S. Army, a corporal, participating in the allied invasion of France. His life being spared in those battles, he became a daily communicant, saying his rosary at least once a day. His answer to hardship and conflict was to pray to St. Jude. Again, it was his magic of believing. He would pray, light candles everyday and often his dreams, our dreams, would become reality.

Every step of the way he supported me. He showed me self-discipline and encouragement in whatever my goals were. I lived to fulfill his expectations but he would never tell me what they were. My dreams had to be my own. Through every campaign and court case or judicial decision, or books or articles, he was always at my side, never asking for anything in return except the satisfaction which he received from our hard work. When I did road work late at night, he would be behind me in a car; he would spot me when I was lifting weights; he would hold the stopwatch during my workouts; drive me to meets and practices. It was because of him that I became a County, State and Eastern Interscholastic Champion and later an NCAA All American, NAIA Champion and Olympic Trials participant. The lesson I learned was hard work equals achievement in sports and life. My father laid a foundation, one brick at a time, President of the Central Nassau Athletic Association and Chairman of Troop 459. It took me to full scholarships at Ohio State University and Adelphi, a training camp in North Jersey for four summers that produced three Olympians and four world records. He sacrificed for me and his grandchildren so that each generation would get better. I am his legacy. My children are also a part of that legacy. They will dedicate themselves to life as I have. They will make a commitment to their children as he did for me, and Wendy and I have for them.

Certainly the development of the internet and the exploration of space have shown us that human potential knows no bounds. In 67 years of marriage and during the 60+ years of my life he never stopped believing that excellence should be pursued and that those who err or weaken in life should be forgiven. They should be given a second chance or the opportunity to work their way back into society. There are exceptions but my dad focused on the good in people.

My father was a pacifist. He did not believe in war except when it is inevitable as in the case of Afghanistan and Al Quaida. Yet, he respected all three current Presidential candidates for their views on that subject. Politics and current events were an abiding interest with my father. His father had been a District Leader in Tammany Hall. We spoke about politics at the dinner table and while my father believed in self-direction, he implied that each of us have a responsibility, a duty to lead and to pursue interests if not careers, in the public sector. He was both a Democratic and Republican Committeeman, each in an effort to help me to pursue politics as a career, to be a true public servant.

In the final analysis where does this take us in answering those imponderable questions? He believed that it takes us to a resolution. What we create during our lifetimes lives on, goes forward in all of its beauty and wonderment, in each of us, in our offspring and in all of us as we launch into new destinies and horizons, not new beginnings but a part of the grand continuum to which our energy, synergy and faith have brought us. My father is speaking to you now through me and he says to each of you to never give up, believe in yourself and your potential. He will see you later when the time is right and the force of your energy is ready to move on.

A few days later *Newsday*, by Ann Givens, and the *Westbury Times*, by Victoria Caruso published my father's obituary. I thank them both for their kindness.

Louis Liotti, 91, Was A Fighter In Every Sense

By Ann Givens

When a group of older boys approached Louis Liotti's son wielding baseball bats nearly 50 years ago, Liotti didn't run to the rescue. Instead, he told the young thugs that if they insisted on fighting, they would have to fight fair. "He'll fight you," Liotti's son, Thomas, recalls him saying. Put down your bats, and who is first?" The boys walked away. Louis Liotti never backed down from a fight, from his early days in the amateur boxing ring, to the beaches of Normandy, to his days as a negotiator for the Communications Workers of America. On April 2, the Westbury resident lost a decade long battle with a heart condition, dying at Winthrop-University Hospital in Mineola at age 91.

He was, in Billy Joel's words, in a perpetual New York state of mind, feisty, scrappy and at times brutally candid in expressing his always independent views and lifestyle," Thomas F. Liotti said in his father's eulogy.

Louis Liotti was born in Manhattan in 1917, the son of Italian immigrants. While he was young, his family moved to Bayside, where Louis played sandlot baseball and was in the minor leagues, Thomas F. Liotti said. He tried out for the Brooklyn Dodgers and the New York Giants.

Louis Liotti attended Stuyvesant High School and graduated from Flushing High School. In the late 1930s, a chance meeting with a beautiful young girl on a bus in Bellerose lead to a 67-year marriage to Eileen Lambe, Thomas F. Liotti said.

Soon after he got married, Liotti was sent to fight in World War II, landing in Normandy and fighting throughout Europe.

Lou in France (1945).

After coming home, he worked for AT&T. He organized and became president of the Communications Workers of

248

America, the Office Workers Local in Manhattan. Those were the early days of the labor movement, Thomas F. Liotti said, and negotiations were not for the faint of heart. Both sides often came to the table with thugs standing behind them ready to inflict physical punishment. But Louis Liotti did not back down, and he usually came away with a fair contract for his members, Thomas F. Liotti said.

Louis Liotti, who was an active member of St. Brigid's Church of Westbury, always dreamed of bringing his love for the fight to the courtroom and often read legal books in his spare time. But he never became a lawyer and instead worked hard to support the legal career of his son, who is now an attorney and the Village Justice in Westbury.

"When I first started trying cases in New York federal court, he would always be there watching, helping me to pick juries and working in my office," Thomas F. Liotti said. "He never left my side and was the best friend I ever had."

In addition to his son Thomas and his wife, Eileen, Liotti is survived by his brother, Mario, Hollywood, Fla., and three grandchildren. See Ann Givens, *Louis Liotti, 91, Was A Fighter In Every Sense*, April 17, 2008, Newsday @ A38.

At the end of July, my mother was taken to Winthrop University Hospital with low blood pressure and a lack of responsiveness to stimuli. We had seen this before, when she could not open her eyes. After a few days she was stabilized and finally moved to the Sands Point Nursing Home on the prestigious Gold Coast. The facility is pristine but is the end of the road for patients like my mother. She had a beautiful room which she never left during the month that she remained there.

She was tended to and kept alive. Her younger sister Carol and her daughter Geralyn Volpe came for a visit, but my mother could barely open her eyes and had no apparent cognition. She was moving out of God's waiting room. A once-beautiful, kind, and generous woman with a most amiable personality was relegated to this state. She was on oxygen, still eating somewhat and getting her medication. She might have continued in this state for years but there was no hope of her ever coming back mentally. I stood next to her and touched her hand. I told her that I loved her. I saw a faint smile, but then it was gone.

It came to me that as her son, I had to decide what she would want. She had told me years ago and so did my father. I signed a DNR (do not resuscitate) form. That meant that she would be kept comfortable, but no more. She was kept on oxygen but was taken off her medication. I waited day after day, calling the nursing home every day and visiting to learn of her status. She was lingering, but was not in pain.

The following is an article which I wrote that was published in the *Daily News*[36] two days prior to my mother's demise:

Letting The Elderly Just Waste Away Denigrates All Of Us

By: Thomas F. Liotti

"On July 14, 2008 I gave a D.N.R. (Do Not Resuscitate) order to my mother's nursing home. They will "keep her comfortable" until "the Lord decides it is time." The Lord may take his time but the experts tell me that he usually decides within three weeks.

My mother has Alzheimer's. She is almost eighty eight and in the advanced stages where she has forgotten how to walk and eat. She no longer recognizes me, her son. She cannot say anything coherently, not even a single word. She is unable to wave hello or goodbye. She has not even smiled in a long time. She is heavily medicated and sleeps most of the time.

My father died in April of this year at the age of ninety one. He had coronary heart disease for many years but did not die from that. Instead, he lost the will to live and starved himself to death.

The costs for maintaining my parents in assisted living prior to my father's death and my mother's entry into a nursing home were running about fifteen thousand dollars a month with one on one care for my mother, twenty four hours a day.

As we advance in age, there are critical issues that we must confront. These have to do with both the short and long term issues of healthcare, but also with the maintenance of a productive quality of life, free of pain, anxiety and depression.

Visiting most assisted living and nursing home facilities presents a scene of patient/residents in various stages of malaise and vegetative states. Drugs may keep them alive for years but few, even with large doses of antidepressant medication, will say that they are happy or that they enjoy their existence. They move about in walkers and wheelchairs often pushed by aides with little formal training and who are, in many cases, illegally in this country. They are good, caring people but their job is to maintain life so that they and their facility will be paid.

I have just given my mother a death sentence. I do not like having to make that decision. I hope that my children will not have to do the same thing for me or if they do, that they will make the right decision.

It is time for us to focus, not merely on health care issues. We must look at health care and quality of life issues. While today we have focused on prolonging life, this by itself does not permit people to enjoy their lives or make them into productive members of society instead of being a drain on it. The elderly are an untapped resource which, if harnessed instead of just waiting to die, may make our nation great again. The challenge for the future is to give them health care and a quality of life that will enable them to continue as productive members of society. I would like to hear Presidential candidates discuss these issues. They need to start by visiting assisted living and nursing home facilities to see for themselves the full nature of this problem. Rhetoric alone will not solve the problem.

Instead of spending more than a trillion dollars on a war we should be putting money into education and research on geriatric care. In the context of medical coverage for all Americans, Presidential candidates should be focusing on how we can meet the extraordinary cost of medical care for the aged. Just as Franklin Delano Roosevelt provided for the enactment of the Social Security Administration, Presidential candidates should be addressing the establishment of an agency or department of the federal government that would provide for long term health care needs for those in need of it."

———————

Aside from the usual reservations that all offspring have in similar circumstances, I had additional layers of conflict to reconcile. Aside from the fiduciary duty that applies to life-and-death decisions and deciding that someone will die sooner rather than later, there were other issues. I do not believe in the death penalty or euthanasia for animals, so exercising the power was anathema to me.

In addition, my father asked me to take care of my mother after he was gone. I promised that I would. Although he was gone, I had a duty to follow his wishes as if he were there. I did not go and see her everyday. I did not sit by her side for hours. That would have served no purpose except to make me more sad.

I also had other issues as an adoptive son—was I exercising my power out of love? Did I harbor anger toward my natural parents, which I might be subconsciously transferring to my adoptive parents? Was I angry for not being told sooner of my adoption? I could not honestly reconcile those feelings, so my decision to sign the DNR form became pragmatic.

After my mother died on August 12, 2008, I was called by the nursing home. "Did I want to see her or spend a few moments with her?" I did not. It would be too painful and she had already gone. If you believe in the spiritual, then her spirit left her body even before her death. As I did with my father who had died four months earlier, I kept the coffin closed with her picture displayed on top. That is how I wanted to remember them. I had to do this because the image of their withered, tortured bodies in their final days is seared in my brain. Those scars could only be made worse if I had consented to open caskets. Why show people the cruel fate that may await them. I chose not to look at their bodies in death, at all. Instead, I put tasteful pictures taken at least ten years before their demise on each of their caskets. Both pictures sit on the credenza in my office. I look at them as they were and as I want to remember them.

I delivered my mother's eulogy at St. Brigids.

EULOGY OF EILEEN F. LIOTTI
(AUGUST 8, 1920-AUGUST 12, 2008)
DELIVERED BY HER SON, THOMAS F. LIOTTI
ON AUGUST 16, 2008

My mother, Eileen F. Liotti, of Scotch-Irish descent, was a beauty, a model in the 1940s. But the outer beauty of a person as we all know, does not reveal much of the person's character. Like the picture of Dorian Gray, beauty may be only skin deep. My mother's inner beauty was even more impressive than what you could see on the outside.

From Mom's portfolio when she was a model in the early 1940's.

My mother was born in 1920. She started her life in Bellerose, where her father owned a bar on Braddock Avenue. The family had a summer home in the Rockaways. All that they had was lost in the Great Depression. My mother, her parents and her younger sister, Carol, were forced to move to a cold water, walk-up flat in Ridgewood, Queens. My mother dropped out of school to work so that her sister could finish.

My mother met my father when she was sixteen and they married five years later in 1941. My father was an Army infantryman, a Corporal in the Second World War. My mother miscarried several times during their marriage and was diagnosed with epilepsy. Yet, her physical frailties still did not reveal the strength of her character. That was shown throughout her life in so many ways. Her true legacy must be the love that she gave to my father and to me.

Like the Blessed Mother, the best symbol of the role of mothers, my mother was special. No matter what the personal achievement, she never sought the limelight, credit or acclaim. She was content to provide unmitigated love and support, albeit always being reserved and in the background, attending all my games, taking me to practices, helping me through the rough spots of college, graduate school, law school, studying for the Bar exam, running for office and providing guidance to me as an attorney, Judge, husband and father. She taught me to read and to swim. She taught me manners, to be polite and to be a gentleman. I could not ask for more. These were important values which she gave to me and which I have endeavored to pass along to my children.

As you may know, my father passed away on April 2, 2008 and I am once again before you sharing a few thoughts on a life worth remembering. Most lives are for the lessons which all of us learn from them. Usually the hard part is to derive meaning from someone else's life. In my mother's case that has been an easy task. The great Greek philosophers, Socrates, Plato and Aristotle encouraged us to examine life's meaning. That is what we do in each eulogy; attempt to answer some of life's questions while raising still more that are then left to the metaphysics of the ages.

I thank all of you for being here with me. You have given me great comfort and the warmth of your friendship and love is felt. So I feel that you are a part of me and that I must cherish this moment and the closeness that I feel for you with some extraordinary facts which I only recently learned and which show the remarkable character of my mother and my father. I plan to publish a book about this, which I have been working on for several months entitled, *Assisted Living*[1]. It is about my upbringing and how I was assisted by these two remarkable people and how my wife, my children and I assisted them at the end of their lives. They lived with us in our home for four and one-half years and then moved into assisted living for 10 months and finally, into a nursing home for a month.

But it will also be about a startling fact that I learned in my sixty—first year, near my parents' end. By last summer my mother had advanced into the final stages of Alzheimer's. She and my father left our home and entered an assisted living facility. As my mother deteriorated, barely recognizing those around her, my father told me that I was adopted by them. I learned that on December 17, 2007, my thirtieth wedding anniversary. It was unsettling. I learned that but for these two extraordinary people that I would have been a ward of the State. These two people, my parents, devoted their entire lives to me, a stranger, not of their blood, but from others as yet still not known to me. So that to me shows the strength of my mother's and father's character. My own character has been strengthened by this revelation. I do not feel rejected by my natural parents as I am told some adopted children do. Rather, I am grateful for witnessing the love that these two people had for each other and for me. My father knew that my mother, like many women

---

[1] Originally I had planned to entitle this book: *Assisted Living: A Ward Of The State*

of her era, needed a child to care for and nurture and brilliantly found a way to adopt me, their only child.

My father explained to me just prior to his death that this secret was kept from me because they thought that "[I] might deny them." Of course that would never be the case due to the strength of character which they gave to me. They turned a negative life experience into a positive one and that is what we must all do. Their legacy is that they did not retreat. Now that I have reflected, I too will not retreat. I dare not turn this moment into a political statement, yet many of us have watched a loved one succumb to a horrible disease. Unfortunately, in the face of that we have prioritized placing a man on the moon by 1969 or conducting wars instead of scientific research and finding cures for these dreaded diseases. In last Sunday's edition of the *Daily News*, I remarked in an Op-Ed article that I was recently compelled to give my mother a death sentence by signing a "Do Not Resuscitate" (DNR) order. Just as President Franklin Delano Roosevelt established the Social Security Administration, so too our Presidential candidates and the Congress should address the need for an agency or department to provide for the long term health care needs of the aged. Why should people who have devoted their lives to making our lives better be left with nothing at the end of the road, wasting away, awaiting death? I have hope that we must do far better. Life in the hereafter may be idyllic but while we wait to discover that determination, let's make life worth living for the aged today.

My mother is gone now, never being told of my father's death or that he told me of my adoption. It is better that way. She goes to her resting place perhaps being uncertain of my love for her, for them. But the strength of my character instilled in me by my mother and father, allows me to say it now, even if unheard: "Mom and Dad, I love you. Thank you for all that you have done to make my life into a good one and to give me your legacy of character."

A few days later, her obituary appeared in *Newsday* and the *Westbury Times*. Zachary Dowdy and Victoria Caruso wrote those pieces and once again, I am forever grateful.

Liotti, 88, Aided Family In Depression

By: Zachary Dowdy

A child of the Depression, Bellerose native Eileen Liotti attended Jamaica High School until the hard economic times forced her to drop out and go to work so that her younger sister might graduate.

It was one of the many sacrifices she made for her family over nearly nine decades of life, during which she married a war veteran, modeled in the high-fashion districts of New York City, became a homemaker and raised a son.

Liotti, of Westbury, died Aug. 12 of Alzheimer's disease. She was 88. "She was a wonderful woman and, like a lot of people from her generation, she worked hard and the most important thing in her life was her family—my father and me," said Thomas F. Liotti, a Garden City attorney and Westbury Village Justice. "She devoted herself to the community and to us."

Born Eileen Lambe in 1920, Liotti and her family enjoyed a home in Bellerose and a summer home in the Rockaways. But the nation's economic low point destroyed the Lambes' restaurant and bar business.

The Lambes moved into a walk-up in Ridgewood, a five-room, railroad-style apartment with a potbelly stove in the kitchen, Thomas F. Liotti said.

Frank Lambe, Eileen Liotti's father, developed Parkinson's disease and could no longer work, forcing the family to scramble to make ends meet.

Liotti's mother, Anna, went to work in a dress pattern factory and Liotti became a secretary, then a clerk and, during and after World War II, she worked as a model in New York City.

At 16, she met Louis J. Liotti, a man who would become an Army infantryman and corporal and fight in World War II. The couple married in 1941 and were together for 67 years until his death last April.

The couple moved to Westbury in 1951, after moving out of a Levitt home in the Salisbury section of East Meadow. Liotti would become a life-long member of the Mercy League of Long Island and was a former member of the Ladies Auxiliary of the Maria Dell'Assunta Society of Westbury, a charitable organization.

For 20 years, she worked for the Nassau County Clerk's office, retiring in 1982.

"She was a lifelong inspiration to me, encouraging me in everything that I have done from teaching me how to swim at the Carmen Avenue pool in Salisbury to becoming an attorney and judge," Thomas F. Liotti said. "She was a powerhouse of support, a beautiful, dignified and elegant woman with exceptional style and grace." Besides her son, Eileen Liotti is survived by a daughter-in-law, Wendy Liotti of Westbury; a sister, Carol Melzig of Bethpage; and three grandchildren.

She was buried Aug. 15 at the Cemetery of the Holy Rood in Westbury.

Donations may be sent to the Alzheimer's Foundation of America or St. Brigid's Church through St. Brigid's Parish Outreach at 75 Post Ave., Westbury, NY 11590. See Zachary R. Dowdy, E. Liotti, 88, Aided Family in Depression, Newsday, August 22, 2008 at A40 and The Westbury Times, Obituaries, August 21, 2008 at 36.

Chapter XXII

<u>The Search</u>

After being told at age 60 that I am adopted, my thoughts turned to whether I should bother to unravel this mystery. I had simultaneous feelings of bewilderment at my sudden loss of a base, a sense of betrayal at not being told and isolation or alienation. But it also awakened a curiosity about myself, my own limits and potential. It gave me an identity with other orphans, wards of the state, outcasts, bastards and others left with no more than swaddling clothes for their heritage.

But what was my heritage in this life or others? I was starting at ground zero. Friends told me, what difference does it make, you are who you are, you have your own identity? That is fortifying, a badge of courage and honor. Where others have had the reinforcement of blood kin, role models, successful siblings to emulate, I had only myself. I did not have a compass or other navigational tools to take me back to my past.

After reading a book given to me by my daughter Francesca on reincarnation therapy, I became more curious about previous lives as an alternative. I was not necessarily a believer, but felt that there was more to this life than meets the eye. There is far too much in the way of ancient beliefs and the science of astrology to entirely discount parapsychology, the supernatural and reincarnation. It gave me hope whereas the other side of the coin was saying when you are dead, you are dead or there is a heaven, a hell and purgatory. On the later, you either passed life's SAT exam or you did not.

The meaning of life or what is known, stands in contrast to the meaning of death, which is unknown. We have set up a reward system for ourselves where the good that we accomplish in this life will give us entrance into the next. Somewhere out there the great book of your life and all others is kept, or, is it?

After my adoptive parents, Louis and Eileen, passed away, I was lost. Gripped by my own bereavement, angry at not being told sooner, yet I was glad that I had not been. My search for a connection to the past was enlivened by my own and my childrens' actual or potential health issues. This, by itself, seemed to be justification for exhuming the past of those who might prefer that it be forgotten. But for them and for me, it could never be. There is a gaping hole in the past which may never be filled.

I arrived an hour early for my appointment scheduled for Sunday, July 19, 2009 at 12:15 p.m. I waited in my car, down the street, reading The New York Times, but having difficulty focusing on the articles, thinking of the unexpected experience that I would soon encounter, how my life has been radically altered by these developments. Uncertainties and self-doubt were comforted by my resolve in deliberately trying to uncover the past. I did not have anxiety but felt relief over the fact that I would pursue the search, somewhat prepared to accept wherever it may lead.

I told a friend at my beach club part of the story and she told me of a "channeler," a former Apostolic Priest who purportedly takes you back in your life and past lives. She asked if my mind was open to it. He communicates with the other side, with the dead. Tom Trotta from Glen Cove, Long Island, does not describe this as a gift. Instead, he refers to himself as "a vehicle." The only information that he had about me beforehand was my date of birth.

I was led into a room in his immaculate suburban home where he cared for his elderly parents. Tom is a trim man perhaps fifty to fifty-five years of age, with jet black hair, thinning slightly at the rear. He was tanned with evidence of red, recent sunning on his face. He wore a blue short sleeved shirt, white shorts and white socks pulled up just below the mid-calf. He had no shoes and looked very comfortable.

In the room which I recall as windowless and painted white, I was told to sit on one side of a coffee table. In front of me on the table I saw an old time tape recorder for the large, blank, sixty minute cassette tape that I was told to bring with me and a small pile of very detailed, printed astrological charts. On one side of the room which was approximately ten by ten feet, I saw bookshelves with titles that I could not read. On the floor was a statue, two to two and one half feet in height of the Blessed Mother. On the other side of the table facing me was Tom's chair and behind him

I saw a few religious artifacts such as some crosses and religious pictures of saints. None of this was distracting or intimidating. It blended in with the surroundings and what lay ahead of me.

Tom closed the door and left the room for a few minutes, telling me to get my tape ready. I was told to bring photos with me. They lay on the floor, face down.

He told me not to volunteer information, not to respond until he spoke to me or pointed his finger at me. He turned sideways in his chair. He looked at the birth dates of my children and my wife on his charts. His head was turned away from me. I could see his profile. His eyes were squinting. His eyelids were flickering. He started saying names and letters asking who they were. I complied wherever I could. After thirty minutes he said: "What is the first question you want answered today?" I only had one question. Who are my biological parents? He said my mother was a young girl. "She met an older man in Little Italy. She did not look like the other people there. He saw the name Kelly around her. At first he thought that my father might be a restaurant owner or Maitre d'. He is dead. My mother is still alive. He could have been a judge, a lawyer or politician. They had an affair. It was a scandal within my family. She was told by him that she had to give me up for adoption or he would ruin her life. His name may have been William L. _."

My adoptive father Louis was speaking to him. He is in heaven. He told me Louis did not tell me the whole story. He lied. He is keeping the secret. He will not give it up. There was a meeting with Cardinal Hayes in 1946 about the adoption. My adoptive mother had two miscarriages during the War.

We spent some time talking about my family and I left it to him to decide whether we should meet again. He said he would have to pray over it.

He asked me what I thought of his room. I told him that he was very sincere and credible. It was a powerful place where something very mystical was occurring. I was living the DaVinci Code. I was in the catacombs, below the Vatican where Popes are buried, unearthing the very secrets of life, possibly eternal life or simply just communicating with the great beyond.

I told Tom at the end of the meeting that I had my doubts as to whether there was an actual adoption. I told him that I felt that there may not be any papers on file. He agreed.

Chapter XXIII

Ethnic Pride

For minorities who have felt the wrath of discrimination themselves or who have ancestors who were the victims of it, ethnic pride is often a justifiable response to prejudice. Each ethnic group advertises the successes of its members while they strive to take better positions in the hierarchy of the "melting pot." My adoptive parents raised me to respect all minorities and to have some resistance to authority. I have referred to it as an uneasy, symbiotic relationship with the establishment. My mother Eileen was of Scotch-Irish descent. Her father, Francis Lambe, was born in Glasgow, Scotland in circa 1880 and her mother, Anna Lambe, nee Burke, traced her ancestry to Dublin, Ireland, although she was born here in circa 1896. I do not know their exact dates of birth.

Certainly I was reminded of the hard lives that the Irish had in assimilating into this country. They were able, through politics and because they were English speaking, to acquire a foothold in the New York City Police and Fire Departments. The Italians had a much more difficult time. They had darker skin tones and did not speak the language, but they were artisans, willing to work with their hands in construction. After all, they built the Roman Empire, Florence and Venice. Many who came to this country were from Calabria and southern Italy. They looked for advantages here that they did not have at home. Most were poor. A few unfortunately gravitated to organized crime, but most were hardworking and content to make their living the old fashioned way, by working hard and earning it.

My mother endured all forms of discrimination even within her own family. One Irish relative remarking that my father was the only "guinea" he ever liked. My mother would wince at the word. It was unspeakable in our household as was any other ethnic slur. My father was willing to start a fight with anyone saying it or if he suspected that they were even thinking it. My mother was a vocal proponent of Italians. She had not an ounce of prejudice within her, neither did her father. My father admired both his father and her's.

When Lee Iacocca, the former Chairman of the Board of Chrysler Corporation championed the redevelopment of Ellis Island, establishing it as a historic landmark in 1986, my parents made sure that both of my grandfathers were enshrined in the Ellis Island Wall of Immigrants. When I first ran for political office I became a member of the Irish American Society and the Ancient Order of Hibernians. I also joined the Sons of Italy in America and later other ethnic groups including the Columbian Lawyers' Association of Nassau County, Inc. where I eventually became their President and received their Distinguished Service Award. In the early days of my legal career, my father came to every legal meeting with me. He talked me up to Sal Spano, the Executive Director of the Association who got me started in the organization by making me an Officer in it. In 1993, I became a member of Tiro A Segno, the oldest ethnic club in the United States, Founded in 1880 and still located in three side by side townhouses at 77 MacDougal Street in Manhattan's Greenwich Village. My father paid my initiation fee there. He supported me in everything I ever did. He was a model of what a good parent should be. He placed my mother first and she placed me first.

My mother could not have children, perhaps because of her medical condition of Epilepsy. But my father was smitten with love to the core of his being, ever protective of my mother, loyal to her in every way.

Chapter XXIV

<u>At Least One Sibling</u>

In a decision by Surrogate Judge Riordan on December 14, 2009, I learned that my natural mother had another child at the time of my birth. I do not know if I have a half brother or sister. If alive, they would be older. I am trying to determine what an encounter with them would be like, the awkwardness of it. I am also trying to imagine what they might be like, how they were raised, what their life experience has been. My gut tells me that I probably do not want to know much about them; that it is unlikely that they could overcome that. I might resent what they may know which I now seek to learn, my identity. Who am I? Where did I come from? What could they tell me about a mother, no a woman, who gave me up at birth, who deserted me? When she did that, did she think that she was giving me a better life or a worse one? What could cause a woman to give up a child that has grown inside of her, to whom she has given birth? Was I simply a burden or were there circumstances that required it? Would she have aborted me if it were legal at the time? Did she give some thought to an illegal abortion or one out of the state or country? What would my life have been if I had been raised by my biological parents? I am grateful for all that I had. I do not imagine that I would have been raised on Park Avenue or gone to the best private schools had I been raised by my biological parents. Would I have been raised as an aristocrat, a member of New York social elite? I doubt it if the superintendent of my parents apartment building in Brooklyn knew of my pregnant mother's plight. Somehow I do not think that my biological parents were close, personal friends with the Rockefellers or Brook Astor.

While I raise these questions about my mother, I have even more concern about my father. My mother did not do this by herself. I cannot blame her alone for the circumstances that gave rise to my birth and adoption. She perhaps recognized her own limits in not being able to care for me. But my father, now that is another story. What responsibility, if any, did he assume? Did he stand tall with honor and dignity by supporting my mother or did he abandon her as many men do, leaving my mother to fend for herself. Did he even know she was pregnant? Did she tell him? Was she able to tell him? Did she know who he was? What did she know about him?

In the final analysis, I would blame my father if it is determined that he mistreated or abandoned the woman who gave birth to me, not for his neglect of me alone. After all, what was I but a life, just a blob of flesh and bones, unable to speak or even walk. The burden that I presented was greater than the joy I might bring. So I was not aborted. I had life. I would be a ward of the state, left in an orphanage or rescued by others who needed the joy I might bring, who would assume the responsibility for me, a stranger. They did not know my fate either, but they agreed to help to determine it.

Chapter XXV

A Lawyer's Work

Being a lawyer I must sometimes remind myself that there are legal processes that we lawyers use to solve problems. My father had told me that the adoption occurred in Nassau County. I met with a friend in Surrogate's Court who explained the process. The Surrogate himself, one of the finest gentleman on the face of this planet, Hon. John Riordan, wrote to me, providing me with two cases that gave me the legal basis for the application. Any application to unseal the adoption records had to be based upon good cause, which I interpreted to mean a medical necessity. I prepared a medical affidavit for my physician to sign. I embellished somewhat. It read:

MEDICAL
AFFIDAVIT CERTIFICATION

STATE OF NEW YORK)

)ss:

COUNTY OF NASSAU)

BRUCE K. LOWELL, M.D., specializing in Internal and Geriatric medicine, with offices at 1000 Northern Blvd., Great Neck, New York, deposes and says under the penalty of perjury:

Thomas F. Liotti, d.o.b. 5/29/47, has been under my care as a patient for several years.

In or about 2005, Mr. Liotti was diagnosed with the onset of cardiac abnormalities which may have a genetic disposition. These abnormalities are known as hypertensive heart disease and high blood pressure. In addition, Mr. Liotti suffers from a condition known as atrial fibrillation or a type of abnormal muscular contraction in which the constituent muscle fibers do not act together as a unit but as separate uncoordinated groups. The term is applied chiefly to describe such an abnormal action of the muscle of the heart, where the situation is further complicated by the special nature of the nerve impulses involved. The resulting beat of the heart is very irregular and unsatisfactory. Atrial fibrillation is due to an abnormal spread of the contraction impulse through the tissue of the atrium. The atrium is one of two receiving chambers by which the blood enters the heart. The contraction impulse is a wave of excitation which, if spread normally, causes the heart to contract rhythmically. In atrial fibrillation, the rhythmical contractions of the atria are replaced by irregular twitching. Mr. Liotti's condition is extremely volatile and precarious, requiring close monitoring. In order to thwart a life threatening situation, Mr. Liotti has been prescribed Hyzaar, an angiotensin II receptor blocker and thiazide diuretic which he takes daily for his high blood pressure. Mr. Liotti is also prescribed Coumadin, 5 mg. daily, an anticoagulent used to treat or prevent harmful blood clots that may occur.

It is my understanding that Mr. Liotti learned on December 17, 2007 that he is adopted and that his file is under seal in the Surrogate's Court in Nassau County. Without access to that file, Mr. Liotti will not be able to learn the identity of his natural parents and their medical and personal histories.

Mr. Liotti's natural son, Louis J. Liotti, born May 25, 1985 is also my patient and recently graduated from Northeastern University. He has signed a professional hockey contract with the American Hockey League's San Jose Sharks.

I am concerned that Louis, a high performance athlete, could have his professional hockey career jeopardized by virtue of the medical and genetic history of his father.

Recently, during"Rookie Hockey Camp"for the San Jose Sharks, Louis was medically tested. Concerns were raised because his heart rate was inappropriately elevated and additional concerns involved suspicions regarding a medical condition known as hypertrophic cardiomyopathy. While it is my understanding that that has been ruled out as a diagnosis for Louis by the San Jose Sharks, nonetheless as their physician I must continue to investigate the causes of any medical abnormalities in Thomas or Louis.

The genetic or medical treatment plan for them as well as Tom's other two children, Carole, born May 25, 1985 and Francesca, born April 30, 1989, may have to do with the ruling in or out of certain diagnoses which are part of the medical, personal and genetic histories of Tom's natural parents. For example, hypertrophic cardiomyopathy is inherited as an autosomal dominant trait and is attributed to mutations in one of a number of genes that encode for one of the sarcoma proteins.

Treatment for such conditions may involve gene therapy, drug treatment with, among other things, beta-blockers. Treatment may also include defibrilator therapy or other surgery.

It is my medical opinion, to a reasonable degree of medical certainty, that information regarding the identities of Tom's natural parents is essential to performing an accurate diagnosis for Tom and his children and to prevent sudden cardiac death or other serious injury by designing an appropriate treatment plan for them.

BRUCE K. LOWELL, M.D.

Al Petraglia's report brought me only slightly closer to the truth. Al is a dear friend who was appointed by Judge Riordan as a Law Guardian in the case. Now I knew the ages of my biological parents when I was born. My mother was 35 and my father was 42, suggesting to me that each had their own families separate from their production of me. I was an inconvenience to them. Looking back on it now and trying to put my own life in perspective and remembering all the times that I had sex just for the fun of it, I resent their irresponsibility, abandonment and neglect of me, not for the sex that they had with each other, but for that I would not exist. What I do object to is their failure to be accountable or take responsibility for me after my birth. How many fathers and mothers put their offspring up for adoption or into orphanages not because of financial reasons, but in order to save themselves from public or private embarrassment or from any of the responsibilities that come in raising a child. Had I known of this earlier in life I may have put my own sexual behavior in check by, for example, either abstaining or using condoms, both of which I never did. Acting on impulse alone may be fun but it is also the height of irresponsibility not toward the partner with whom you are having sex because they too also acted on impulse, but to the child that may be brought into the world by their liaison.

In my chauvinistic brain, I have given little thought to the dilemmas which my natural mother may have faced. But I am compelled to consider the fact that she may have been raped, a real and possibly, unreported fact in that era. My anger soars when I think of the man who might have done that to her. Indeed, he deserved to be beaten and tortured, to teach him a lesson, to give him and men like him a wake up call. I would like to give him that beating. I would be relentless. I can see me throwing body punches at him now. Just the thought of it gives me satisfaction. Then, I must look in the mirror at myself. Until now, I was never taught that lesson. I never raped a woman but I have certainly been irresponsible in my sexual encounters. This is no doubt one of the great disparities of our times, of the ages, of our civilization—women bearing responsibility and some men walking away from theirs'. It is an outrage, a sadness which we must endure as a people in recognizing all the children who were not properly nurtured by their natural parents from birth, who were not loved by them or have their self-esteem built from the ground up.

I was one of the lucky ones, having adoptive parents who loved and cared for me with their all. But what of those who never had that? It makes me think that that is the obvious reason why our moral or ethical teachings tell us that pre-marital sex is wrong. That is not the problem. The problem is in not being responsible for the consequences of your actions after having had sex. If the only consequence is a good time for both partners, then fine. There are thresholds of consequences that often ensue thereafter including an emotional response which may elevate into a more profound psychological consequence. For the male it may be little more than another notch on his sexual gun belt, but for the woman it can be and often is, much more. These may be relatively minor consequences of the sexual encounter if a child or children are the by-product of the union. The birth of a child takes it to a much higher level, one that cannot be simply ignored or from which any man should be allowed to blithely walk away.

What are the consequences, if any, that society, our courts, legislatures and judges should impose in the event of adoption. Financial consequences may be considered given the financial circumstances of the natural parents, but if they are too severe then we may be unwittingly encouraging abortions to occur with greater frequency. We should ask ourselves why there should not be an ongoing relationship between natural parents and adoptive parents. Is that any worse than the current state of affairs of confusion on the part of adopted children. A consequence of adoption should be the full disclosure of all pertinent information to the court overseeing that adoption and the realization that the information can be made available to the offspring at a later time.

Biological parents today should provide pedigree and background information but also DNA and blood samples should be a condition of adoption.[37] The disclosure of medical and birth records as well as medical histories should be made. These should be updated periodically so that adopted children will know of what diseases they may be more susceptible. HIV, drug, I.Q. and other psychological testing should also be part of the adoption process.

The current adoption process is outmoded and antiquated. It does not take advantage of modern science and is mired in a byzantine bureaucracy that can no longer be justified. Myths and taboos should be re-evaluated given the social dynamics in which we live. Adopted children today should not be victimized by biological parents who may wish to hide their past. The mysteries surrounding adoptions should be removed in favor of an open society, one where we share our problems and joys. Giving up a child for adoption may be a sad event for biological parents, but it is a joyful one for adoptive parents.

The stigma of being a bastard, a child born out of wedlock, an adopted child, should be put to rest. It cannot be if adoptions are shrouded in secrecy.

Chapter XXVI

Discoveries

The search for my identity, my origins is misleading and inhibiting. The unknown presents more promise. I am not building on someone else's foundation or living off of a legacy. A recent article in the Sunday Magazine Section of The New York Times presents the bewildering fact that psychological therapy may teach a great deal about analysis but less about your own condition.[38] A recent book by David Remnick, *The Bridge, The Life And Rise Of Barack Obama* (Alfred A. Knopf, New York, 2010) at 242, provides some insight into the President's search for his own identity as the product of two highly intelligent parents, one white (his mother) and one black (his father). He knew little about his father and had almost no interaction with him. His father died in Africa as a broken man, an alcoholic. Remnick writes:

> "As a well-read student who is coming of age in the era of multiculturalism and critical theory, Obama is keenly aware of the academic notions that identity is, in some measure, a social construction. Race is a fact, a matter of genetics and physical attributes, but it is also a matter of social and self-conception. A commanding theme of the book (referring to Obama's first book) is a young man's realization that he has a say in all of this; that he is not merely a "product" of family history; he has to make sense of his circumstances and his inheritances, and then decide what he wants to make of it all and who he wants to be. Identity and race are matters over which he has some influence."

Unlike President Obama, with whom I identify, I do not have the benefit of knowing much of anything about my biological mother and father. It is here that I have hit a brick wall but where I differ from President Obama in that his search for identity is both internal and external. Internally he must figure out who he is. Externally he must look to life experiences, genetics and his father's rejection or neglect, but he still has a basis upon which he may proceed. It is not a complete vacuum.

My ability to collect and analyze similar information externally and therefore internally, is limited, if not a vacuum. That is a significant difference that adopted children without information about their biological parents must face. For many it is an insurmountable task.

In some respects I am mired in all the inhibitors, warnings and cautionary instructions that children receive from their biological parents when they are breaking away and trying to establish their own unique identities. I then have the additional protective shield that my adoptive parents placed over me as their only child. While these factors have placed limits on me, the lack of inhibitors from biological parents and the fact that my adoptive parents helped me to be self-determinative and to set my own course, has been liberating. In retrospect it has not added to my ego or my grandiosity but rather added to my role as a confident leader who is prepared to exist, survive, discover and excel on my own terms.

The abandonment that I in some respects feel is less important than the personal tragedies of others who have had far less of a compass upon which to govern their own lives. I have been lucky and I am lucky still. None of us should ever feel alone. We are all in this together whether we are living or whether we are dead. Like the great explorers who ventured into unchartered waters and lands, I am going into the unchartered waters and lands of the inner self, the mind and body. Many surprises no doubt await me. I am rejuvenated by the exciting discoveries that await me.

I cannot say enough praise for the compassion, understanding, wisdom and care that Surrogate John Riordan; his esteemable Chief Clerk Michael Ryan, Esq.; Guardian Ad Litem Albert Petraglia and the investigator and former homicide Detective Tom Allen showed during the course of these events. I will never be able to thank them enough for their efforts.

My biological mother was 35 when she had me. She reportedly was unmarried and had no other children as of the time of my birth. Her name was Anne Ferguson and she added the additional name of Smith. I was born in Doctors Hospital in Brooklyn on May 29, 1947. I do not know the whereabouts of those records. Apparently the first name given to me at birth, if in fact I had one at all, was Donald Ferguson Smith. My mother lived in Brooklyn until 1977 and then moved to Port Washington, Long Island, not far from where I was raised. She lived there until 1997 when she moved to Cleveland and died there in 2000. We have her Social Security number and the addresses of where she lived, but we have been unable to find a picture of her or an obituary. I do not know why she moved to Cleveland or if I have any brothers or sisters.

There is scant information about my biological father whose name was indicated as John Smith, probably fictitious in whole or in part. He was allegedly 42 at the time of my birth and my mother indicated that he was from England. This too may be fictitious. I have little else to go on, not even pictures of them. I thought of securing a DNA test but have not yet done so. I doubt that I will. After speaking with my friend, co-author and DNA scientist, Dr. Larry Koblinsky, I do not see this as a tool that will aid in my search.

I am seemingly at the end of my search, bewildered by not having more information available and doubtful that I will ever learn more. This lacuna is then added to the cache of essentially meaningless facts provided by my biological mother apparently without consideration for how more details might influence my physical or mental well being. For example, was the reason that I was offered for adoption economic; was it because she did not want to rear a child or thought of herself as inept as a mother or otherwise incapable of caring for me perhaps due to the onset of a dreaded disease or disability or was she shielding herself or my biological father from embarrassment or did she so detest him and his abandonment of me that I too painfully reminded her of him.

I was not officially adopted until November 13, 1951 when I acquired the name of Thomas Francis Liotti, named after my adoptive grandfathers. Thomas F. Liotti and Francis Lambe. With this knowledge I will continue my search for my inner self and stay strong so that I may help others to do likewise.

To me it seems that as a society we have misinterpreted the need to protect biological and adoptive parents from disclosure of important facts to adopted children. The timing of full disclosure, the impact of it on those involved deserves much more study by developmental and other psychologists. Society should then decide whether disclosure and the extent of it should be decided as a matter of law or whether it should be left to the discretion of adoptive and biological parents. Arbitrary and capricious abuses of discretion can be guarded against by more research, studies, counseling and advice from behavioral scientists. This is too important a subject to be left to the whims of well intentioned amateurs alone and clearly, adoptive children who have been heretofore unheard, deserve a say in determining their own heritage and destiny.

Chapter XXVII

<u>Epilogue</u>

So now I have the unresolved issues with which to concern myself. I have a wife and three children so first, as a responsible person, no matter how unsettling or shattering these revelations have been, I have to be strong for them, for my office staff, and for those who will watch my actions in dealing with their own crises. I say that in a complimentary way not as if I have to prove my fortitude to anyone. I say it because the strength and thoughtfulness which I demonstrate may help others through their own turmoil.

A very dear friend who is an attorney, married with children and a few years younger than I, learned of his own adoption years ago. It has been a catastrophic revelation for him. He is having severe problems and in having relationships even with his children. One graduated from a prominent University and my friend could not bring himself to attend the graduation ceremonies. He has become reclusive, a chain smoker, and a diabetic, resulting in the loss of body parts due to the condition not being treated. He was in a nursing home and rehabilitation center. He recently retained an investigator to search for his natural parents. For adoptive children the saga never ends due to prevalent non-disclosure.

I have some curiosity about my natural parents, but I am torn there also—in wanting to know more. I might be let down in my expectations once learning of them. I cannot pass judgment on them because I know not what problems caused them to put me up for adoption. Certainly an out-of-wedlock child in that era would have marked them as pariahs. I was very lucky to find two people who loved and cared for me better than my natural parents did.

Oddly, although I might have been aborted, my views on a woman's right to decide these issues remains unchanged. Thankfully, my natural mother, perhaps because she had no choice about it or felt that she had none, decided to give me life. I can only imagine what that decision must have meant to her throughout her life, whether she was tortured by it or somehow found a way to reconcile her feelings. She may have been tormented by her feelings that she had made a mistake or acted out of lust or love. And what about that not just from her standpoint, but from my natural father's? Did he have any regrets or was he simply relieved by the adoption and content to move on, unfettered by this little disturbance in his life? What legacy did they give to me? Was I simply an unwanted pregnancy, a bastard, to be discarded and rejected at birth? Even if I learn about them or if I had the opportunity to have met them before their death, these questions can never be answered. If that is so, why ask them in the first place, even in my own mind? It is as Plato remarked in 400 B.C., "to know that I do not know." That is a positive step. It provides a peaceful unification with my natural and adoptive parents, adoptive children and all others, alive or dead, who have contemplated such questions. On some levels we are all one and we come from the same stock. For me, just being a part of the human race has made me proud. But each of us make our own way, establish our own unique identities. We can have support and assisted living along the way, but after thousands of years of the human existence, the gene pool in each of us is not limited to our natural parents or confined by those who raised us. Not knowing who may be responsible for what, takes away an anchor, but it can also set you free. It has done that for me.

I plan to make further inquiries and to do DNA testing, but I also view this time in my life almost as a rebirth. There is a freedom that I feel, separated from the genetic constraints that all of us come to accept when we know who our natural parents are. But the excitement of not knowing is creating a whole new outlook on life for me. It has, for example, caused me to consider the spiritual much more, to think in terms of reincarnation and immortality. I can think of and imagine these things now because I am freed from my foundation, not entirely and not adrift, but finding out you are adopted this late in life opens new vistas for how I look at the world and the space beyond it. It also provides me with a duty to think independently, not knowing whether my thoughts are genetic, the result of social engineering by society or my adoptive parents, or simply original in all respects. These revelations, I suspect will permit me to explore my potential without the shackles and chains that my conventional upbringing wrought. I will have fewer inhibitions, but I will not be self-destructive. I will be kinder to others and try to help them wherever I can. The people who have expressed their heartfelt condolences to me have really shown me a better way. I feel as if they are a part of my family. They are the family that I know. I love and I cherish them as the parents I did not know and those that I did.

As we develop, most of us go through a rebellious period where we seek to break away from our parents and establish our own independence. This is a totally natural part of life. Everyone goes through it in a matter of degrees, some rebelling more than others. But none of that produces an identity crisis, because you still know from whence you came. You may be angry about where you came from or how you were raised. That reaction may produce both constructive and destructive behavior.

Since I was not from Louis and Eileen, they were protective but they never knew what to expect from me. Since I have no baseline of heritage to work from, I do not know what to expect in myself. Therefore, and in that sense, potential becomes limitless. And isn't that how each of us should proceed through life, without the limits, the inhibitions that we acquire by ancestors, lineage and tradition? Each of us must break the shackles that stop us from exploring our potential and the unknown. I have no fear in the loss of identity since I have none, except what I create, thanks in part to my natural parents and Louis and Eileen.

I cannot speak for all adoptive children and I cannot address how this revelation might have affected me earlier in my life. Now though, I have only my own identity—what I have or will create. I may never be able to quantify how much of what I am is genetic or the result of the nurturing which I received. I feel that I have an obligation, not to myself or to my adoptive or natural parents, but to establish my own identity, for others, to lead and to tell what I have learned, known by some, unknown by others. Hopefully the courage to do that is in me somewhere. What I do know is that my search for my own identity is counterproductive unless it points to the future. In the future, what becomes important, at least for me, is not the search for my identity but rather establishing the future on my own, creating it through words and actions. At the same time I think all of us should do that and never lapse into complacency by thinking that we know who we are because we know from where we came. I see a great adventure ahead, without limits. My hopes and dreams are alive. I see no end to them. I see no reason to despair. I thank those who have assisted my living, but I have my own identity—that is who I am and who I will continue to be. I hope to inspire all others to join with me in this journey in trying to discover the unknown about ourselves and what we can and will become.

This book might have been entitled: *"Who Am I?"* But that implies that I do not know who I am. My genes and life experiences tell me part of the story. The future will be based upon my past or as George Santayana once said: "Those who do not know history, are condemned to relive it." I do not need a GPS to take me back or forward. I do not know the starting or finishing points. Guided by words of caution from my parents and Jiminy Cricket, I get to determine my own course and where I will wind up at the end of this life. In many ways these revelations have given me a new lease on life, and perhaps the freedom and independence that many humans seek but can never achieve. They are held back by the inhibitions which they have been taught. Self preservation and survival for all humans comes first. After that, what's important? Where do we go from here? I now get to decide that for myself.

Sometimes I chide myself for holding back, for not crying or opening up to someone. But how would that help me or another by showing my feelings, my regrets, my sorrows or my tears. Maybe I do need that release and the fact that I have not cried through all of this is simply the product of my defense mechanisms at work. The fact that I am adopted has made me more reflective. Death has resulted in a controlled, analytical response by me. Maybe that is cold and one day I will cry, but for right now, the answers to my questions are more important. I am not afraid to cry. I have just put that on hold for the time being.

Endnotes

[1] See A book review by Thomas F. Liotti of Boom! Voices of the Sixties, Personal Reflections on the 60's and Today by Tom Brokaw, Random House (662 pp, $28.95). The Attorney of Nassau County, March, 2008 at 7.

[2] See Brian L. Weiss, M.D., Many Lives, Many Masters, Simon & Schuster, Inc. (1988).

[3] See Robert A. Caro, *The Power Broker: Robert Moses and the Fall of New York*, published by Alfred A. Knopf, Inc. in 1974.

[4] See Thomas F. Liotti, The Lawyer's Bookshelf, Lost Boys, Why Our Sons Turn Violent and How We Can Save Them by James Garbarino, Ph.D., Anchor Books, Edition, August 2000, 274 pp., $13.00 paper bound. The book review appeared in The New York Law Journal on March 30, 2001 at 2.

[5] My college coach Bill Irwin, from Rutgers University won the Eastern Intercollegiate Swimming Championships in 1948 at 50 yards freestyle, in a time of 23.5 seconds. Bill is nineteen years older than me.

[6] See David McCullough, *1776*, Simon & Schuster (2005).

[7] Terry Laughlin, *Total Immersion—The Revolutionary Way to Swim Better, Faster, and Easier*, Simon and Schuster (2004).

[8] Years later when I had a syndicated newspaper column for a community newspaper, I wrote a column about him. Thomas F. Liotti was a Syndicated Community Newspaper Columnist for Anton Community Newspapers (18 publications) from September, 1994-October, 1995.

[9] See Seymour Mellman, *Pentagon Capitalism* (McGraw Hill, 1970). Professor Mellman was an Industrial Engineer at Columbia University who described the fact that the Pentagon was underwriting the cost of research at many leading universities

which then furthered what Dwight D. Eisenhower, a former President of Columbia University referred as a "Military-Industrial Complex." See Military-Industrial Complex Speech, Dwight D. Eisenhower, 1961.

[10] General Curtis Emerson LeMay, *Points of Rebellion.*

[11] <u>Never Stop Running, Allard Lowenstein And the Struggle to Save American Liberalism by</u> William H. Chafe, 556 pp.,Basic Books, A Division of Harper Collins Publishers, Inc. (N.Y., N.Y.). Reviewed by Thomas F. Liotti in Criminal Courts Bar Association Newsletter, April, 1994, Vol. 2, No. 4 at 4.

[12] See *U.S. v. David T. Dellinger, et al.*, 472 F.2d 340 (1972). There was an eighth defendant, Bobby Seale, who Hoffman had gagged in the courtroom. See also *Disturbing the Universe*, a movie about the life of William Kunstler.

[13] William O. Douglas, *Points of Rebellion,* Random House (1969).

[14] See *Go East, Young Man: The Early Years: The Autobiography of William O. Douglas*, Random House (1974).

[15] Many students at the time believed that it was also apart of a Government conspiracy that rock 'n roll icons such as Janis Joplin, Jimi Hendrix and Jim Morrison had all died mysteriously by drug overdoses. Similarly, Marilyn Monroe's purported suicide raised questions particularly after Senator Ted Kennedy was able to escape liability following the death of Mary Jo Kopechne at Chappaquiddick in 1969.

[16] See contra, a book review by Thomas F. Liotti of *Boom! Voices of the Sixties, Personal Reflections on the 60's and Today*, written by Tom Brokaw, Random House (662 pp, $28.95), The Attorney of Nassau County, March, 2008 at 7. My criticism of Brokaw in this review is that he reported as a journalist and never placed himself at risk in the 1960's and 70's. One of the things that I did not like about Tom Brokaw's book and his television specials on the same topic are that he never put himself at risk with a committed political ideology. He also said that our generation was "unrealized", that we did not achieve our potential or the promises we made. First of all, I think Brokaw is wrong about that. We made great strides in changing political ideology, ultimately making it possible for Barack Obama to be elected. To the extent that we did not achieve all that we envisioned or set out to do, the

process is not yet over but it was also people like Brokaw, nice but uncommitted, who prevented us from achieving more.

[17] See Charles A. Reich, *The Greening of America*, Random House, Inc., New York (1970) at pp. 394-395.

[18] See, Mollison, Andrew and Kerins, Annabelle, 2 Candidates: Young But At Odds, Newsday, May 1, 1971.

[19] See *The Report of the President's Commission on Campus Unrest* (Avon Books, a division of The Hearst Corporation, 1971).

[20] See Special Citizens' Commission Report of Attica Prison Riot, September 11, 1972.

[21] In 2008 I changed my registration to "Blank."

[22] See William L. Shirer, *The Rise and Fall of the Third Reich, A History of Nazi Germany* (Simon and Schuster, New York, 1960) at 319.

[23] See Robert A. Caro, *The Power Broker: Robert Moses and the Fall of New York*, Alfred A. Knopf, Inc., 1974.

[24] Weeks' held a Master's in Law degree from Duke University.

[25] Published Student Note—"An Historical Survey of Federal Incorporation," published in the Delaware Journal of Corporate Law (Vol. I, 1976). The Note was reprinted in the Congressional Record of the United States at the request of former Congressman James V. Stanton (D-Ohio) and described therein as the definitive work on Federal Incorporation. See, Congressional Record of the United States of America, Proceedings and Debates of the 94th Congress, Second Session, September 21, 1976, Vol. 122, No. 143 (H10738-H10745).

[26] At the end of 2008 and during the recession that was upon us in 2009, federal incorporation seems like an idea whose time has finally come.

[27] See Bruce Lambert, *G.O.P. Poised To Lose Voter Lead In Nassau*, The New York Times (Long Island and The Region Section) September 14, 2008 at 1.

"For most of a century, running as a Democrat in Nassau County was not merely an uphill battle. It was like climbing a political Mount Everest."

"As recently as 1998, the Republican Party had 340,333 enrolled voters—a daunting lead of nearly 100,000 over the Democratic enrollment of 240,735."

"That is no longer true. In just a decade, the Republican plurality has all but vanished and is down to several thousand voters."

28   See Thomas F. Liotti, Service Clubs: It's Time to Admit Women, Op-Ed Article, Long Island Section of the Sunday, The New York Times, September 25, 1983 at 22.

29   It is not the purpose of this book to write of cases in which I have been involved. They will be the subject of future writings.

30   See The American Lawyer Magazine, Connie Bruck, March, 1980 at 1, 12 and 13, "Fraiman Defendant Pursued By State and Federal Prosecutors" and "Review Of Judge Fraiman Still In Committee."

31   Village, Town and District Courts in New York", Practice Guide, (1995-Present), Lawyers Cooperative Publishing Company, Rochester, New York (now Thompson-Reuters, St. Paul, Minnesota).

32   *People v. Ventura*, 3 Misc.3d 1107(A), 787 NYS2d 680 (NY Just. Ct., 2004); New York Law Journal, May 25, 2004 at 1, 17, 19 & 20, Evidence of Overcrowded, Illegal Two-Family Home Suppressed as Exceeding Search Warrant and *People v. Ventura (#2)*—6 Misc. 3d 1001(A), 800 NYS2d 354 (2004), NY Slip Op 51695(u). (Just. Ct., Dec. 10, 2004, Liotti, J.).

33   *People v. Rafael Quiroga-Puma*, 18 Misc.3d 731, 848 NYS2d 853 (NY Just. Ct., 2008). This decision declared New York's unlicensed operation of motor vehicles law unconstitutional.

34   Stuart Vincent, Kunstler `Disinvited' By Nassau Attorneys, Newsday, Wednesday, May 29, 1991 at 23 and 24. See also, New York Law Journal, May 28, 1991 at 1 on the same subject. Both articles concerned the canceling of a speech scheduled before the Criminal Courts Bar Association of Nassau County. Liotti as the Program Chair invited William Kunstler and stood firmly behind the invitation alleging that the speech was canceled for political reasons.

35   Grievance Comm. for the Ninth Judicial Dist. v. Mogil (In re Mogil), 97-04366, Supreme Court of New York, Appellate Division, Second Department, 250 A.D.2d 343; 682 N.Y.S.2d

70 (1998) LEXIS 13540, December 16, 1998, Decided. See, Freedman, Mitchell, Newsday, September 11, 1995, Did Judge Harass Lawyer?; Tayler, Letta, Newsday, September 13, 1995, Markings Cited In Threat Letters; Tayler, Letta, Newsday, September 14, 1995, Lawyer, Judge Square Off; Tayler, Letta, Newsday, September 15, 1995, Lawyer Accused of Judge Bias; Kowal, Jessica, Newsday, September 16, 1995, Judge Claims Fax Is a Phoney; Tayler, Letta, Newsday, September 18, 1995, Public Battle at the Bar; Tayler, Letta, Newsday, September 18, 1995, Judicial Hearings Are Rare; Tayler, Letta, Newsday, September 19, 1995, Judge Denies Devilish Threats; Kowal, Jessica, Newsday, September 19, 1995, Around The Island—Crime & Courts, Rare Decision Makes Judge's Case Public; Newsday, Editorial, September 20, 1995, Hearings on Judges' Misconduct Should Be Public; Kowal, Jessica, Newsday, September 20, 1995, Mogil: Liotti Asked to See Gun; Kowal, Jessica and Tayler, Letta, Newsday, September 21, 1995, Devil Of A Time At Hearing; Kowal, Jessica, Newsday, September 22, 1995, Of Lawyers and 'Looney Tunes'; Kowal, Jessica, Newsday, September 23, 1995, Judge Contradicted; Topping, Robin, Newsday, Around The Island, Crime & Courts, September 28, 1995, Judge Is Flying Too High for Low Profile; Tayler, Letta, Newsday, October 10, 1995, Flamboyant Judge's Battle; Kowal, Jessica, Newsday, December 22, 1995, Ruling Against Judge; photo and caption, Disciplinary Panel Urged to Recommend Nassau Judge's Removal, January 12, 1996 at 6; Topping, Robin, Mogil's Fax To Foe Questioned, Newsday, January 12, 1996 at A7; Topping, Robin, Newsday, February 22, 1996, State Panel Wants Judge Removed; Milton, Pat, Daily News, February 22, 1996, Judge Linked To Threats Axed; Goldstein, Matthew, New York Law Journal, February 22, 1996, Removal of Nassau County Judge Urged by Judicial Conduct Panel; Hoffman, Jan, The New York Times, February 22, 1996, The Judge and the Lawyer: Some Not-So-Judicious Letters; Matter of the Proceeding Pursuant to '44, subdivision 4, of the Judiciary Law in Relation to B. Marc Mogil, a Judge of the County, Court, Nassau County, New York Law Journal, Disciplinary Proceedings (for full decision), February, 26, 1996; Daily News, Long Island Section, 'Hate Mail' Judge Suspended,

March 27, 1996 at A24; New York Law Journal, Today's News, March 27, 1996 at 1; Miller, A. Anthony, The Attorney of Nassau County, Judge Marc Mogil Appeals Ouster, March, 1996; Bowles, Peter, Judge Fails To Win LI Libel Case, Newsday, Long Island, August 21, 1996 at A23; Slackman, Michael, Newsday, High Court Reviews Ouster Case, September 6, 1996 at A16; The Associated Press, Judge's 60M Suit Is Tossed, Daily News, Long Island, October 2, 1996 at QLI 1; Topping, Robin, Suspended Judge's Lawsuit Tossed Out, Newsday, October 7, 1996 at A18; Bowles, Pete, Deposed Judge Loses Pistol Permit, Newsday, October 31, 1996 at A28; Miller, A. Anthony, Court Of Appeals Ousts Mogil, The Attorney of Nassau County, October, 1996 at 1; New York State Bar Association, New York State Law Digest, Vendetta Against Lawyer, Both Overt and Secretive, and Lying to Commission on Judicial Conduct, Costs County Judge His Job, No. 443, November, 1996 at 3; Miller, A. Anthony, Court Strips Former Judge's Law License, August, 1997 at 3; Suspension and prosecution for disbarment ordered by the Appellate Division, Second Department (By Mangano, P.J.; Bracken, Rosenblatt, Miller and Ritter, J.J.). The Appellate Division, among other things, stated: "The respondent also committed actions involving dishonesty, fraud, deceit, or misrepresentation in that he repeatedly gave false testimony under oath to the Commission on Judicial Conduct during its investigation and reported false information to the Nassau County Police Department." See New York Law Journal, August 1, 1997 at 23; Topping, Robin, Stop Practicing Law, Mogil Told, Newsday, August 6, 1997 at A22. An article concerning the suspension of former Judge Mogil from the practice of law and the Appellate Division authorizing the Grievance Committee to initiate disbarment proceedings against Mogil. See Today's News, New York Law Journal, August 6, 1997 at 1. See also, Former Nassau County Court Judge B. Marc Mogil, Removed From The Bench in 1996 for His Bizarre Harassment of Garden City Attorney, Thomas F. Liotti, Has Been Disbarred, New York Law Journal, December 28, 1998 at 1 and 9; Kara Bond, Suspended Nassau Judge Disbarred For Conduct, Newsday, December 29, 1998 at A27 and A. Anthony Miller, Appellate Division Disbars Mogil, The Attorney of Nassau

County, January, 1999 at 3. New York Court of Appeals decision, Matter of Mogil, 88 N.Y.2d 749, 673 N.E.2d 896, 650 N.Y.S. 2d 611 (1996). Docket number for Appellate Division disciplinary matter (97-04366). Hearing held on March 23, 1997 and October 15, 1997 before Special Referee, Hon. Morrie Slifkin re: disbarment proceeding of B. Marc Mogil. Letter To the Editor, Newsday, April 27, 2000 at A46 entitled: Witness Protection. The letter suggests Judicial Disciplinary Hearings may be open to the public, as Newsday suggested in an editorial, providing complaints are screened, pass preliminary stages and negative character testimony about complaining witnesses, unless germane to the charges, should be disallowed. See also Michael Frazier, Attorney Fights Reinstatement of Former Judge, October 31, 2007 at www. newsday.com and Michael Frazier, Target of Judge's Ire Fights Restoring Law License, Newsday, November 2, 2007 at A18.

See also, Thomas F. Liotti, *Judge Mojo: The True Story of One Attorney's Fight against Judicial Terrorism* published through iUniverse. The book may be ordered through www.iuniverse.com and www.bn.com for $25.95 U.S. The book has been described by Ronald Kuby, Esq., media talk show host, commentator and renowned civil rights attorney as "a fascinating and frightening book that chronicles the brave struggle of a prominent civil rights attorney to fight back against a terrorist in black robes. Judge Mojo provides a terrifying look at what happens when the Judge is angry, armed and psychotic. A must-read for every law student and every student of the law." March 5, 2008 appeared on WGBB radio, 1240 AM, Street Wise, the Lou Telamo Show for a discussion about the book. See Just Published. Judge Mojo: The True Story of One Attorney's Fight against Judicial Terrorism by Thomas F. Liotti, American Board of Criminal Lawyers, The Roundtable, Vol. MMVIII, No. 3, March, 2008 at 5. See book review by Herald Price Fahringer and Erica T. Dubno, The Roundtable, a publication of the American Board of Criminal Lawyers, April, 2008, Vol. MMVIII, No. 4 at 2 and The Attorney of Nassau County, April, 2008 at 9. On April 11, 2008, Mr. Liotti was interviewed by Marlene Smith on her radio show, Marlene's Electronic Salon, KBOO, FM out of Portland, Oregon. See also,

Cory Twibell, <u>Liotti's Mojo Cites Details Of Judge Conflict</u>, The Westbury Times, July 1, 2010 at 3.

[36] Thomas F. Liotti, <u>Letting The Elderly Just Waste Away Denigrates All Of Us,</u> The Daily News, Be Our Guest Column, August 10, 2008 at 33.

[37] See Ruth Padawar, *Losing Fatherhood, Cheap and Accurate DNA Tests Have Led Men To Discover That They Are Not The Biological Fathers Of The Children They Raised. What Has Also Been Revealed Is Just How Murky Our Notions Of Fatherhood Really Are*, The New York Times Magazine, November 22, 2009 at 1 and 38.

[38] Daphne Merkin, *My Shrunk Life—What 40 Years Of Talking To Analysts Has—And Hasn't Done For Me*, August 8, 2010 at 1 and 28, *et seq.*

Richie Havens

1969 – Lyrics from the song Freedom - Live From Woodstock

Freedom
Freedom

Freedom
Freedom

Freedom
Freedom

Freedom
Freedom

Sometimes I feel
Like a motherless child

Sometimes I feel
Like a motherless child

Sometimes I feel
Like a motherless child

A long
Way
From my home, yeah
Yeah

Sing
Freedom
Freedom

Freedom
Freedom

Freedom
Freedom

Freedom
Freedom

Freedom
Freedom

Sometimes I feel
Like I'm almost gone

Sometimes I feel
Like I'm almost gone

Sometimes I feel
Like I'm almost gone, yeah
A long, long, long
Way
Way from my home, yeah
Yeah

Clap your hands
Clap your hands

Clap your hands
Clap your hands

Clap your hands
Clap your hands

Clap your hands, yeah
Clap your hands

Hey, hey, hey, hey
Hey, yeah yeah yeah yeah
Hey, yeah, yeah, yeah
Hey, yeah yeah yeah yeah

I got a telephone in my bosom
And I can call him up from heart

I got a telephone in my bosom
And I can call him up from heart

When I need my brother / (Brother)
Brother / (Brother)

When I need my father / (Father)
Father, hey / (Father)

Mother / (Mother)
Mother, hey / (Mother)

Sister / (Sister)
Yeah / (Yeah)

When I need my brother / (Brother)
Brother, hey / (Brother)

Mother / (Father)
Mother / (Mother)
Mother / (Mother)

Hey, yeah, yeah, yeah
Yeah-yeah, yeah yeah yeah yeah yeah

Hey, yeah, yeah, yeah
Hey, yeah, yeah, yeah

Hey, yeah, yeah, yeah
Hey, yeah, yeah, yeah

Appendix

September 29, 2008 letter to Hon. John B. Riordan

October 6, 2008 letter from Hon. John B. Riordan

Petition for Access to Sealed Adoption Records

November 4, 2009 letter to Albert W. Petraglia, Esq. from Michael P. Ryan

Notice of Appearance and Guardian Ad Litem Report

Decision and Order of the Court

Certificate of Birth

Final Guardian Ad Litem Report

Notification of Adoption

Petition for Adoption

Order of Adoption

Adoption Papers

Affidavit of Natural Mother, etc.

Agreement of Adoption

Ferguson Family Crest and Name History

Letter from Harriet Meirs, Counsel to the President

Thomas F. Liotti

LAW OFFICES OF

THOMAS F. LIOTTI, LLC

600 OLD COUNTRY ROAD - SUITE 530
GARDEN CITY, NEW YORK 11530

TELEPHONE: (516) 794-4700
FACSIMILE: (516) 794-2816
WEBSITE: www.tliotti.com

THOMAS F. LIOTTI◆

LUCIA MARIA CIARAVINO
JENNIFER L. McCANN
EDWARD A. PALTZIK
DRUMMOND SMITH

MARIA ALBANO
Office Manager/Legal Assistant

JEAN LAGRASTA
ELLEN LUXMORE
Paralegals

September 29, 2008

<u>Personal & Confidential</u>

Hon. John B. Riordan
Nassau County Surrogate's Court
262 Old Country Road
Mineola, NY 11501

Your Honor:

I write to request access to my adoption files. My date of birth is apparently May 29, 1947 and I was allegedly adopted soon thereafter by my adoptive parents, Louis J. and Eileen F. Liotti (nee Lambe). Both of my adoptive parents passed away in 2008. My adoptive father informed me of this on December 17, 2007.

I am requesting this information for health reasons. Thank you.

Very truly yours,

Thomas F. Liotti

TFL:ma

294

CHAMBERS OF THE SURROGATE
COUNTY OF NASSAU
MINEOLA, N.Y. 11501

JOHN B. RIORDAN
SURROGATE

October 6, 2008

Thomas F. Liotti, Esq.
600 Old Country Road
Suite 530
Garden City, NY 11530

Re: <u>Unsealing of Adoption Records</u>

Dear Mr. Liotti:

I write in response to your inquiry regarding access to an adoption file. Please be advised that adoption records are sealed in New York State as a matter of public policy. The operative statute is Domestic Relations Law § 114, particularly subdivisions (2) and (4). The statute does authorize unsealing adoption records for medical reasons, but, as drafted, your letter does not satisfy the "good cause" standard required to unseal the record. I have taken the liberty of enclosing copies of two decisions emanating from this court which I believe are illustrative of the burden which must be met to justify unsealing an adoption record. I hope they will be helpful to you.

If I can be of any further assistance, please feel free to contact me at your convenience.

Very truly yours,

JOHN B. RIORDAN

JBR:ks

Encls.

Westlaw.

801 N.Y.S.2d 781 (Table)   Page 1
8 Misc.3d 1005(A), 801 N.Y.S.2d 781 (Table), 2005 WL 1473951 (N.Y.Sur.), 2005 N.Y. Slip Op. 50936(U)
Unreported Disposition
(Cite as: 8 Misc.3d 1005(A), 801 N.Y.S.2d 781, 2005 WL 1473951 (N.Y.Sur.))

(The decision of the Court is referenced in a table in the New York Supplement.)

Surrogate's Court, Nassau County, New York.
In the Matter of the Adoption of RAYMOND E.E.T.,
Anonymous.
No. 276A.

June 22, 2005.

JOHN B. RIORDAN, J.

***1 This is an application by an adult adoptive child to unseal adoption records, based upon alleged medical necessity. The adoptive child has not submitted any supporting documentation from physicians, however, he avers that he recently lost consciousness and was taken to a hospital where he was unable to provide medical history which might have assisted the doctors with their diagnosis. In addition, the adoptive child is concerned that his lack of knowledge of his medical history will present similar difficulties for his children and grandchildren.

The adoptive child made a previous application to the court requesting the same relief. By decision dated February 15, 1990, the court appointed Joseph Carrieri, Esq. as guardian ad litem to take reasonable steps to locate the whereabouts of the biological parents and to review any and all medical records and family history in the court's file. The adoptive child avers that a private investigator was hired to assist in the search, but his efforts were unsuccessful and the biological parents were not located. The adoptive parents are now both deceased.

Domestic Relations Law § 114 requires that adoption records be sealed. The purpose is to protect and ensure confidentiality which is "vital to the adoption process" (*Matter of Hayden,* 106 Misc.2d 849 [1981]). The confidential nature of the adoption process serves many purposes--to foster a stable and secure home for the adoptive child, to ensure that the biological parents will be able to start a new life

without fear of the past intruding on their ability to do so, conversely, to allow the adoptive parents to go on without fear that the biological parents will intrude into their lives, and to shield the adoptive child from possibly disturbing facts regarding his birth or background (*Golan v. Louise Wise Services,* 69 N.Y.2d 343 [1987]; *Matter of Walker,* 64 N.Y.2d 354 [1985]; *Matter of Linda F.M.,* 52 N.Y.2d 236 [1981], *appeal dismissed* 454 U.S. 806 [1981]; *Matter of Hayden,* 106 Misc.2d 849 [1981]). The statutory sealing requirements have been held to be constitutional and do not violate the adoptive child's 14th amendment right to equal protection (*Matter of Linda F.M.,* 52 N.Y.2d 236 [1981], *appeal dismissed* 454 U.S. 806 [1981]; *Matter of Romano,* 109 Misc.2d 99 [1981]).

Despite the strong policy in favor of confidentiality, the courts and the legislature have recognized that, under certain circumstances, an adoptive child may need information concerning his or her medical background (*Matter of Chattman,* 57 A.D.2d 618 [1977]; *Juman v. Louise Wise Services,* 159 Misc.2d 314 [1994], *affd* 211 A.D.2d 446 [1995]; *Matter of Harrington,* NYLJ, Mar. 31, 1993, at 25). Nevertheless, "[a] rule which automatically gave full disclosure to any adopted person confronted with a medical problem with some genetic implications would swallow New York's strong policy against disclosure ..." (*Golan v. Louise Wise Services,* 69 N.Y.2d 343, 349 [1987]). Thus, the courts and the legislature have attempted to strike a balance between the conflicting interests of the biological parents to maintain anonymity and the interests of adopted children and their adoptive parents in having access to medical information (Domestic Relations Law § 114; *see Matter of Marino,* 291 A.D.2d 849 [2002]). The legislature, recognizing the adoptive child's need for such information, in 1983 enacted Social Services Law § 373-a which requires certain information, including information on medical histories, to be provided by the biological parents.

***2 Based on the same rationale, Domestic

801 N.Y.S.2d 781 (Table)   Page 2
8 Misc.3d 1005(A), 801 N.Y.S.2d 781 (Table), 2005 WL 1473951 (N.Y.Sur.), 2005 N.Y. Slip Op. 50936(U)
Unreported Disposition
(Cite as: 8 Misc.3d 1005(A), 801 N.Y.S.2d 781, 2005 WL 1473951 (N.Y.Sur.))

Relations Law § 114(2) provides that adoption records may be unsealed upon a showing of "good cause." A prima facie case of good cause on medical grounds may be established under Domestic Relations Law § 114(4). Domestic Relations Law § 114(4) provides as follows:

"4. Good cause for disclosure or access to and inspection of sealed adoption records and orders and any index thereof, hereinafter the 'adoption records,' under this section may be established on medical grounds as provided herein. Certification from a physician licensed to practice medicine in the State of New York that relief under this subdivision is required to address a serious physical or mental illness shall be prima facie evidence of good cause."

The certification must also identify the information required to address such illness. Moreover, in order to maintain the anonymity of the biological parents, Domestic Relations Law § 114 requires the appointment of a guardian ad litem to review the records or, if the records are insufficient, to contact the biological parents.

The type of certification required under Domestic Relations Law § 114(4) was found to exist in *Matter of Howard* (N.Y.LJ, Dec. 28, 1998, at 27). There, the adoptive child had medical problems, which according to his doctors, were inherited. The doctor averred that information concerning both parents' medical history, as well as the medical condition of the adoptive child at birth, was necessary to provide proper medical care to the adoptive child and his issue. Pursuant to the procedure set out in Domestic Relations Law § 114(4), the court appointed a guardian ad litem to review the records and to contact the biological parents if the record was insufficient. The court held that the biological parents, if located, should be given the option to disclose the information sought by the adoptive child as well as the option to consent to the examination of his or her medical records.

Here, the adoptive child has not submitted the type of certification to establish prima facie "good cause" under Domestic Relations Law § 114(4) for the inspection of sealed adoption records on medical grounds. An adoptee who does not meet the requirements of Domestic Relations Law § 114(4) may, nevertheless, pursue his application under

Domestic Relations Law § 114(2). Domestic Relations Law § 114(2) provides for the unsealing of adoption records on good cause shown and on due notice to the adoptive parents and to such additional persons as the court may direct. Here, the only assertion made in support of the application is that of the adoptive child who claims that such medical information would be helpful. The adoptive child has not submitted any supporting doctor's affidavit. While the court recognizes that both adoptive parents are deceased, the court must still consider the harm that might be caused to the biological parents (*Matter of Donald*, NYLJ, Sept. 5, 1991 at 23, col.1) and finds that the adoptive child's unsupported assertions are insufficient to meet his initial burden to establish good cause on medical grounds under Domestic Relations Law § 114(2).

***3** The adoptive child has also failed to establish good cause under Domestic Relations Law § 114(2), (4) to learn the identity of his adoptive parents (see *Matter of Rubin*, NYLJ, Mar. 26, 1999, at 31). "Mere curiosity or desire to learn the identity of one's biological parents does not alone constitute good cause" (*Matter of Rubin*, NYLJ, Mar. 26, 1999, at 31). To establish good cause to allow identification of biological parents the adoptive child must show that he suffers from "concrete psychological problems ... specifically connected to the lack of knowledge about ancestry...." (*Matter of Linda F.M. v. Dept. of Health*, 52 N.Y.2d 236 [1981], appeal dismissed 454 U.S. 806 [1981], see also, *Matter of Donald*, NYLJ, Sept. 5, 1991, at 23, col. 1; *Matter of Romano*, 109 Misc.2d 99 [1981]). The adoptive child has not met this burden. His application is accordingly denied.

This constitutes the decision of the court.

8 Misc.3d 1005(A), 801 N.Y.S.2d 781 (Table), 2005 WL 1473951 (N.Y.Sur.), 2005 N.Y. Slip Op. 50936(U) Unreported Disposition

END OF DOCUMENT

Westlaw.

Not Reported in N.Y.S.2d
Not Reported in N.Y.S.2d, 2003 WL 21302907 (N.Y.Sur.), 2003 N.Y. Slip Op. 50967(U)
(Cite as: 2003 WL 21302907 (N.Y.Sur.))

C Surrogate's Court, Nassau County.
In the Matter of the ADOPTION OF CAMILLE
C.C.B.
No. 223.

June 3, 2003.

Background: Adopted child brought petition to unseal adoption records.

Holdings: The Surrogate Court, Nassau County, Riordan, J., held that:
(1) adopted child failed to demonstrate "good cause" for unsealing of adoption records,
(2) grandson's symptoms of attention deficit hyperactivity disorder (ADHD) and obsessive compulsive disorder (OCD) were not serious, existing physical or mental illnesses; and
(3) statute requiring that adoption records remain sealed except upon showing of good cause did not deny equal protection to adoptees.
Petition denied.

West Headnotes

[1] Records 32
326k32 Most Cited Cases
Adopted child failed to demonstrate "good cause" for unsealing of adoption records, on basis of her own medical need, where child was in general good health but suffered from minor ailments, such as hypertension, high cholesterol, and irritable bowel syndrome, which were not uncommon for person who had aged 64 years. McKinney's DRL § 114(2), (4).

[2] Records 32
326k32 Most Cited Cases
Adopted child failed to demonstrate "good cause" for unsealing of her adoption records, on basis of grandson's medical need, although grandson had symptoms of attention deficit hyperactivity disorder (ADHD) and obsessive compulsive disorder (OCD). McKinney's DRL § 114(2), (4).

[3] Constitutional Law 3740
92k3740 Most Cited Cases
(Formerly 92k225.1)

[3] Records 32
326k32 Most Cited Cases
In view of the legislative goal of encouraging the adoption of children and in
view of the privacy interests of the natural parents, statute requiring that adoption records remain sealed except upon a showing of good cause does not deny equal protection to adoptees. U.S.C.A. Const.Amend 14; McKinney's DRL § 114.

JOHN B. RIORDAN, Judge.

*1 In this petition to unseal adoption records, the petitioner is the adoptive child who is now a woman of 64 years of age. She was adopted pursuant to an order of this court dated January 18 1939. The court notes that the petitioner has sought access to her adoption records since the date she made her first application therefor in 1968. Because the instant petition seeks an order directing the hospital in which she was born, as well as the City of Glen Cove, the Nassau County Health Department and the New York State Department of Health to open their records to the petitioner's inspection, the court directed service of citation upon each of them. The Office of the Attorney General of the State of New York has appeared on behalf of the New York State Department of Health and opposes the application. For the reasons that follow, the petition is denied.

[1] The petitioner bases this application on medical need which is a ground upon which the court can grant an application to unseal adoption records.

Not Reported in N.Y.S.2d
Not Reported in N.Y.S.2d, 2003 WL 21302907 (N.Y.Sur.), 2003 N.Y. Slip Op. 50967(U)
(Cite as: 2003 WL 21302907 (N.Y.Sur.))

Domestic Relations Law § 114[2] provides that no person shall be allowed access to sealed adoption records except upon an order of a judge or surrogate, and no order for disclosure may be granted except on good cause shown. The good cause requirement can be satisfied upon presentation of a certification from a physician licensed to practice medicine in the State of New York that release of the information is required to address a serious physical or mental illness; the certification must identify the information required to address the illness (Domestic Relations Law § 114[4]).

With regard to disclosure based on the petitioner's own medical need, the court finds that there is none. The certification presented by the petitioner's doctor advises the court that the petitioner is in "generally good health" but that she does "suffer from hypertension, high cholesterol, and has irritable bowel syndrome." The certification goes on to provide that the inability to identify the genetic makeup and medical history of the petitioner's parents unnecessarily hampers the doctor's ability to evaluate the petitioner's health and prognosis. The fact that the petitioner's doctor would like to have the medical histories of her parents in order to treat the petitioner does not satisfy the statute's good cause requirement. The doctor admits that the petitioner is in general good health but suffers from minor ailments which the court finds are not uncommon for a person the petitioner's age. The petitioner is not facing a serious physical or mental illness the treatment of which requires or would be greatly enhanced by knowledge of the medical histories of the petitioner's parents.

[2] Regarding the health issues of the petitioner's grandson, it appears from the affidavit of the neurological psychologist whose affidavit is submitted in support of the application, that the petitioner's grandson, a 10- year-old boy, shows symptoms of several conditions, including attention deficit hyperactivity disorder (ADHD), obsessive compulsive disorder (OCD), and autism. The certification does not advise the court that the boy has been diagnosed with autism; rather, it provides that the boy "appears to have more significant current symptoms of attention deficit disorder." While the court is not unsympathetic to either the boy's condition or the petitioner's desire to obtain access to her adoption files, the public policy of this State, as reflected in its legislative enactments, is that sealed adoption records are not be made available except upon a showing of need to treat a serious, existing physical or mental illness. The court finds that the petitioner has failed to meet that burden.

*2 [3] Regarding the petitioner's argument that her inability to review her own birth and adoption files violates her rights of equal protection under the Fourteenth Amendment to the United States Constitution, the Court of Appeals has held that it does not (Matter of Linda F.M., 95 Misc.2d 581, 409 N.Y.S.2d 638, aff'd 72 A.D.2d 734, 442 N.Y.S.2d 963, aff'd 52 N.Y.2d 236, 437 N.Y.S.2d 283, 418 N.E.2d 1302).

Accordingly, the petition is denied.

Not Reported in N.Y.S.2d, 2003 WL 21302907 (N.Y.Sur.), 2003 N.Y. Slip Op. 50967(U)

END OF DOCUMENT

SURROGATE'S COURT OF THE STATE OF NEW YORK
COUNTY OF NASSAU
---X

In re: THOMAS F.,   **PETITION FOR ACCESS**
                                                     TO SEALED ADOPTION
                          Petitioner,   **RECORDS**

FOR THE UNSEALING AND DISCLOSURE   **File No.: 3803**
OF ADOPTION RECORDS,

                                                     <u>**Request for Filing Under Seal**</u>
---X

TO THE SURROGATE'S COURT OF THE COUNTY OF NASSAU

    The Petitioner respectfully alleges to this Court that:

    1.   I am the child who was adopted in the above-entitled proceeding.

    2.   I reside at 34 Lexington Street, Westbury, New York 11590.

    3.   Upon information and belief, I was born in Brooklyn, New York on or about May

29, 1947 A certified copy of my birth certificate is attached as Exhibit "A".

    4.   Upon information and belief, I was adopted in Nassau County Surrogate's Court.

    5.   A request for information has been made of the Adoption Information Registry.

    6.   The names and dates of death of the adoptive parents, are as follows:

Louis J. Liotti - date of death - April 2, 2008;

Eileen F. Liotti - date of death: August 12, 2008.

    7.   I am requesting access to sealed adoption records (this Court's File No.: 3803) on

medical grounds pursuant to D.R.L. §114(4) and as provided in the attached Medical Certificate

and my accompanying affidavit.

    8.   No previous application has been made for the relief requested herein. I understand

that the Court may appoint a guardian *ad litem* for the purpose of reviewing the file and determining whether the information being sought is in the file and to undertake such other and further instructions that the Court may require. I further understand that I will be responsible to pay guardian *ad litem* fees, if any.

WHEREFORE, for the reasons stated above, I respectfully request access to the sealed adoption records and information sought above and for such other and further relief as this Court deems just and proper.

_____
THOMAS F. LIOTTI
Petitioner

STATE OF NEW YORK)
)ss:
COUNTY OF NASSAU)

THOMAS F. LIOTTI, being duly sworn, says that he is the Petitioner in the above-named proceeding and that the foregoing petition is true to his own knowledge, except as to matters stated to be alleged on information and belief and as to those matters he believes them to be true.

_____
THOMAS F. LIOTTI
Petitioner

Sworn to before me this

18th day of August, 2009.

_____
Notary Public

SURROGATE'S COURT
COUNTY OF NASSAU
---X

In re: THOMAS F.,   **AFFIDAVIT**

                     Petitioner,   **File No.: 3803**

FOR THE UNSEALING AND DISCLOSURE
OF ADOPTION RECORDS,

                                    <u>Request for Filing Under Seal</u>
---X

STATE OF NEW YORK)
                     ss.:
COUNTY OF NASSAU)

THOMAS F. LIOTTI, ESQ., an attorney duly admitted to practice within the State of New York deposes and says under penalty of perjury as follows:

1.   I am the petitioner herein and as such I am fully familiar with the facts and circumstances of this matter. I am also an attorney in the State of New York.

2.   The purpose of this application is to unseal my adoption records pursuant to D.R.L. §114(4) which, upon information and belief, are on file in this court. This application is made for extremely good cause and medical reasons. I am attaching as Exhibit "B" a medical affidavit and certification from my personal physician Bruce K. Lowell, M.D., attesting to said good cause and medical necessity.

3.   On December 17, 2007 at the age of 60 years, I learned for the first time that I was adopted. My adoptive father, Louis J. Liotti, told me. He was then in an assisted living facility suffering from a severe heart condition and some other maladies including dementia. He was born on March 22, 1917 and died in April, 2008 at the age of 91 years and 10 days. A copy of

his obituary from Newsday is attached as Exhibit "C".

4.   Prior to entering into an assisted living facility in September, 2007, my adoptive father and my adoptive mother, Eileen F. Liotti, had lived with me and my family for 4 ½ years where I, my wife and live-in help became their exclusive caretakers. My adoptive mother, Eileen F. Liotti, born on August 8, 1920, suffered from the advanced stages of Alzheimer's Disease where by September, 2007 she had little cognitive abilities. Sadly, by December, 2007, at the time of my father's disclosure, my mother did not recognize me, her husband or anyone else, including her sister. She was incontinent and spoke gibberish. She had no understanding or knowledge of my adoptive father's disclosure to me. She and he were intermittently in and out of hospitals and tragically, separated from each other and confined to wheelchairs and bed rest, each taking a vast array of medication each day. At the time I had three children in college and an active law practice to maintain.

5.   In August, 2008 at the age of 88 years, my adoptive mother died. She had been confined to a bed and the Sands Point Nursing Home for the last 2 ½ months of her life. Her condition had so deteriorated that I was compelled to issue a heartbreaking DNR (Do Not Resuscitate) order and she expired soon thereafter. See article attached as Exhibit "D". Her obituary then appeared in the newspaper. See obituary attached as Exhibit "E". At her funeral mass I delivered the following eulogy, revealing my adopted status to those present:

EULOGY OF EILEEN F. LIOTTI
(AUGUST 8, 1920 - AUGUST 12, 2008)
DELIVERED BY HER SON, THOMAS F. LIOTTI ON AUGUST 16, 2008

My mother, Eileen F. Liotti, of Scotch-Irish descent, was a beauty, a model in the
1940s. But the outer beauty of a person as we all know, does not reveal much of
the person's character. Like the picture of Dorian Gray, beauty may be only skin

303

deep. My mother's inner beauty was even more impressive than what you could see on the outside.

My mother was born in 1920. She started her life in Bellerose, where her father owned a bar on Braddock Avenue. The family had a summer home in the Rockaways. All that they had was lost in the Great Depression. My mother, her parents and her younger sister, Carol, were forced to move to a cold water, walk-up flat in Ridgewood, Queens. My mother dropped out of school to work so that her sister could finish.

My mother met my father when she was sixteen and they married five years later in 1941. My father was an Army infantryman, a Corporal in the Second World War. My mother miscarried several times during their marriage and was diagnosed with epilepsy. Yet, her physical frailties still did not reveal the strength of her character. That was shown throughout her life in so many ways. Her true legacy must be the love that she gave to my father and to me.

Like the Blessed Mother, the best symbol of the role of mothers, my mother was special. No matter what the personal achievement, she never sought the limelight, credit or acclaim. She was content to provide unmitigated love and support, albeit always being reserved and in the background, attending all my games, taking me to practices, helping me through the rough spots of college, graduate school, law school, studying for the Bar exam, running for office and providing guidance to me as an attorney, Judge, husband and father. She taught me to read and to swim. She taught me manners, to be polite and to be a gentleman. I could not ask for more. These were important values which she gave to me and which I have endeavored to pass along to my children.

As you may know, my father passed away on April 2, 2008 and I am once again before you sharing a few thoughts on a life worth remembering. Most lives are for the lessons which all of us learn from them. Usually the hard part is to derive meaning from someone else's life. In my mother's case that has been an easy task. The great Greek philosophers, Socrates, Plato and Aristotle encouraged us to examine life's meaning. That is what we do in each eulogy, attempt to answer some of life's questions while raising still more that are then left to the metaphysics of the ages.

I thank all of you for being here with me. You have given me great comfort and the warmth of your friendship and love is felt. So I feel that you are a part of me and that I must cherish this moment and the closeness that I feel for you with some extraordinary facts which I only recently learned and which show the remarkable character of my mother and my father. I plan to publish a book about this, which I have been working on for several months entitled: Assisted Living.

It is about my upbringing and how I was assisted by these two remarkable people and how my wife, my children and I assisted them at the end of their lives. They lived with us in our home for four and one-half years and then moved into Assisted Living for 10 months and finally, into a nursing home for a month. But it will also be about a startling fact that I learned in my sixty first year, near my parents' end. By last summer my mother had advanced into the final stages of Alzheimer's. She and my father left our home and entered an assisted living facility. As my mother deteriorated, barely recognizing those around her, my father told me that I was adopted by them. I learned that on December 17, 2007, my thirtieth wedding anniversary. It was unsettling. I learned that but for these two extraordinary people that I would have been a ward of the State. These two people, my parents, devoted their entire lives to me, a stranger, not of their blood, but from others as yet still not known to me. So that to me shows the strength of my mother's and father's character. My own character has been strengthened by this revelation. I do not feel rejected by my natural parents as I am told some adopted children do. Rather, I am grateful for witnessing the love that these two people had for each other and for me. My father knew that my mother, like many women of her era, needed a child to care for and nurture and brilliantly found a way to adopt me, their only child.

My father explained to me just prior to his death that this secret was kept from me because they thought that "[I] might deny them." Of course that would never be the case due to the strength of character which they gave to me. They turned a negative life experience into a positive one and that is what we must all do. Their legacy is that they did not retreat. Now that I have reflected, I too will not retreat. I dare not turn this moment into a political statement, yet many of us have watched a loved one succumb to a horrible disease. Unfortunately, in the face of that we have prioritized placing a man on the moon by 1969 or conducting wars instead of scientific research and finding cures for these dreaded diseases. In last Sunday's edition of the Daily News, I remarked in an Op-Ed article that I was recently compelled to give my mother a death sentence by signing a "Do Not Resuscitate" (DNR) order. Just as President Franklin Delano Roosevelt established the Social Security Administration, so too our Presidential candidates and the Congress should address the need for an agency or department to provide for the long term health care needs of the aged. Why should people who have devoted their lives to making our lives better be left with nothing at the end of the road, wasting away, awaiting death. I have hope that we must do far better. Life in the hereafter may be idyllic but while we wait to discover that determination, let's make life worth living for the aged today.

My mother is gone now, never being told of my father's death or that he told me of my adoption. It is better that way. She goes to her resting place perhaps being uncertain of my love for her, for them. But the strength of my character instilled in me by my mother and father, allows me to say it now, even if unheard: "Mom and Dad, I love you. Thank you for all that you have done to make my life into a good one and to give me your legacy of character."

6. My adoptive parents were fine and loving people who treated me like their own. I was an only child in their household.

7. I am not seeking to unseal these adoptive records out of curiosity or to confront, embarrass or bother anyone. But I am primarily seeking this information for good cause and medical reasons involving my health, my children's and any future generations that may follow me. See *Application of Anonymous*, 1977, 92 Misc.2d 224, 399 N.Y.S.2d 857; *Alma Soc. Inc. V. Mellon*, C.A.N.Y. 1979, 601 F.2d 1225, *cert. denied* 100 S.Ct. 531, 444 U.S. 995, 62 L.Ed.2d 426; *Golan v. Louis Wise Services*, 1987, 69 N.Y.21d 343, 514 N.Y.S.2d 682, 507 N.E.2d 275; *Chattman v. Bennett*, 1977, 57 A.D.2d 618, 393 N.Y.S.2d 768; *Matter of Wilson*, 1989, 153 A.D.2d 748, 544 N.Y.S.2d 886 and *Juman v. Louise Wise Services*, 1994, 159 Misc.2d 314, 608 N.Y.S.2d 612.

8. When my father told me of my adoption, I inquired of him as to what knowledge he had of my biological parents. He told me that he had no records; that the adoption took place in Nassau County and that the Surrogate's Court records are under seal. Upon information and belief, my adoptive parents lived in Brooklyn until 1951 when they moved to the Salisbury part of Westbury in the East Meadow School District. At that time they purchased a Levitt home at 26 Lace Lane, Westbury, New York.

9. My adoptive father told me that my birth certificate showed a date of birth of May 29, 1947. A copy is attached as Exhibit "A". I am not absolutely certain that I was actually, legally adopted since I have no papers to that effect. Understandably this has caused a great deal

of uncertainty and consternation within my own immediate family including my wife and children. I am informed by this court that there is a sealed adoption file, number 3803, in this court that relates to my adoption.

10. The attached birth certificate issued to my adoptive parents on October 25, 2001 shows a date of birth of May 29, 1947 out of Brooklyn Doctors Hospital. The original report of my birth was apparently filed on June 2, 1947 and was later approved for a further filing on November 19, 1951 under the name Thomas Francis Liotti. I do not know what name, if any, I may have had other than this one, from May 29, 1947 to November 19, 1951. The aforementioned birth certificate seems to suggest that I was not formally adopted until 1951 in Nassau County where my parents were then residing. Yet, the early photos of me indicate that my adoptive parents had taken custody of me either at birth or close to it. (Copy of photo attached as Exhibit "F"). I do not know what happened during that four and one-half year interlude between my stated birth date of May 29, 1947 and November 19, 1951.

11. My adoptive father told me that my adoptive mother had several miscarriages and suffered from Epilepsy. Thus, she was apparently unable to conceive. He also informed me that they had a meeting with Cardinal Hayes in the early 1940's concerning adoption and until 1946, he was the Archbishop of New York.

12. My adoptive father said that he had few details about my adoption; that had I not been adopted I would have been an orphan, a ward of the state. While he did not say so, since he was a very religious person and told me of the meeting with Cardinal Hayes and had few details about my biological parents, I tend for those reasons to believe that I may have been adopted through Catholic Charities or some other Roman Catholic faith-based organization. My adoptive

mother was of Scotch-Irish descent. She was not a religious person and followed her father's faith from the Episcopalian religion.

13.   My adoptive father told me that my natural mother was a young married woman and nurse from Garden City with the last name of Smith. However, Smith being a common name and my place of birth being Brooklyn, would suggest otherwise. According to my adoptive father, she had another child born before me, a boy. She had me out of wedlock as a result of an extra-marital affair with an attorney from downtown New York City. My adoptive parents used as their attorney, Jules Buckbinder, Esq., who had an office in the Woolworth Building in New York City. I believe he has since died and the location of any of his files have long since vanished. Finally, my adoptive father stated that he had learned from the Superintendent or co-tenant of the apartment building in which my adoptive parents were living at the time, on Martense Street in Brooklyn, that he, a "Mr. Krause" knew of my biological mother and her condition. He may have acted as the intermediary between my parents and my biological mother. How my biological mother lost custody of me is a mystery.

14.   These scant facts were told to me by my adoptive father and he said that the only one who could verify any of the information was my adoptive mother's sister, Carol, then 83 and residing in Bethpage, New York. I then attempted to verify this information through her. She said that she thought the information was correct, but had no other details. I know of no other sources to obtain said information although I intend to pursue other possible avenues of discovery such as DNA testing and if necessary, the retention of a genealogist. I am attempting to secure any municipal records that may be available. I have even been referred to and consulted with a so-called "Channeler", a former Apostolic Priest from Canada, now residing in

Glen Cove, Thomas Trotta. This later endeavor was of course highly subjective and involved his attempts to contact the dead. In meeting with him he claimed to have been in contact with my adoptive father who he said is now in heaven. He said my adoptive father did not tell me the whole story, that he is still holding onto the secret which he described as a "scandal within the family." He claimed that my biological mother and father met in New York City in Little Italy and that she was a young girl who did not look like the people living in the area at that time, namely Italians. According to Mr. Trotta they met in a restaurant and my biological father may have been a politician, lawyer or judge. Prior to meeting Mr. Trotta he had received only my date of birth and was unaware of my last name or any other information about me. He did consult very detailed astrological charts during our meeting.

15.   I am not necessarily a believer or disbeliever in parapsychology, the paranormal, astrology, reincarnation or the extraterrestrial. I am also not agnostic. I believe that all things are possible, but I offer this information only to impress upon the Court the seriousness of my endeavors primarily for medical reasons and that I am pursuing all potential avenues for information. Obviously, the information that I am seeking here, if available, would be of considerable importance to me since I would be able to use it to possibly trace the medical histories of my biological parents to, for example, determine their causes of death, if they are deceased. Mr. Trotta told me that my biological father is deceased but that my mother is still alive. If the scenario is correct that my biological father was a politician, attorney or judge, then he may have in fact been older than my mother as both Mr. Trotta, my adoptive father and my adoptive mother's sister stated. Therefore, he would appear to be deceased.

16.   On May 29, 1947, the purported date of my birth, my adoptive parents, Louis was

309

30 and Eileen was 26. It is entirely possible, even likely, that my biological mother was younger than both of them, perhaps a minor and this could also explain the reason for me becoming an orphan or ward of the state. It is my belief that my biological mother is most likely in her late 70's or early 80's and still alive. If I can locate her true identity, I will make every effort to delicately contact her. Mr. Trotta stated: "You take from your father, not your mother."

17.   When I asked my adoptive father why he did not inform me sooner, he stated: "We thought that you would deny us."

18.   These facts and circumstances have been very disturbing and unsettling for me. But, at the same time not knowing my origins, I am also uncertain as to my background, my gene pool and my limitations. Mr. Trotta told me that I would die in 15-18 years, suddenly of a heart attack. If believed, that would mean that I will die between the ages of 77-80, a very short life expectancy by today's standards, further suggesting that more medical information about my biological parents may extend that.

WHEREFORE, I respectfully request for good cause shown herein that if my adoption records exist in this Court, that they be unsealed and revealed to me.

THOMAS F. LIOTTI

Sworn to before me this

/8 day of August, 2009.

Notary Public

9

THE CITY OF NEW YORK
VITAL RECORDS CERTIFICATE

Certificate of Birth

Certificate No. 29694

1. Full name of child (Print or Typewrite)

THOMAS	FRANCIS	LIOTTI
First name	Middle name	Last name

2. Sex **Male**

3. Date of birth — Month **May** day **29** **1947**

4. PLACE OF BIRTH
(a) NEW YORK CITY; (b) Borough **Brooklyn**
(c) Name of Hospital or Institution **Brooklyn Doctors** (If not in hospital or institution, give street and number)

9. USUAL RESIDENCE OF MOTHER: (a) State **New York**
(b) Co. **Nassau** (c) Town or City **Westbury**
(d) No. **26 Lace Lane** Ave. St.

5. Full name **FATHER** **LOUIS J. LIOTTI**

6. Color or race **White**

7. Birthplace (city or place and State, or country) **N.Y. N.Y.C. USA**

8a. Usual Occupation **Analyst**
8b. Kind of business or industry in which work was done **Western Electric Co.**

10. Full maiden name **MOTHER** **EILEEN FRANCES LAMBE**

11. Color or race **White**

12. Birthplace (city or place and State, or country) **NY NYC USA**

13a. Usual Occupation **Housewife**
13b. Kind of business or industry in which work was done **own home**

This certificate is filed pursuant to paragraph three of subdivision a. of Section 567-2.0 of the Administrative Code of the City of New York.

Approved for Filing _November 19, 1951_ (Signed) _____ Father
(Signature) (Title) _Eileen F. ___ Mother

Date of Original Report _June 2_ 19 _47_ Address _26 Lace Lane, Westbury, L.I._

BUREAU OF RECORDS AND STATISTICS   DEPARTMENT OF HEALTH   CITY OF NEW YORK

This is to certify that the foregoing is a true copy of a record on file in the Department of Health. The Department of Health does not certify to the truth of the statements made thereon, as no inquiry as to the facts has been provided by law.

Steven P. Schwartz, Ph.D., City Registrar

Do not accept this transcript unless it bears the security features listed on back. Reproduction or alteration of this transcript is prohibited by §3.21 of the New York City Health Code if the purpose is the evasion or violation of any provision of the Health Code or any other law.

DATE ISSUED **OCTOBER 25, 2001.**   DOCUMENT No. **E187752**

ANY ALTERATION OR ERASURE VOIDS THIS CERTIFICATE

311

MEDICAL AFFIDAVIT
CERTIFICATION

STATE OF NEW YORK   )
)ss:
COUNTY OF NASSAU   )

BRUCE K. LOWELL, M.D., specializing in Internal and Geriatric medicine, with offices at 1000 Northern Blvd., Great Neck, New York, deposes and says under the penalty of perjury:

1.   Thomas F. Liotti, d.o.b. 5/29/47, has been under my care as a patient for several years.

2.   In or about 2005, Mr. Liotti was diagnosed with the onset of cardiac abnormalities which may have a genetic disposition. These abnormalities are known as hypertensive heart disease and high blood pressure. In addition, Mr. Liotti suffers from a condition known as atrial fibrillation or a type of abnormal muscular contraction in which the constituent muscle fibers do not act together as a unit but as separate uncoordinated groups. The term is applied chiefly to describe such an abnormal action of the muscle of the heart, where the situation is further complicated by the special nature of the nerve impulses involved. The resulting beat of the heart is very irregular and unsatisfactory. Atrial fibrillation is due to an abnormal spread of the contraction impulse through the tissue of the atrium. The atrium is one of two receiving chambers by which the blood enters the heart. The contraction impulse is a wave of excitation which, if spread normally, causes the heart to contract rhythmically. In atrial fibrillation, the rhythmical contractions of the atria are replaced by; irregular twitching. Mr. Liotti's condition is extremely volatile and precarious, requiring close monitoring. In order to thwart a life threatening situation, Mr. Liotti has been prescribed Hyzaar, an angiotensin II receptor blocker

312

and thiazide diuretic which he takes daily for his high blood pressure. Mr. Liotti is also prescribed Coumadin, 5 mg. daily, an anticoagulent used to treat or prevent harmful blood clots that may occur.

3.   It is my understanding that Mr. Liotti learned on December 17, 2007 that he is adopted and that his file is under seal in the Surrogate's Court in Nassau County. Without access to that file, Mr. Liotti will not be able to learn the identity of his natural parents and their medical and personal histories.

4.   Mr. Liotti's natural son, Louis J. Liotti, born May 25, 1985 is also my patient and recently graduated from Northeastern University. He has signed a professional hockey contract with the American Hockey League's San Jose Sharks.

5.   I am concerned that Louis, a high performance athlete, could have his professional hockey career jeopardized by virtue of the medical and genetic history of his father.

6.   Recently, during "Rookie Hockey Camp" for the San Jose Sharks, Louis was medically tested. Concerns were raised because his heart rate was inappropriately elevated and additional concerns involved suspicions regarding a medical condition known as hypertrophic cardiomyopathy. While it is my understanding that that has been ruled out as a diagnosis for Louis by the San Jose Sharks, nonetheless as their physician I must continue to investigate the causes of any medical abnormalities in Thomas or Louis.

7.   The genetic or medical treatment plan for them as well as Tom's other two children, Carole, born May 25, 1985 and Francesca, born April 30, 1989, may have to do with the ruling in or out of certain diagnoses which are part of the medical, personal and genetic histories of Tom's natural parents. For example, hypertrophic cardiomyopathy is inherited as an autosomal

dominant trait and is attributed to mutations in one of a number of genes that encode for one of the sarcoma proteins.

8.   Treatment for such conditions may involve gene therapy, drug treatment with, among other things, beta-blockers. Treatment may also include defibrilator therapy or other surgery.

9.   It is my medical opinion, to a reasonable degree of medical certainty, that information regarding the identities of Tom's natural parents is essential to performing an accurate diagnosis for Tom and his children and to prevent sudden cardiac death or other serious injury by designing an appropriate treatment plan for them.

BRUCE K. LOWELL, M.D.

Sworn to before me this

30   day of July, 2009

Notary CHARLTON BUEE
Notary _____ New York
_____ County
Commission Expired **07/23/20**

24   THE WESTBURY TIMES - APRIL 17, 2008

POLICE BLOTTER

The following was submitted by the Third Precinct:

Stolen Cars

March 27
'95 Acura Integra, Fulton Avenue, Uniondale.
'95 Nissan Maxima, Prospect Avenue, New Cassel

March 30
'94 Honda, Liberty Boulevard, Uniondale
'97 Honda Civic, Monitor Street, New Cassel

April 4
'91 Buick Century, Hempstead Turnpike, East Meadow

April 6
'99 Audi, Grant Street, Mineola
'95 Honda Civic, Lee Avenue, Albertson

Burglaries

March 31
At North Street, New Hyde Park, a subject removed the alarm box and threw it in the back yard, resulting in the loss of jewelry.
Unknown amount was removed from a residence on Nassau Boulevard, Garden City Park. Apparently, a male opened the back screen door, rang the bell and then walked to the front. He left and returned with another subject and eventually entered the residence.

April 1
At Bagels & A Whole Lot More, Hillside Avenue, New Hyde Park, a cash register was removed.

April 2
At Old Country Road Bagels, Carle Place, $8,000 was removed from the cash register.
A male was arrested for removing cigars from Costco, Old Country Road, Westbury.

April 3
Copper piping was removed throughout a house waiting to be demolished on Sheridan Street, New Cassel.
Cash in the amount of $100 was removed from Pine Cleaners register located on Jericho Turnpike, Mineola.
Police responded to an alarm call at Westbury Pharmacy, Post Road, Westbury and the cash register containing $150 was removed.
Copper pipes were removed from a location on Prospect Avenue, New Cassel.

April 4
A resident on Morris Drive, Garden City Park, heard a loud bang, then his alarm went off. No loss reported at this time.

April 5
A victim was waiting for a friend to come visit him at Harrison Avenue but buzzed in a large male with a gun who removed his wallet.
Three men were arrested at Target for removing iPods.

April 6
A previous arrestee, from Westbury, was found in Costco, Corporate Drive, Westbury, and arrested again.
Jewelry in the amount of $6500 and a Sony TV were removed from a residence on Lynton Road, Albertson.

DONOHUE CECERE

OBITUARIES

Louis J. Liotti

Louis J. Liotti of Westbury passed away April 2, 2008 from complications of a heart condition. He was 92 years old.

Mr. Liotti was born on March 22, 1917 in lower Manhattan. His father immigrated to New York from Italy and owned a barbershop on 9th Avenue. Later the family moved to a farm in New Jersey and then to a home in Bayside where Mr. Liotti played sandlot baseball and was in the minor leagues, trying out for the New York Giants. He attended Stuyvesant High School and graduated from Flushing High School.

Mr. Liotti served in the United States Army in World War II reaching the rank of corporal and landing in Normandy and then fighting throughout the European Theater. After the war he went to work for AT&T. He organized and became the president of the Communication Workers of America, the Office Workers Local, and later became a contract negotiator on behalf of Western Electric Corporation.

Mr. Liotti moved to Long Island from Brooklyn and, in 1951, bought a Levitt home on Lace Lane in the Salisbury section of Westbury. About 10 years later he moved to a home in the Incorporated Village of Westbury, which he resided in for some 45 years.

LOUIS J. LIOTTI

Mr. Liotti was friends with Alex Rose, president of the International Ladies Garment Workers Union, and the late United States Senator Robert Wagner Sr. He was also an extremely active member of the community. He served as president of the Central Nassau Athletic Association, building it from just a Little League to a Pony League, Babe Ruth League and Connie Mack League while also helping to add a basketball league. Mr. Liotti also served as chairman of Boy Scout Troop 459 and was both a Democratic and later Republican Committeeman.

Mr. Liotti was active in St. Brigid's R.C. Church, serving as an usher and a daily communicant for many years, and was an active member of the Knights of Columbus, the Holy Name Society and the Sons of Italy. He was also a swimming

coach with the championship Levittown Carmen Avenue Team through which his son, Thomas, was introduced to the sport and went on to become an NCAA All-American and Olympic Trials participant. Mr. Liotti was also president of the Adelphi University Parents' Association and succeeded in bringing an FM radio station, WBAU to Adelphi.

Mr. Liotti is survived by Eileen, his wife of 67 years; his son and daughter-in-law Thomas and Wendy Liotti; three grandchildren, Louis, Carole and Francesca; and his brother Mario of Hollywood, FL.

Of his father, Thomas Liotti, a Garden City-based attorney and Westbury Village Justice, said, "He was devoted to his family, his church and his community. He was a tough man, a rugged individual living with severe heart problems and other ailments for over a decade. He taught me to be an athlete, a leader and independent. He was incredibly honest, moral, ethical and the fiercest fighter for the underdog and minorities that I have ever known. He encouraged me in sports, in life and in the law. When I first started trying cases in New York Federal Court, he would always be there watching, helping me to pick juries and working in my office. He never left my side and was the best friend I ever had."

315

Death Notices

BANASZAK - Patricia Diver. Loving wife of Walter. Devoted mother of Matthew, Kathleen, and Dorothy Loose. Caring sister of Dr. John & Stella Loose and Catherine Loose Fletcher, predeceased by her father John Loose. 9:30 pm at the Bayport-Blue Point Funeral Home, 683 Montauk Hwy., and Sunday 2-4/7-9. St. Ann's Cemetery, Sayville. www.raynordandre.com

BARATTA - BODIE ANNE 2002. Born in Farmingdale, NY. Devoted manager after 34 years of retired caring in the Woodward Parkway School, Farmingdale. Also will receive relatives and friends. (Steven) Diane Fond sister of the late Diane Fond. Cherished grandmother of Christopher, Michelle, and Melissa. Juliet (Adam), Jillian, Lisa, Nina, Andrew and Philip. Also survived by five grandchildren, nieces and nephews. Memorial Park. As an alternative to floral tributes, donations. 6800 Jericho Tpke, Suite 200W Syosset NY 11791 in memory of Bobbie Anne Baratta.

BARELLA - Albert of Gilbert, Arizona, formerly of Hicksville, NY. Beloved husband of the late Max. Loving father of Cynthia and Frank. Cherished grandfather of John Kim, Robert, Michael, Matthew, Adored great-grandfather of Zachary, Justin, Ethan and Harrison, Sarah, Allison, Jaclyn. Memorial Home 125 Old Country Road Hicksville on Saturday 1:00-3:00pm. Religious service 2:30pm at the Funeral Home.

CEVINA - Heienrose. of Wantagh, April 1, 2008. (Born February) Beloved wife of the late Frank. Loving mother of Robert (Heather). Cherished grandmother of Amanda and Ella. Devoted longtime companion of the late John Ronsheim. Dear Anita Seaglione. Fond sister of Gene and Vincent Rosenblatt and Arlene Gritto. Friday 2-4:30 & 7-9:30 PM. at James Funeral Home 540 Broadway Massapequa, NY. Funeral Saturday 9 AM. Interment Greenwood Cemetery Brooklyn, NY

CLANCY - Donald J. of Island Park on April 1, 2008, age 63. Beloved husband of Eileen (nee Gillespie). Devoted father of Donald Jr., Maryanne Lamond. Dear Grandfather of 4. Fond uncle, cousin and friend. Retired Sergeant, Long Island Railroad. Member of Ancient Order of Hibernians. Proud Vietnam Veteran. Family will receive friends Funeral Home 333 Atlantic Ave. Mass Monday. Interment National Cemetery.

COMERFORD - Agnes Decdue. (nee Murphy) of Rockville Centre, NY on April 7, 2008. Beloved wife of the late Eugene F. Decue and the

He was a long time resident of Sayville, on April 2, 2008. Customer Service Representative for Verizon. In addition to his parents, Mr. Carr was preceded in death in 2005 by his wife, Theresa and Gregory Carr and his wife Ann of New Fairfield, CT; two grandsons, John Carr of Manassas, VA; Carr; two sister Miriam Russel and Pauline Bolk; and several nieces and nephews. A funeral St. Patrick Catholic Church with member of St. James Catholic Church. www.raynordandre.com

D'Andrea Funeral Home, 245 neral Mass Monday 11:00am at Kohler, Northport Fire Department. St. John Nepomucene R.C. Church, Bohemia. Interment Long Island National Cemetery, Pinelawn, LI

DAMM - Dorothy Joan Corr, age 81, passed away in 2008 at Sind Stone Regional Medical Center. Mrs. Damm was born in Brooklyn, NY, the daughter of the late Bernard Regional Medical Center. The spending books, traveling. She was predeceased by a brother, Bernard Corr. Surviving are her loving husband, Kenneth Damm of Dobwik, three daughters, Deborah Magic and husband Joseph of New York, Ann Kleinman and Dennis of Mary land, and Dorothy Bivona and husband Michael of Arkansas; six grandchildren Brendan, and Matthew, A Memorial Service will be held 11:30 AM Friday at St. James Catholic Church with Father officiating. Burial will be at a later date at St. Charles Cemetery in Westbury. Dear father-in-law of Karen Mary, Christopher. Sign, a guestbook at goldfinchfuneralhome.com

EVERS - Patrick J. of HICKSVILLE on April 1, 2008. (Born February) Beloved husband of Mary (Nolen). Loving father of Marie, Dustin (Rick) Longford, Ireland.) Beloved husband of Mary (Nolen). Loving father of Marie, Dustin (Rick) macule. Cecily, Tony and the late Laurence. Cherished grandfather of Sara, Brian, Haley, Ellyn, Michael. Visitation at the Thomas F. Dalton Funeral Homes Hicksville Chapel, 47 Jerusalem Ave. Mass. Interment St. Charles R.C. Church. Interment St.

GARIBALDI - Rita Susan on April 3, 2008 of East Northport, LI. Beloved wife of the late Liborio. Loving mother of Richard, Michael and his wife Marie and the late Peter. Cherished grandmother of Victoria Parcasa. John (Cathy) Paredes, Rosemarie (Joseph) Giorgi, Deborah (Al) Bernard, Dana Paredes and Lisa (Ron) Paddett. Beloved son of Josephine Paredes and the late John and Grace Paredes. Beloved

brother of Jeanne Martin, Kathy and the late Lorraine Radicella, Tony Joseph Picone & Sons, Inc. In Farmingdale where she retired in 2005 at age 88. Her love for travel Asia, and Africa. Beloved wife of the late Joseph. Loving Mother of Kurt and the late J., Craig Mendenhofer of Connor and Chelsea. Reposing Saturday April 5, 4-8pm Lindenhurst Funeral Home, Inc. 422 South Wellwood Ave. Saturday afternoon. Cremation private.

LIOTTI - Louis J. of Westbury on April 2, 2008 in his 92nd Year. Beloved husband of Eileen. For 67 years. Loving father of Honorable Veteran of WWII, serving in the European Theater. the Family #1-8 PM at the Donohue Cecere Funeral Home 290 Post Avenue, Westbury. Mass at Christian Burial Monday 10 AM at St. Brigid's R.C. lowing in Holy Rood Cemetery. In lieu of flowers donations in Louis memory would be appreciated. Reach 25 Post Avenue Westbury NY 11590. Guestbook at www.donohue-cecere.com

NAWROCKI - Frank C. of Port Jefferson Station, on April 1, 2008 at the age of 82. Loving husband of Stanley DeGeorge, Patricia (Barry), and the late Laura the Thomas M. mother of Francis (Zeynep), Jennifer (Steve) and Jeffrey Runge. Interment Monday, 9:45 AM at the Connell Funeral Home 934 New York Ave., Huntington Station. Religious Services on Monday.

RICHMOND - Neal W. age 95 on March 23, 2008. Born in Vermont. 1912-95. Veteran. Surviving by his wife, Pauline, sons, Nicholas and Peter, and grandchildren Jessica and Mindy.

RIZZI - Joseph J., 83, of Casselberry April 1, 2008. Beloved husband of Betty, loving father of Catherine, McWilliams, Anthony (Phyllis), William (Catherine), Laura Frankie Dakota, Erik and Ali. Dear brother of Steven (Mary). p.m. at Raynor & Andrea Funeral Home, 245 Montauk Hwy., West Sayville. St. Ann's Cemetery. Altamonte Springs, FL 32714, are appreciated.

RUNGE - Elizabeth of Huntington formerly of Richmond Hill on April 1, 2008. Loving wife of the late John (Francesco) and Dorothea mother of Francis (Zeynep), Jennifer (Steve) and Jeffrey Runge.

SCHWARTZ - Jerome, M.D. 92 of Hewlett Harbor New York passed away on March 30, 2008. Beloved husband of Ellen, father of Seth and his wife Sharyon, Edwin and Grandfather of Ann, Amy, Lauren, Erica, Jennifer, Stephany, Shane, Grandchildren, Mona and Marlene Edelman. Services on Monday.

In Memoriam

STRUZZIERI - Peter J., age 91, of Pompano Beach, Fl. passed away on Thursday, April 3, 2008. Mr. Struzzieri was born on February and operated the Bell Furniture Moving Co. in Queens, N.Y. and for the railroad. Peter is survived by his wife, the former Margaret Clarke, and friends may call from sons Peter, John, and Thomas Struzzieri; 2 daughters Margaret Pace and Patricia Struzzieri; James and Michael, 5 sisters Julia Zotto, Dorothy Parretti, and Antoinette Zotto, 24 grandchildren; step son Walter Miller. 2 brothers Kraeer Funeral Home, 200 N. Federal Highway, Pompano Beach, Fl. 33062. Funeral Services will be held at Forest Lawn North Cemetery.

THOMAS - Beatrice M. 86 Sun City Ctr. FL suddenly 3/25/08. Loving daughter of George & Catherine Thomas. Roslyn Heights NY. Res, Direction Mass. Church at St. Ct. FL Burial 4/5/08 at 10AM at Holy Rood Cemetery. Survived by cousins Margaret Hannigan, Catherine Monahan Flaherty & 14 other cousins.

nydailynews.com　　**DAILY NEWS**　　Sunday, August 10, 2008

Page 33

BE OUR GUEST

Letting the elderly just waste away denigrates all of us

By Thomas F. Liotti

recently gave my mother a death sentence. I handed a Do Not Resuscitate Order — known as DNR — to her nursing home. The staff there will only "keep her comfortable" until "the Lord decides it is time." The Lord may take his time, but the experts tell me that he usually decides within three weeks.

My mother has Alzheimer's. She is almost 88 and in the advanced stages of the disease. She has forgotten how to walk and eat. She no longer recognizes me, her son. She cannot say anything coherently; not one, single word. She is unable to wave hello or goodbye. She has not smiled in a very long time. She is heavily medicated and sleeps most of the time.

My father died in April. He was 91. He had coronary heart disease but did not die from that. Instead, he lost the will to live and starved himself to death.

The costs for maintaining my parents in assisted living prior to my father's death and my mother's entry into a nursing home were running about $15,000 a month, with one-on-one care for my mother, 24 hours a day.

As we advance in age, there are critical issues that we must confront. These have to do with both the short- and long-term issues of health care, but also with the maintenance of a productive quality of life, free of pain, anxiety and depression.

Visiting most assisted living and nursing home facilities presents a scene of patient-residents in various stages of malaise and vegetative states. Drugs may keep them alive for years, but few, even with large doses of antidepressant medication, will say that they are happy or that they enjoy their existence. They move about with walkers and in wheelchairs, often pushed by aides with little formal training and who are, in many cases, in this country illegally. They are good, caring people, but their job is to maintain life so that they and their facility will be paid.

I do not like having to give my mother a death sentence. I hope that my children will not have to do the same thing for me or, if they do, that they will make the right decision.

It is time for us to focus not merely on health care issues. We must look at health care and quality-of-life issues. Although today we have focused on prolonging life, this by itself does not permit people to enjoy their lives or make them interesting or productive members of society instead of being a drain on it.

The elderly are an untapped resource that, if harnessed instead of just waiting to die, may make our nation great again. The challenge for the future is to give them health care and a quality of life that will enable them to continue as productive members of society. I would like to hear presidential candidates discuss these issues. They need to start by visiting assisted living and nursing home facilities to see for themselves the full nature of this problem. Rhetoric alone will not solve the problem.

Instead of spending more than a trillion dollars on a war, this

Leaders need to address long-term care

country's leaders should be putting money into education and research on geriatric care. In the context of medical coverage for all Americans, presidential candidates should be focusing on how we can meet the extraordinary cost of medical care for the aged. Just as President Franklin D. Roosevelt provided for the enactment of the Social Security Administration, Sens. Barack Obama and John McCain should be addressing the establishment of an agency or department of the federal government that would provide for the long-term health care of those in need of it.

Liotti, a lawyer, is village justice for Westbury, L.I.

OBITUARIES

EILEEN F. LIOTTI

Eileen F. Liotti

Eileen F. (nee Lambe) Liotti of Westbury died on Aug. 12, 2008. She was 88 years old and suffered from Alzheimer's disease.

Born Aug. 8, 1920 in Queens, Eileen attended Jamaica High School until the Great Depression when she was forced to drop out of school in order to work so that

her younger sister, Carol, might graduate. Her father, Francis Lambe, was born in Glasgow, Scotland and her mother Anna Burke, was a second generation implant from Dublin, Ireland.

Just prior to the Depression, Eileen's parents had a beautiful home in Bellerose and a summer home in the Rockaways. During the Depression, Frank Lambe's restaurant and bar business on Braddock Avenue in Queens failed and the family moved to a walkup, cold water flat in Ridgewood. It was a five-room, railroad- style apartment with a potbelly kitchen stove. Frank Lambe became afflicted with Parkinson's disease and was unable to work so, in order to support the family, Eileen's mother went to work in a dress pattern factory and Eileen became a secretary, clerk and during and after World War II, worked as a model in New York City.

In 1941, Eileen married Louis J. Liotti and, at the time of his death on April 2, 2008, they were together for 72 years, 67 of which they were married. The Liottis moved to Westbury in 1951, first buying a Levitt home in the Salisbury section and later moving to the Incorporated Village of Westbury where Eileen was a lifelong member of the Mercy League of Long Island and a former member of the Ladies Auxiliary of the Maria Del'Assunta Society of Westbury.

Eileen worked for the Nassau County Clerk's Office for 20 years and retired in

1982. Her son, Thomas F. Liotti, an attorney in Garden City and a Westbury Village Justice, said, "She was a lifelong inspiration to me. She encouraged me in everything I did – from teaching me how to swim at the Carmen Avenue Pool in Salisbury to becoming an attorney and a judge. She was a powerhouse of support and a beautiful, dignified and elegant woman, with exceptional style and grace," said Thomas Liotti.

He added, "My mother was afflicted with Alzheimer's, one of the worst diseases known. I am hopeful that a cure may be found because no one should have to finish their lives as my mother did. I plan to spend some portion of my remaining life trying to help those afflicted with this

terrible disease."

Eileen Liotti is survived by her son and daughter-in-law, Thomas F. and Wendy Liotti; three grandchildren, Louis, Carole and Francesca; and a sister, Carol Melzig of Bethpage. Arrangements were made by the Donohue Cecere Funeral Home, 290 Post Avenue, Westbury. A Mass took place at St. Brigid's Church followed by interment at Holy Rood Cemetery. Donations in Mrs. Liotti's memory can be sent to either the Alzheimer's Foundation of America, 322 Eighth Avenue, 7th Floor, New York, NY 10001 or, St. Brigid's Church through St. Brigid's Parish Outreach, 75 Post Avenue, Westbury, NY 11590.

Craft Vendors Wanted

Craft Vendors Wanted for the St. Brigid/OLH School Fall Crafts Festival, a fun family event, to be held on Sept. 27 on Maple Ave. in the Village of Westbury from 10

RELIGIOUS SERVICES

JEWISH
Old Westbury Hebrew Congregation
(Conservative)
21 Old Westbury Rd.
Old Westbury, NY 11568
www.owhcong.org
office@owhcong.org
Rabbi Michael Stanger
Cantor Yosef Karavani
Services:
Monday - Friday 6:50 a.m. except
legal holidays 9 a.m.
Friday 8:30 p.m.
Saturday 9 a.m.
Sunday 9 a.m.
Call office for Saturday evening
Havdalah Service dates and times
and special

Jr. Congregation Saturday morning
10 to 11:30 a.m.
Torah for Tots and Mini Minyan first
Saturday of each month 10:30 to
11:30 a.m. (Sept.-June)
Friday night programs
Tot Shabbat and Mini Minyan
Nursery School 333-5949
Religious School for Kindergarten
through high school 997-4630

Temple Beth Torah
(Conservative)
243 Cantiague Rd.
Westbury, NY 11590
334-7980
www.templebethtorah.org
Rabbi Michael Katz
Cantor Kiannan Fliegelman
Services:
Friday 8:30 p.m.

First Friday of each month family
service at 8:30 p.m.
Monthly family services 8 p.m.
Saturday 9:45 a.m. and sundown
Sunday 9 a.m. and 8:30 p.m.
Monday - Thursday daily Minyan
8:30 p.m.

QUAKER/RELIGIOUS
SOCIETY OF FRIENDS
Westbury Friends Meeting
Southeast corner of Jericho Tpke.
and Post Ave.
Westbury, NY 11590
333-3178
http://westburyquakers.org
Services:
The meeting starts at 11 a.m.
on Sundays for silent,
meditative worship

Changes made twice, yearly: July and September. Sabbath changes for summer hours by the end of June and when to revert back by the end of August.

THE WASHINGTON POST

Manny Farber, an influential film critic whose writings punctured the self-serious veil of arthouse favorites Orson Welles and François Truffaut while celebrating the less-studied but more-entertaining work of Laurel & Hardy and Howard Hawks, has died.

Farber, 91, who also had a long career as an artist, died of bone cancer Monday at his home in the San Diego suburb of Leucadia.

Often mentioned with movie critics James Agee and Pauline Kael in impact, Farber drew admirers for his fierce opinions. Susan Sontag called him "the liveliest, smartest, most original film critic this country has ever produced . . . (his) mind and eye change the way you see."

Farber offered a high-spirited attack on pretentiousness in movies and extolled the value of such marginalized genres as film noir and slapstick comedy.

He was the first critic to champion the work of Hawks ("The Big Sleep"), Don Siegel ("Dirty Harry") and Samuel Fuller ("Fixed Bayonets"), as well as "Looney Toons" animator Tex Avery, among others.

He wrote for the New Republic, Time, the Nation, the New Leader, and Artforum among others.

He is survived by his wife, painter and installation artist Patricia Patterson; a daughter from his second marriage, Amanda Farber; and a grandson.

...nger and Ronkonkoma resident whose voice was so versatile he was able to compete as a bass, baritone and tenor, died at age 50 after a brief illness, his management company said.

Lundberg died Aug. 15 at Stony Brook University Medical Center, said Stuart Wolferman of Herbert Barrett Management. The cause of death wasn't released.

Lundberg sang bass, then baritone, for many years before making the transition to dramatic tenor roles. He competed at the regional finals of the Metropolitan Opera National Coun- cil Auditions as a bass, baritone and tenor, according to the Pittsburgh Opera, where Lund-

Lundberg had three ranges.

"He was a fine singer who made a great contribution to the opera stages of the world," Christopher Hahn, general director of the Pittsburgh Opera, told the Pittsburgh Post-Gazette.

Born in Denver, Lundberg studied at Indiana University under opera singer Margaret Harshaw. His roles in the 1980s and '90s included Samson, Daga in "The Black Mask" and Bacchus in "Ariadne auf Naxos." A significant milestone in Lundberg's career was his debut with the Theatre de la Monnaie in Brussels in the

man said. Survivors include his wife Anya, and four children.

Wolferman said a memorial service was held at Christ the King Roman Catholic Church in Commack on Tuesday. Full Anglican services are scheduled for today at St. Simon Episcopal Church in Arlington Heights, Ill. In lieu of flowers the family requested contributions to the Stained Glass Window Fund at Christ the King, or to the Memorial Garden Fund at St. Simon in Arlington Heights, Ill.

This story was supplemented with Newsday staff reporting.

LONG ISLAND

E. Liotti, 88, aided family in Depression

BY ZACHARY R. DOWDY
zachary.dowdy@newsday.com

A child of the Depression, Bellerose native Eileen Liotti attended Jamaica High School until the hard economic times forced her to drop out and go to work so that her younger sister might graduate.

It was one of the many sacrifices she made for her family over nearly nine decades of life, during which she married a war veteran, modeled in the high-fashion districts of New York City, became a homemaker and raised a son.

Liotti, of Westbury, died Aug. 12 of Alzheimer's disease. She was 88.

"She was a wonderful woman and, like a lot of people from her generation, she worked hard and the most important thing in her life was her family — my father and me," said Thomas Liotti, a Garden City attorney and Westbury Village justice. "She devoted herself to the community and to us."

Born Eileen Lambe in 1920, Liotti and her family enjoyed a home in Bellerose and a summer home in the Rockaways. But the nation's economic low point destroyed the Lambes' restaurant and bar business.

The Lambes moved into a walk-up in Ridgewood, a five-room, railroad-style apartment with a potbelly stove in the kitchen, Thomas Liotti said.

Frank Lambe, Eileen Liotti's father, developed Parkinson's disease and could no longer work, forcing the family to scramble to make ends meet. Liotti's mother, Anna, went to work in a dress pattern factory and Liotti became a secretary, then a clerk and, during and after World War II, she worked as a model in New York City.

At 16, she met Louis J. Liotti, a man who would become an Army infantryman and corporal and fight in World War II. The couple married in 1941 and were together for 67 years until his death last April.

The couple moved to Westbury in 1951, after moving out of a Levitt home in the Salisbury section of East Meadow.

Liotti would become a lifelong member of the Ladies League of Long Island and was a former member of the Maria Dell'Assunta Society of Westbury, a charitable organization.

For 20 years, she worked for the Nassau County clerk's office, retiring in 1982.

"She was a lifelong inspiration to me, encouraging me in everything that I have done from teaching me how to swim at the Carmen Avenue pool in Salisbury to becoming an attorney and judge," Thomas Liotti said. "She was a powerhouse of support, a beautiful, dignified and elegant woman with exceptional style and grace."

Besides her son, Eileen Liotti is survived by a daughter-in-law, Wendy Liotti of Westbury; a sister, Carol Melzig of Bethpage; and three grandchildren.

She was buried Aug. 15 at the Cemetery of the Holy Rood in Westbury.

Donations may be sent to the Alzheimer's Foundation of America or St. Brigid's Church through St. Brigid's Parish Outreach, at 75 Post Ave, Westbury, NY 11590.

Eileen Liotti

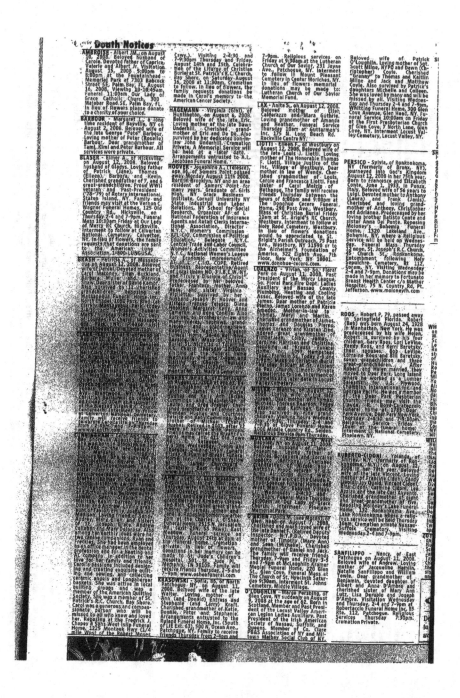

File No.: 3803

SURROGATE'S COURT OF THE STATE OF NEW YORK
COUNTY OF NASSAU
--X

In re: THOMAS F.,

                                        Petitioner,

FOR THE UNSEALING AND DISCLOSURE
OF ADOPTION RECORDS,
--X

PETITION FOR ACCESS TO SEALED ADOPTION RECORDS AND AFFIDAVIT

THOMAS F. LIOTTI, ESQ.
Petitioner *Pro Se*
600 Old Country Road, Suite 530
Garden City, New York 11530
Telephone Number: (516) 794-4700
Facsimile Number: (516) 794-2816

NASSAU COUNTY SURROGATE'S COURT
Hon. John B. Riordan
Surrogate

262 Old Country Road
Mineola, New York 11501
516.571.2082
Facsimile: 516.571.2997

Michael P. Ryan, Esq.
Chief Clerk

Michael J. Murphy
Deputy Chief Clerk

John T. Moore, Esq.
Principal Law Clerk

Mary L. Meyer
Daniel Zimmerman
Court Clerk Specialists

Law Department
516.571.2042

Andrew L. Martin
Chief Court Attorney

Patrick E. Castelluccio
Sally M. Donahue
Peter K. Kelly
William A. Mapes
Gail B. Singer
Lori A. Sullivan
Anne E. Tozier
Nomi N. Zornick

November 4, 2009

Albert W. Petraglia, Esq.
Rivkin Radler, LLP
926 Rexcorp Plaza
Uinondale, N.Y. 11556

File No: 3803
G.A. L. Appointment Date: November 4, 2009

Dear Counselor:

You have been appointed guardian ad litem for persons under a disability and interested in a proceeding in the above estate. Please report to this office as soon as possible to indicate your acceptance by signing your consent to act, pursuant to Section 207.13 of the Uniform Rules for the Surrogate's Court. Also note that an order appointing you as a fiduciary has been submitted to the fiduciary clerk listed below to monitor compliance with UCS rules covering such appointments. Please give this matter your immediate attention.

Persons appointed as fiduciaries pursuant to Part 36 of the Rules of the Chief Judge must comply with the filing requirements of that Part. Attached please find the form required by Part 36, the UCS-872 (Notice of Appointment and Certification of Compliance). Also included is a Data Collection form, the filing of which is voluntary. Please be sure to review the Chief Judge's Rules regarding eligibility to accept this appointment. Also note that Uniform Court Rule 207.13 (b) requires that where the payment of money or delivery of property is to be made to the ward, the Guardian Ad Litem must file a supplemental report within 60 days after the decree settling the account showing whether the decree has been complied with in so far as it affects the ward.

Please note: You are no longer required to file the UCS-875 form (Statement of Approval of Compensation). That form will be filed by the Fiduciary Clerk directly with the Office of Court Administration. You must, however, include in your Guardian ad Litem's Report the number of hours which have been spent on the particular matter for which you have been appointed.

*YOU MUST APPEAR AT THE COURT TO SIGN YOUR CONSENT AND COMPLETE THE NOTICE OF APPOINTMENT AND CERTIFICATION OF COMPLIANCE FORM WITHIN TEN (10) DAYS OF YOUR APPOINTMENT OR YOUR APPOINTMENT MAY BE REVOKED. PLEASE SUBMIT THESE FORMS TO:*Michael P Ryan, Esq.

Fiduciary Clerk
Surrogate's Court - Nassau County
262 Old Country Road
Mineola, NY 11501

Very truly yours,

MICHAEL P RYAN
Fiduciary Clerk

cc: **Atty (Pro Se):** Thomas F. Liotti, Esq., 600 Old Country Rd., Ste. 530, Garden City, N.Y. 11530 (516-794-4700)

Thomas F. Liotti

SURROGATE'S COURT OF THE STATE OF NEW YORK
NASSAU COUNTY
--X
In the Matter

THOMAS I.I.F.,

Anonymous

For the Unsealing and Disclosure of
Adoption Records.

--X

<u>NOTICE OF</u>

<u>APPEARANCE</u>

File No. 40

Dec. No. 681

     PLEASE TAKE NOTICE, that the undersigned attorney appears as Guardian Ad

Litem for the purpose of examining certain adoption records to ascertain if medical

information relating to the adopted child is contained therein and demands that copies

of all papers filed with the Court be sent to the undersigned.

Dated: November 19, 2009

                             Rivkin Radler LLP
                             926 RXR Plaza
                             Uniondale, New York 11556
                             (516) 357-3178

                             By:_____
                               ALBERT W. PETRAGLIA

To: Thomas Liotti, Esq.
    600 Old Country Road
    Garden City, NY 11530

2313862 v1

STATE OF NEW YORK
SURROGATE'S COURT: NASSAU COUNTY
---X
In the Matter

GUARDIAN *AD LITEM* REPORT

THOMAS I.I.F.,   File No. 40

                    Anonymous   Dec. No. 681

For the Unsealing and Disclosure of
Adoption Records.
---X

TO THE SURROGATE'S COURT OF THE STATE OF NEW YORK,
COUNTY OF NASSAU:

I, Albert W. Petraglia, the undersigned Guardian *ad Litem*, in the above-entitled

proceeding, respectfully reports as follows:

APPOINTMENT OF THE GUARDIAN *AD LITEM*

By Order of the Honorable John B. Riordan, Judge of the Surrogate's Court of Nassau

County, made on November 4, 2009, I was appointed Guardian *ad Litem* for the purpose of

examining certain adoption records to ascertain if medical information relating to the adopted

child is contained therein. Upon receipt of my Order of Appointment, I appeared at the Nassau

County Surrogate's Court to sign my Consent To Act and filed my Notice of Appointment

pursuant to Part 36 of the Rules of the Chief Judge of the State of New York, along with my

Certificate of Compliance. On November 19, 2009, I filed my Notice of Appearance and sent a

copy to the Petitioner, Thomas F. Liotti.

325

NATURE OF THE PROCEEDING.

The adopted parents Louis J. Liotti and Eileen F. Liotti are both deceased, having died respectively on April 2, 2008 and August 16, 2008. The Petitioner who is seeking to unseal the court's adoption records relies on Domestic Relations Law § 114 Sub. 2, which permits the unsealing of adoption records when good cause is shown.

The Petitioner has made a *prima facie* showing of "good cause" for medical reasons. He has provided the court with a Medical Affidavit Certification by Bruce K. Lowell, M.D., in which Dr. Lowell describes the medical condition affecting the Petitioner and potentially affect his children.

EXAMINATION OF THE COURT'S ADOPTION FILE.

I have reviewed the entire court's file, which included the Petition for Adoption signed by the adoptive parents and the Agreement of Adoption signed by the adoptive parents and the natural mother. I also observed in the file the natural mother's affidavit and the affidavit of the attorney for the adoptive parents. The only other documents in the file are the Order of Adoption and a statement by the home investigator. There was absolutely no medical information contained in the file, nor was there any information concerning the identity of the natural father. There is only minimal information identifying the natural mother, contained in the Petitioner's original birth certificate.

CONCLUSION AND RECOMMENDATION.

The original birth certificate contains the ages of the natural parents at the time of birth. From this information, I am able to report to the court that the natural mother, if alive, would be

97 years old this year. The natural father, if alive, would be 102 years of age. Unfortunately, there is no medical information contained in the court's file, which would help the Petitioner in this matter. Further, it is unlikely that either the natural father or the natural mother are still living at this late date. Based upon the court's records, it is clear that the natural father's identity is unknown and, if alive, his whereabouts, cannot be ascertained. While the likelihood of the natural mother still being alive is remote, if directed by the court, the Guardian *ad Litem* will engage the services of a genealogist/investigator in an effort to locate her.

Dated: Uniondale, New York
     November 19, 2009

Respectfully submitted:

Albert W. Petraglia, Guardian Ad Litem
Rivkin Radler LLP
926 RXR Plaza
Uniondale, NY 11556
(516) 357-3178

TO: Thomas Liotti, Esq.
       600 Old Country Road
       Garden City, NY 11530

SURROGATE'S COURT OF THE STATE OF NEW YORK
COUNTY OF NASSAU
--X
In the Matter of

              THOMAS I.I.F.,

                Anonymous,

For the Unsealing and Disclosure of
Adoption Records.
--X

File No. 40

Dec. No. 681

      This is an application by an adult adoptive child to unseal adoption records, based upon alleged medical necessity. The application is supported by a letter submitted by a physician, which reveals that the adopted child suffers from a diagnosed medical condition. Both the adoptive father and adoptive mother are deceased.

      Domestic Relations Law §114 requires that adoption records be sealed. The purpose is to protect and insure confidentiality which is "vital to the adoption process" (*Matter of Hayden*, 106 Misc 2d 849 [Sup Ct, Albany County 1981]). The confidential nature of the adoption process serves many purposes - to foster a stable and secure home for the adoptive child, to ensure that the natural parents will be able to start a new life without fear of the past intruding on their ability to do so, to allow the adoptive parents to go on without fear that the natural parents will intrude into their lives, and to shield the adoptive child from possibly disturbing facts regarding his birth or background (*Golan v Louise Wise Services*, 69 NY2d 343 [1987]; *Matter of Walker*, 64 NY2d 354 [1985]; *Matter of Linda F.M.*, 52 NY2d 236 [1981], *appeal dismissed* 454 US 806 [1981]; *Matter of Hayden*, 106 Misc 2d 849 [Sup Ct, Albany County 1981]). The statutory sealing requirements have been held to be constitutional and do not violate the adoptive child's 14th amendment right to equal protection (*Matter of Linda F.M.*, 52 NY2d 236 [1981], *appeal dismissed* 454 US 806 [1981]; *Matter of Romano,* 109 Misc 2d 99 [Sur Ct, Kings County 1981]).

Despite the strong policy in favor of confidentiality, the courts and the Legislature have recognized that, under certain circumstances, an adoptive child may need information concerning his or her medical background (*Matter of Chattman,* 57 AD2d 618 [2d Dept 1977]; *Juman v Louise Wise Services,* 159 Misc 2d 314 [Sup Ct, New York County 1994], *affd* 211 AD2d 446 [1st Dept 1995]; *Matter of Harrington,* NYLJ, Mar. 31, 1993, at 25, col 6 [Sur Ct, Westchester County]). Nevertheless, "[a] rule which automatically gave full disclosure to any adopted person confronted with a medical problem with some genetic implications would swallow New York's strong policy against disclosure ..." (*Golan v Louise Wise Services,* 69 NY2d 343, 349 [1987]). Thus, the courts and the Legislature have attempted to strike a balance between the conflicting interests of the biological parents to maintain anonymity and the interests of adopted children and their adoptive parents in having access to medical information (Domestic Relations Law §114; *see Matter of Marino,* 291 AD2d 849 [4th Dept 2002]). The Legislature, recognizing the adoptive child's need for such information, in 1983 enacted Social Services Law §373-a which requires certain information, including information on medical histories, to be provided by the biological parents.

Based upon the same rationale, Domestic Relations Law §114 (2) provides that adoption records may be unsealed upon a showing of "good cause." A prima facie case of good cause on medical grounds may be established under Domestic Relations Law §114 (4). Domestic Relations Law §114 (4) provides as follows:

> . "4. Good cause for disclosure or access to an inspection of sealed adoption records and orders and any index thereof, hereinafter, the 'adoption records,' under this section may be established on medical grounds as provided herein. Certification from a

physician licensed to practice medicine in the State of New York that relief under this subdivision is required to address a serious physical or mental illness shall be prima facie evidence of good cause."

The certification must also identify the information required to address such illness. Moreover, in order to maintain the anonymity of the biological parents, Domestic Relations Law §114 [4] requires the appointment of a guardian ad litem to review the records or, if the records are insufficient, to contact the biological parents.

The type of certification required under Domestic Relations law §114 (4) was found to exist in *Matter of Howard* (NYLJ, Dec. 28, 1998, at 27, col 5 [Sur Ct, New York County]). There, the adoptive child had medical problems which, according to his doctors, were inherited. The doctor averred that information concerning both parents' medical histories, as well as the medical condition of the adoptive child at birth, was necessary to provide proper medical care to the adoptive child and his issue. Pursuant to the procedure set out in Domestic Relations Law §114 (4), the court appointed a guardian ad litem to review the records and to contact the biological parents if the record was insufficient. The court held that the biological parents, if located, should be given the option to disclose the information sought by the adoptive child as well as the option to consent to the examination of their medical records.

According to the doctor's affidavit in the instant case, the adoptive child's condition is "extremely volatile and precarious, requiring close monitoring." The doctor also states that there are concerns regarding the health of the adoptive child's son. The doctor concludes that it is his medical opinion that information regarding the adoptive child's natural parents is "essential to performing an accurate diagnosis for the adopted child and his children [and] to prevent sudden cardiac death or other serious injury by designing an appropriate treatment plan for them."

The adoptive child has provided the type of certification required to establish prima facie "good cause" under Domestic Relations Law §114 (4). The doctor's affidavit confirms that the medical records of the adoptive child's biological parents may be helpful in treating the adoptive child's condition. Accordingly, the court will appoint a guardian ad litem to represent the interests of the biological parents concerning the application. The adoptive child has stated that he shall pay the reasonable fees and expenses of the guardian ad litem if one is appointed.

Once appointed, the guardian ad litem shall examine the adoption records to ascertain if the medical information the adoptive child seeks is contained therein. The adoptive child shall not be permitted to personally inspect the records at this time. The guardian ad litem shall preserve the anonymity of the biological parents. If the guardian ad litem discovers that the records are insufficient for the purpose of obtaining medical information, the guardian ad litem shall follow the procedure set forth in Domestic Relations Law §114 (4). The guardian ad litem shall undertake further efforts to locate and contact the biological parents and offer them the option of disclosing the medical information sought by the adoptive child, as well as the option of granting consent to examine their own medical records, and the option to contact the adoptive child directly.

The guardian ad litem shall report his findings to the court within sixty (60) days of the date of this decision.

This constitutes the order of the court.

Dated: November 𝒜 , 2009

JOHN B. RIORDAN
Judge of the
Surrogate's Court

SURROGATE'S COURT OF THE STATE OF NEW YORK
COUNTY OF NASSAU
---x
In the Matter of

             File No. 3803

        THOMAS J.J.F.,

                Anonymous.
---x

This is an application by an adult adoptive child to unseal adoption records, based upon alleged medical necessity.

The court previously found by decision dated November 2, 2009 (Dec. No. 681) that the adoptive child provided the type of certification required to establish prima facie "good cause" under Domestic Relations Law §114(4). Accordingly, the court appointed a guardian ad litem to represent the interests of the biological parents and to examine the adoption records to ascertain if the medical information the adoptive child is seeking is contained therein. The court further directed that, if the records were insufficient to obtain medical information, the guardian ad litem should undertake efforts to locate the biological parents.

Thereafter, the guardian ad litem submitted his initial report. The guardian ad litem reported that there was no medical information in the file that would aid the petitioner and asked for authorization to engage the services of a genealogist/investigator. By decision dated December 14, 2009 (Dec. No. 912), the court authorized the guardian ad litem to engage the services of a genealogist/investigator to attempt to locate the birth mother and birth father, or, if neither was living, to locate any issue of theirs in order to determine whether such issue are in possession of medical information which would assist the petitioner. The court also directed the guardian ad litem to submit a supplemental report detailing the results of the investigation.

The guardian ad litem has filed his final report. The guardian ad litem states that the investigation confirmed that the biological mother is deceased. In addition, the guardian ad litem reports that "[a]s far as the natural father is concerned his identity was shadowy at best from the information on the petitioner's birth certificate." He further states that, if the information on the birth certificate is, in fact, accurate, the birth father would be in excess of 100 years of age.

The guardian ad litem also reports that, although the birth certificate indicates that the birth mother had another child at the time she gave birth to the petitioner, the investigator was unable to ascertain whether or not the birth mother had any other children or whether they are still living.

The guardian ad litem concludes that since the birth parents are deceased, the protection afforded them under DRL §114 is no longer applicable or necessary. Accordingly, he recommends that the court exercise its discretion in making its file available to the petitioner in the event the petitioner has a sibling who may provide helpful medical information.

The court accepts the recommendation of the guardian ad litem and hereby exercises its discretion to allow the petitioner access to the file in accordance with DRL §114.

With respect to the guardian ad litem's fee, the guardian ad litem has submitted contemporaneous time records showing that he rendered a total of 7.5 billable hours at the rate of $300.00 per hour, for a total of $2,250.00. The guardian ad litem also incurred disbursements of $39.25, all of which are disallowed (*see Matter of Corwith*, NYLJ, May 3, 1995, at 35, col 2 [Sur Ct, Nassau County]). The guardian ad litem's services included reviewing the file, preparing an initial report, meeting with the investigator, and preparing a final report. The court finds the proposed fee to be reasonable in light of the governing criteria found in *Matter of Freeman* (34 NY2d 1 [1974]) and *Matter of Potts* (123 Misc 346 [Surr Ct, Columbia County 1924], *affd* 213

Thomas F. Liotti

App Div 59, affd w/o opn 241 NY 593 [1925]). The fee shall be paid within twenty (20) days of the date of this decision.

This constitutes the decision and order of the court.

Dated: April 23, 2010

JOHN B. RIORDAN
Judge of the
Surrogate's Court

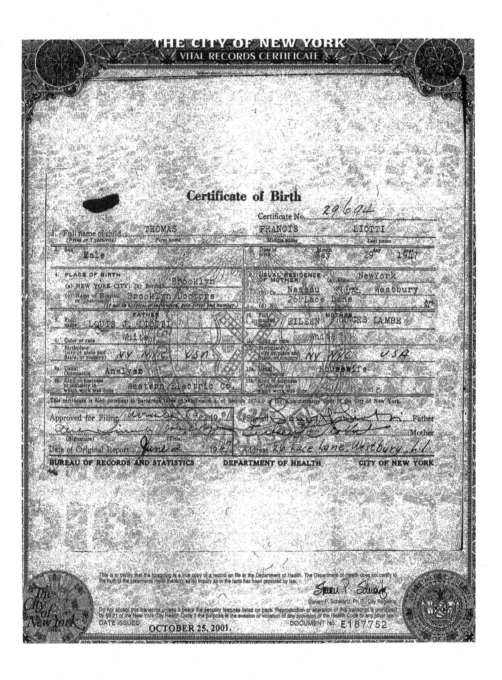

THE CITY OF NEW YORK
VITAL RECORDS CERTIFICATE

Certificate of Birth

Certificate No. 29694

1. Full name of child... THOMAS   FRANCIS   LIOTTI
   (Print or Typewrite)   First name   Middle name   Last name

2. Sex   Male   Date of Birth   Month May   Day 29   1947

4. PLACE OF BIRTH
  (a) NEW YORK CITY (b) Borough Brooklyn
  (c) Name of Hospital Brooklyn Doctors
  or Institution *(If not in hospital or institution, give street and number.)*

5. USUAL RESIDENCE OF MOTHER (a) State New York
  (b) Co. Nassau   (c) City or vil. Westbury
  (d) No. 26 Lace Lane

9. FATHER   Full name LOUIS J. LIOTTI
10. MOTHER   Full maiden name EILEEN FRANCES LAMBE

6. Color or race White
11. Color of race Wht

7. Birthplace (City or place and State, or country) N.Y. NYC USA
12. Birthplace (City or place and State, or country) NY NYC USA

8a. Usual Occupation Analyst
8b. Kind of business or industry in which work was done Western Electric Co.

13a. Usual Occupation Housewife
13b. Kind of business or industry in which work was done Home

This certificate is filed pursuant to paragraph three of subdivision a. of Section 367-2.0 of the Administrative Code of the City of New York.

Approved for Filing _____ 19__   (Signed) _____ Father
(Signature) _____ Title _____   _____ Mother
Date of Original Report June 2 19 47   Address 26 Lace Lane, Westbury, L.I.

BUREAU OF RECORDS AND STATISTICS   DEPARTMENT OF HEALTH   CITY OF NEW YORK

This is to certify that the foregoing is a true copy of a record on file in the Department of Health. The Department of Health does not certify to the truth of the statements made thereon, as no inquiry as to the facts has been provided by law.

Steven P. Schwartz
Steven P. Schwartz, Ph.D., City Registrar

Do not accept this transcript unless it bears the security features listed on back. Reproduction or alteration of this transcript is prohibited by §3.21 of the New York City Health Code if the purpose is the evasion or violation of any provision of the Health Code or any other law.

DATE ISSUED OCTOBER 25, 2001.   DOCUMENT NO. E187752

STATE OF NEW YORK
SURROGATE'S COURT: NASSAU COUNTY
---X
In the Matter

FINAL
***GUARDIAN AD LITEM* REPORT**

THOMAS I.I.F.,   File No. 40

Anonymous

For the Unsealing and Disclosure of
Adoption Records.
---X

TO THE SURROGATE'S COURT OF THE STATE OF NEW YORK,
COUNTY OF NASSAU:

I, Albert W. Petraglia, the undersigned Guardian *ad Litem*, in the above-entitled

proceeding, respectfully reports as follows:

APPLICATION TO EXAMINE ADOPTION FILE

The petitioner asking to unseal the Court's adoption files is an adult adoptive child who

supported his application with a medical affidavit from his physician. The Court determined that

he made a prima facie showing of "good cause" to unseal the adoption records based upon

medical reasons.

By decision dated November 4, 2009, I was appointed Guardian Ad Litem for the natural

parents in order to examine the adoption records of the petitioner to ascertain certain medical

information that might be helpful in connection with the petitioner's medical condition.

INITIAL GUARDIAN AD LITEM REPORT

Pursuant to the Court's decision (No. 681) of November 4, 2009, I was directed to review

the Court's file. In the event there was no medical information available, I was given the authority to locate and contact the biological parents. They would have the option of disclosing the medical information sought by the adoptive child or consent to an examination of their own medical records or the option of contacting the adoptive child directly. In my Initial Report, dated November 19, 2009, I reported that the Court's file contained no medical information. Based upon the petitioner's birth records, both natural parents would be of advanced years and unlikely to have survived to this date. Nevertheless, I reported that in the event the Court wished me to locate the natural parents with the remote likelihood that at least the natural mother is still alive, I would engage the services of a genealogist/investigator in that effort.

INVESTIGATIVE SERVICES

In a subsequent decision dated December 14, 2009 (Decision No. 912) I was directed to engage the services of a genealogist/investigator in order to locate the birth mother and birth father, or if not living, to locate any issue of theirs. The Court's Decision further stated that the fee for the genealogist/investigator would be paid by the petitioner. I was further directed not to release the identities of the birth mother and birth father to the petitioner and to file a supplemental report detailing the results of my investigation.

Having resolved the fee issue with the petitioner beforehand, I engaged the services of ACI Investigation Services Inc. an established company involved in investigative services with offices located in Nassau County, New York and Wellington, Florida.

Before hiring ACI Investigation Services Inc. I obtained a confidentiality agreement from the president of the company that all information gathered was to be kept strictly confidential and only divulged to me as Guardian Ad Litem. A copy of the confidentiality agreement is attached hereto as Exhibit "A".

I have now received a detailed report from the investigator which shows the following information:

Through personal interviews and by accessing different databases such as the Social Security death index, the investigator was able to trace the petitioner's mother. The petitioner's birth certificate shows that the natural mother's name is Anne Ferguson. The identity of the father from the birth certificate is indiscernible and most likely his name is fictitious. We know that the natural mother, eventually moved to Port Washington, New York. She lived there between 1978 and 1993. Through the use of additional database searches the investigator located the natural mother's next address in Cleveland, Ohio. The investigator called the phone number attached to the Ohio address and was able to speak to the current residents who stated that they had purchased the house from one Anne Ferguson sometime in 1997. They further advised the investigator that they believed that Anne Ferguson had died in the year 2000. Through the use of the Social Security Death Index, the investigator was able to confirm that Anne Ferguson died on January 30, 2000. The information further listed her date of birth as February 17, 1912 which was a birth date consistent with the age of the natural mother on the petitioner's birth certificate. We are unable to obtain a certified death certificate for the natural mother because it will only be released to family members. It should be noted that ACI Investigation Services was thorough and professional in every aspect of it's investigation. A copy of the ACI Investigation Services report has been attached hereto as Exhibit "B.

CONCLUSIONS AND RECOMMENDATIONS

As a result of my own investigation and the exhaustive investigation done by ACI Investigation Services, I am convinced that the natural parents of the petitioner are deceased. The natural mother was traced to Ohio, and her death is confirmed by Social Security records and statements made by persons who met her. As far as the natural father is concerned his identity was shadowy at best from the information on the petitioner's birth certificate. In any event, if the age of the father is accurate as stated on the petitioner's birth certificate, then he would be a person in excess of 100 years of age. It is highly unlikely that he is still alive. While it is not certain that Anne Ferguson, the petitioner's mother had any other children, the possibility does exist from the information contained on the petitioner's birth certificate. Under § 19(b) of the birth certificate: "number of children born previous to this pregnancy and now living" there appears the number 1. Unfortunately, the investigator was unable to ascertain whether or not the natural mother had any other children or whether they are still living. Pursuant to Domestic Relations Law § 114 " . . . if the guardian or other disinterested person appointed has not obtained the medical information sought by the petitioner, such guardian or disinterested person shall make a report of his or her efforts to obtain such information to the court. Where further efforts to obtain such information are appropriate, the court may in its discretion authorize direct disclosure access to an inspection of the adoption records by the petitioner." Since it is clear that the Petitioner's natural parents are deceased, the protection afforded them under DRL § 114 is no longer applicable or necessary. In the event the petitioner has a sibling who may provide helpful medical information, I respectfully recommend that the Court exercise it's discretion in making its file available to the petitioner in accordance with the authority set forth in DRL §114.

I further recommend that I be permitted to make my Final Guardian Ad Litem's Report available to the petitioner.

Dated: Uniondale, New York
    March 10th , 2010

Respectfully submitted:

Albert W. Petraglia, Guardian Ad Litem
Rivkin Radler LLP
926 RXR Plaza
Uniondale, NY 11556
(516) 357-3178

2344522 v2

STATE OF NEW YORK
SURROGATE'S COURT: NASSAU COUNTY
---X
In the Matter

          THOMAS I.I.F.,   File No. 40

                    Anonymous

For the Unsealing and Disclosure of
Adoption Records.
---X

Confidentiality Agreement

    Thomas Allen, on behalf of ACI Investigation Services, Inc., agrees to investigate certain kinship information concerning the above referenced Surrogate's Court matter. Such information shall be furnished on a confidential basis to the Guardian Ad Litem, Albert W. Petraglia, Esq. only, with the understanding that all such information will be kept strictly confidential.

    The information obtained will not be divulged to any third party without prior decision or order of Nassau County Surrogate's Court.

    The undersigned acknowledges that he is authorized to execute this Confidentiality Agreement on behalf of his company.

Dated: January 19, 2010

                                        ACI Investigation Services, Inc.

                                        BY: _____
                                            Thomas Allen
                                            President

Josephine M. Ponella

Sworn to before me
this 19th day of January, 2010

JOSEPHINE M PONELLA
Notary Public, State of New York
No. 01PO5077025
Qualified in Nassau County
Commission Expires April 28,20__

341

Thomas F. Liotti

ACI
ACI Investigation Services, Inc.

830 Shore Road
Suite 2J
Long Beach, NY 11561
(917)886-4121

2165 Wingate Bend
Wellington, Fl. 33414
(561) 723-2240

March 1, 2010

RivkinRadler
926 RexCorp Plaza
Uniondale, NY 11556

Attention: Albert Petraglia, Esq.

Re: File No. 40 – Dec. No. 681

PRIVILEGED AND CONFIDENTIAL

Anne Ferguson
a/k/a/ Anna Ferguson
a/k/a/ Anne Smith

After reviewing the Birth Certificate and the other documents you provided, which indicated that the birth mother's information was accurate and the birth father's information was fictitious, I conducted numerous data base searches in an attempt to locate the current whereabouts of the birth mother. Due to the large number of persons named Anne Ferguson and the lack of comprehensive database information from the time period in question, those searches proved inconclusive.

84 Garfield Place
Brooklyn, NY

On January 26, 2010, I responded to the captioned address in an attempt to locate someone who may have been acquainted with Anne Ferguson. I interviewed the current residents of the building, Maria Olavarria; Liza Escott and Michael Farley. None of those persons were able to provide any useful information.

I then attempted to locate a person who lived in the neighborhood in 1947 and who may have known Anne Ferguson. I interviewed a mail carrier who stated that he was "filling in on the route for the day" and could not help.

I remained in the area and interviewed several persons who appeared to be old enough to have lived in the area circa 1947 with negative results.

Between February 1st and February 16th I returned to the area of Garfield Place on several occasions in an attempt to locate the regular mail carrier and to interview persons of suitable age who I found in the area. None of the persons interviewed were helpful. On February 17th I located the regular mail carrier, Charles Smith. He advised me that the only person who may have lived in the area since 1947, was a woman named Grossman residing at 97 Garfield Place. He described her as being elderly and having lived in the area for her entire life.

I went to 97 Garfield Place and found an elderly woman leaving the location. She identified herself as Mrs. Grossman. When I asked her how long she had lived in the neighborhood she stated that she had lived there her entire life. She would not give me her age but she appeared to be in her eighties. When I asked about Anne Ferguson she stated, "of course I knew her. She used to babysit for me sometimes." Mrs. Grossman told me that the last time she saw her that "Anne and her husband were moving out to Long Island." At first she did not recall where on Long Island. After we spoke for a while she recalled that they had moved to Port Washington sometime in the mid 1970's. When I began to ask about children or anyone else who may have known Anne Ferguson, Mrs. Grossman stated, "I've probably said too much already" and ended the conversation by walking away. Mrs. Grossman seemed confused during parts of this interview, but was Adamant that he knew Anne Ferguson.

Additional Database Searches

I then conducted additional database searches utilizing the above information. I was able to locate an Anne Ferguson who resided at 10 Hawthorne Avenue in Port Washington from 1978-1993, having previously lived in Brooklyn. I was able to ascertain that her Social Security number was 102-10-3759 and that that number was issued in New York between 1936 and 1951.

Albert Petraglia, Esq.
Re: File No, 40 – Dec. No. 681
Page 3

10 Hawthorne Ave. Port Washington	On February 26, 2010, I responded to the captioned address and spoke to a female resident who refused to give her name She did state that she and her husband had purchased the home from Mr. and Mrs. Ferguson and that they had moved to, "Somewhere in Ohio". She the refused to answer any additional questions.
31089 Shaker Blvd. Cleveland, Ohio	I then conducted additional database searches and found that an Anne Ferguson resided at the captioned address in 1994, having moved there from 10 Hawthorne Avenue, Port Washington.
	I was able to get a telephone number, 216-292-1060, for the current occupants, Mr. and Mrs. Jeffrey Wahl. I interviewed Mrs. Wahl and she confirmed that they had purchased the home in 1997 from Anne Ferguson. She stated that Anne Ferguson was elderly and in poor health at the time of the sale. The only other information she could offer was that she had heard that Anne Ferguson had died sometime around the year 2000.
Ohio Office of Vital Records	I was able to ascertain that Anne Ferguson, Social Security Number 102-10-3759, had died on January 30, 2000. Her date of birth is February 17, 1912. That date of birth is consistent with the birth mother's age on the original birth certificate.
	I have been unable to secure a copy of the death certificate due to the confidentiality requirements of the Office of Vital Records.

If you have any questions, or require any additional information, please contact me.

Sincerely yours,

Thomas Allen

G90-1M-7-49

NO. 3803

IN THE MATTER OF THE ADOPTION OF

Donald Smith aka
Thomas Francis Liotti

BY ORDER THEREAFTER KNOWN AS

Thomas Francis Liotti

BY

Louis J. Liotti

Eileen F. Liotti

ORDER DATED *Nov. 13. 1951*

I HEREBY ORDER THIS ENVELOPE TO BE SEALED AND OPENED ONLY ON ORDER OF THE SURROGATE.

SURROGATE

NOTIFICATION. ☑ MAILED ☐ WAIVED

10 *Bklyn*

ADOPTION CLERK

345

Thomas F. Liotti

O142-25C-3-51

SURROGATE'S COURT, NASSAU COUNTY

In the matter of the adoption

of

DONALD SMITH a/k/a THOMAS
FRANCIS LIOTTI

a minor ~~xxxx~~ under the age of fourteen years,

by LOUIS J. LIOTTI and EILEEN F.
LIOTTI

PETITION FOR ADOPTION

To THE HONORABLE LEONE D. HOWELL,

SURROGATE OF THE COUNTY OF NASSAU:

The petition of LOUIS J. LIOTTI and
EILEEN F. LIOTTI

, his wife, respectfully shows:

1. That your petitioner s are over the age of twenty-one years, and are citizen s

of the United States, and ~~xxxxxxxx~~ legally married, living together as husband and wife.

2. That the post-office address and place of residence of your petitioner s is
26 Lace Lane
Westbury, L.I., N.Y.

3. That your petitioners are desirous of adopting as their own child

DONALD SMITH a/k/a THOMAS FRANCIS LIOTTI, a male minor child, born on the 29th

day of May , 19 47 at Brooklyn Doctors Hospital,
Brooklyn, New York

4. That the religious faith of said minor child is Roman Catholic ;

that the religious faith of the parent of said child as petitioner s are informed and

verily believe is Roman Catholic ; that the religious faith of petitioner s

is Roman Catholic

346

5. That your petitioner s ' family residing with petitioner consists of petitioners and infant child herein.

6. That said minor child has resided continuously with petitioner since June 6, 1947.

(State briefly nature of business or profession, average income, and other facts relative to financial condition of ALL petitioners.)

7. That the occupation of your petitioner , LOUIS J. LIOTTI is Analyst employed by Western Electric Company, 195 Broadway, New York City, New York, for the past ten years. That petitioner's annual income is approximately $4,300.00, per annum. That petitioner, EILEEN F. LIOTTI is a housewife. That petitioners own their own home at 26 Lace Lane, Westbury, L.I., N.Y.

*State names, residences and any relevant facts.

When used in connection with institutional proceedings state relevant facts regarding agency and qualifications to place children for purpose of adoption. Also, give facts Re: instrument of surrender by parent or parents to said agency.

8. ~~That the names of said minor child~~ That upon information and belief, ANNE FERGUSON of 84 Garfield Place, Brooklyn, New York City, unmarried, is the mother of the infant child herein.

(Where adoption is sought on consent of only one natural parent, set forth facts upon which dispensation of other natural parent's consent is based.)

9. That your petitioner s   obtained custody of the minor child in the following manner:

On or about June 6, 1947, ANNE FERGUSON, brought the infant child herein to the home of LOUIS J. LIOTTI and his wife, EILEEN F. LIOTTI, and left the said child with them for them to take care of and maintain the said infant. That since the said time the said foster parents have cared for and maintained the said minor child. That ANNE FERGUSON, the mother of the said child, upon information and belief, on June 6, 1947, was unmarried, and had so been unmarried for at least one year prior to May 29, 1947.

OI45-2500-6-50

AT A SURROGATE'S COURT, held in and for the County of Nassau, at the Surrogate's Court, County Court House, at Mineola, in said County, on the *13th* day of *November* in the year ·one thousand nine hundred and *fifty-one*

PRESENT:

   HON. LEONE D. HOWELL,

            SURROGATE.

In the matter of the adoption

of

DONALD SMITH a/k/a
THOMAS FRANCIS LIOTTI

a minor ~~over~~ under   the age of fourteen years

by   LOUIS J. LIOTTI and
     EILEEN F. LIOTTI

ORDER OF ADOPTION

On the petition of   LOUIS J. LIOTTI   and

EILEEN F. LIOTTI   , his wife, adult s , duly verified

before me the   *13th*   day of *November*   , 19 51 , and the

affidavit of   MARK K. LEEDS   , Attorney-at-Law,

duly sworn to, and the above-named parties having severally appeared before me together with

DONALD SMITH a/k/a THOMAS FRANCIS LIOTTI   a minor, and

said parties constituting all of the parties required to appear before me pursuant to the provisions of an

Act relating to the domestic relations, constituting chapter fourteen of the Consolidated Laws, as amended,

and said parties having been examined by me, as required by said law, and said parties having presented

to me an instrument containing substantially the consents required by said law, an agreement on the part

of the foster parent s to adopt and treat the minor as   their   own lawful child, and a statement

of the date and place of birth of the minor to be adopted, as nearly as the same can be ascertained, the

religious faith of the parent   of the minor, the manner in which the foster parent s obtained the minor,

and said instrument having been duly signed, sealed and acknowledged as required by law by each person

whose consent is necessary to the adoption;*

348

would give me full knowledge as to the desirability of approving said adoption, and the said investigator, having made his report in writing, and the same having been filed in this court; and said investigator having reported that the facts and conditions as set forth in the petition, the instrument or agreement of adoption and other papers in this proceeding are true and are fairly stated, and further reporting that in his opinion the adoption of the said minor, Donald Smith a/k/a THOMAS/ FRANCIS LIOTTI , as prayed for in the petition herein would be for the best interests of said minor;

And it appearing to my satisfaction that the moral and temporal interests of the minor, Donald Smith a/k/a THOMAS FRANCIS LIOTTI , will be promoted by granting the petition of said LOUIS J. LIOTTI and EILEEN F. LIOTTI his wife, and allowing and approving the proposed adoption; and it appearing to my satisfaction that there is no reasonable objection to the change of name proposed,

NOW, ON MOTION OF MARK K. LEEDS , attorney for the petitioner s herein, it is

ORDERED that the petition of LOUIS J. LIOTTI and EILEEN F. LIOTTI , his wife, for the adoption of DONALD SMITH a/k/a THOMAS FRANCIS LIOTTI , a minor, born on the 29th day of May , 19 47 , in Brooklyn Doctors Hospital, Brooklyn, New York City, New York

be and the same is hereby granted and that such adoption and the agreement therefor submitted upon this application be and the same hereby are in all respects allowed and approved, and it is

FURTHER ORDERED that the minor, DONALD SMITH a/k/a THOMAS FRANCIS LIOTTI shall be henceforth regarded and treated in all respects as the child of said LOUIS J. LIOTTI and EILEEN F. LIOTTI , his wife and be known and called by the name of THOMAS FRANCIS LIOTTI

_____
Surrogate

349

Thomas F. Liotti

In Re: Adoption of:

Smith BY _Liotti_

Phone No._____

PETITION: ✓   9/28

AGREEMENT: ✓

AFFIDAVITS: ✓

AFFIDAVIT OF ATTORNEY: ~~done~~

ORDER OF ADOPTION: _due_

CUSTODY COMPLETE: ✓

C.C. ORG. BIRTH CERTIFICATE: ~~done~~

NEW BIRTH CERTIFICATE: ✓

NOTIFICATION TO ~~State~~ City HEALTH DEPT. ✓
~~Other~~

- -

INVESTIGATION: 11/14   ATTORNEY ADVISED BY:

HEARING: N.M.   ~~Mail~~)
         N.P. _____ Phone) on 10/10
                    Counter)

         F.P. 11/13 10 a Entered In
                          Diary _____ ✓ BY _/_

- -

ATTORNEY _Mark K Leeds_ Carbon_____ Photo_____   250
Address _305 Bdway nyc_ Rec. No. _1245/_ Bill_____   Pd
Telephone _Worth 2-166_ ✓ Taken_____ Mail_____

- -

EXHIBITS: _____

REMARKS: _____

Code# 10   November 6, 1951

In the Matter of the Adoption of

DONALD SMITH a/k/as THOMAS LIOTTI,

an infant under 14

By- LOUIS J. LIOTTI and EILEEN F. LIOTTI

        On Sunday, November 4, 1951, your investigator
visited petitioners and infant at their home 26 Lace Lane.
Westbury, N.Y.

        Mr. Liotti is an Analyst for Western Electric
Company earning approx 4300. per annum. Mrs. Liotti is a
housewife. They have been married for ten years. Their religious
faith is Roman Catholic.

        Petitioners have had custody of said infant since
June 6, 1947.

        All facts and allegations set forth in the moving
papers were duly verified. The granting of the relief herein
sought would appear to be in the best interest of the infant.

        Respectfully submitted,

                                    Willoe R. Gregory
                            Willoe R. Gregory

Thomas F. Liotti

SURROGATE'S COU

    ADOPTIO

2.

3.

4.

Please refer to —

Sur. Ct. 130 M-1699 6/85

IN THE MATTER OF THE ADOPTION OF

Donald Smith

BY ORDER THEREAFTER KNOWN AS

Thomas Liotti

BY

Louis Liotti

Eileen Liotti

RNEY   pro se

(516) 794-4700

IO 3 803

) BE SEALED AND

SURROGATE

JUDGE OF THE SURROGATE'S COURT

NOTIFICATION OF ADOPTION ORDER   MAILED _____

                           WAIVED _____

PLACE OF BIRTH ____ Brooklyn NY

ORDER GRANTED ____ 11/13/1951

ADOPTION CLERK

SURROGATE'S COURT : NASSAU COUNTY

- X

In the Matter of the Adoption

of

DONALD SMITH a/k/a THOMAS FRANCIS
LIOTTI

a minor under the age of 14 years, by

LOUIS J. LIOTTI and EILEEN F. LIOTTI, his
wife

- X

STATE OF NEW YORK)
COUNTY OF *New York*) ss.:

      ANNA FERGUSON, being duly sworn, deposes and says:

      1. That she is the mother of DONALD SMITH, birth
certificate No. 29694, Brooklyn, New York City Department of
Health, *and that she is also known as ANNA FERGUSON SMITH.*

      2. That Donald Smith was born to your deponent on May
29, 1947, at Brooklyn Doctors Hospital, Brooklyn, New York.

      3. That at the time of said birth, and for at least one
(1) year prior thereto, deponent was unmarried.

      4. That the name of "JOHN SMITH" which appears on said
certificate of birth is fictitious, as is also the other information in said certificate regarding "JOHN SMITH".

      5. That this affidavit is made at the request of Louis
J. Liotti and in connection with his application to adopt DONALD
"SMITH".

Sworn to before me this

4th day of *Sept*, 1951.   *(Mrs) Anne Smith*

      Anne Ferguson

DAVE GORDON
Notary Public St. of New York
No. 24-1800800
Qualified in Kings County
Cert. filed with Kings, N.Y. Co. Clk. & Reg.
Commission Expires March 30, 1953

*Sworn to before me this
15th day of November 1951*

SURROGATE

353

Thomas F. Liotti

354

GI44-25C-9/50

SURROGATE'S COURT, NASSAU COUNTY

In the matter of the adoption

of

DONALD SMITH a/k/a
THOMAS FRANCIS LIOTTI

a minor ~~over~~ under the age of 14 years, by

LOUIS J. LIOTTI

and

EILEEN F. LIOTTI

, his wife

AFFIDAVIT OF ATTORNEY

MARK K. LEEDS , being duly sworn, deposes and says:

That he is an attorney at law duly licensed to practice under the laws of the State of
New York and has his office at 305 Broadway, New York 7, New York

That he knows LOUIS J. LIOTTI and
EILEEN F. LIOTTI his wife,

and knows that the y are the same persons described in and who executed the foregoing
instrument and who are now present before the Surrogate.

That he believes that the adoption by the proposed foster parents, LOUIS J. LIOTTI
and EILEEN F. LIOTTI
of the said minor, DONALD SMITH a/k/a THOMAS F. LIOTTI, will be for the
best moral and temporal interests of the said minor.

That he believes that the proposed foster parents, LOUIS J. LIOTTI
and EILEEN F. LIOTTI , are persons of sufficient means, and fit
and proper persons to have the care and custody of the said minor.

Sworn to before me this 13th
day of ~~August~~ December , 19 51.

....

....
Surrogate, Nassau County

O14-25C-3-51

SURROGATE'S COURT, NASSAU COUNTY

In the matter of the adoption
of
DONALD SMITH a/k/a THOMAS
FRANCIS LIOTTI

a minor ~~over~~ under the age of fourteen years,

by LOUIS J. LIOTTI and EILEEN
F. LIOTTI

AGREEMENT OF ADOPTION

*(Insert names
and addresses
of parties.)

AGREEMENT made and dated this ~~Fourth (4th)~~ *13th*
day of ~~July~~ ~~September~~ *November* , 19 51 , between* LOUIS J. LIOTTI and his
wife, EILEEN F. LIOTTI, both of 26 Lace Lane, Westbury, L.I., N.Y.
and ANNA FERGUSON of 84 Garfield Place, Brooklyn, New York.

WHEREAS, LOUIS J. LIOTTI   and

EILEEN F. LIOTTI   are ~~his~~

desirous of adopting, pursuant to the provisions of law, DONALD SMITH a/k/a THOMAS
FRANCIS LIOTTI
a minor child ~~over~~ under the age of fourteen years, and to regard and treat such minor in all

respects as their own lawful child, and

WHEREAS, ANNA FERGUSON , ~~xxon~~

approve s and consents to said adoption.

NOW, THEREFORE, in consideration of the premises and of the mutual convenants
hereinafter expressed, it is agreed as follows:

FIRST: That said LOUIS J. LIOTTI and EILEEN F. LIOTTI
covenant and agree to adopt, and do hereby adopt, said minor child,

356

and covenant and agree to treat and regard ~~xxxx~~ him in all respects as their own lawful child, hereby extending and assuring to such child all rights, benefits and privileges incident to such relation, and hereby assume and engage to fulfill all of the responsibilities and duties of parent in respect to such child.

SECOND: The said ANNA FERGUSON hereby consent s to said adoption, and covenant s and agree s to acquiesce therein and to refrain from doing or causing to be done any act or thing whatsoever which will in any way interfere with the rights, duties and privileges of said child when so adopted.

THIRD: That the name of said minor child shall be changed to
THOMAS FRANCIS LIOTTI

*(Insert religious faith.)

FOURTH: That said minor child shall be reared in the* Roman Catholic faith

*(Strike out if child is under 14 years of age.)

~~FIFTH: The said minor child,~~

~~, hereby consents to such adoption.~~

THE FOLLOWING FACTS ARE AFFIRMED BY THE PARTIES HERETO:

A. Said minor child was born on the 29th day of May

1947, at Brooklyn Doctors Hospital, Brooklyn, New York

B. The religious faith of the parents of said child is Roman Catholic

The religious faith of said minor is Roman Catholic

The religious faith of the foster parent s is Roman Catholic

(Where adoption is sought on consent of only one natural parent, set forth facts upon which dispensation of other natural parent's consent is based.)

When used in connection with institutional proceedings state relevant facts regarding agency and qualifications to place children for purpose of adoption. Also, give facts Re: instrument of surrender by parent or parents to said agency.

C. The foster parents obtained custody of said minor child as follows:
On or about June 6, 1947, ANNA FERGUSON, brought the infant child herein to the home of LOUIS J. LIOTTI and his wife, EILEEN F. LIOTTI, and left the said child with them for them to take care of and maintain the said infant. That since the said time the said foster parents have cared for and maintained the said minor child. That ANNA FERGUSON, the mother of the said child, upon information and belief, on June 6, 1947, was unmarried, and had so been unmarried for at least one year prior to May 29, 1947.

D. Said minor child has resided continuously with LOUIS J. LIOTTI

and EILEEN F. LIOTTI

since June 6, 1947.

IN WITNESS WHEREOF, the parties have set their hands and seals the day and year first above written.

In presence of

In presence of

STATE OF NEW YORK
COUNTY OF NASSAU } ss. :

On this 13th day of November in the year one thousand nine hundred and fifty one before me personally appeared

Louis J Liotti & Eileen F. Liotti

proven to me by the oath of Mark K. Leeds

counselor-at-law, to be the individual described in and who executed the foregoing instrument, and they acknowledged to me that they executed the same.

Surrogate

STATE OF NEW YORK
COUNTY OF NASSAU } ss. :

On this 13th day of November in the year one thousand nine hundred and fifty one before me personally appeared

Anne Ferguson aka Anne Smith

proven to me by the oath of Mark K Leeds

counselor-at-law, to be the individual described in and who executed the foregoing instrument, and she acknowledged to me that she executed the same.

Surrogate

STATE OF NEW YORK }
COUNTY OF } ss. :

On the   day of   , one thousand nine hundred and

before me came   to me known, who, being by me duly sworn, did depose

and say that he resides at   in   ;

that he is the   of

the corporation described in, and which executed, the foregoing

instrument; that he knows the seal of said corporation; that the seal affixed to said instrument is such corporate

seal; that it was so affixed by order of the Board of   of said corporation, and that he

signed h name thereto by like order.

Notary Public, State of New York,
Qualified in................County.
No. ....Com. Exp..............

....MARK K. LEEDS...................

305 Broadway...................

New York 7, New York
Attorney for Petitioner.

359

House of Names.com

Ferguson Family Crest and Name History

☐ Text Size ☐ ✗ 🖨 🖂

Origins Available: Irish, Scottish-All, Scottish

Where did the Scottish Ferguson family come from? What is the Scottish coat of arms/family crest? When did the Ferguson family first arrive in the United States? Where did the various branches of the family go? What is the history of the family name?

The ancestors of the Ferguson family come from the ancient Scottish kingdom of Dalriada. Their surname comes from the Scottish surname MacFergus, which means "son of Fergus".

Medieval spelling was at best an intuitive process, and translation between Gaelic and English was no more effective. These factors caused an enormous number of spelling variations in Dalriadan names. In fact, it was not uncommon to see a father and son who spelled their name differently. Over the years, Ferguson has been spelled Ferguson, Fergusson, Ferguson, Fargerson, Fargusson and many more.

First found in Galloway, where they held a family seat from very ancient times, some say well before the Norman Conquest and the arrival of Duke William at Hastings in 1066 A.D.

◻ More

Settlers from Scotland put down roots in communities all along the east coast of North America. Some moved north from the American colonies to Canada as United Empire Loyalists during the American War of Independence. As clan societies and highland games started in North America in the 20th century many Scots rediscovered parts of their heritage. Early North American records indicate many people bearing the name Ferguson were among those contributors: Daniel Ferguson who settled in New England in 1651; Duncan Ferguson settled in Virginia in 1716; Robert Ferguson settled in Virginia in 1716; Thomas Ferguson settled in Barbados in 1678..

Motto Translated: Sweeter after difficulties

For more information on the last name Ferguson, the PDF Surname History is available for purchase as well as other products.

Some noteworthy people of the name Ferguson
- Elsie Ferguson (1885-1961), American actress
- Homer Samuel Ferguson (1889-1982), American politician and lawyer, Senator from Michigan
- Alex Ferguson, Scottish soccer manager
- Adam Ferguson (1723-1816), Scottish philosopher
- James Ferguson (1710-1776), Scottish astronomer
- Sir John Ferguson (1832-1907), Scottish statesman
- Patrick Ferguson (1744-1780), Scottish soldier
- Robert Ferguson (1637-1714), Scottish conspirator
- Sir Charles Ferguson, of Kilkerran
- Harry George Ferguson (1884-1960), Irish engineer
- John Douglas Ferguson, Surgeon
- Sarah Ferguson (b. 1959), British ex-wife of Prince Andrew
- Fergie Ferguson (b. 1959), British noble, ex-wife of Prince Andrew
- Sir Samuel Ferguson (1810-1886), Irish poet
- Al Ferguson (1888-1971), English (Irish born) actor, and director

Ferguson Clan Badge

A clan is a social group made up of a number of distinct branch-families that actually descended from, or accepted themselves as descendants of, a common ancestor. The word clan means simply children. The idea of the clan as a community is necessarily based around this idea of heredity and is most often ruled according to a patriarchal structure. For instance, the clan chief represented the hereditary "parent" of the entire clan. The most prominent example of this form of society is the Scottish Clan system...

◻ More

Septs of the Distinguished Name Ferguson
Caddy, Chedday, Cheddie, Cheddy, Falredge, Fairege, Feiredge, Fairege, Felridge, Fairies, Faidge, Faids, Faidsh, Fairlich, Feradge, Farage, Fareadge, Fareage, Faredge, Fareedge, Fareege, Farega, Fereldge, Fareles, Fareige, Fards, Fareish, Fereilch, Fargason, Fargerson, Fargie, Fargoson, Fargus, Farguson, Fargusson, Fargyson, Faridge, Faries, Farige, Faris, Farish, Farlich, Farradge, Farrage, Farrass, Farredge, Farrass, Farress, Fergus, Farridge and more.

Tell Me More About Family Crests

Family Crests: the Heraldic Artist

We have researched the Ferguson family crest in the most recognized sources. Before an artist or craftsmen can render a family crest, it must exist. In other words the crest must have been designed and recorded by the heralds from time immemorial.

Heraldic designs malcirculated by the lay-artist in many cases becomes uninspired, meretricious and even ugly...

◻ More

Family Crests: Timeline

Many of the symbols adopted into armory have been used since the time of the ancient Egyptians, but heraldry itself did not begin until the 11th century. In continental Europe, the most ancient recorded family crest was discovered upon the monumental effigy of a Count of Wasserburg in the church of St. Emeran, at Ratisbon, Germany...

◻ More

Family Crests: Elements

In the Ferguson coat of arms as in all coat of arms the crest is only one element of the full armorial achievement. Again the Family Crest is just part of the story of Coats of Arms or Heraldry. Heraldry is defined as the hereditary art or science of blazoning, the description is appropriate technical terms of Coats-of-Arms and other heraldic and armorial insignia, and is of very ancient origin...

◻ More

3/12/2010

Family Crests and Genealogy: how they relate

We encourage you to study the Ferguson genealogy to find out if you descend from someone who bore a particular family crest. Anyone making a study of heraldry usually becomes interested in Genealogy or seeking legal claim to a particular family crest. No families, not even the royal houses, can make sound claim to the right to bear arms unless a proven connection is established through attested Genealogical records...

◐ More

Ferguson Family Crest Products

Anniversary	Anniversary products for the name Ferguson.	**Popular Products**
Apparel	Apparel revealing the Ferguson family crest.	Armorial History With Coat of Arms
Armorial histories	Armorial histories for the name Ferguson.	
Ceramics	Ceramics revealing the Ferguson family crest.	Coat of Arms & Surname History Package
Clan Badges	Clan Badges for the name Ferguson.	
Coat of Arms	Coat of Arms for the name Ferguson.	Family Crest Image (jpg) Heritage Series - 300 DPI
Downloads	Downloads revealing the family crest for the surname Ferguson.	
Family Crest	Family Crest for the name Ferguson.	
Family Tree	Family Tree featuring the Ferguson family crest.	Key-chain
Hand Painted Plaques	Hand Painted Plaques emphasing the Ferguson family crest.	
Keychains	Keychains emphasing the Ferguson family crest.	Coffee Mug
Mouse pads	Mouse pads revealing the Ferguson family crest.	
New Products	New Products emphasing the family crest for the name Ferguson.	Armorial History with Frame
Packages	Packages featuring the Ferguson family crest.	
Plaques and Frames	Plaques and Frames showing the Ferguson family crest.	Framed Surname History and Coat of Arms
Surname Histories	Surname Histories for the name Ferguson.	
Symbolism	Symbolism with a Ferguson family crest.	
Travel Mugs	Travel Mugs for the Ferguson family crest.	

The Ferguson Family Crest was acquired from the Houseofnames.com archives. The Ferguson Family Crest was drawn according to heraldic standards based on published blazons. We generally include the oldest published family crest once associated with each surname.

Tools

E-Newsletter: Email Address   [Sign Up Now]

Last Updated Friday, March 12, 2010

Home | About Us | Our Guarantee | Privacy Statement | Contact Us | Name Search | Site Map

Call us Toll free: 888-488-7086 x1 222 or (912)384-9986 x1 222

THE WHITE HOUSE

WASHINGTON

November 30, 2005

Dear Mr. Liotti:

Thank you for your recommendation of your son Tom for a Federal judgeship. Please be assured that he, and your views, are being given appropriate consideration.

In the event that additional information from you would be helpful to the selection process, we will contact you directly. In the meantime, please accept my thanks for your input.

Sincerely,

Harriet Miers
Counsel to the President

Mr. Louis J. Liotti
34 Lexington Street
Westbury, NY 11590

I know you are proud and rightly so! Your son

INDEX